Epic Films

SECOND EDITION

Epic Films

Casts, Credits and Commentary on
Over 350 Historical Spectacle Movies

Second Edition

GARY ALLEN SMITH

Foreword by STEPHEN PAPICH

McFarland & Company, Inc., Publishers
Jefferson, North Carolina, and London

ALSO BY GARY ALLEN SMITH

Uneasy Dreams:
The Golden Age of British Horror Films, 1956–1976
(McFarland, 2000)

Frontispiece: Claudette Colbert as the wicked empress Poppaea in
Cecil B. DeMille's *The Sign of the Cross* (1932).

LIBRARY OF CONGRESS CATALOGUING-IN-PUBLICATION DATA

Smith, Gary A., 1950–
Epic films : casts, credits and commentary on over 350 historical
spectacle movies / Gary Allen Smith ;
foreword by Stephen Papich.—2nd ed.
p.   cm.
Includes bibliographical references and index.

ISBN 0-7864-1530-4 (illustrated case binding : 50# alkaline paper)

1. Historical films—History and criticism.
2. Epic films—History and criticism.   I. Title.
PN1995.9.H5S55   2004   791.43'658—dc22   2003019131

British Library cataloguing data are available

On the cover: Charlton Heston as Moses leads the Exodus from Egypt
in *The Ten Commandments* (1956); background ©1998 PhotoDisc

Manufactured in the United States of America

McFarland & Company, Inc., Publishers
Box 611, Jefferson, North Carolina 28640
www.mcfarlandpub.com

For my dear friends Glenn and Richard

Acknowledgments

Many thanks to the usual suspects including Werner Lehmann, Mike Meriano, Marty Kearns, Pete at Larry Edmund's Bookstore and, most importantly, Michael Hirschbein for his constant love and support.

Contents

Foreword:
Choreographing Antiquity

Stephen Papich

During the Golden Age of Hollywood Epics in the 1950s, Mr. Papich served as choreographer on four of the most prestigious productions of the era. His efforts in creating "specialty dances" for these films helped set the mood for these excursions into the distant past.

My Hollywood career began when I was hired as a contract dancer at 20th Century–Fox in 1952. In those days, Fox kept 40 dancers under contract at all times. When we weren't dancing, we also played bit parts in films to keep us busy. I was in *Stars and Stripes Forever*, *The President's Lady* and *Gentlemen Prefer Blondes* as a dancer, a bit player, or both.

In 1953 Fox began filming *The Robe*, which would be a very expensive and complicated production. This was the first CinemaScope movie and each scene was filmed twice, once in widescreen and then again for a standard screen version. The lighting setup had to be changed drastically for each shot as CinemaScope required more lighting. Every day a driver in a limousine would arrive at the studio with the CinemaScope lens, and every evening he would return the lens to the company that owned it. Everybody available on the lot was pressed into service for the crowd scenes in *The Robe*. I was one of the Roman soldiers gambling with Richard Burton at the foot of the cross during the crucifixion scene.

A scene in the Roman baths called for some minor choreography involving a dancing girl played by Virginia Lee. Casting director George Light suggested me because he thought I would be able to choreograph to a "click track," which is really little more than a beat like a metronome. I had worked with the Katharine Dunham Dance Company, and many of the dances had been done only to drum beats. This was my first job as a film choreographer, but I didn't receive any screen credit. Credit often depended on the number of seconds your work was featured on screen, and I was too naive to demand it.

My next picture was the first one on which I got a credit: *Demetrius and the Gladiators*. *The Robe* was so expensive that Darryl Zanuck wanted to make use of the sets for another movie, so a sequel was planned before the first picture had wrapped. I had a lot more to do on this film, and I wanted to make it as authentic as possible. The director, Delmer Daves, had a collection of antique Roman vases which were painted with pictures of dancers. I used these for my inspiration.

Once again, the dances were choreographed to a click track. I was amazed at how perfectly they matched the final music

Stephen Papich and Carmen de Lavallade on the set of *The Egyptian* (1954).

by Franz Waxman. Waxman had worked closely with me and altered the tempo of the click track to fit the movements of my dancers. For a scene in the gladiatorial school we needed dancing girls, and I had chosen one of them specifically for her height. It was Julie Newmar, who was just then beginning her career.

After *Demetrius*, I was loaned out to MGM for a 12-week stint as a dancer in *Seven*

Brides for Seven Brothers. My first day on the set the choreographer, Michael Kidd, took an instant dislike to me and had me fired. I had a contract, so MGM had to pay me for the entire time whether I worked on the picture or not. So I collected my 12 weeks pay and went back to Fox.

One day Darryl Zanuck saw me and asked me what I was doing back on the lot. I told him what had happened, and he told me to go and pick up the script for *The Egyptian*, which was my next film.

This turned out to be an even bigger production than *The Robe*. In addition to the choreography, I also orchestrated all of the procession scenes. I hired Carmen de Lavallade to do an Egyptian specialty dance. This was one of the only times the dancer actually danced to the music. A non-union African drummer was brought in specifically to accompany Carmen's dance for the scene in Nefer's house.

The Egyptian had an especially good cast. I had worked with Edmund Purdom in *Titanic*, and he was an extremely nice fellow. Bella Darvi was very beautiful and a pleasure to work with as well.

After *The Egyptian*, I worked on *Desiree*, starring Marlon Brando as Napoleon. Then, at the suggestion of Franz Waxman, I was loaned out to Warner Bros. to work on *The Silver Chalice*. At my first meeting for *The Silver Chalice*, I carried on about all of these elaborate plans I had for a banquet scene in Nero's court. I was sure nobody paid any attention, but the next time I arrived at the lot they were digging a huge hole in the soundstage floor so my dancers could be catapulted out of it.

The sets for *The Silver Chalice* were enormous and quite stylized. They had borrowed Rolf Gerard from the Metropolitan Opera to design the production, and he did some remarkable things.

The film had a very interesting cast. Virginia Mayo worked hard and was always pleasant. Paul Newman seemed totally indifferent to everything going on. Jack Palance was impossibly temperamental and, on one occasion, walked off the set and didn't come back for several days.

When I returned to Fox I worked on *Untamed*, again with Franz Waxman. Alfred Newman was the head of the music department at Fox, and he always hired the most talented composers. Waxman was my favorite because he worked with me more closely than the others. Bernard Herrmann was also a great guy. Once we ended up sitting next to each other on a plane to New York, and he regaled me with stories of his experiences in Hollywood.

I took a leave of absence from Fox to go to Paris and work with the great Josephine Baker. I later accompanied her back to America where she was immediately arrested by the FBI for being a Communist, which wasn't true. A judge dismissed the charges. Later, when I attempted to go back to Fox, I found that I had been barred from the lot because of my association with Josephine Baker.

At the time we worked on these pictures, it was just another job. Few of us realized the importance of the work we were doing or the lasting effect it would have. Although my Hollywood career ended abruptly, I recall it with great fondness, and I'm proud to have been associated with many films which are now regarded as classics.

Stephen Papich
Hollywood, California

Preface

Back in 1989 and 1990 when I was writing the first edition of this book, a great many of the films were not yet available for home video viewing. I had to rely on my recollections of several of the movies which I had not seen for many years. Frankly, some of those memories did not do justice to the films. Movies like Roger Corman's bargain-basement epics *Viking Women and the Sea Serpent* and *Atlas* deserved far more credit than I originally gave them. When the publishers agreed to do a second edition of *Epic Films*, I was delighted. It isn't often in life that you are given a second chance. At any rate, the difference between memory and reality will account for any drastic changes of opinion that readers of the first book may encounter.

In this second edition I have included 355 films; 222 appeared in the first edition. I have also expanded the credits and information on many of the entries that did appear previously. The list of titles that fit into the epic genre is seemingly endless, and although I have attempted to include as many as possible, I apologize for any omissions.

Credits Abbreviations

P—Producer
D—Director
W—Screenwriter
M—Composer
C—Cinematographer
E—Editor
PD—Production Designer
AD—Art Director
CD—Costume Designer
SVE—Special Visual Effects

Introduction

The dictionary defines the word "epic" as "a poem of elevated character, describing the exploits of heroes and composed in a lofty narrative style." Whether produced on a shoestring budget like *Sins of Jezebel* or at a cost of millions like the 1963 version of *Cleopatra*, all epics are concerned with momentous events and larger-than-life characters. The historical and mythological events portrayed in the films covered by this text take place during the period of time from the creation to the thirteenth century—from cavemen to the Crusades.

The ancient world has always held a strong fascination for both filmmakers and filmgoers. Bringing distant times and places to life through the magic of motion pictures allows modern audiences a glimpse into the historic or mythical past. Such depictions of antiquity are the subjects of some of the earliest movies. In 1907 the famous French illusionist Georges Méliès directed and appeared in a short film entitled *Shakespeare Writing Julius Caesar*. In it Méliès, as the Bard, visualizes the assassination of Julius Caesar in ancient Rome. The same year saw an unauthorized two-reel version of the popular novel *Ben-Hur*, directed by Sydney Olcott. A feature length version of the Oberammergau Passion Play appeared in 1910 and enjoyed considerable financial success. D.W. Griffith directed the four-reel *Judith of Bethulia* in 1913, starring Blanche Sweet and Henry B. Walthall. This became the forerunner of all the Hollywood biblical epics that were to follow.

Elaborate as it was, Griffith's movie was overshadowed by a twelve-reel Italian version of *Quo Vadis* (1912), released in America at the same time Griffith was filming *Judith*. In 1914 the Italians topped their production of *Quo Vadis* with *Cabiria*, directed by Giovanni Pastrone and written by Gabriele D'Annunzio. *Cabiria* introduced the enduring character of the strongman Maciste to the screen in the person of Bartolomeo Pagano. This hero would eventually assume mythical proportions in Italian cinema and reappear in many films throughout the coming years.

It took D.W. Griffith to outdo the Italians in terms of spectacle. With his production of *Intolerance* in 1916, Griffith set a standard for screen spectacle that has seldom been equaled. The film tells four stories simultaneously, and its "Fall of Babylon" sequence hit a new high in cinematic opulence. At the time of its release, *Intolerance* proved unpopular with audiences and resulted in a financial disaster for Griffith. His career would never fully recover from this blow. His problems, however, did not deter other directors from making their contributions to the epic genre.

The following decade brought such notable productions as *The Queen of Sheba* (1921), another imported *Quo Vadis* (1924) and MGM's *Ben-Hur* (1925). It was Cecil B. DeMille who best realized the potential of the epic with his productions of *The Ten Commandments* (1923) and *The King of Kings* (1927). DeMille had hit on the perfect formula with his mixtures of sex, splendor and the sacred. With these two films he became the undisputed "King of the Spectacle," a title he would retain throughout his long career.

Michael Curtiz's mammoth retelling of *Noah's Ark* (1929) was the last of the great silent spectaculars, but by the time it was released to theatres the advent of sound had already destroyed any chances for box office success. The last-minute addition of some sound sequences did little to improve the situation.

During the thirties, DeMille almost singlehandedly kept the epic alive with his films *The Sign of the Cross* (1932), *Cleopatra* (1934) and *The Crusades* (1935). It was unusual for a director to return time and again to this particular type of film. Most of the major Hollywood directors were tempted to tackle the epic at least once in their careers, but only DeMille built his entire reputation on filming spectaculars. The one film which might have threatened DeMille's eminence was Alexander Korda's production of *I, Claudius* (1937), but this was never completed.

The forties were an especially lean period for epics. Even DeMille temporarily abandoned ancient history for Americana. World War II had audiences much more interested in the present than the past. *The Sign of the Cross* was reissued during this time, with a modern prologue and epilogue showing American bombers flying over Rome while a chaplain compares Mussolini to Nero.

In 1949 DeMille returned to the Bible for inspiration, and the result was *Samson and Delilah*, the biggest film of his career up to that time. It also turned out to be one of the most successful. *Samson and Delilah* broke all box office records for Paramount studios.

During the early fifties the epic film flourished as never before; extravagance increased with each new production. In 1953, as Hollywood began to realize that large-scale historical spectaculars might be the way to lure audiences away from their tele-vision sets, 20th Century–Fox added further inducement by introducing the CinemaScope widescreen process in *The Robe*. CinemaScope turned out to be the perfect medium for this type of film. Most of the major studios quickly adopted CinemaScope for their new films, and those who didn't invented their own widescreen processes. Eventually, DeMille outdid them all with his VistaVision and Technicolor remake of *The Ten Commandments* (1956). Apparently this was a tough act to follow because the genre had no notable contributions until the 1959 releases of *Solomon and Sheba* and *Ben-Hur*.

That same year, promoter Joseph E. Levine bought the U.S. distribution rights to a modestly budgeted Italian film about Hercules, starring the former Mr. Universe, Steve Reeves. Levine backed the film with an extensive publicity campaign, the cost of which exceeded the entire budget of the film he was publicizing. The gamble paid off. *Hercules* was a runaway box office bonanza, and Steve Reeves became, for a brief time, one of the most popular actors in the world.

It was as if a dam had burst: Dozens of inexpensive sword-and-sandal potboilers began to pour out of Europe at an alarming rate. The French began to categorize them with the term "Peplum," referring to the skirts worn by men and women alike in these shoestring spectaculars. These films glutted the market to such an extent that occasionally an outstanding production such as *Jason and the Argonauts* (1963) got lost in the shuffle and was sadly neglected by audiences.

Many of the peplum films never made it into U.S. theatres at all and were directly released to television in packages from Embassy or Medallion Pictures. In Los Angeles the local TV station KHJ had a highly rated Saturday night show called *David the Gladiator*. This was hosted by champion bodybuilder Dave Draper, who presented "The World's Biggest Movies." More often than not these included the likes of *Son of Samson*

Victor Mature succumbs to the temptations of Hedy Lamarr in *Samson and Delilah* (1949).

or *Gladiator of Rome*, but occasionally a genuine blockbuster like *Helen of Troy* or *Alexander the Great* would sneak in.

Those Euro-epics that were given a theatrical release were usually highly publicized. The film companies had learned from Joe Levine's example: Dazzle the public into seeing the picture with an avalanche of publicity rather than trying to sell the film on its own dubious merits. The pub-

Body Builder Dave Draper was the Los Angeles television host "David the Gladiator."

licity campaign for one relatively minor effort, *Sword of the Conqueror* (1962), employed a float, complete with muscular gladiator and pretty handmaiden, which traveled to major cities across the country. This stunt is especially worth noting because the gladiator was a young Peter Lupus, who shortly thereafter went to Europe to star, as Rock Stevens, in a series of peplum films.

In 1963 the notorious production problems and $40 million cost of *Cleopatra* nearly destroyed 20th Century–Fox studios and the epic genre. Escalating production costs indicated that the heyday of this type of film was drawing to a close. Big budget box office failures like *The Fall of the Roman Empire* (1964), *The Greatest Story Ever Told* (1965) and *The Bible … In the Beginning* (1967) dealt the final blows. The few theatrical releases in the ensuing years, such as *King David* (1985), seemed anachronistic and met with slim success both critically and financially. The Italian film industry attempted to revive the peplum films during the early eighties with a series of movies usually featuring Lou Ferrigno or Sybil Danning, but the genre stubbornly refused to be resuscitated.

During the past two decades the epic film has flourished on television. It is ironic that the type of film once used to combat the growing threat of television has been kept alive by that same medium. In the nineties two companies emerged as leaders in the production of epic TV films. The Italian company Lube/Lux Vide produced a series of made-for-television biblical films ranging from *Genesis* to *Jesus*. Hallmark Entertainment contributed new versions of such classic tales as *The Odyssey* and *Jason and the Argonauts*, in addition to a remake of *Cleopatra*.

The new millennium saw the triumphant return of the epic genre to the big screen with the release of Ridley Scott's *Gladiator*. This mega-budgeted Roman spectacle was no doubt a gamble, but it paid off handsomely for everyone involved. In addition to being a tremendous winner at the box office, *Gladiator* also won the Academy Award for Best Picture. Despite its success, however, *Gladiator* has spawned few imitators. So far, one of the few movies which has surfaced as a direct result of *Gladiator* is a hardcore gay porno movie set in ancient Rome and entitled *Conquered* (Chi Chi Larue; 2002). With this film, the basically innocent homoerotic images of the peplum movies are taken to the opposite extreme, and the epic film finds a niche in yet another genre.

A more mainstream compromise may be reached with a new film version of the life of Alexander the Great. A trio of historical novels by Valerio Massimo Manfriedi was responsible for generating considerable interest in a new Alexander biopic. An HBO mini-series about Alexander, produced by and starring Mel Gibson, was cancelled when Gibson dropped out. Martin Scorsese briefly showed interest in helming a film about Alexander with Leonardo DiCaprio in the lead. Later, DiCaprio was set to star as Alexander in a Dino De Laurentiis production to be directed by Baz Lurmann. As of this writing, the only Alexander project which has actually gone into production is being directed by Oliver Stone for release by Warner Bros. in November 2004. Colin Farrell beat out Jude Law, Tom Cruise, and Heath Ledger for the lead role. Apparently, Oliver Stone will not shrink from addressing Alexander's homosexuality as Jared Leto is cast as the youthful Greek conqueror's first general and longtime lover.

Amidst all the Alexander hubbub comes the uninspiring news that Tom Cruise may play the title role in a new version of *El Cid* and that Vin Diesel is set to star in a film about Hannibal. More encouraging are Warner Bros. *Troy*, directed by Wolfgang Petersen and Mel Gibson's controversial $30 million movie *The Passion of Christ*. Further in the future is the George Clooney–produced *Gates of Fire*, based on Steven Pressfield's best selling novel about the Battle of Thermopylae. The epic film marches on.

THE FILMS

1 A.D.

(Anno Domini)
A BBC TV/Vincenzo Labella Production
U.S.–NBC TV Network (1985)

P–Vincenzo Labella/D–Stuart Cooper/W–Anthony Burgess, Vincenzo Labella/M–Lalo Schifrin/C–Ennio Guarnieri/E–John Martinelli/PD–Enzo Bulgarelli/CD–Enrico Sabbatini

Cast–James Mason (Tiberius), Ava Gardner (Agrippina), Jack Warden (Nerva), David Hedison (Porcius), Susan Sarandon (Livilla), Richard Kiley (Claudius), Jennifer O'Neill (Messalina), Anthony Andrews (Nero), John McEnery (Caligula), Millie Perkins (Mary), Colleen Dewhurst (Antonia), Dennis Quilley (Peter) with Ben Vereen, Richard Roundtree, Fernando Rey, Ian McShane, Anthony Zerbe, Amanda Pays, Michael Wilding, Jr.

Producer Vincenzo Labella hoped to repeat the success of his *Jesus of Nazareth* and capitalize on the popularity of the TV series *I, Claudius* with this twelve-hour mini-series. The plot relates the fates of Jesus' disciples following his death. This is told against the background of Rome during the reigns of the emperors Tiberius, Caligula, Claudius and Nero. *A.D.* is a slow moving and labored affair which manages to reduce the same era so fascinatingly portrayed in *I, Claudius* to utter boredom. The cast is large but uniformly unmemorable. An interesting footnote in movie history is the presence of Elizabeth Taylor's son Michael Wilding, Jr., as Jesus.

2 Abraham

A Turner/Lube/Lux Vide/Beta Film/Rai Uno Production
U.S.–TNT Network (1994) 175 min.
Color

P–Gerald Rafshoon, Lorenzo Minoli/D–Joseph Sargent/W–Robert McKee/M–Marco Frisina/C–Raffaele Mertes/E–Michael Brown/PD–Enrico Sabbatini, Paolo Biagetti/CD–Enrico Sabbatini

Cast–Richard Harris (Abraham), Barbara Hershey (Sarah), Maximilian Schell (Pharaoh), Vittorio Gassman (Terah) Carolina Rossi (Hagar), Andrea Prodan (Lot), Gottfried John (Eliezer), Kevin McNally (Nahor) with Jude Alderson, Simona Ferro Chartoff, Tom Radcliffe, Paolo Bonacelli, Christian Kohlund

After a voice speaks to him in the desert, Abram rejects the gods of his family and takes his wife and followers on a pilgrimage to a new land. He leads them to the beautiful land of Canaan but, unfortunately it is already occupied by others. Abram and his people cross the desert and arrive in Egypt. Abram's wife Sarai attracts the attention of the Pharaoh, who allows the nomads to stay in Egypt if she will join his household. An affliction comes over the Pharaoh and his Egyptians. Believing the desert tribe to be the cause, Pharaoh returns Sarai to her people and they are driven out of Egypt. Abram leads them back to Canaan, where they are accepted by the inhabitants. After many years the tribe becomes so numerous that Abram's nephew Lot takes his family and followers out of Canaan to live in the city of Sodom. More time passes and Sarai, unable to conceive a child, gives her Egyptian servant Hagar to Abram as a surrogate mother. Hagar has a child who is named Ishmael. Contention grows between Sarai and Hagar until, in her old age, Sarai conceives Isaac. Because of his abiding faith, God changes Abram's name to Abraham, which means the Father of Nations, and Sarai to Sarah. Although it is well produced and generally well acted *Abraham* often seems as dry and long as the Hebrews trek through the desert. This was the first in the Turner series of Italian produced Bible movies, although the Lux Vide production *Genesi: La Creazione e il Diluvio* (*Genesis: The Creation and the Flood*; 1994) preceded it. Directed by Ermanno Olmi, *Genesi* was shown on Italian television but was not imported as part of the Turner Bible series.

3   *The Adventures of Hercules*

(Hercules II)
A Golan-Globus Production
Cannon Italia (1983) 89 min
Technicolor
U.S.–MGM/UA (1984)
P–Alfredo Pecoriello/D/W–Lewis Coates (Luigi Cozzi)/M–Pino Donaggio/C–Alberto Spagnoli/E–Sergio Montanari/PD–Antonello Geleng/CD–Adriana Spadaro/SVE–Jean-Manuel Costa
Cast–Lou Ferrigno (Hercules), Sonia Viviani (Glaucia), Milly Carlucci (Urania), Charlotte Green (Athena), William Berger (King Minos), Claudio Cassinelli (Zeus), Nando Poggi (Poseidon), Maria Rosaria Omaggio (Hera), Laura Lenzi (Flora), Margi Newton (Aphrodite) with Venantino Venantini, Cindy Leadbetter, Raffaele Baldassarre, Serena Grandi, Eva Robbins, Sandra Venturini, Andrea Nicole

Italian director Luigi Cozzi (aka Lewis Coates) strikes again with this sequel to his 1983 film *Hercules*. The Adventures of Hercules covers much of the same ground as its predecessor, even repeating the "highlights" of the first film during the opening credits. Lou Ferrigno stars again as Hercules and William Berger returns as his archenemy King Minos. Cozzi is a big fan of horror and science fiction films and many of his ideas are taken from other movies and incorporated into the plot. The dread fire monster is a dead ringer for "The Monster from the ID" from *Forbidden Planet*. Hercules slays a gorgon in a sequence

Lou Ferrigno stars as the mythical strongman for the second time in *The Adventures of Hercules* (1984).

highly reminiscent of *Clash of the Titans* and King Minos is resurrected from the dead in a scene right out of the Hammer Film *Dracula— Prince of Darkness*. The special effects are marginally better this time around. The slim storyline involves Hercules attempts to recover seven magic thunderbolts stolen from Zesus by three jealous goddesses.

4 *The Affairs of Messalina*

(Messalina)
Produzione Gallone, Rome–Filmsonor, Paris (1951)
  108 min.
U.S.–Columbia (1953)
  P/D–Carmine Gallone/W–Carmine Gallone, Albert Valentin, Vittorio Nino Novarese, Pierre Laroche/M–Renzo Rossellini/C–Anchise Brizzi/ E–Niccolo Lazzari/AD–Gastone Medin/CD–Vittorio Nino Novarese
  Cast–Maria Felix (Messalina), Georges Marchal (Caius Silius), Memo Benassi (Claudius), Jean Tissier (Mnester), Jean Chevrier (Valerius Asiaticus), Michel Vitold (Narcissus), Giuseppe Vari (Pallas), Germaine Kerjean (Ismene), Delia Scala (Cinzia), Erno Crisa (Timus), Camillo Pilotto (Octavius) with Carlo Ninchi, Ave Ninchi, Cesare Barbetti, Gino Saltamerenda

The popular Mexican actress Maria Felix made a bid for international stardom as the dissolute Messalina in this uninspired depiction of the wanton empress's rise and fall. In this free adaptation of historical fact, the emperor Claudius divorces his wife when a fortune-teller predicts the death of Messalina's husband. Messalina weds Caius Silius, a young aristocrat with whom she conspires to overthrow the emperor. Claudius has Silius killed, thereby fulfilling the prediction, and Messalina commits suicide. An impressive production and good cast cannot overcome the dullness of the screenplay. Director Carmine Gallone was a pioneer in Italian cinema.

Maria Felix plans new iniquities in *The Affairs of Messalina* **(1953).**

During his long career, which began in 1913, he directed several epic films over a span of some three decades. The first of these was the 1926 version of *The Last Days of Pompeii*, which he co-directed with Amleto Palermi. He was chosen by Benito Mussolini to helm *Scipio Africanus* (1937) and ended his epic film career with *Carthage in Flames* (1960).

5 Age of Treason

Columbia Pictures Television (1993) 93 min.
U.S.–Cable television release
Color
P/W–Lee David Zlotoff/D–Kevin Connor/ Based on the novel *The Silver Pigs* by Lindsey Davis (uncredited)/M–Ken Thorne/C–Ronnie Taylor/ E–Barry Peters/PD–Franco Fumagalli/AD–Taieb Jallouli/CD–Paolo Scalabrino

Cast–Bryan Brown (Falco), Matthias Hues (Justus) Amanda Pays (Helena), Patricia Kerrigan (Druida), Anthony Valentine (Vespasian), Art Malik (Pertinax), Richard Sharpe (Petro), Sophie Okonedo (Niobe) Jamie Glover (Domitian), Peter Jonfield (Simplex) with Alan Shearman, William Hootkins, Ian McNeice, Shirley Stelfox

Set in Rome A.D. 69, the plot of *Age of Treason* concerns Falco, who refers to himself as a "private investigator." He is hired by a noblewoman to find her missing brother. Falco turns up the brother's corpse, the first clue in what is eventually revealed to be a plot to murder the emperor Vespasian. The scriptwriter took a clever idea and totally ruined it by not being able to decided what type of story he was trying to tell. Is it a mystery, epic, or comedy? Consequently the movie lumbers along in a schizophrenic state for most of its running time. To give some measure of credit, *Age of Treason* has authentic looking sets and costumes and a certain amount of atmosphere. However, the poor quality of the dialogue, delivered by a mind boggling hodge podge of accents, overcomes any virtues the movie might have. Bryan Brown as Falco is perhaps the greatest liability. He speaks all of his lines with the broadest possible Australian accent. This is apparently met to be humorous but instead it is annoying. Major beefcake is provided by German bodybuilder Matthias Hues as Falco's gladiator sidekick, Justus. At least a reason for his accent is given but this still doesn't prevent him from looking like

something out of the W.W.F. SmackDown. Author Lindsey Davis, who has written several Falco novels, was so displeased by the finished film that his name was removed from the credits.

6 Aida

An Oscar Production (1953) 110 min.
FerraniaColor
U.S.–I.F.E. Releasing–Pathé Pictures (1954) 96 min.
P–Ferruccio De Martino, Federico Teti/D–Clemente Fracassi/W–Clemente Fracassi, A. Gobbi, G. Salviucci
Based on the opera by Giuseppe Verdi/Music Supervision–Renzo Rossellini/C–Piero Portalupi/E–Mario Bonotti/AD–Flavio Mogherini/ CD–Maria De Matteis

Cast–Sophia Loren (Aida), Lois Maxwell (Ameneris), Luciano Della Marra (Radames), Afro Poli (Amonasro), Antonio Cassinelli (Ramfis), Enrico Formichi (Pharaoh) with Alba Arnova, Victor Ferrari, Ciro Di Pardo

Aida is an early and largely successful attempt at bringing grand opera to the motion picture screen. Impresario Sol Hurok was responsible for importing this Italian production to the United States. At the time he stated, "This is the first time in my career that I have presented a motion picture. I have done so because I believe that this film has made a spectacular advance in translating opera from stage to the screen." It is a venture that has honorable intentions but is sometimes naive in its execution. For the U.S. release, 14 minutes were cut from *Aida* and narration, which is often irritating and unnecessary, was added. But these are relatively minor annoyances in a film that does have much to recommend it, not the least of which is nineteen-year-old Sophia Loren in the title role. Loren, in one of her earliest starring parts, is beautiful and mimes the dubbed singing voice of Renata Tebaldi to perfection. Luciano Della Marra plays Radames, with the singing voice of Giuseppe Campora. Della Marra was an unknown construction worker when he was chosen for this major role. The best performance is given by Lois Maxwell as the jealous Princess Ameneris (voiced by Ebe Stignani). This Canadian actress later gained fame as the original Miss Moneypenny in the James Bond films. Obviously no effort was spared in bringing the familiar story of the Ethiopian princess, Aida, and her love for the young Egyptian army officer, Radames, to the screen. The impressive production features colossal sets, which are very inaccurate despite publicity to the contrary, and the requisite cast of thousands.

Motion Picture: Lovers of grand opera will find a rare treat in this rendition of Verdi's highly melodious classic. It's even calculated to please movie-goers with no special fondness for opera—there's not one heavy-weight diva in sight.

7   Alexander the Great

United Artists (1956) 141 min.
CinemaScope/Technicolor
P/D/W–Robert Rossen/M–Mario Nascimbene/C–Robert Krasker/E–Ralph Kemplen/ AD–Andre Andrejew/CD–David Ffolkes

Cast–Richard Burton (Alexander), Fredric March (Philip), Claire Bloom (Barsine), Barry Jones (Aristotle), Harry Andrews (Darius), Stanley Baker (Attalus), Nial MacGinnis (Parmenio), Danielle Darrieux (Olympias), Peter Cushing (Memnon), Michael Hordern (Demosthenes), Marisa De Lerza (Eurydice), Gustavo Rojo (Cleitus), Peter Wyngarde (Pausanias) with Ruben Rojo, William Squire, Helmut Dantine, Frederich Ledebur, Virgilio Teixeira, Teresa Del Rio

Robert Rossen's *Alexander the Great* is both literate and lavish; what it isn't is lively. Originally titled *Alexander the Conqueror*, this biography of the youthful Greek warrior is told with restraint, a quality which Richard Burton would have done well to employ to some degree in his characterization of the title role. Instead he rants, raves and chews the beautiful Spanish scenery. Burton's histrionics aside, there are some interesting performances, including a pre–Frankenstein Peter

Cushing as Memnon, a Greek officer who joins the Persians in opposition to Alexander. Myriad other characters come and go with alarming rapidity, due, no doubt, to the fact that United Artists cut the film by forty-five minutes before its release. The most interesting part of *Alexander the Great* is the first half when Alexander and his father Philip (a barely recognizable Fredric March) engage in a heated rivalry for power, spurred on by Alexander's conniving mother Olympias. With the death of Philip, the film loses much of its momentum and begins to seem like one prolonged battle scene. Rossen does manage to use the CinemaScope screen to its fullest potential and provides some impressive panoramas of warring armies.

Photoplay: Rich in pageantry and the clash

Richard Burton as the youthful Macedonian leader *Alexander the Great* (1956).

of ancient battles, this saga of a mighty warrior also has an air of true history, thanks in part to Richard Burton's commanding presence.

8   Alfred the Great

A Bernard Smith-James R. Webb Production
Metro-Goldwyn-Mayer (1969) 122 min.
Panavision/MetroColor
  P–Bernard Smith/D–Clive Donner/W–James R. Webb, Ken Taylor/M–Raymond Leppard/C–Alex Thomson/E–Fergus McDonnell/PD–Michael Stringer/AD–Ernest Archer/CD–Jocelyn Richards
  Cast–David Hemmings (Alfred), Michael York (Guthrum), Prunella Ransome (Aelhswith), Colin Blakely (Asher), Sinead Cusack (Edith), Ian McKellen (Roger) with Julian Glover, Vivian Merchant, Peter Vaughan, Alan Dobie, Peter Blythe, Julian Chagrin, Jim Norton

Alfred the Great is an interesting cinematic portrait of the Saxon warrior who became a king. In A.D. 871 a Viking invasion of England prompts the youthful warrior Alfred to mobilize the local farmers into an army to stave off the attack. The valorous Alfred is crowned King of Wessex and he takes the beautiful Aelhswith to be his queen. Guthrum, leader of the Norsemen, abducts Aelhswith and she soon finds herself hopelessly drawn to him. The film emphasizes the youth-oriented attitudes which prevailed in the sixties. To quote a press release, *"Alfred the Great* is essentially the story of a young man who at first staggers under the weight of the responsibilities history had to thrust on him, but who learns through youth tenacity to shoulder them." *Alfred the Great* failed in its attempts to capture the youth market and quickly faded into obscurity. This failure is unfortunate as there are several elements in the film which make it worth recommending. The Irish location photography is splendid and the two major battle sequences are extremely well staged. David Hemmings and Michael York display great skill in presenting the complexities of their characters and the remainder of the cast is admirable.

Michael York as Guthrum, arch rival of *Alfred the Great* (1969).

9   Alone Against Rome

(Solo Contro Roma/Vengeance of the Gladiators)
Atlantica Cinematografica (1962) 100 min.
Totalscope/Eastman Color
U.S.–Medallion (1963)
  P–Marco Vicario/D–Herbert Wise (Luciano Ricci)/W–Ennio Mancini, Gianni Astolfi, Gasted Green/Based on the novel *The Gladiator* by Gasted Green/M–Armando Trovajoli/C–Silvano Ippoliti/E–Roberto Cinquini/AD–Piero Poletto/CD–Paolo Caraco
  Cast–Rossana Podesta (Fabiola), Lang Jeffries (Brenno), Philippe Leroy (Silla), Gabriele Tinti (Goruk) with Luciana Angelillo, Renato Terra, Federico Hungar, Angelo Bastianoni, Rinaldo Zamperla, Giorgio Nenadova, Giancarlo Bastianoni, Alfredo Davesi, Franco Nonibasti

Marco Vicario produced *Alone Against Rome* especially for his wife Rossana Podesta. He wanted to showcase her in the type of film for which she had become famous. Fabiola, a Christian convert, gives herself to be the mistress of a ruthless Roman governor in order to save the life of the man she loves. Unfortunately, this noble sacrifice is lost on her lover, Brenno, who rejects her because he mistakenly believes she has willingly joined the enemy. Podesta suffers stoically throughout these misunderstandings until the climax in the arena when she is reunited with her sweetheart. The exciting arena sequences were staged by Riccardo Freda. The script is much better than many of its type and the three leading players give above average performances. Philippe Leroy, as the Roman governor Silla, is particularly good in his role, showing considerable depth of character. Instead of the usual raving despot, which became a standard for these films, Silla is a hardened military officer. When he takes Fabiola as his mistress she is merely the spoils of yet another conquest. He later grows to admire her courage and selflessness and tries to truly win her love. When he thinks she has betrayed his trust and made a fool of him, he becomes pitiless. Lang Jeffries, as the gladiator Brenno, is given less to work with by the screenwriters but he does well with a fairly standard hero role. The scene in which Fabiola sneaks away to visit her wounded lover and is then rejected by him, is well played by both Jeffries and Podesta. This is easily the dramatic highlight of the film.

10 *The Amazons*

(Le Guerriere dal Seno Nudo; Warriors of the Naked Breast/War Goddess)

U.S.–American-International (1973) 89 min. Technicolor

P–Nino Krisman/D–Terence Young/W–Dino Maiuri, Massimo De Rita, Serge De La Roche/ Based on a story by Robert Aubrey and Robert Graves/M–Riz Ortolani/C–Aldo Tonti/E–Roger Dwyer/PD–Mario Garbuglia/CD–Giorgio Desideri

Cast–Alena Johnston (Antione), Sabine Sun (Oreitheia), Rossana Yanni (Penthesileia), Helga Line (High Priestess), Godela H. Meyer (Molpadia), Luciana Paluzzi (Phaedra), Angelo Infanti (Theseus), Rebecca Potok (Melanippe), Malisa Longo (Leuthera), Franco Borelli (Perithous) with Fausto Tozzi, Angel Del Pozzo, Benito Stefanelli, Lucy Tiller, Almet Berg, Virginia Rhodes, Veronique Floret

Once a year the Amazons are forced to endure the embraces of the Greek warriors for the sake of propagating their race of women. Antione, Queen of the Amazons, mates with the Greek king, Theseus, and becomes pregnant with his child. Oreitheia, the half-sister of Antione, suspects that the queen has fallen in love with Theseus, and plans to depose her. When Antione rejects her female lover, Oreitheia's suspicions are confirmed. Antione and Theseus continue to make clandestine love

Alena Johnston (left) as the queen of *The Amazons* (1973).

until one day she arrives unexpectedly to find her lover in the arms of his wife. Antione allies with Oreitheia in a scheme to take revenge on the Greeks. The plot backfires and the Amazons are taken to Greece in defeat. Antione vows to establish more freedom in society for the Grecian women. Terence Young, who had directed three highly successful James Bond films prior to *The Amazons*, had less good fortune with this curious combination of spectacle, women's lib and sexploitation. Despite plans for a massive campaign to promote *The Amazons*, AIP found scant playdates for the film. Retitling it *War Goddess* didn't help and the movie remains largely unknown today.

11 *Amazons and Gladiators*

Beyond Films / Drotcroft Ltd / MBP (2000) 89 min.
U.S.–Lions Gate Video
Color
    P–Fred Weintraub, Maxwell Meltzer, Tom Kuhn / D / W–Zachary Weintraub / M–Tim Jones / C–Thomas Hencz / E–Eric Torres / PD–Galius Klicius / CD–Daiva Petrulyte
    Cast–Patrick Bergin (Crassius), Jennifer Rubin (Ione), Nichole Hiltz (Serena), Richard Norton (Lucius), Wendi Windburn (Gwyned), Melanie Gutteridge (Briana), Mary Tamm (Zenobia) with Darius Miniotas, Janina Matekonyte, Tomas Ereminas, Gabija Danileniciute

The army of the Roman general Crassius invades a small village and the parents of the young girl Serena are both killed. Serena is taken to be sold as a slave and her older sister is spirited off to the household of Crassius. Ten years later, Serena has become a palace dancing girl. When a Roman nobleman attempts to force his attentions on her, she stabs him to death. Serena flees the city with the help of Ione, an Amazon warrior. Together they go to the Amazon tribe and Serena trains to become one of them. Serena's main ambition is to avenge her family and, to this end, she goes to the palace of Crassius to assassinate him. There, her identity is betrayed by her sister, who has become the cruel general's mistress. Serena is taken captive and forced to fight with the gladiators in Crassius' private arena. This bargain basement epic was filmed in Lithuania and has nothing to recommend it. One-time "Robin Hood" Patrick Bergin is

one of the few recognizable performers. He is surrounded by a bevy of untalented, and often unclothed, buxom actresses. The Amazons, however, are a singularly unattractive lot and fortunately keep their clothes on throughout. Love interest is supplied by Australian Judo expert Richard Norton. If unlucky enough to view *Amazons and Gladiators*, take note of the opening and closing narration. It is filled with more historical inaccuracies than a dozen peplum films put together.

12 *Amazons of Rome*

(Le Vergini di Roma; The Virgins of Rome / Warrior Women)
Criterion Films S.A., Regina S.A., Paris–Cine Italia, Rome (1962) 93 min.
Eastman Color
U.S.–United Artists (1963)
    P/D–Carlo Ludovico Bragaglia / W–Leo Joannon, Luigi Emmanuele, Gaetan Loffredo, Pierre O'Connell / M–Marcel Landowski / C–Marc Fossard / E–Michel Leroy / AD–Raymond Gabutti
    Cast–Louis Jourdan (Drusco), Sylvia Syms (Cloelia), Ettore Manni (Horatio) with Nicole Courcel, Renaud Mary, Jean Chevrier, Nicholas Vogel, Carlo Giustini, Paola Falchi, Corrado Pani, Michel Piccoli

Another version of the conflict between the newly established city of Roman and the Etruscan leader Lars Porsena (see *Hero of Rome*). Cloelia and three hundred Roman women are given over to the Etruscans as hostages to ensure peace. Drusco, a barbarian leader whose troops are allies of the Etruscans, is assigned the task of safeguarding the captive women. Drusco falls in love with Cloelia and protects the women when they are caught in an escape attempt. Cloelia eventually leads her women across the Tiber back to Rome where they take arms to help fight the Etruscans. Many of the elements from the legend of Cloelia are present but they are handled to greater effect in *Hero of Rome*, which itself is a distorted interpretation. As in that film, Caius Mucius fails in his attempt to assassinate Lars Porsena and burns his own arm as punishment but, rather than build an entire film around this event, *Amazons of Rome* presents it as a minor incident. The bulk of the story is cen-

Sylvia Sims defends the women of Rome from invading Etruscans in *Amazons of Rome* (1963).

tered on Cloelia and her rather masculine group of women warriors. As Cloelia, Sylvia Syms is spirited, if a trifle androgenous. Ettore Manni is wasted in the minor role of the famed Roman general Horatio. Louis Jourdan gives an irritating performance as Drusco. His particular brand of Gallic charm is at a distinct variance with his part as a barbarian overlord. To further undermine the role, he plays every scene with a self-satisfied smirk on his face that would try the patience of even the most charitable viewer.

13   *Androcles and the Lion*

R.K.O. (1952) 98 min.
   P–Gabriel Pascal / D–Chester Erskine / W–Chester Erskine, Ken England / Based on the play by George Bernard Shaw / M–Frederick Hollander / C–Harry Stradling / E–Roland Gross / PD–Harry Horner / AD–Albert D'Agostino, Charles F. Pike / CD–Emile Santiago
   Cast–Jean Simmons (Lavinia), Victor Mature (The Captain), Robert Newton (Ferrovius), Maurice Evans (The Emperor), Alan Young (Androcles), Elsa Lanchester (Magaera), Reginald Gardiner (Lentulus), Lowell Gilmore (Metellus), Noel Willman (Spintho) with Jim Backus, Alan Mowbray, Gene Lockhart, John Hoyt and Jackie the Lion

   This was the last of the Gabriel Pascal–produced films based on the works of George Bernard Shaw. Although Shaw participated in discussions about a film version of his play, he died before actual production got under way. His guidance is sorely missed as this is the least satisfying of the Shaw / Pascal collaborations. Following the wholesale extravagance of *Caesar and Cleopatra*, Pascal could no longer find financial backing in England. He tried to finance the film in Mexico City with Cantinflas as Androcles and Diego Rivera as the Production Designer but negotiations fell through. He then took the project to R.K.O. Pictures in Hollywood. R.K.O. agreed to finance the film but Pascal was forced to economize on production costs. When compared to its costly predecessor, *Androcles and the Lion,*

Victor Mature and Jean Simmons in *Androcles and the Lion* (1952), the first of several epic films they would appear in together.

filmed in black and white, has a decidedly inexpensive look. The script strikes a poor balance between comedy and drama. Victor Mature, as a Roman captain, and Jean Simmons, as his Christian lady love, often seem to have wandered into the wrong movie. Their dramatic scenes are in conflict with the comic tone of the remainder of the film, but this is the fault of the screenwriters and not the performers. Harpo Marx was to have played Androcles and Alan Young makes a poor substitute. More effective are Robert Newton, as an impassioned Christian convert, and Elsa Lanchester, as Androcles' shrewish wife. At the time of its release, R.K.O. publicized the film as a dramatic spectacle ("Pleasure-mad Rome, scarlet symbol of history's most sin-swept era ... comes to wicked life again!") and all but ignored the comic aspects in the advertising campaign. Critical response was negative and Pascal never made another motion picture.

Photoplay: Androcles demands delicately balanced screen adapting, playing and direction. The film version is sorely lacking in these elements.

Motion Picture: It's transformation from the printed page to the screen has not been entirely successful. En route, it seems to have lost much of its sharp Shavian wit, and thus emerges as a somewhat slapstick spectacle.

14   *Antony and Cleopatra*
A Peter Snell Production
Rank Film Distributors (1972) 160 min.
Todd-AO 35 / Technicolor
P–Peter Snell / D–Charlton Heston / Based on the play by William Shakespeare / Adapted by Charlton Heston / M–John Scott, Augusto Alegero / C–Rafael Pacheco / E–Eric Boyd-Perkins / PD–Maurice Pelling / AD–Jose Alguero, Jose Ma Alarcon / CD–Wendy Dickson

Cast–Charlton Heston (Marc Antony), Hildegard Neil (Cleopatra), Eric Porter (Enobarbus), John Castle (Octavius), Fernando Rey (Lepidus), Carmen Sevilla (Octavia), Freddie Jones (Pompey), Jane Lapotaire (Charmian), Douglas Wilmer (Agrippa), Julian Glover (Proculeius) with Peter Arne, Roger Delgado, Warren Clarke, Juan Luis Galiardo, Fernando Bilbao, Sancho Gracia, Garrick Hagan, Monica Peterson, Joe Melia

Plans to film Shakespeare's famous historical tragedy *Antony and Cleopatra* started to form during the filming of *Julius Caesar* (1970). Charlton Heston worked at adapting the play for the screen, while both he and producer Peter Snell began searching for a director and an actress to play Cleopatra. Jack Gold and Peter Glenville were early choices for director but Heston hoped to obtain the services of Orson Welles. When Welles declined, Heston decided to direct the film himself. Welles had advised that without a great actress the play couldn't be done. Irene Papas, Susannah York, Barbara Jefford and Glenda Jackson were early considerations for the part. When Anne Bancroft was finally offered the role she turned it down. With the production ready to shoot, British actress Hildegard Neil was hastily tested and signed for the role, despite some misgivings on the part of Heston. Although filmed in Spain on a modest budget, *Antony and Cleopatra* has a truly epic quality that more expensive films have failed to achieve. Due to the restricted budget, Heston purchased outtakes from *Ben-Hur* to use in the sea battles and this helps give the film added scope. As Mark Antony, Charlton Heston gives one of the finest performances of his career. It is obviously a part he cares deeply about. Although Hildegard Neil was maligned by some critics she is, nevertheless, quite good as Cleopatra. The supporting cast is uniformly excellent and John Scott's evocative score is one of the best of the seventies. Charlton Heston's directorial debut was, unfortunately, a financial failure due to poor worldwide distribution. Obviously a great deal of creative energy was spent to bring *Antony and Cleopatra* to the screen and it is a pity that it went virtually unseen in the United States until the home video release in 1985.

Variety: It is impressively mounted and well played, and though lengthy, it sustains well. The finished film is a neat balance of closeup portraiture and panoramic action. But Heston's particular achievement is that he has kept the love story in primary focus.

15 *Aphrodite, Goddess of Love*

(Afrodite, Dea dell'Amore/ Slave Women of Corinth)
Schermi Produzione, Rome (1958) 103 min.
Schermiscope/Eastman Color
U.S.–Embassy (1960) 86 min.
P–Alberto Manca/D–Mario Bonnard/W–Ugo Moretti, Mario Bonnard, Sergio Leone, Mario Dinardo/M–Giovanni Fusco/C–Tino Santoni/E–Nella Nanuzzi/AD–Saverio D'Eugenio/CD–Giancarlo Bartolini Salimbeni
Cast–Isabelle Corey (Lerna), Antonio De Teffe (Demetrius), Irene Tunc (Diala), Ivo Garrani (Antigonus), Giulio Donnini (Erastus), Carlo Tamberlani (Matthew), Andrea Aureli (Kibbur) with Germano Longo, Paul Muller, John Kitzmiller, Matteo Spinola, Mino Doro, Massimo Serato, Clara Calamai

Rome rules the city of Corinth in the person of Antigonus, an appointee of the emperor Nero. Demetrius, a famous artist, comes to Corinth to sculpt a statue of the goddess Aphrodite. Diala, the mistress of Antigonus, becomes the model for the statue and falls in love with the handsome young sculptor. Demetrius, however, is in love with Lerna, a Christian girl who is Diala's handmaiden. Diala convinces Antigonus to persecute the Christians and Lerna is sent to prison. When the unexpected death of Nero brings about the end of Antigonus and Diala, Demetrius

and Lerna are reunited. Often confused with *The Goddess of Love* which was made the same year, *Aphrodite, Goddess of Love* is the inferior film, lacking the star presence of the former vehicle's Jacques Sernas and Belinda Lee. Director Mario Bonnard reportedly auditioned over one thousand actresses before choosing Irene Tunc as the perfect women to pose for the statue of Aphrodite.

16 *The Arena*

(La Rivolta della Gladiatrici/Naked Warriors)
New World Pictures (1973) 83 min.
Techniscope/Technicolor
P–Mark Damon/D–Steve Carver/W–John William Corrington, Joyce Hooper Corrington/M–Francesco De Masi/C–Aristide Massaccesi/E–Joe Dante
Cast–Pam Grier (Mamawi), Margaret Markov (Bodicia), Lucretia Love (Diedre), Maria Louise (Livia), Paul Muller (Lucilius), Sara Bay (Cornelia), Mary Count (Lucinia), Daniele Vargas (Timarchus), Sid Lawrence (Priscium) with Dick Palmer, Jann Fox, Vic Karis, Anthony Vernon, Anna Melita, Pietro Torrisi

The Arena was the logical step for the epic film genre to take in the newly permissive atmosphere of the late sixties and early seventies. Distributed by Roger Corman's recently formed company New World Pictures, *The Arena* is an exploitation, sexploitation and blaxploitation picture all in one package. It is also a pseudo-peplum film as it contains many of the trappings and performers of the European epics of the early sixties. However, after years of semi-clothed muscular heroes we are now given naked and semi-naked heroines. A brief prologue shows Roman invaders in Britain where they capture a Druid priestess named Bodicia and again in Africa where they take captive the beautiful Nubian, Mamawi. The main story begins in the city of Brundisium where the captives are sold as slaves to the local gladiatorial school. Here they are raped, beaten and eventually forced to fight each other to the death. Bodicia and Mamawi lead the women in a bloody revolt against their cruel masters. Despite the fact that *The Arena* is blatantly exploitative of women, the filmmakers have attempted to inject a women's lib element. Something for everyone, so to speak. What does save this from being a mere

The Arena: **Roman legions on the march (1973).**

peep show is the presence of several players from the heyday of the peplum films a decade before. Rosalba Neri (Sara Bay) is Cornelia, the cruel mistress of Timarchus (Daniele Vargas, in his usual villainous role). Even the ever-present Mimmo Palmara (Dick Palmer) puts in a brief appearance as a Roman centurion. In the small role of a gladiator is Pietro Torrisi who, using the name of Peter McCoy, starred in a series of Conan type films during the eighties (*Sword of the Barbarians, Throne of Fire* etc.). In addition to these familiar faces in front of the cameras, there is an even more familiar name behind the scenes. Joe Dante was the editor on this and several other New World releases before Roger Corman gave him the chance to direct *Piranha* (1978). Dante later went on to direct such popular films as *The Howling* and *Gremlins*. Although direction of *The Arena* is credited to Steve Carver, it was actually directed by Joe D'Amato (real name: Aristide Massaccesi). In Europe the direction of the film is credited to Michael Wotruba, which was Massaccesi's pseudonym prior to

using Joe D'Amato. Confused? In 2001, Roger Corman's current company, New Concorde, released a direct to video remake of *The Arena* starring Playboy playmates Lisa Dergan and Karen McDougal.

17   *Atlantis, the Lost Continent*

Galaxy Productions Inc.
Metro-Goldwyn-Mayer (1961) 90 min.
MetroColor
    P/D–George Pal/W–Daniel Mainwaring/Based on the play *Atlanta* by Sir Gerald Hargreaves/M–Russell Garcia/C–Harold E. Wellman/E–Ben Lewis/AD–George W. Davis, William Ferrari/SVE–Projects Unlimited
    Cast–Anthony Hall (Demetrios), Joyce Taylor (Antillia), John Dall (Zaren), Edward Platt (Azor), Frank De Kova (Sonoy), Barry Kroeger (Surgeon), Jay Novello (Xandros) with Bill Smith, Edgar Stehli, Wolfe Barzell, Buck Maffei, Peter Pal

    Producer George Pal had planned to make a motion picture about the legendary Atlantis while he was under contract to Paramount studios during the early fifties. He purchased the rights to an unproduced play by Sir Gerald Hargreaves but when he presented it to the studio executives they refused to support the project. Several years later, after moving to MGM studios, Pal attempted to revive his plans to film the Atlantis story. This time he met with success. However, he was forced to rush the movie into production without the benefits of an acceptable screenplay or adequate budget. Consequently, several of the more complex special effects sequences had to be scrapped. The financial restrictions are evident in the extensive use of stock footage from *Quo Vadis* and previous Pal productions. The sets and costumes are, for the most part, recycled from *The Prodigal*. Despite these obvious limitations, the film does have its share of imaginative touches, such as an Atlantean submarine and a giant crystal death ray machine. These effects are beautifully designed and well executed. The plot concerns a Greek fisherman named Demetrios, who rescues the princess of Atlantis when she is shipwrecked. When they return to her homeland, he discovers an advanced civilization about to embark on a plan of world conquest. The world is saved when a volcanic eruption sinks Atlantis to the bottom of the ocean. The final destruction, impressive given the small budget, was later reused in Pal's *Seven Faces of Dr. Lao* as the destruction of the city of Woldercan. Anthony Hall (real name: Sal Ponti), was a former songwriter for teen idols Fabian and Frankie Avalon. *Atlantis, the Lost Continent* was his only starring role.

Anthony Hall and Joyce Taylor are an attractive pair of lovers in George Pal's fantasy *Atlantis, the Lost Continent* (1961).

18   *Atlas*

A Filmgroup Presentation (1961) 84 min. VistaScope/Eastman 52-50 Color

P/D–Roger Corman/W–Charles Griffith/M–Ronald Stein/C–Basil Maros/E–Michael Luciano/CD–Barbara Comeau

Cast–Michael Forest (Atlas), Barboura Morris (Candia), Frank Wolff (Praximedes), Walter Maslow (Garnis), Christos Exarchos (Indros), Andreas Filipiddis (Talectos) with Theodore Dimitriou, Miranda Kounelaki, William Jolley, Jean Moore, Robert Hudson, Kent Whitley, James Carleton, Charles Stirling, Sascha Dario

Roger Corman, the "B" movie king, went to Europe in 1960 to negotiate with EMI for a film he hoped to make in London. The deal fell through but Corman figured that while he was in Europe he should do a film anyway. *Hercules* was still pulling in the big bucks in the United States so Corman decided to make a muscleman epic in Greece to capitalize on the

trend toward beefcake. A Greek producer agreed to put up a considerable amount of money for the filming, but later backed out on the deal. This left Corman in Greece with his actors and a $75,000 budget. He also didn't have a muscleman to star. Never one to be deterred by such a minor detail, Corman starred Michael Forest in the title role. Forest, though not muscle-bound like the other peplum stars, did have a handsome face, a nice physique and, as an added bonus, could also act. Due to the very restricted budget, the production had a fifteen-day shooting schedule and used actual locations in lieu of sets. The lack of money is especially evident in the costumes and props and the small number of extras used in the battle scenes. Corman was even forced to don a toga and appear in a couple of shots. Although *Atlas* suffers from its "cast of tens, cost of hundreds" look, Corman does his best with the material at hand. What he does have is a thoughtful script by Charles Griffith and some solid acting by his principal players. Barboura Morris, in particular, gives a charming, and often touching, performance as a world weary ex-priestess who is now the mistress of a tyrant. The plot is a simple conflict of right and wrong, herein called "creation and destruction." The evil Praximedes enlists the strength of a reluctant Atlas to help him overthrow a Greek city. There is more to Atlas than his muscles, as Praximedes' paramour Candia points out: "He has a beautiful body and an even more beautiful mind." She knows of what she speaks and Atlas soon comes to realize the duplicitous nature of Praximedes. He and Candia join the rebel forces who oppose the tyrant and eventually destroy him. Ronald Stein, the underrated composer for many B-movies, must have been happy to compose music for something other than a horror film because he provides one of his best ever scores for *Atlas*.

New York Herald Tribune: Michael Forest, as Atlas, is earnest enough, but stacked up against Steve Reeves, he generates far fewer oohs and ahs.

New York Times: Roger Corman produced and directed the activities, ostensibly on Greek location sites. They provide an additional source of nostalgia for the grandeur that was Rome.

Show Business Illustrated: A dreadful Grecian epic patterned after early Joe Levine.

19 *Atlas Against the Cyclops*

(Maciste nella Terra dei Cyclopi; Maciste in the Land of the Cyclops)
A Panda Films Production (1961) 100 min.
Dyaliscope/Eastman Color
U.S.–Medallion
P–Ermanno Donati, Luigi Carpentieri/D–Antonio Leonviola/W–Oreste Biancoli, Gino Mangini/M–Carlo Innocenzi/C–Riccardo Pallottini/E–Mario Serandrei/AD–Alberto Boccianti/CD–Giuliano Papi
Cast–Gordon Mitchell (Atlas/Maciste), Chelo Alonso (Capys), Vira Silenti (Penope), Dante Di Paolo (Ifito), Paul Wynter (Mumba), Aldo Bufi Landi (Sirone), Aldo Padinotti (Cyclops) with Germano Longo, Giotto Tempestini, Raffaella Pelloni, Massimo Righi, Tullio Altamura, Antonio Meschini, Little Fabio

The descendants of Circe the Enchantress and Polyphemus the Cyclops still want revenge on the descendants of Ulysses for the wrongs done to their forebears. The last of Ulysses' line is an infant boy who is taken to Maciste (he is never referred to as Atlas in the film) for protection. The baby's mother is taken captive by the vengeful Queen Capys who tries unsuccessfully to discover the whereabouts of the child. Maciste comes to rescue the mother and Capys soon falls under the spell of his muscular charms ("I'm no longer a queen, I'm a woman!"). Her jealous henchman drugs Maciste's wine with a truth serum and thus learns where the child is hidden. The baby and his mother are then taken to the island of the Cyclops and thrown into the monster's lair. Maciste follows and slays the one-eyed giant to save them. Gordon Mitchell (real name: Charles Pendleton), was a former school teacher and somewhat older than many of the other musclebound peplum stars when he received the call to go to Europe to appear in this film. Unfortunately, his film debut is marred by Leonviola's typically tepid direction and the overlong running time. The film was later distributed under the title

Opposite: **Atlas (Michael Forest, in black with sword) reviews his meager troops in *Atlas* (1961).**

Atlas Against the Cyclops (1961): Gordon Mitchell in a typical peplum pose.

Monster from an Unknown World in an attempt to attract horror film aficionados.

20   *Attila*

An Alphaville/Michael R. Joyce Production
USA TV Network (2001) 177 min.
Color
   P–Michael R. Joyce, Sean Daniel, James Jacks, Caldecot Chubb/D–Dick Lowry/W–Robert Cochran/M–Nick Glennie-Smith/C–Steven Fierberg/E–Tom Fuerman/PD–Roy Forge Smith/CD–Jane Robinson
   Cast–Gerard Butler (Attila), Powers Boothe (Flavius Aetius), Alice Krige (Placidia), Simmone Jade Mackinnon (N'Kara/Ildico), Tim Curry (Theodosius), Reg Rogers (Valentinian), Steven Berkoff (Rua), Tommy Flanagan (Bleda), Pauline Lynch (Galen), Sian Phillips (Grandmother), Liam Cunningham (King Theodorie), Andrew Pleavin (Orestes) with Jolyon Baker, Kirsty Mitchell, Jonathan Hyde, Rollo Weeks

   In this elaborate TV mini-series filmed in Lithuania, Attila, the ruler of the Huns, is leading his barbarian hordes toward Rome. Since he has conquered everything in his path, the emperors of the divided Roman empire are understandably worried that Attila may be victorious over them as well. The treacherous Roman general Flavius Aetius is released from prison in the hope that he can defeat Attila before he descends on Rome. The culture clash between the civilized Romans and the barbaric Huns is made all the more obvious when the two warring nations attempt an uneasy alliance which is ultimately a failure. Gerard Butler is certainly the most handsome movie Attila we have seen thus far. He portrays the infamous Hun as a hirsute stud with a weakness for hot baths and red headed slave girls. The latter proves to be his downfall.

   Variety: Although basically factual, the mini offers a mixed bag of lush visuals and hokey melodrama. The film would serve as an entertaining educational tool if it weren't for excessive blood and a generous amount of exposed skin.

21   *Attila the Hun*

(Attila, Flagello di Dio; Attila, Scourge of God)
Ponti-De Laurentiis, Italy–Lux Film, France (1955)
 83 min.
Technicolor
U.S.–A Joseph E. Levine Presentation
Warner Bros. (1958)

 P–Carlo Ponti, Dino De Laurentiis/D–Pietro Francisci/W–Ennio De Concini, Primo Zeglio/M–Enzo Masetti/C–Aldo Tonti/E–Leo Cattozzi/AD–Flavio Mogherini/CD–Veniero Colasanti

 Cast–Anthony Quinn (Attila), Sophia Loren (Honoria), Henri Vidal (Ezio), Irene Papas (Grune), Eduardo Ciannelli (Onegesius), Ettore Manni (Bleda), Claude Laydu (Valentinian), Colette Regis (Galla Placidia) with George Brehal, Guido Celano, Carlo Hinterman, Mario Feliciani, Piero Pastore, Aldo Pini, Christian Marquand, Marco Guglielmi

 This Ponti–De Laurentiis follow-up to their financially successful production of *Ulysses* failed to duplicate the previous film's box office draw with audiences. *Attila the Hun* wasn't even picked up for American release until three years after it was produced. Even then, only Sophia Loren's growing popularity ensured its distribution in the United States. In A.D. 451 the barbarian chieftan, Attila, leads his army of warriors across Northern Europe, leaving a path of destruction in his wake. In the city of Ravenna, capital of the Western Roman empire, the court of Emperor Valentinian is alarmed to hear of Attila's approach. Valentinian's ambitious sister, Honoria, offers herself to Attila as his bride so that, together, they can wrest the throne from her brother. Attila rejects her proposal of marriage but keeps her as his mistress. The armies of Attila relentlessly advance toward Rome but the intervention of Pope Leo causes the barbarian

Poster art for *Attila the Hun* with Anthony Quinn and Sophia Loren (1958).

hordes to retreat. Though not the accomplished actress she would later become, Sophia Loren gives a credible performance as the traitorous beauty who gives herself to Attila and is killed for her efforts. Anthony Quinn is properly fierce as the infamous Hun. Director Pietro Francisci would soon score his greatest success with the film *Hercules*, starring Steve Reeves. In 1961, Warner Bros. and Joseph E. Levine reissued *Attila the Hun* on a double bill with *Hercules*: "The Mightiest Men in All the World! … The Mightiest Show in All the World!"

22　*The Avenger*

(La Leggenda di Enea; The Legend of Aeneas
Conquerants Heroiques; Conquering Heroes / The
　Last Glory of Troy)
Europa Cinematografica, Rome–Les Films Modernes, Paris (1962) 108 min.
Euroscope / Eastman Color
U.S.–Medallion (1964)
　P–Giorgio Venturini / D–Giorgio Rivalta, Albert Band (Alfredo Antonini) / W–Ugo Liberatore, Luigi Mangini, Arrigo Montanari / M–Giovanni Fusco / C–Angelo Lotti / E–Antonietta Zita / AD–Arrigo Equini
　Cast–Steve Reeves (Aeneas), Carla Marlier (Lavinia), Liana Orfei (Camilla), Gianni Garko (Turno), Giacomo Rossi Stuart (Euralio) Mario Ferrari (Latino) with Nerio Bernardi, Enzo Fiermonte, Luciano Benetti, Maurice Poli, Pietro Capanna, Adriano Vitale

The Avenger is a sequel to *The Trojan Horse* with Steve Reeves reprising his role of Aeneas. The story provides the link between the fall of Troy and the birth of Rome. Aeneas and his followers, all survivors of the Trojan War, arrive at the banks of the Tiber River and hope to build a new city there. Latino, king of a neighboring city, gives Aeneas permission to settle the land but another local chieftain, Turno, opposes the plan and attempts to destroy the encampment of the Trojans. The ensuing war takes its toll on both sides until Aeneas proposes a hand-to-hand combat between Turno and himself. This is an interesting film dealing with a period of history seldom depicted on screen. It was to be Steve Reeves' final encounter with antiquity. After *The Avenger*, he starred in two films as the pirate Sandokan and in the western *A Long Ride from Hell* (1969). He then retired to his horse

ranch in Southern California where he lived until his death in 2000 at the age of 74.

23　*The Bacchantes*

(Le Baccanti)
Vic Films, Rome (1960) 100 min.
Techniscope / Technicolor
U.S.–Medallion (1961)
　D–Giorgio Ferroni / W–Giorgio Stegani, Giorgio Ferroni / Based on *The Bacchae* by Euripedes / M–Mario Nascimbene / C–Pier Ludovico Pavoni / CD–Nadia Vitale
　Cast–Tania Elg (Dirce), Pierre Brice (Dionysus), Alessandro Panaro (Manto), Alberto Lupo (Pentheus) with Akim Tamiroff, Nerio Bernardi, Erno Crisa, Gerard Landry, Miranda Campa

Supposedly based on a classic Greek drama, *The Bacchantes* is closer in spirit and execution to the sword and sandal action adventures than it is to Euripedes. Pentheus, the new King of Thebes, refuses to acknowledge Dionysus; so the God of Wine brings drought and famine to the land of Boeotia. When Pentheus continues to oppose Dionysus, a group of women who worship the god flee into the forest to escape persecution. These women become the magical Bacchantes, who dance in tribute to Dionysus and avenge the wrongs done to him. The portrayal of the Bacchantes is decidedly different from their literary personae. The mythological Bacchantes (also known as the Maenads) were mad women who danced wildly and destroyed any living creatures they came in contact with by tearing them to pieces and devouring the flesh. In the film version they are a group of beautiful women, led by ballerina Tania Elg, who fight on the side of good. The choreography is by Herbert Ross, who later became the director of such diverse films as *The Owl and the Pussycat* and *The Turning Point*.

24　*Barabbas*

(Barabba)
A Dino De Laurentiis Production
Columbia (1962) 134 min.
Technirama / Technicolor
　P–Dino De Laurentiis / D–Richard Fleischer / W–Christopher Fry / Based on the novel by Par Lagerkvist / M–Mario Nascimbene / C–Aldo Tonti / E–Raymond Paulton / AD–Mario Chiari / CD–Maria De Matteis

A captive Pierre Brice is comforted by Tania Elg in *The Bacchantes* (1961).

Cast–Anthony Quinn (Barabbas), Silvana Mangano (Rachel), Arthur Kennedy (Pontius Pilate), Katy Jurado (Sara), Harry Andrews (Peter), Valentina Cortese (Julia), Vittorio Gassman (Sahak), Jack Palance (Torvald), Ernest Borgnine (Lucius), Norman Wooland (Rufio), Roy Mangano (Christ), Douglas Fowley (Vasasio) with Arnoldo Foa, Laurence Payne, Robert Hall, Ivan Triesault, Joe Robinson, Michael Gwynn

An impressive but slow-moving account of the fate of Barabbas. Pontius Pilate offers to spare a prisoner from crucifixion and the people of Jerusalem choose to free the murderer and thief, Barabbas, and send Jesus to the cross in his place. Barabbas returns to a life of crime and is again captured by the Romans. This time he is sentenced to be a slave in the sulfur mines in Italy. After twenty years of labor, he is sent to a gladiator school to be trained for the arena. His audacity as a fighter soon earns him his freedom. When Rome is set aflame, he joins the Christians who have been wrongly accused of setting the fires. He is taken prisoner and condemned to die on the cross. At the moment of his death he realizes the enduring truths of Jesus and accepts him as his Savior. The screenplay by poet/ playwright Christopher Fry is based on the 1951 novel by Swedish Nobel Prize winner Par Lagerkvist. The book was first brought to the attention of Dino De Laurentiis by Federico Fellini when they were filming *La Strada* in 1954. The director had hoped to eventually direct Anthony Quinn in a movie version. By the time Dino De Laurentiis decided to film the story, Fellini was involved in other projects. *Barabbas* was over two years in preparation and, according to studio publicity, employed a total of 66,175 extras. The Roman arena in Verona was restored for use in the gladiatorial sequences and these scenes alone featured over 9,000 extras. Anthony Quinn is fine in the title role but it is Silvana Mangano who makes the most of her brief scenes as a former prostitute who has become a Christian. Peplum star Joe Robinson can be seen briefly as a gladiator.

Motion Picture: This over long, but frequently exciting spectacle falls short of being one of the "great ones," but, once again, Anthony Quinn gives a dynamic performance.

Cosmopolitan: As a spectacle, the movie is first-rate; as a study of a man torn between God and evil, it is confused and superficial.

Modern Screen: Filled with virile adventure and authentic spectacle, this Italy-produced drama still focuses on the believable human being strongly portrayed by Quinn.

25   Battle of the Amazons

(Amazzoni: Donne d'Amore e di Guerra; Amazons: Women of Love and War)
Roas Produzioni, Rome–Pelimex S.A., Madrid (1973) 92 min.
Techniscope / Technicolor
U.S.–American-International
    P–Riccardo Billi / D–Al Bradly (Alfonso Brescia) / W–Mario Amendola, Bruno Corbucci, Fernando Izcaino Casas / M–Franco Micalizzi / C–Fausto Rossi / AD–Bartolomeo Scavia
    Cast–Lincoln Tate (Zeno), Lucretia Love (Eraglia), Paola Tedesco (Valeria), Robert Vidmark (Ilio), Benito Stefanelli (Erno), Mirta Miller (Melanippe), Genia Woods (Antiope), Giancarlo Bastianoni (Filodos), Luigi Ciavarro (Turone), Pilar Clement (Elperia), Solvi Stubing (Sinade) with Francisco Brana, Sonia Ciuffi, Riccardo Pizzuti, Marco Steffani, Franco Ukmar

A soldier, Zeno, is taken captive by the Amazons and made a slave. He escapes, but is wounded in the attempt. Eraglia, the daughter of a tribal chieftain, finds Zeno and tends to his wounds. After Zeno returns to his band of fellow soldiers, Eraglia's village is raided by the Amazons and her father is killed. Eraglia enlists the aid of Zeno and his men in helping train her villagers to fight against the Amazons. This violent, repulsive film has no redeeming qualities whatsoever. It is ugly to look at and, due to an awful background score, just as ugly to hear. The storyline includes all of the standard Amazon clichés with the cruel warrior women pillaging neighboring villages and kidnapping the menfolk for slaves and the abhorrent, but necessary, act of procreation. The plot is merely an excuse for showing bare breasts and acts of sadism. Why AIP decided to give *Battle of the Amazons* a widespread release and neglect the vastly superior *The Amazons* is a puzzlement.

26   Beast of Babylon Against the Son of Hercules

(L'Eroe di Babilonia; Hero of Babylon / Goliath–King of Slaves)
C.I.R.A. & F.I.A., Rome–Gladiator Film, Paris (1964) 86 min.
Euroscope / Eastman Color
U.S.–Embassy
    D–Siro Marcellini / W–Gian Paolo Callegari, Siro Marcellini, Albert Valentin / M–Carlo Savina / C–Pier Ludovico Pavoni / E–Nella Nannuzzi / AD–Pier Vittorio Marchi / CD–Mario Giorsi
    Cast–Gordon Scott (Nippur), Genevieve Grad (Tamira), Moira Orfei (Ura), Mario Petri (Cyrus) with Piero Lulli, Celina Cely, Andrea Scotti, Andrea Aureli, Giuseppe Addobbati, Paolo Petrini, Consalvo Dell'Arti, Oreste Lionello

A flaming comet appears in the skies over Babylon and Ura, the high priestess of Ishtar, predicts the fall of the great city. In an attempt to thwart this prediction, King Belshazzar decrees that all the beautiful young maidens of Babylon must be sacrificed to Ishtar. Prince Nippur, the rightful heir to the thone of Babylon, has been living under the protection of Cyrus, the King of Persia. A group of slaves who are planning a revolt send one of their leaders to bring Nippur back to Babylon. Nippur confronts his cruel cousin Belshazzar and demands that he take account for his evil actions. The rebels plan to assassinate Belshazzar while he attends a sacrificial ceremony. Realizing the futility of this plan, Nippur foils the assassination attempt but is wounded as he is escaping. He is found by soldiers from Cyrus' army, which is marching on Babylon. Nippur agrees to organize a revolt within the walls of Babylon while Cyrus attacks from without. Together, they defeat Belshazzar and Nippur assumes his rightful place on the throne. If Steve Reeves was the king of the peplum films then Gordon Scott must certainly have been the Crown Prince, by virtue of quantity if not quality. Films such as *Tyrant of Lydia*, *Beast of Babylon* and *Conquest of Mycenae* begin to blend together with interchange-

Beast of Babylon Against the Son of Hercules (1964): **The Prince of Babylon (Gordon Scott, left) fights to regain his throne.**

able sets, costumes and performers until one becomes almost indistinguishable from the other.

27　*Ben-Hur*

Metro-Goldwyn-Mayer (1925) 148 min.

P–Louis B. Mayer, Irving Thalberg, Samuel Goldwyn/D–Fred Niblo/W–June Mathias, Bess Meredyth, Carey Wilson/Based on the novel by General Lew Wallace/M–David Mendoza, William Axt/C–Rene Guissart, Percy Hilburn, Karl Struss, Clyde de Vinna/E–Lloyd Nosler/AD–Cedric Gibbons, Horace Jackson/CD–Hermann J. Kaufmann

Cast–Ramon Novarro (Judah Ben-Hur), Francis X. Bushman (Messala), May McAvoy (Esther), Claire McDowell (Princess of Hur), Kathleen Key (Tirzah), Carmel Meyers (Iras), Nigel De Brulier (Simonides), Betty Bronson (The Virgin Mary), Mitchell Lewis (Ilderim), Frank Currier (Quintis Arrius) with Leo White, Charles Belcher, Dale Fuller, Winter Hall

Ben-Hur, based on the popular 1880 novel by General Lew Wallace, had already been a successful stage play and an unauthorized 1907 two-reeler directed by Sidney Olcott when the Goldwyn Company purchased the movie rights in 1922. The film was to be made in Italy by director Charles Brabin from a screenplay by June Mathias. The stars were George Walsh as Ben Hur and Francis X. Bushman as Messala. With the formation of MGM in 1924, Louis B. Mayer and Irving Thalberg viewed the rushes of Brabin's footage and realized that they had a potential disaster on their hands. Charles Brabin was replaced by Fred Niblo. Bess Meredyth and Carey Wilson were brought in to rewrite the scenario. George Walsh was replaced by Ramon Novarro. Filming continued in Italy for many months and rumors persisted that the lives of several men were lost as a result of the dangerous stunts

Ramon Novarro as *Ben-Hur* (1925).

Stephen Boyd (Messala) Hugh Griffith (Shiek Ilderim), Martha Scott (Miriam), Cathy O'Donnell (Tirzah), Sam Jaffe (Simonides), Finlay Currie (Balthasar), Frank Thring (Pontius Pilate), Andre Morell (Sextus), Marina Berti (Flavia), Terence Longden (Drusus), George Relph (Tiberius) with Adi Berber, Stella Vitelleschi, Jose Greci, Laurence Payne, Mino Doro, Robert Brown, Duncan Lamont, Dervis Ward, Claude Heater, Richard Coleman, John Horsley, Ferdy Mayne

required in the sea battle and chariot race sequences. The chariot race footage shot in Italy proved inadequate so the company returned to Hollywood where a new set was built and the race restaged. Released in December 1925, *Ben-Hur* is the apex of the silent screen epic. The film's two exciting set pieces are the sea battle and the famous chariot race. The former has the advantage over the same scene in the 1959 remake, as it boasts full-size ships and not unconvincing miniatures. *Ben-Hur* also has the novelty of several sequences filmed in two-strip Technicolor. Novarro and Bushman are good as the hero and antagonist but the film fails badly in the presentation of the two major women's roles. May McAvoy as Esther is decked out in Mary Pickford curls and Carmel Myers as Iras is a typical twenties style vamp. William Wyler, who directed the 1959 remake, was an assistant director on this version.

28   Ben-Hur

Metro-Goldwyn-Mayer (1959) 217 min.
  P–Sam Zimbalist / D–William Wyler / W–Karl Turnberg / Based on the novel by General Lew Wallace / M–Miklos Rozsa / C–Robert Surtees / E–Ralph E. Winters, John D. Dunning / AD–William A. Horning, Edward Carfagno / CD–Elizabeth Haffenden
  Cast–Charlton Heston (Judah Ben-Hur) Jack Hawkins (Quintus Arrius), Haya Harareet (Esther),

In 1955 MGM began plans for a remake of their silent classic *Ben-Hur*, to be directed by Sidney Franklin. When filming actually began a few years later William Wyler was in the director's chair. One of Wyler's first acts was to suggest Charlton Heston for the part of the villainous Messala. He had recently directed Heston in the large-scale western *The Big Country* and was impressed with the talented actor's performance. Rock Hudson was to be borrowed from Universal for the part of Ben-Hur. Negotiations for Hudson fell through and MGM suddenly found themselves without a leading man. Several newcomers, including British actor George Baker, were tested for the part but none proved satisfactory. Wyler, who had been considering Heston for the lead from the very first, convinced MGM to put him in the title role. This turned out to be a happy twist of fate for everyone involved except, perhaps, Rock Hudson. Other members of the cast were Stephen Boyd as Messala, Israeli actress Haya Harareet as Esther, Jack Hawkins as Quintus Arrius and Marie Ney as Miriam. With the major casting out of the way, Wyler turned his attention to Karl Turnberg's screenplay, which he felt needed some refinement. Maxwell Anderson, S.N. Behrman and Gore Vidal all did rewrites, but Wyler was still not satisfied with the script. Wyler bought in poet / playwright Christopher Fry to further revise the screenplay. Fry remained on hand throughout the entire filming in Rome to supply any necessary script changes. Those involved with the production have stated that his contributions helped the film immeasurably. Controversy regarding the extent of Gore Vidal's involvement still continues, with Vidal claiming much of the credit for the final screenplay. Several months into the filming, Wyler replaced Marie Ney as Miriam and refilmed all of her scenes with Martha Scott in the part. Wyler had decided that he wanted British actors for the Romans and American actors for the Jews and Marie Ney had been an exception to this. Two other cast members had reason to be unhappy. Kamala Devi was to have played the part of Iras, a temptress who is employed by Messala to seduce Ben-Hur. All of the scenes involving her character were eliminated from the final script. Marina Berti fared only slightly better in the role of Flavia, a Roman beauty who falls in love with Ben-Hur while he is living in Rome. All of her lines were cut from the final print but she can be seen at Ben-Hur's side during the scene at Arrius' party. Filming was completed at Cinecitta Studios at a cost of $15 million and *Ben-Hur* went on to become one of the most successful motion pictures of all time, winning a record-breaking eleven Academy Awards. Sadly, producer Sam Zimbalist died during the filming and never saw the finished movie. The major credit for the film's tremendous success must be given to director William Wyler who never substitutes spectacle for intimacy. The characters are the focal point of the story and Wyler never loses sight of this all-important detail.

Marina Berti and Charlton Heston in a scene cut from *Ben-Hur* (1959).

AA Nominations: Best Picture*, Actor (Charlton Heston)*, Supporting Actor (Hugh Griffith)*, Direction*, Screenplay, Editing*, Color Art Direction* Color Cinematography*, Color Costume Design*, Special Effects*, Sound*, Musical Score*

Red Book: *Ben-Hur* is long, it has too much of everything and it is gory, but it is also a magnificent spectacle.

29   *The Bible ... In the Beginning*

(La Bibbia)
A Dino De Laurentiis Production
20th Century–Fox (1967) 174 min.
Dimension-150 / Color by DeLuxe

P–Dino De Laurentiis / D–John Huston / W–Christopher Fry / M–Toshiro Mayuzumi / C–Giuseppe Rotunno / E–Ralph Kemplen / AD–Mario Chiari / CD–Maria De Matteis

Cast–Stephen Boyd (Nimrod), Ava Gardner (Sarah), Richard Harris (Cain), John Huston (Noah), Peter O'Toole (The Three Angels), Michael Parks (Adam), George C. Scott (Abraham), Zoe Sallis (Hagar), Eleonora Rossi Drago (Lot's Wife), Franco Nero (Abel), Ulla Bergryd (Eve), Gabriele Ferzetti (Lot) with Robert Rietty, Grazia Maria Spina, Claudie Lange

In 1961 producer Dino De Laurentiis announced his grand plan to film *The Bible* as a

Director John Huston and Ulla Bergryd (as Eve) on the set of *The Bible* (1967).

multi-director, ten hour film with highlights from the Old and New Testaments. It would be filmed over a period of three years to be shown in three parts. Laurence Oliver, John Gielgud and Ralph Richardson were possible stars. Orson Welles and Charlie Chaplin were mentioned as two of the directors. The estimated cost was $25 million, which would have made it the costliest film ever, in those pre-*Cleopatra* days. Eventually De Laurentiis had to settle for one director and the book of Genesis from the Creation through the story of Abraham. Despite the efforts of John Huston and an all-star cast, the film tends to be pretentious and boring. Huston does triple duty as director, Noah, and the voice of God. After an uninspired, though beautifully photographed, version of the Creation, we are given a very modern Adam and Eve in the persons of Michael Parks and Ulla Bergryd. Most of their time is spent jumping from bush to bush to prevent the viewers from getting a glimpse of their genitals. Richard Harris, as Cain, chews the scenery and kills his brother Abel (Franco Nero in his first English-language film). The Great Flood is the most memorable and entertaining sequence with John Huston's comic interpretation of Noah, a role originally intended for Charlie Chaplin. This brings the first half of the film to a very satisfying conclusion. The second half begins with the story of the Tower of Babel, featuring Stephen Boyd as King Nimrod in heavy mascara. This sequence is closest in

spirit to the grand style of DeMille. The final and longest portion features George C. Scott as Abraham and Ava Gardner as his wife, Sarah. These two fine performers are mired in the dullest part of the entire film. Even the bizarre antics on view in Sodom and Gomorrah can't do anything to enliven it. *The Bible* ends on this sour note and its failure at the box office brought an end to the lengthy cycle of biblical films which had begun in 1949 with *Samson and Delilah*.

AA Nomination: Best Musical Score

Variety: An achievement which will endure for generations. People will see it as children, as teenagers and later as parents taking their children.

30   *The Big Fisherman*

A Centurion Films Production (1959) 180 min. Buena Vista

P–Rowland V. Lee / D–Frank Borzage / W–Howard Estabrook, Rowland V. Lee / Based on the novel by Lloyd C. Douglas / M–Albert Hay Malotte / C–Lee Garmes / E–Paul Weatherwax / PD–John De Cuir / CD–Renie

Cast–Howard Keel (Simon), Susan Kohner (Fara), John Saxon (Voldi), Martha Hyer (Herodias), Herbert Lom (Herod), Ray Stricklyn (Deran), Marian Seldes (Arnon), Alexander Scourby (David), Beulah Bondi (Hannah), Jay Barney (John the Baptist), Charlotte Fisher (Rennah), Mark Dana (Zendi), Rhodes Reason (Andrew), Henry Brandon (Menicus) with Brian Hutton, Thomas Troupe, Marianne Stewart, Jonathan Harris, Leonard Maudie, James Griffith, Peter Adams

By all rights *The Big Fisherman* should have been a classic motion picture. Based on Lloyd C. Douglas' semi-sequel to *The Robe*, produced and directed by men long associated with quality film fare, and starring talented veteran performers plus some attractive and competent newcomers, the film had all the earmarks of greatness. What went wrong? Producer Rowland V. Lee had retired from motion picture production in the forties but decided to return when he was able to acquire the screen rights to Douglas' novel. He then began to mount one of the biggest productions ever assembled in Hollywood. Seventy-three sets were built in the San Fernando Valley near Hollywood. Thousands of props and costumes were designed and executed for the mammoth undertaking. The plot focuses on

Howard Keel questions the motives of Susan Kohner in *The Big Fisherman* (1959).

Fara, a princess of Arabia. Upon learning that she is the daughter of King Herod, Fara sets out on a mission to revenge herself on the father who deserted her. Along the way she is befriended by John the Baptist and Simon called Peter, the Big Fisherman. The teachings of Jesus remove the hatred for Herod from her heart and she willingly joins the multitudes who follow the Nazarene. Despite what might have been an interesting storyline, dramatically the film is wanting. The dialogue is stilted and the performances are generally mediocre. Susan Kohner does have some opportunity to shine as Princess Fara and manages to overcome the limitations of the script. Kohner made only a handful of films but she was very good in all of them. Howard Keel is a major disappointment as Simon Peter. Best know for his singing roles, he has shown himself to be a capable actor in several nonmusical films. Although physically perfect for the part, it seems beyond his range

of acting ability. John DeCuir's exquisite production design is the highlight of the motion picture.

AA Nomination: Color Art Direction, Color Costume Design

Motion Picture: A dazzling spectacle illuminates the beginnings of Christianity. John Saxon and Susan Kohner provide the romance.

31 *The Black Rose*

A 20th Century–Fox Ltd/London Film Studios
  Production
20th Century–Fox (1950) 120 min.
Technicolor
  P–Louis D. Leighton/D–Henry Hathaway/W–Talbot Jennings/Based on the novel by Thomas B. Costain/M–Richard Addinsell/C–Jack Cardiff/E–Manuel Del Campo/AD–Paul Sheriff, W. Andrews/CD–Michael Whittaker
  Cast–Tyrone Power (Walter), Orson Welles (Bayan), Cecile Aubry (Maryam), Jack Hawkins (Tristram), Finley Currie (Algar), Michael Rennie

(King Edward), Herbert Lom (Anthemus), James Robertson Justice (Simeon), Laurence Harvey (Edmund) with Mary Clare, Alfonso Bedoya, Gibb McLaughlin, Henry Oscar, Torin Thatcher, Hilary Prichard, George Woodbridge, Carl Jaffe, Ley On, Bobby (Robert) Blake

Based on one of those expansive novels of historical fiction so beloved by the producers at 20th Century–Fox, *The Black Rose* was originally announced for filming by the studio in 1946 with Cornel Wilde as the star. Eventually produced in England to utilize Fox funds being held there, *The Black Rose* reunited stars Tyrone Power and Orson Welles, who had just appeared together in *Prince of Foxes*, filmed by the same studio in Italy the previous year. The complicated story, set in the thirteenth century, involves many characters and traverses a great deal of geography during the course of its running time. Walter of Gurnie, a deposed Saxon nobleman who is weary of his country's Norman rule, leaves England hoping to find his fortune in distant Cathay. He is joined on this journey by his friend Tristram. They buy passage with a caravan led by the fierce Mongol warrior Bayan of the Hundred Eyes, who is marching his army toward China. Also with the caravan is the beautiful slave girl Maryam, known as the Black Rose. Her father was an English Crusader and she hopes someday to go to his homeland. Walter is temporarily blinded by Bayan's dreams of conquest and power, despite Tristram's argument the he is not following an honorable quest. *The Black Rose* is a beautifully produced film with some outstanding location color photography. Tyrone Power manages to convincingly play the part of the young adventurer, although he was thirty-six years old at the time the movie was made. *The Black Rose* was met with more than its share of critical lambasts, most of which seem overly severe in light of the films obvious merits.

32   *Blue Paradise*

(Adamo ed Eva, la Prima Storia d'Amore; Adam and Eve, the First Love Story)
Alex Film International, Rome–Arco Film, Madrid (1982) 90 min.
Telecolor
U.S.–Trans World Entertainment
  P–Enzo Doria/D–John Wilder (Luigi Russo)/

W–Domenico Raffle, Luigi Russo, Donald Forrest, Eugenio Benito/M–Guido and Maurizio De Angelis/C–Martin Janssen/E–Alan O'Neal/AD–Xavier Fernandez/CD–Rossana Romanini
  Cast–Mark Gregory (Adam), Andrea Goldman (Eve) with Vito Fornari, Constantino Rossi, Angel Alcazar, Pierangelo Pozzato, Liliana Gerace, Leda Simonetti, Antonio Adolfi, Andrea Aureli, Patrizia Rubeo

Surely the strangest version of Adam and Eve on film. This hodgepodge of fundamentalism, Darwinism and pure idiocy could have been subtitled "Adam and Eve Meet One Million Years B.C. in the Blue Lagoon." The movie opens with the creation of man and proceeds in a manner not very different in approach from *The Sin of Adam and Eve*. Adam and Eve are a very contemporary looking couple of kids with gorgeous physiques and trendy hairstyles. They play around innocently in the Garden of Eden until Eve becomes bored and hopes to find excitement by eating the forbidden fruit. A volcanic eruption (lifted from *One Million Years B.C.*) ensues. Adam and Eve are almost crushed by a huge rolling boulder (in a scene right out of *Raiders of the Lost Ark*) but escape to find themselves in a harsh prehistoric world. They are attacked by a pterodactyl (also courtesy of *One Million Years B.C.*) and encounter a variety of primitive tribes in various stages of evolution. Following one of their endless quarrels, Adam and Eve go their separate ways. Eve takes up with one of the more highly developed humanoids (in an extremely bad wig credited to "Sexy Wigs" in the end titles) and together they invent "infidelity." Adam returns and sends Eve's gentleman caller packing. Suddenly the Ice Age is upon them but Adam tells Eve not to fear because he knows that "something is going to happen soon." Sure enough, the Ice Age ends as suddenly as it began. Eve is pregnant and gives birth in the warm ocean waters to the strains of a dreadful pop song. Mark Gregory (aka Marco Di Gregorio) went on to become a popular action hero in Italian cinema, starring in several films as "Thunder Warrior."

33   *The Boys from Syracuse*

Universal (1940) 73 min.
  P–Jules Levy/D–A. Edward Sutherland/W–

Paul Gerard Smith, Leonard Spiegelgass / Based on the play by George Abbott / Songs: Music by Richard Rodgers, Lyrics by Lorenz Hart / C–Joseph Valentine / E–Milton Carruth / PD–John Otterson / CD–Vera West

Cast–Allan Jones (Antipholus), Joe Penner (Dromio), Martha Raye (Luce), Rosemary Lane (Phyllis), Charles Butterworth (Duke of Ephesus), Irene Harvey (Adriana), Eric Blore (Pinch), Alan Mowbray (Angelo) with Samuel Hinds, Tom Dugan, Spencer Charters, Bess Flowers

The successful 1938 Broadway musical was brought to the screen by Universal in an abbreviated version which, despite some lovely Rodgers and Hart songs, is never anything more than mediocre. The plot, which was adapted from Shakespeare's *Comedy of Errors*, concerns a war between the Greek cities of Ephesus and Syracuse. Antipholus and Dromio of Ephesus, have twins in Syracuse. When the twins show up in Ephesus they cause no end of confusion for Antipholus, Dromio and their wives, Luce and Adriana. Martha Raye steals the show with some energetic dance routines.

34   *Braveheart*

An Icon Productions / Ladd Company Production
Paramount (1995) 177 min.
Panavision / Color by DeLuxe

P–Mel Gibson, Alan Ladd Jr, Bruce Davey / D–Mel Gibson / W–Randall Wallace / M–James Horner / C–John Toll / E–Steven Rosenblum / PD–Tom Sanders / CD–Charles Knode

Cast–Mel Gibson (William Wallace), Sophie Marceau (Isabelle), Patrick McGoohan (King Edward), Catherine McCormack (Murron), Peter Hanly (Prince Edward), Brian Cox (Argyle), Sean Lawlor (Malcolm), James Cosmo (Campbell) with James Robinson, Sandy Nelson, Sean McGinley, Stephen Billington, Angus MacFayden

This is the story of William Wallace, one of Scotland's greatest patriots, who fought against England for the independence of his country. Fed up with the tyranny of King Edward I, Wallace engineered a resistance movement which culminated in 1297 at the Battle of Stirling Bridge. This was actor Mel Gibson's second directorial effort. It was a mammoth undertaking which, in addition to his own acting duties, involved maneuvering as many as seventeen hundred extras for the battle scenes. He was rewarded with an Oscar for

Best Director. Author Randall Wallace (a possible descendant) became interested in William Wallace in 1983 and, after reading the medieval manuscript *The Wallace*, began to develop a screenplay which was eventually purchased by producer Alan Ladd, Jr. This well written film has all of the key elements of a great epic—valor, treachery, romance and tragedy. The outstanding direction and excellent performances put it in a class with the best of the genre.

AA Nominations: Best Picture*, Director*, Screenplay, Cinematography*, Sound, Musical Score, Editing, Costume Design, Makeup*, Sound Effects Editing*

35   *Brennus, Enemy of Rome*

(Brenno, il Nemico di Roma / Battle of the Valiant)
Victory Films (1963) 92 min.
Ultrascope / Eastman Color
U.S.–American-International

P–Luigi Mondello / D–Giacomo Gentilomo / W–Arpad De Riso, Nino Scolaro / M–Carlo Franci / C–Oberdan Trojani / E–Gino Talamo / AD–Piero Filippone / CD–Virgilio Ciarlo

Cast–Gordon Mitchell (Brennus), Tony Kendall (Quintus Fabius), Ursula Davis (Nissia), Margherita Girelle (Catulla), Erno Crisa (Vatinius) with Massimo Serato, Carlo Lombardi, Nerio Bernardi, Andrea Aureli, Roland Gray, Anna Maria Pace, Marco Vassilli, Michael Gaida, Lucio De Santis, Aldo Cecconi, Goffredo Unger, Pietro Tordi, Aldo Pini, Carla Calo

In 390 B.C. Brennus the Gaul leads his army of barbarians into Italy. When he lays siege to the city of Clusium he offers to spare the place in exchange for the beautiful Nisia, who has captured his fancy. Secretly he plans to take both the girl and the city before marching his troops on to Rome. Brennus' plans are thwarted and he is killed by Nisia's lover Fabius before he can invade the Eternal City. Gordon Mitchell enacts the title role, this time a muscular villain instead of his usual role as a muscular hero. He is equally adept at playing either type of character. This versatility provided him with continual employment during the heyday of the peplum films and beyond. Mitchell was a frequent participant in Spaghetti Westerns as well as Hollywood productions such as John Huston's *Reflections in a Golden Eye* (1967). He died in 2003.

36 Cabiria

Itala Films (1914) 150 min.

P–Giovanni Pastrone/D–Piero Fosco (Giovanni Pastrone)/W–Giovanni Pastrone, Gabriele D'Annunzio/M–Manlio Massa, Ildebrando Pizzetti/C–Segundo de Choman

Cast–Umberto Mozzato (Fulvio Axilla), Bartolomeo Pagano (Maciste), Lidia Quaranta (Cabiria), Gina Marangoni (Croessa), Dante Testa (Karthalo), Raffaele Di Nipoli (Bodastoret), Emilio Vardannes (Hannibal), Italia Almirante Manzini (Sofonisba), Edoardo Davesnes (Hasdrubal)

Produced at the extravagant cost of $100,000, Giovanni Pastrone's *Cabiria* was a milestone for the Italian film industry and epic filmmaking. Spectacular and innovative, *Cabiria* set the precedent that directors, such as Griffith and DeMille, would strive to equal or surpass. The plot involves the child Cabiria who is separated from her parents during an eruption of Mount Etna. She is sold at the slave market in Carthage to the high priest who plans to sacrifice her to the god Moloch. The sacrifice is interrupted when the Roman officer Fulvio Axilla and his servant Maciste rescue the child. During their escape they place her in the care of Sofonisba, the beautiful daughter of the Carthaginian king. Fulvio, Maciste and Cabiria are separated until a chain of events reunites them some ten years later. This fictional story incorporates such historical incidents as Hannibal crossing the Alps, Archimedes harnessing the sun's rays to defeat the Roman fleet at Syracuse and the fall of Carthage to the Romans. *Cabiria* succeeds magnificently as pure spectacle, but as drama it often falls short of the mark. A myriad of major characters makes for a confused storyline and events are often not tied together logically. Perhaps *Cabiria*'s most enduring contribution to the epic genre was the introduction of Maciste. The character proved so popular that it made a star of an unknown Italian dockworker named Bartolomeo Pagano. Pagano went on to play Maciste in a series of films following *Cabiria*. In the Sixties the character reappeared in countless peplum films, portrayed by a variety of musclebound actors. *Cabiria* was first shown in the United States in May 1914 at the Astor Hotel in New York City. A month later it opened at the Knickerbocker Theatre where it played for six months.

New York Times: The picture, in fact, brings a rather vague part of history vividly to life. It is absorbingly interesting. It is so well directed that it serves to animate for all what otherwise would be a purely historical work of limited appeal.

37 Caesar

A DeAngelis Group and Five Mile River Films Production

U.S.–TNT Network (2003) 178 min.

Color

P–Lorenzo Minoli, Guido De Angelis, Russell Kagen, Jonas Bauer, Piria Paolo, Giuseppe Pedersoli/D–Uli Edel/W–Peter Pruce, Craig Warner/M–Carlo Siliotto/C–Fabio Cianchetti/E–Mark Conte/PD–Francesco Bronzi/AD–Ino Bonello/CD–Simonetta Leoncini

Cast–Jeremy Sisto (Julius Caesar), Christopher Noth (Magnus Pompey), Richard Harris (Sulla), Christopher Walken (Cato), Valeria Golino (Calpurnia), Heino Ferch (Vercingetorix), Sean Pertwee (Labienus), Ralph Brown (Xanthus), Samuela Sardo (Cleopatra), Ian Duncan (Brutus), Jay Rodin (Mark Antony), Kate Stevenson-Payne (Portia), Tobias Moretti (Cassius) with Paolo Briguglia, David Langham, Pamela Bowen, Daniela Piazza, Nicole Grimaudo, Christian Kohlund

This $18 million mini-series was miraculously shot in only twenty-seven days in Bulgaria and Malta (which seems to have replaced Morocco as the epic location of choice). It is, quite simply, one of the best of its type. At times it seems too good and too grand for the confines of the television screen. The movie begins with the much neglected early life of Caesar. Prior to this, the only film within memory to show a youthful Caesar was *Spartacus* and in that his character is merely a "supporting player." The young Gaius Julius Caesar is a courageous man with high principals and strong convictions. He stands up to the tyrannical Sulla and, were it not for the intervention of the noble general Pompey, would have lost his life for it. After Sulla dies, Caesar becomes a favorite of the people, if not the Senate. The center part of the story shows his campaigns against the Gauls and eventual capture of their leader, Vercingetorix. Caesar returns to Rome in triumph but his new ambitions have incurred the hatred of Pompey, who flees to Egypt seeking asylum. Pompey is murdered by the Egyptians and Caesar, pur-

Claude Rains bids farewell to Vivien Leigh in *Caesar and Cleopatra* (1946).

suing his enemy, meets Cleopatra. The remainder of *Caesar* relates incidents far more familiar to filmgoers, but the presentation is always fresh and engaging. In addition to a literate script, *Caesar* has a fine cast with many outstanding actors. Chief among them is Jeremy Sisto as Caesar. His commanding performance never falters, even when saddled with some rather unconvincing aging makeup. This was Richard Harris' final film.

38   *Caesar and Cleopatra*

A Gabriel Pascal Production for the Rank Organisation (1945) 123 min.
Technicolor
U.S.–United Artists (1946)
P/D–Gabriel Pascal/W–George Bernard Shaw/ M–Georges Auric/C–F.A. Young, Robert Krasker, Jack Hildyard, Jack Cardiff/E–Frederick Wilson/ AD–John Bryan/PD/CD–Oliver Messel
Cast–Claude Rains (Caesar), Vivien Leigh (Cleopatra), Flora Robson (Ftatateeta), Francis L. Sullivan (Pothinus), Basil Sydney (Rufio), Cecil

Parker (Britannus), Stewart Granger (Apollodorus), Raymond Lovell (Lucius Septimus) with Anthony Eustrel, Ernest Thesiger, Anthony Harvey, Michael Rennie, Leo Genn, Esme Percy, Stanley Holloway, Robert Adams, John Bryning, Alan Wheatley, John Laurie

Hungarian producer Gabriel Pascal had begun his collaboration with George Bernard Shaw in 1937 and together they crafted the film versions of Shaw's plays *Pygmalion* and *Major Barbara* with varying degrees of success. In 1944 Pascal announced that their next project would be an adaptation of *Caesar and Cleopatra*. The prestigious J. Arthur Rank Organisation had agreed to finance the production to the tune of £250,000. Pascal chose Vivien Leigh as Cleopatra and Shaw chose Claude Rains as Caesar. From the outset, the filming was plagued with problems. Pascal did not get along with Claude Rains and Vivien Leigh was pregnant, necessitating that the shooting schedule be changed to film all of her scenes first. Pascal later insisted that Vivien Leigh perform a strenuous scene without the benefit of a double and two days later she miscarried. Leigh blamed Pascal and for the remainder of the filming she constantly tried to have him replaced as director. In addition to not getting along with his two stars, Pascal also had to contend with the German rocket bombings on wartime London and several months of inclement weather. By the time *Caesar and Cleopatra* was completed, the cost had risen to £1.25 million, five times the estimated budget and equal to over $3 million. Parliament condemned Pascal for unnecessary extravagance and consequently he never produced another film in England. His close partnership with Shaw was also ended. Contemporary critical and audience reaction to *Caesar and Cleopatra* was generally negative and the film lost a fortune for the Rank Organisation. Time has been kind and it is now regarded as a classic. Vivien Leigh is marvelous as the childish Cleopatra who becomes a queen with the help of Caesar, played with equal amounts of wit and wisdom by Claude Rains. The large supporting cast features a number of soon-to-be famous players in minor roles, such as Leo Genn, Stanley Holloway and Michael Rennie. Jean Simmons makes her film debut as a harp-playing slave girl. Originally James Mason had been offered the part of Apollodorus but turned it down and Stewart Granger was cast in his place. George Bernard Shaw adapted his play with little change for the transfer from stage to screen. Additional material written for the movie by Shaw totals only thirteen minutes. Technically the film is astonishing, with dazzling Technicolor photography and spectacular sets.

AA Nomination–Best Color Art Direction

The Commonweal: As a spectacle *Caesar and Cleopatra* merits high praise; but as a movie, it is dull. Regardless of the heights GBS may have reached as a playwright, this film shows that motion picture writing is not one of his talents.

39   *Caesar the Conqueror*

(Giulio Cesare, il Conquistatore delle Gallie; Julius Caesar, the Conqueror of Gaul)
Metheus Film, Rome (1962) 103 min.

Julius Caesar (Cameron Mitchell, center) leads his troops to victory in *Caesar the Conqueror* (1962).

CinemaScope / Eastman Color
U.S.–Medallion

P–Roberto Capitani / D–Amerigo Anton / W–Arpad De Riso, Nino Scolaro / M–Guido Robuschi, Gian Stellari / C–Romolo Garroni / E–Beatrice Gelici / AD–Amedeo Mellone / CD–Maria Luisa Panaro

Cast–Cameron Mitchell (Julius Caesar), Rik Battaglia (Vercingetorix), Bruno Tocci (Marc Antony), Dominique Wilms (Astrid), Nerio Bernardi (Cicero), Raffaella Carra (Publia), Ivo Payer (Claudius) with Carla Calo, Giulio Donnini, Cesare Fontoni, Fedele Gentile, Aldo Pini, Carlo Tamberlani, Lucia Randi, Enzo Petracca

Julius Caesar and his armies attempt to quell the rebellion in Gaul led by Vercingetorix. Publia, the ward of Caesar, is taken captive by Vercingetorix along with Claudius, one of Caesar's lieutenants. When Claudius is tortured, Publia reveals Caesar's secret plan of attack to save him. Publia and Claudius escape and attempt to reach Caesar to warn him that Vercingetorix has knowledge of his battle plans but Caesar and his troops are already marching against the Gauls. The Roman army suffers a great defeat at the hands of the Gauls but, when all seems lost, Claudius arrives with reinforcements. Vercingetorix is captured and the battle is won. As a reward for his valor, Caesar grants Claudius permission to marry Publia.

40　*Caligula*

Felix Cinematografica S.R.L.
Penthouse Films International (1979) 148 min.
Color

P–Bob Guccione, Franco Rossellini / D–Tinto Brass / Additional sequences directed and photographed by Giancarlo Lui and Bob Guccione / Adapted from a screenplay by Gore Vidal / M–Paul Clement with themes from Aram Khachaturian and Sergio Prokofiev / C–Silvano Ippoliti / E–Nino Baragli / AD / CD–Danilo Sonati

Cast–Malcolm McDowell (Caligula), Peter O'Toole (Tiberius), Teresa Ann Savoy (Drusilla), Helen Mirren (Caesonia), John Gielgud (Nerva), Guido Mannari (Macro), John Steiner (Longinus), Paolo Bonacelli (Chaerea), Leopoldo Trieste (Charicles), Giancarlo Badessi (Claudius), Adriana Asti (Ennia), Mirella D'Angelo (Livia) with Richard Parets, Paula Mitchell, Donato Placido, Lori Wagner, Anneka Di Lorenzo

It is said that everyone has their price and I can think of no better example of this than the presence of Malcolm McDowell, Peter O'Toole and John Gielgud in this sorry mess of a movie. One could argue that the film was tampered with and none of them knew what they had gotten into, but there is enough evidence on view during the sequence in the grotto of Tiberius to disprove this theory. McDowell and O'Toole seem to be having a great time; to his credit, John Gieldud does not. The fact that this was not the end of their careers speaks well of their talent as actors. The widespread success of the BBC series *I, Claudius* in the mid-seventies led *Penthouse* magazine publisher, Bob Guccione to believe that the time was ripe for a film version of Gore Vidal's play about the dissolute emperor Caligula. Vidal adapted his work into a screenplay and an impressive cast of players was assembled to star in what would be entitled *Gore Vidal's Caligula*. Three-time Academy Award winner Danilo Donati designed the imaginative sets and costumes. The end result is probably filmdom's most expensive turd. Obviously, the story of Caligula could not be told truthfully without some depiction of the perverted attitudes which prevailed throughout his reign, but these excesses are dwelt upon to a nauseating extent. When principal photography had been completed by director Tinto Brass, Bob Guccione decided that the film needed an extra "something" to give it added box office appeal. Guccione and Giancarlo Lui proceeded to film hardcore sex scenes which were then edited into the existing footage. Both Tinto Brass and Gore Vidal were horrified at the results and demanded that their names be removed from the finished product. The credits were altered but their names remain. *Caligula* is a curious hodgepodge of material—too lurid for the average filmgoer and too highbrow for the porno circuit crowd. For a brief time it drew curious audiences (where else could you see a legitimate film star urinate in full view of the camera?) but word of mouth soon killed its already limited potential.

41　*Camelot*

Warner Bros.–Seven Arts (1967) 179 min.
Panavision / Technicolor

P–Jack Warner / D–Joshua Logan / W–Alan Jay Lerner / Based on the play by Alan Jay Lerner and Frederick Loewe and the novel *The Once and Future*

King by T. H. White/Songs: Music by Frederick Loewe, Lyrics by Alan Jay Lerner/C–Richard Kline/E–Folmar Blangsted/PD–Edward Carrere, John Truscott/CD–John Truscott

  Cast–Richard Harris (Arthur), Vanessa Redgrave (Guinevere), Franco Nero (Lancelot), David Hemmings (Mordred), Laurence Naismith (Merlin), Lionel Jeffries (Pellinore) with Pierre Olaf, Estelle Winwood, Gary Marshal, Anthony Rogers, Peter Bromilow, Nicholas Beauvy, Sue Casey

The original play of *Camelot* opened on Broadway December 3, 1960, and ran for 873 performances. The musical starred Richard Burton as Arthur, Julie Andrews as Guinevere, and Robert Goulet as Lancelot. When Jack Warner decided to make a movie version he jettisoned the three theatrical leads and, in a move typical when adapting Broadway musicals for film, he cast three non-singers in the lead roles. True that Burton was no singer himself, but at least he had a pleasant way of putting the songs across. Richard Harris, on the other hand, poses and mugs his way through the songs while looking directly into the camera. Vanessa Redgrave warbles her tunes and the singing voice of Franco Nero is dubbed. The singing abilities of the stars isn't the only thing wrong with *Camelot*. Despite the fact that it is filmed in Panavision, director Joshua Logan shoots much of the film in closeup, all but ignoring the sumptuous sets and costumes. Instead we are treated to greatly magnified shots of runny noses and silver tooth fillings. The movie version opens on the eve of battle, with King Arthur ruminating on his fateful relationship with Guinevere. Three hours later the story comes full circle with Arthur remembering that "once there was a fleeting wisp of glory called Camelot" ... in closeup, of course.

  AA Nominations: Best Cinematography, Sound, Costume Design★, Art Direction★, Musical Adaptation (Alfred Newman, Ken Darby)★

42   *Carry On Cleo*

A Peter Rogers Production (1965) 92 min.
Exoticolor
U.S.–Governor Films
  P–Peter Rogers/D–Gerald Thomas/W–Talbot Rothwell/M–Eric Rogers/C–Alan Hume/E–Archie Ludski/AD–Bert Davey/CD–Julie Harris
  Cast–Sidney James (Mark Antony), Amanda Barrie (Cleopatra), Kenneth Williams (Julius Caesar), Joan Sims (Calbpurnia), Kenneth Connor (Hengist), Charles Hawtrey (Seneca), Jim Dale (Horsa), Julie Stevens (Gloria), Sheila Hancock (Senna) with Victor Maddern, David Davenport, Michael Ward, Tanya Dinning, Francis De Wolff, Tom Clegg, Jon Pertwee, Brian Oulton, Warren Mitchell

Britain's "Carry On" gang, in their first color film, spoofs Fox's ultra-expensive *Cleopatra*. Beginning with *Carry On Sergeant* in 1958, this zany group appeared in a lengthy series of movies which were a tremendous success in their native England but soon lost their novelty with American filmgoers. In *Carry On Cleo* all attempts at historical fact are cheerfully thrown to the wind and the results are typically delirious. Amanda Barrie is the kittenish Cleo fought over by series regulars Sidney James and Kenneth Williams. Worth noting is the reuse of many costumes and props from the 1963 version of *Cleopatra*. Writer Talbot Rothwell continued his brand of epic silliness with the British television series *Up Pompeii* in 1970.

43   *Carthage in Flames*

(Cartagine in Fiamme)
Lux Film S.p.A–Gallone S.r.L, Rome–Lux C.C.F., Paris (1960) 110 min.
Technirama/Technicolor
U.S.–Columbia (1961) 93 min.
  P–Guido Luzzato/D–Carmine Gallone/W–Carmine Gallone, Ennio De Concini, Duccio Tessari/Based on the novel by Emilio Salgari/M–Mario Nascimbene/C–Piero Portalupi/E–Niccolo Lazzari/AD–Guido Fiorini/CD–Veniero Colasanti
  Cast–Anne Heywood (Fulvia), Pierre Brasseur (Sidone), Jose Suarez (Hiram), Daniel Gelin (Phegor), Ilaria Occhini (Ophir), Paolo Stoppa (Astarito) Mario Girotti (Tsour) with Erno Crisa, Cesare Fantoni, Ivo Garrani, Edith Peters, Aldo Silvani, Gianrico Tedeschi

At the time of the Third Punic War, as Rome threatens the city of Carthage, the high priest arranges for the sacrifice of the Roman hostage Fulvia to the god Baal-Moloch. The sacrificial rites are disrupted when Hiram, an exiled Carthaginian warrior, rescues Fulvia. Five years earlier, Fulvia had saved the life of Hiram when he was seriously wounded in battle. Although Fulvia loves him desperately, Hiram's heart belongs to the Carthaginian maiden Ophir. Ophir has been promised in marriage to Tsour and when Hiram attempts to prevent the wedding he is taken captive by the soldiers of the villainous Phegor. Knowing he desires her, Fulvia offers herself to Phegor if he will agree to spare Hiram's life. Hiram is pardoned by the Carthaginian council and goes off to help defend Carthage from the invading Roman legions. Phegor betrays the city to the Romans and the Carthaginian troops are slaughtered. Fulvia escapes from Phegor only to discover Hiram mortally wounded on the battlefield. Returning to the city as the Romans are setting fire to Carthage, Fulvia traps Phegor in the conflagration, sacrificing herself to avenge her beloved Hiram. A dramatic story and an impressive production did little to set *Carthage in Flames* apart from the vast number of European epics which were being imported to America in the early sixties. The film was quite successful in Europe and has a considerable reputation there. Perhaps the lack of recognizable name stars is the reason it was neglected in the United States. Although Anne Heywood later enjoyed a brief period of international fame, at the time of her appearance in *Carthage in Flames*, she was virtually unknown outside her native country of England. A star of the caliber of Sophia Loren would have elevated the power of the film considerably. "Star power" aside, *Carthage in Flames* has some magnificent production values. Guido Fiorini's sets are as imaginative as they are opulent and a sea battle with full-scale ships is a spectacular highlight. Composer Mario Nascimbene contributes one of his finest epic scores, greatly enhancing the dramatic impact of the tragic tale. In British prints of *Carthage in Flames*, Hiram survives the battlefield and final destruction of the city to sail off into the sunset with his lover Ophir. The original downbeat ending is far more in keeping with the tone of the rest of the film.

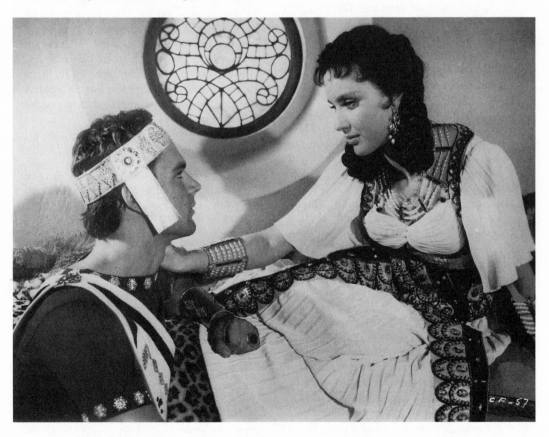

Mario Girotti hopelessly loves Ilaria Occhini in *Carthage in Flames* (1961).

44 The Castilian

A Cinemagic–M.D. of Spain Co-Production (1963)
129 min.
Panacolor by Eastman
U.S.–Warner Bros.

P–Sidney Pink/D–Javier Seto/W–Paulino Rodrigo, Javier Seto, Luis De Arcos/M–Jose Buenagu/C–Mario Pacheco/E–Richard G. Meyer, Margarita De Ochoa/AD–Jose De La Guerra/CD–Jose Azmora

Cast–Cesar Romero (Jeronimo), Spartaco Santony (Fernando Gonzalez), Teresa Velasquez (Sancha), Broderick Crawford (Don Sancho), Alida Valli (Queen Teresa), Frankie Avalon (Jerifan), Fernando Rey (King of Leon) with George Rigaud, Julio Pena, Hugo Pimental, Herman Cobos, Tomas Blanco, Rafael Doran, Beni Deus, Pepe Calvo, Lola Alba, Soledad Miranda

In tenth century Spain only the provinces of Leon, Castile and Navarre have not yet come under the control of the Moors led by Caliph Abderrman. Instead of uniting against the common enemy, the Spaniards continually fight each other. Fernando Gonzalez, the Count of Castile, falls in love with Princess Sancha, daughter of Don Sancho, the King of Navarre. Unfortunately, during a dispute, Fernando kills Don Sancho, incurring the ire of his beloved Sancha and her brother the crown prince. All differences are forgotten when the Moors begin a major assault. Fernando, assisted by two patron saints of Spain, leads the newly united Spaniards to victory against the Moors in a long and bloody battle in the Valley of the Swords. The Castilian was a major departure for producer Sidney Pink, who was usually responsible for such esoteric film fare as Reptilicus, Pyro and Journey to the 7th Planet. Originally filmed under the title The Valley of the Swords, this large-scale historical drama suffers badly from slow pacing. To make matters worse, inserted scenes feature Frankie Avalon as a strolling minstrel who sings about what has happened or is going to happen. This adds more running time to a movie which could only have benefited by some additional editing to begin with.

45 Caveman

A Turman-Foster Co. Production
United Artists (1981) 92 min.

P–Lawrence Turman, David Foster/D–Carl Gottlieb/W–Ruby De Luca, Carl Gottlieb/M–Lalo Schifrin/C–Alan Hume/E–Gene Fowler, Jr./AD–Jose Rodriguez Granada/CD–Robert Fletcher/SVE–David Allen

Cast–Ringo Starr (Atouk), Barbara Bach (Lana), Dennis Quaid (Lar), Shelley Long (Tala), Jack Gilford (Gog), Avery Schreiber (Ock), John Matuszak (Tonda), Cork Hubbert (Ta), Mark King (Ruck), Miguel Angel Fuentes (Grot) with Paco Morayta, Evan Kim, Ed Greenberg, Carl Lumbly, Erica Carlson

Caveman is a parody of the Hammer prehistoric films and might have been more timely and effective had it been made a decade earlier. The story, set in "One Zillion B.C.," is a standard caveman yarn with two tribes, herein known as the "Misfit Tribe" and the "Hostile Tribe," at odds with each other. Barbara Bach is the gorgeous cavewoman who stirs the desire of both Ringo Starr and John Matuszak. Shelley Long is the "cavegirl-next-door" type who secretly loves Starr. More silly than clever, Caveman never reaches any real heights of comedy and most of the humor is of the lowbrow variety. The excellent special effects include several stop-motion dinosaurs courtesy of animator David Allen. These sequences are the highlights of Caveman and Allen infuses his creations with just the right touch of goofy drollery. The Puerto Vallarta location provides an appropriately rugged background.

46 The Centurion

(Il Conquistatore di Corinto; The Conqueror of Corinth; La Bataille de Corinthe; The Battle of Corinth)
Europe Cinematografica, Rome–Comptoir Français, Paris (1961) 77 min.
Euroscope/Eastman Color
U.S.–A William Hunter Presentation for Producers International (1962)
ColorScope

P–Alberto Dionisi/D–Mario Costa/W–Nino Stresa/M–Carlo Innocenzi/C–Pier Ludovico Pavoni/E–Antonietta Zita/AD–Antonio Visone/CD–Mario Giorsi

Cast–John Drew Barrymore (Dieos), Jacques Sernas (Caius Vinicius), Genevieve Grad (Ebe), Gianna Maria Canale (Artemide), Gordon Mitchell (Metellus), Gianni Santuccio (Critolaos), Nando Tamberlani (Callicratos), Ivan Staccioli (Ippolitus) with Andrea Fantasia, Gianni Solaro, Jose Jaspe, Vassili Karamesinis, Dina De Santis, Milena Vukotic, Adrian Vianello

In A.D. 146 the Greek people revolt against the Roman rule. Caius Vinicius, a centurion and emissary of Rome, goes to the city of Corinth in an attempt to make peace between the Romans and the Macedonians. Caius' plea is rejected and, in the ensuing fight, he is wounded. He escapes the fracas and makes his way to a nearby villa. Unknown to Caius, this is the home of Critolaos, the chief spokesman of the Roman opposition. Critolaos' daughter, Ebe, finds the handsome centurion and protects him. The Roman general Metellus is sent to quell the rebellion by force of arms. Caius joins his fellow Romans and leads them through the subterranean passageways into the city. As Corinth is put to the torch, Caius saves Ebe from the destruction of the city. Filmed in southern Greece near sites where the actual battle of Corinth took place, *The Centurion* makes good use of the spectacular scenery. Studio publicity stated that twenty-six men lost their lives during the six weeks of filming the battle scenes. A doubtful statement and, if true, a dubious fact to use to promote a motion picture. Gordon Mitchell is billed in this film as "Mitchel Gordon."

47   *The Clan of the Cave Bear*

A Jozak/Decade Production for Producers Sales Organization
Warner Bros. (1986) 98 min.
Technivision/Technicolor
  P–Gerald I. Isenberg/D–Michael Chapman/W–John Sayles/Based on the novel by Jean M. Auel/C–Jan De Bont/E–Wendy Greene Bricmont/PD–Anthony Masters/CD–Kelly Kimball
  Cast–Daryl Hannah (Ayla), Pamela Reed (Iza), James Remar (Creb), John Doolittle (Broud), Curtis Armstrong (Goov), Paul Carafotes (Brug) with Thomas G. Waites, Martin Doyle, Tony Montanaro, Mike Muscat, Keith Wardlow, John Wardlow, Karen Austin

Thirty-five thousand years ago mankind was in the process of evolving from the Neanderthals into Cro-Magnon man. For a time, both species occupied the earth. As a child, Ayla loses her mother in an earthquake and is adopted by the kindly medicine woman of a passing tribe of Neanderthals. The clan is reluctant to accept the blonde Cro-Magnon child but when she stumbles across a cave dwelling for them, it is believed that the good spirits are with her and she is allowed to remain. When Ayla grows into a woman she is continually harassed by the clan stud, Broud. Eventually he rapes her and she becomes pregnant. Ayla breaks a tribal taboo by using a man's hunting weapon and is banished to have her baby alone. When she returns to the clan with her child, Broud is more hostile than ever. Several years pass and Ayla accompanies the tribe to a meeting of the clans. There, she encounters a man with blue eyes like her own but her chances of romance are abruptly ended when his head is bitten off by an enraged cave bear. Broud is made leader of the clan and banishes Ayla, forcing her to leave her son. Ayla fights Broud and, surprisingly, she wins. Broud must step down as leader and Ayla walks off into the sunset knowing that her son will one day take his place as head of the clan. Jean M. Auel's novel was a best seller but what looks good on the written page doesn't always translate successfully to the screen. Despite a screenplay by John Sayles which is faithful to the source, the movie often comes across as a pastiche of scenes from Hammer's prehistoric films. What is missing are the babes, beasts and fur bikinis. Daryl Hannah does get to wear an off-the-shoulder fur number that looks like a leftover from *Flashdance*, but that's about as good as it gets. The extensive narration is spoken by Salome Jens.

48   *Clash of the Titans*

A Charles H. Schneer Production
MGM/UA (1981) 118 min.
MetroColor
  P–Charles H. Schneer, Ray Harryhausen/D–Desmond Davis/W–Beverly Cross/M–Laurence Rosenthal/C–Ted Moore/E–Timothy Gee/PD–Frank White/AD–Don Picton, Peter Howitt, Giorgio Desideri, Fernando Gonzalez/CD–Emma Porteous/SVE–Ray Harryhausen
  Cast–Harry Hamlin (Perseus), Judi Bowker (Andromeda), Laurence Olivier (Zeus), Burgess Meredith (Ammon), Maggie Smith (Thetis), Claire Bloom (Hera), Ursula Andress (Aphrodite), Sian Phillips (Cassiopeia), Jack Gwillim (Poseidon), Susan Fleetwood (Athena), Tim Pigott-Smith (Thallo) with Flora Robson, Freda Jackson, Anna Manahan, Neil McCarthy, Pat Roach, Donald Houston, Vida Taylor, Harry Jones

Aphrodite (Ursula Andress) and Zeus (Laurence Olivier) discuss the fate of mere mortals in *Clash of the Titans* (1981).

Ray Harryhausen's final special effects extravaganza prior to his retirement was a long-awaited return to Greek mythology originally to have been called *Perseus and the Gorgon's Head*. In the post–*Star Wars* years fantasy had gained new respectability. Thus, for the first time in his career, Harryhausen had a nearly carte-blanche budget at his disposal and an impressive roster of topflight stars. Unfortunately, most of these stars are given little to do other than stand around on Mount Olympus looking bored. Harry Hamlin and Judi Bowker, as the earthbound hero and heroine, are given the bulk of the film's acting duties. The plot is a liberal adaptation of the story of Perseus and Medusa. Cassiopeia, queen of the city of Joppa, offends the goddess Thetis and, as punishment, her daughter Andromeda is condemned to be sacrificed to a terrible sea beast. Perseus, son of Zeus and a mortal woman, embarks on a perilous journey to find the one thing that may help him defeat the monster–the head of the dread Gorgon,

Medusa. So hideous is the Gorgon that to look directly on her features will turn living flesh to stone. The confrontation between Perseus and Medusa is especially effective in building tension and succeeds, where most stop-motion sequences have failed, in being truly frightening. Also on hand are an entire menagerie of animated creatures, including the flying horse Pegasus. The special effects sequences were so extensive that, for the first time in his career, Ray Harryhausen was forced to engage the services of assistants (Jim Danforth and Steven Archer) to help him with the animation. The fine effects work and interesting story are marred by the inclusion of a totally unmythological R2D2–like mechanical owl named Bubo. As a whole, *Clash of the Titans* never attains the grand heights reached by Harryhausen's earlier foray into Greek mythology, *Jason and the Argonauts* (1963), but it is an entertaining motion picture.

Motion Picture Herald: The plot, loosely

based on classical mythology, is secondary to Ray Harryhausen's marvelously old-fashioned special effects. *Clash of the Titans* is unsurprising and predictable. But the film delivers exactly what it sets out to, and entertains despite its limitations.

49 *Cleopatra*

Helen Gardner Picture Players (1912)

P–Helen Gardner/D–Charles L. Gaskill/W–Victorien Sardou, Charles L. Gaskill/C–Lucien Tainguy/E–Helen Gardner/AD–Arthur Corbault/CD–Helen Gardner, Madame Stippange

Cast–Helen Gardner (Cleopatra), Pearl Sindelar (Iras) with James Waite, Helene Costello, Harley Knowles

This first feature film version of *Cleopatra* was produced at Tappan-on-the-Hudson, New York, by the then popular actress Helen Gardner. For Miss Gardner this was certainly a "hands on" production for, in addition to starring in the title role, she designed her own costumes and did the editing as well. Despite a disclaimer vindicating the writers use of dramatic license, the plot sticks surprisingly close to that of Shakespeare's *Antony and Cleopatra*. The major exception is the inclusion of a Greek fisherman named Pharon (played by someone billed simply as "Mr. Howard" in the credits). Pharon is given a lot of screen time and why the screenwriters felt compelled to include this tiresome fictitious character is anybody's guess. Pharon is loved by Cleopatra's handmaiden Iras but he only has eyes for the Egyptian queen. To amuse herself, Cleopatra tells Pharon that she will love him for ten days if he agrees to kill himself at the end of that time. He accepts the offer but Iras prevents his death and he is, unfortunately, around for the rest of the film. The production and acting are horribly stilted and, like many movies from this time period, the scenes are presented as a succession of tableaus. It is a miracle that this version of *Cleopatra* survives while the next has apparently been lost forever.

50 *Cleopatra*

Fox (1917) 125 min.

P–William Fox/D–J. Gordon Edwards/W–Adrian Johnson/C–John Boyle/E–Edward McDermott

Theda Bara played the title role in the 1917 version of *Cleopatra*.

Cast–Theda Bara (Cleopatra), Fritz Liber (Caesar), Thurston Hall (Antony), Henri de Vries (Octavius) with Dorothy Drake, Genevieve Blinn, Herschel Mayall, Delle Duncan, Hector Sarno, Albert Roscoe, Art Acord

William Fox conceived of his 1917 production of *Cleopatra* as a "Super Deluxe Picture" and, as such, reportedly spent $500,000 filming it. In the title role was Fox's resident "Vamp" Theda Bara. Bara had come to public attention in 1916 when she was chosen to play the lead in *A Fool There Was*. Born Theodosia Goodman, studio publicity claimed that she was the daughter of a French father and Egyptian mother, although in reality she came from Ohio. The cardboard backdrops of the previous Helen Gardner version of the story were replaced with extensive exterior sets which included the city and waterfront of Alexandria, the Roman Senate and even an expanse of the Nile river. Highlights of the film were the battle of Actium (filmed in Southern California's Newport Bay) and a scene in which Cleopatra wins a chariot race to impress the Romans. Despite the extravagance of the production, the critics and public seemed most impressed with Theda Bara's fifty elaborate, and often revealing, costumes. With a running time in excess of two hours, *Cleopatra* was given a "Road Show" release with inflated admission prices. Fox's big gamble paid off handsomely and the film grossed a million dollars. Sadly, no prints of *Cleopatra* are known to exist today. It has been conjectured that all of the prints and negatives were destroyed in a 1937 fire at Fox studios. All that remains are the intriguing stills which show a very curious vision of ancient Egypt. In 1918 Theda Bara and director J. Gordon Edwards teamed again for another Fox spectacular, *Salome*, co-starring Albert Roscoe as John the Baptist.

51   *Cleopatra*

Paramount (1934) 101 min.
  P/D–Cecil B. DeMille/W–Waldemar Young, Vincent Lawrence/M–Rudolph Kopp/C–Victor Milner/E–Anne Bauchens/CD–Travis Banton

Cast–Claudette Colbert (Cleopatra), Warren William (Julius Caesar), Henry Wilcoxon (Marc Antony), Gertrude Michael (Calpurnia), Joseph Schildkraut (Herod), Ian Keith (Octavian), C. Aubrey Smith (Enobarbus), Ian Maclaren (Cassius), Arthur Hohl (Brutus), Leonard Mudie (Pothinos), Irving Pichel (Apollodorus), Claudia Dell (Octavia), Eleanor Phelps (Charmian) with Grace Durkin, John Rutherford, Robert Warwick, Edwin Maxwell, Charles Morris, Harry Beresford

Cleopatra is Cecil B. DeMille at his most entertaining. It entirely lacks the sermonizing evident in many of his other historical subjects. The screenplay is one part Shaw, one part Shakespeare and two parts DeMille. By "telescoping history," as he called it, DeMille was able to accomplish in less than two hours most of what it takes the 1963 version over four hours to achieve. Claudette Colbert is superb as the Queen of the Nile—kittenish with Caesar, romantic with Antony and regal when faced with her destruction. Warren William is a trifle stuffy as Julius Caesar but Henry Wil-

Marc Antony (Henry Wilcoxon) is seduced by Cleopatra (Claudette Colbert) on her barge in DeMille's *Cleopatra* (1934).

coxon is both handsome and dashing as Marc Antony. Wilcoxon became one of DeMille's favorite performers. He would appear in the majority of the director's subsequent films, eventually attaining the position of associate producer on DeMille's last three motion pictures. Although *Cleopatra* is a lavish looking production, it is actually one of DeMille's less expensive films. Following the unexpected success of *The Sign of the Cross* in 1932, De-Mille directed two box office flops in a row, *This Day and Age* (1933) and *Four Frightened People* (1934). Both were modern day stories and their failure convinced DeMille to return to the historical spectacle genre. Paramount studio head Adolf Zukor was unwilling to spend a great deal of money on what could well be another DeMille disaster. As a result, the normally extravagant director was forced to economize. The Roman sets are left over from *The Sign of the Cross* and several of the battle sequences include scenes lifted from the 1923 version of *The Ten Commandments*. Many of the deceptively vast crowd scenes were accomplished with the aid of mirrors. In other areas, seemingly no expense was spared. The art-deco Egyptian sets are magnificent, in particular, Cleopatra's palace with it giant winged scarab throne. The justifiably famous barge scene, when Cleopatra seduces Antony, is one of the most memorable sequences in the history of cinema, as well as being a high point in DeMille's career.

AA Nominations: Best Picture, Sound Recording, Editing, Cinematography*, Assistant Director (Cullen Tate)

Vanity Fair: Unconsciously hysterical synthesis of Minsky burlesk, grand opera, the Beaux Arts costume ball and amatur theatricals of the Knights Templer—all mixed up together in one incredibly lavish spectacle.

Variety: DeMille adds nothing to his directorial rep in this one ... though he does provide one of the finest examples of rhythm in a picture yet to be exploited. This comes when the barge of Cleopatra moves out of the port to carry the enchantress and Marc Antony to Egypt.

52 *Cleopatra*

MCL Films, S.A. and Walwa Films, S.A.
20th Century–Fox (1963) 246 min.
Todd-AO / Color by DeLuxe

P–Walter Wanger / D–Joseph L. Mankiewicz / W–Joseph L. Mankiewicz, Ranald MacDougall, Sidney Buchman / Based on *The Life and Times of Cleopatra* by C. M. Franzero / M–Alex North / C–Leon Shamroy / E–Dorothy Spencer / AD–Jack Martin Smith, Hilyard Brown, Herman Blumenthal, Elven Webb, Maurice Pelling, Boris Juraga / PD–John De Cuir / CD–Irene Sharaff, Vittorio Nino Novarese, Renie

Cast–Elizabeth Taylor (Cleopatra), Richard Burton (Mark Antony), Rex Harrison (Julius Caesar), Roddy McDowall (Octavian), Pamela Brown (High Priestess), George Cole (Flavius), Hume Cronyn (Sosigenes), Cesare Danova (Apollodorus), Kenneth Haigh (Brutus), Andrew Keir (Agrippa), Martin Landau (Rufio), Robert Stephens (Germanicus), Jean Marsh (Octavia), Francesca Annis (Eiras), Gregoire Aslan (Pothinos), Martin Benson (Ramos), Isabelle Cooley (Charmian), Carroll O'Connor (Casca), John Hoyt (Cassius) with Herbert Berghof, John Cairney, Jacqui Chan, John Doucette, Andrew Faulds, Michael Gwynn, Michael Hordern

In September 1958, 20th Century–Fox studio head Spyros Skouras decided to remake their 1917 production of *Cleopatra* which had featured Theda Bara in the title role. He conceived of the new film as a modestly budgeted picture starring studio contract actress Joan Collins. When Walter Wanger was brought on as producer he convinced the Fox executives that they should increase the budget and make a quality film, not just another "naked dame on a couch" sex-and-sand epic. Fox contract players Dana Wynter, Suzy Parker, Joanne Woodward and even Marilyn Monroe, were considered for the lead but Wanger wanted Elizabeth Taylor as the Queen of Egypt. He also suggested Laurence Oliver as Julius Caesar and Richard Burton as Mark Antony. Fox executives countered with Cary Grant as Caesar and Burt Lancaster as Antony. Skouras was still adamant about using a contract player as Cleopatra and planned to announce Susan Hayward would play the part. Wanger eventually won out and Elizabeth Taylor was signed, for a million dollar fee, to begin filming as soon as she completed work on *Butterfield 8*, the final film under her MGM contract obligations. The other leads would be Peter Finch as Caesar, Stephen Boyd as Antony, and Keith Baxter as Octavian. Rouben Mamoulian would direct the film, now budgeted at $4 million. Huge sets were constructed at a cost of $600,000 on the backlot

Richard Burton and Elizabeth Taylor rehearse a scene from *Cleopatra* (1963).

of Pinewood Studios in England and in September 1960 filming finally started. Ten weeks later $7 million had been spent and only ten minutes of usable footage was in the can. Consistently bad weather had delayed shooting and Elizabeth Taylor was stricken with a near-fatal case of pneumonia. By the time she had recovered, Mamoulian had resigned as director and Peter Finch, Stephen Boyd and Keith Baxter had been replaced by Rex Harrison, Richard Burton and Roddy McDowall, respectively. Joseph L. Mankiewicz was

Joseph L. Mankiewicz directs Elizabeth Taylor's death scene in *Cleopatra* (1963).

brought in to take over as director and it was decided to move the production from England to Italy, where the climate was more favorable. The filming dragged on for months with Mankiewicz shooting by day and rewriting the script by night. He envisioned the proj-ect as two three-hour features to be released a few months apart. Meanwhile, the Elizabeth Taylor/Richard Burton love affair had begun and became public knowledge. This kept *Cleopatra* in the news with a surfeit of bad publicity. Before filming was completed the budget had climbed to an unprecedented $40 million, two marriages were in ruins, Spyros Skouras resigned as head of Fox and Walter Wanger was fired as producer. In additon to all of this, the new head of Fox, Darryl F. Zanuck, objected to Mankiewicz's concept of two pictures and ordered two hours to be cut from the finished film. Included in the excised footage were the entire performances of genre regulars Finlay Currie as Titus the Moneylender, and Marina Berti as the Queen of Tarsus. Despite these adversities, *Cleopatra* has withstood the test of time and remains one of the most intelligent and spectacular motion pictures ever made. The sheer scope is staggering and it is doubtful if anything quite like it will ever be seen again. The script is literate but never dull, and the performances are uniformly excellent, with Rex Harrison and Roddy McDowall as standouts. Following the initial roadshow engagements, *Cleopatra* was further cut to 194 minutes for its general release. In recent years there has been much talk of restoring the two hours of missing footage to comply with Mankiewicz's original intentions.

AA Nominations: Best Picture, Actor (Rex Harrison), Sound, Editing, Musical Score, Special Effects*, Color Cinematography*, Color Art Direction*, Color Costume Design*

Time: Physically, *Cleopatra* is as magnificent as money and the tremendous Todd-AO screen can make it. As drama and as cinema, *Cleopatra* is raddled with flaws.

New York Times: The memorable thing about this picture is that it is a surpassing entertainment, one of the great epic films of our day.

Life: 20th Century–Fox has mixed an unsuccessful pousse-cafe—gorgeous to look at, with occasional sweet sips, but, in the end, a mixed-up disappointment.

53 *Cleopatra*

Hallmark Entertainment/Babelsberg International
 Film
ABC TV Network (1999) 139 min.
Color

P–Robert Halmi Sr., Robert Halmi, Jr., Dyson Lovell/D–Franc Roddam/W–Stephen Harrigan, Anton Diether/Based on the book *Memoirs of Cleopatra* by Margaret George/M–Trevor Jones/

C–David Connell/E–Peter Coulson/PD–Martin Hitchcock/CD–Enrico Sabbatini

Cast–Leonor Varela (Cleopatra), Timothy Dalton (Caesar), Billy Zane (Antony), Rupert Graves (Octavian), John Bowe (Rufio), Nadim Sawalha (Mardian), Art Malik (Olympus) with Owen Teale, Philip Quast, Daragh O'Malley, Bruce Payne, Sean Pertwee, David Schofield, Indira Ove

Near the end of the twentieth century, the discovery of Cleopatra's palace beneath the waters near Alexandria caused renewed interest in Egypt's most famous queen. A new film version of her story was inevitable. Almost as inevitable was that it would be a TV movie produced by Hallmark Entertainment. This company's epic output ranges from the good (*The Odyssey*) to the awful (*Noah's Ark*). *Cleopatra* falls somewhere in between. With a $30 million budget, this extravagant production cost nearly as much as the 1963 Fox version but lacks the one element essential to this oft filmed slice of history; a captivating Cleo. In the title role newcomer Leonor Varela is beautiful but devoid of the charisma necessary to bring the part off and hold the story together. While some of the production is visually magnificent (the city of Alexandria), some is dreadful (the battle of Actium fought with obvious miniatures). Many of the situations and much of the dialogue are total rip-offs of the 1963 version. In the second half, Leonor Varela and Billy Zane seem to be playing Elizabeth Taylor and Richard Burton rather than Cleopatra and Antony. They are not up to the task. There is a lot of lust but very little romance or passion between them. In one of the most ridiculous scenes, Cleopatra suddenly grabs a sword and comes on like Xena: Warrior Princess, dispatching a Roman soldier with a fatal stab to the crotch. In another attempt at originality, Cleopatra's death is by cobra rather than asp, but this is likely to leave any viewer who knows the story wondering why they would bother to change this familiar detail.

Variety: Camp without being lame or buffoonish, "Cleopatra" is a lusty, tasty treat from start to finish. You just rarely get an opportunity to watch people this unctuously earnest wearing get-ups this insanely gaudy.

Ettore Manni rescues Debra Paget from being buried alive in *Cleopatra's Daughter* (1963).

54   *Cleopatra's Daughter*

(Il Sepolcro dei Re; The Tomb of the King/La Val-
lée des Pharons; The Valley of the Pharaohs)
Explorer Film, Rome–C.F.P.C., Paris (1961) 102 min.
Ultrascope/Eastman Color
U.S.–Medallion (1963)

P–Bruno Turchetto/D–Fernando Cerchio/W–
Damiano Damiani, Fernando Cherchio/M–Gio-
vanni Fusco/C–Anchise Brizzi/E–Antonietta
Zita/PD–Carlo Gentili/AD–Arrigo Equini/CD–
Giancarlo Bartolini Salimbeni

Cast–Debra Paget (Shila), Robert Alda (Inuni),
Ettore Manni (Resi), Corrado Pani (Nemorat),
Erno Crisa (Kefren), Yvette Lebon (Taja), Andriena
Rossi (Tegi), Ivano Staccioli (Mana), Renato Mam-
bor (Tabor) with Betsy Bell, Rosalba Neri

The forces of the pharaoh Nemorat defeat
the Assyrian army and the royal family is
taken prisoner and brought to Egypt. Shila is
an Assyrian princess who is spared when the
rest of her family is executed. She reluctantly
agrees to marry the pharaoh in order to save
the Assyrian nation from extinction. When
the young pharaoh suddenly dies, Shila is accused of having poisoned him. She is condemned to be buried alive in the tomb of her
husband. The court physician, Resi, is in love
with Shila and knows that she is innocent. He
conceives of a plan in which she will seemingly take poison and die but, in actuality, it
will be a sleeping potion which causes a state
resembling death. Resi will then take her body
from the coffin and revive her before she can
be buried with the pharaoh. The plan goes
awry and Shila awakens in her coffin within
the tomb. Resi enlists the aid of a band of
grave robbers and forces Inuni, the architect
who designed the tomb, to help him rescue
his beloved. Resi and Shila escape together
and, in a scene right out of *Land of the Pharaohs*, Inuni seals himself and the grave robbers in the tomb alive. Produced in Europe in
1961, the film was released to American cine-
mas two years later when the mania over the

20th Century–Fox version of *Cleopatra* was in high gear. To capitalize on this, the film was retitled *Cleopatra's Daughter*. The title was explained in the opening narration which states that Shila was the daughter of Cleopatra and Mark Antony. She was sent to the rulers of Assyria in order to escape the fate of her parents at the hands of the Roman conquerors. This would be plausible except that the story obviously takes place in a period well before the post–Cleopatra era. I guess you can't blame the distributors for trying. Casting any pretense towards historical accuracy aside, what remains is an entertaining romantic adventure. Debra Paget, already a veteran of two Hollywood spectacles set in Egypt, is as strikingly beautiful as ever. She also suffers convincingly. Robert Alda, the other Hollywood expatriate in the cast, is second billed

but his role is a relatively minor one. As is often the case, it is Ettore Manni who successfully shoulders most of the dramatic responsibility. Director Fernando Cerchio spent a good part of 1961 in ancient Egypt. That same year he also directed *Queen of the Nile*.

55 *Colossus and the Amazon Queen*

(La Regina delle Amazzoni; The Queen of the Amazons)
Glomer Film–Galatea S.p.A. (1960) 100 min.
Dyaliscope / Eastman Color
U.S.–American-International (1964) 94 min.
  P–Enzo Merolle / D–Vittorio Sala / W–Ennio De Concini, Fulvio Foa, Vittorio Sala, Duccio Tessari, Vittorio Nino Novarese, Giorgio Mordini / M–Roberto Nicolosi / C–Bitto Albertini / E–Mario Serandrei / AD–Ottavio Scotti / CD–Gaia Romanini

Daniela Rocca and Rod Taylor share an intimate moment in *Colossus and the Amazon Queen* (1964).

Kirk Morris threatens Laura Brown in *Colossus and the Headhunters* (1963).

Cast–Rod Taylor (Perious), Ed Fury (Colossus/Glaucus), Dorian Gray (Antiope), Gianna Maria Canale (Amazon Queen), Daniela Rocca (Melitta), Ignazio Leone (Sofo) with Alberto Farnese, Adriana Facchitti, Alfredo Varelli, Gino Buzzanca, Renato Tagliani, Paolo Falchi

A perfectly awful sword and sandal film played strictly for laughs. A band of Greeks led by Colossus (Glaucus, in European versions) and his cynical sidekick Perious arrive on the island of the Amazons. Here they discover that the men are weak and ineffectual, performing the duties of housewives. The domineering Amazon women are fascinated with the gang of brawny newcomers and soon succumb to the joys of male chauvinism. Trouble arises when Perious steals the Sacred Girdle of the Amazons. In the end everyone must unite to fight the ruthless pirates who are trying to rob the Amazons of their trea-

sure. Among the film's atrocities are a terrible Busby Berkeley–type production number with dozens of dancing Amazons, and a wise-cracking parrot. As if this wasn't bad enough, when the picture was picked up for TV distribution by AIP they deleted most of Roberto Nicolosi's original score and substituted an uncredited comic one. Obviously Rod Taylor's career was at a low point when he agreed to do this film. Fortunately he got back on track with *The Time Machine*, which was made the same year as *Colossus and the Amazon Queen*.

56   Colossus and the Headhunters

(Maciste Contro i Cacciatori di Teste; Maciste Against the Headhunters)
R.M.C. Produzione Cinematografica, Rome (1962)
79 min.

CinemaScope/Eastman Color
U.S.–American-International (1963)
  P–Giorgio Marzelli/D/W–Guido Malatesta/
M–Gian Stellari, Guido Robuschi/C–Domenico
Scala/E–Enzo Alfonsi/AD–Giuseppe Ranieri
  Cast–Kirk Morris (Maciste), Laura Brown
(Amoa) with Frank Leroy, Demeter Bitenc, Alfredo
Zammi, Ines Holder, Giovanni Pazzafini, Mina
Oliveri, Corine Capri, Letizia Stephan, Alessio Pre-
garc

The island kingdom of King Sandor is destroyed by a volcanic eruption (lifted from *Fire
Monsters Against the Son of Hercules*) but some
of his people are rescued by Maciste with his
convenient raft. They sail to the country of
the Urias, a people who have been subjugated
by a tribe of headhunters led by the traitorous
Kermes. Although Maciste and the islanders
are first met with hostility and suspicion,
Amoa, the queen of the Urias, soon realizes
they may be of help in overcoming the headhunters. Amoa falls in love with Maciste but
Kermes wants to marry her to insure his claim
to the throne. In a hysterical highlight, Amoa
attempts to delay the marriage ceremony by
having her handmaiden dance to appease the
gods. The dance goes on and on and on.
Maciste eventually arrives as the Urias are engaging the headhunters in battle. Maciste sur-
veys the scene and then topples over a
wooden tower on nobody in particular. Big
help! *Colossus and the Headhunters* is definitely
one of the worst peplum films and features
some of the most ridiculous dialogue ever
dubbed. As Queen Amoa says of Maciste,
"I'm sure his words had nothing to do with his
thoughts." In France they tried to pass this off
as a Tarzan film entitled *Tarzan Contre les
Coupeurs de Têtes.*

57   *The Colossus of Rhodes*

(Il Colosso di Rodi)
Cineproduzioni Associate, Rome–Procusa, Madrid–
C.F.P.C. and C.T.I., Paris (1961) 142 min.
Supertotalscope/Eastman Color
U.S.–Metro-Goldwyn-Mayer (1961) 129 min.
  P–Michaele Scaglione/D–Sergio Leone/W–
Ennio De Concini, Sergio Leone, Cesare Seccia,
Luciano Martino/M–Angelo Francesco Lavag-
nino/C–Antonio Ballesteros/E–Eraldo Da Roma/
AD–Jesus Mateos
  Cast–Rory Calhoun (Dario), Lea Massari (Diala),
Georges Marchal (Peliocles), Angel Aranda

(Koros), Conrado San Martin (Thar), Mabel Karr
(Mirte), Jorge Riguad (Lissipo), Roberto Camardiel
(Serse), Mimmo Palmara (Ares), Felix Fernandez
(Carete) with Carlo Tamberlani, Alfio Caltaviano,
Jose McVilches, Antonio Casas, Yann Lavor, Fer-
nando Calzado

After several years of contributing to the
screenplays of various European Epics, Sergio Leone was finally given the opportunity to
direct one of his own, with the able assistance
of Michele Lupo. *The Colossus of Rhodes* has
much of the same frantic energy and drive of
Leone's "Spaghetti Westerns." It also has the
same penchant toward cruelty and violence
that dominates his western films. Rory Calhoun is Dario, a Greek visiting his uncle in
the seaport city of Rhodes. After witnessing
two assassination attempts on the king in one
day, he decides to leave the "quiet" city and return home to Athens. But the king has forbidden anyone to leave Rhodes until he can
discover who has made the threats on his life.
Dario hires a boat to take him from the city
anyway. Unknown to him, the crew is made
up of members of the band of patriots who
want to free Rhodes from the tyrannical rule
of the king. The escape is foiled and Dario is
accused of being a traitor. Dario begins to realize that the rebels have the right idea. The
film is filled with bizarre touches such as the
sudden revelation that the heroine is actually
in league with the villains. *The Colossus of
Rhodes* also includes some rather gruesome
torture sequences which are given an unusu-
ally generous amount of screen time. The
Colossus itself is a wonderful set piece with
shots of soldiers clambering out of its enormous ear and running along the arms. The
top half of the Colossus was constructed
along the highway to the Barajas Airport near
Madrid while the bottom half was built in the
port of Laredo, Spain, where the navel scenes
were shot. The climactic earthquake is impressive but the actual destruction of the
Colossus is a bit of a disappointment. The Italian version has a longer running time and includes even more blood and violence, including a ghastly scene where a dog licks the gore
from the head of a man who has been crushed
in the earthquake.

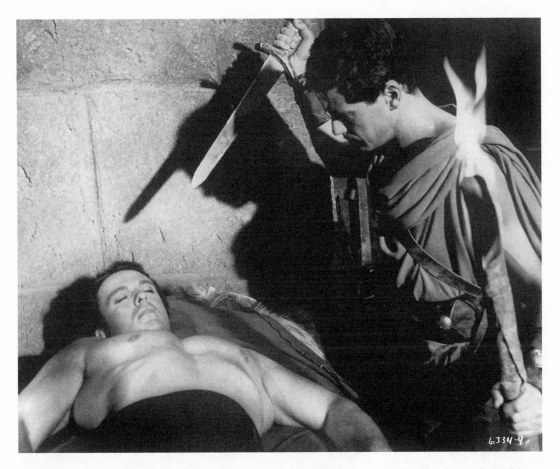

In *Colossus of the Arena* (1964), Maciste (Mark Forest, left) is unaware that death may be only inches away.

58 *Colossus of the Arena*

(Maciste, il Gladiatore Più Forte del Mondo;
 Maciste, the Greatest Gladiator in the World/
 Death in the Arena)
Leone Film (1962) 99 min.
Totalscope/Technicolor
U.S.–American-International (1964)
  D–Michele Lupo/W–Lionello De Felice, Er-
nesto Guida/M–Francesco De Masi
  Cast–Mark Forest (Maciste), Scilla Gabel (Tal-
ima), Dan Vadis (Sidone) with John Chevron, Jose
Greci, Erno Crisa, Germano Longo, Harold Brad-
ley, Vittorio Sanipoli, Carlo Pisacane, Maurizio
Conti, Calisto Calisti, Umberto Silvestri, Ciccio
Barbi

A wealthy merchant hires seven brutal gladiators to perform at the coronation of Princess Talima. Actually the gladiators are to be
used in a plot by Talima's sister and an evil
courtier to take over the throne. The valiant
Maciste joins the gladiators in order to discover their true motives. When Maciste rescues the youngest and most handsome gladiator from a runaway chariot, it appears to be
love at first sight. Maciste is given a sleeping
potion in his wine and the young gladiator is
told to kill him. As the gladiator holds his
sword over the sleeping strongman, Maciste's
lips part in a sigh and the would-be assassin
can't bring himself to carry out his task. This
is definitely one of the oddest moments in all
of peplumdom. Meanwhile, Talima is imprisoned and the gladiators fight in the arena to
celebrate her sister's triumph. Maciste enters
the arena and, one by one, kills the treacherous gladiators. Talima is liberated and crowned
as queen. Despite three appealing leads, *Colossus of the Arena* is mediocre at best. On the

Susan Hayward, Thomas Gomez, John Wayne between takes on the set of *The Conqueror* (1956).

plus side is Dan Vadis in his peplum debut. He plays the meanest gladiator of them all and engages in two major fight scenes with Mark Forest. Unfortunately, these scenes are marred by the excessive use of a very obvious stunt double for Forest. The film also features the most annoying chimpanzee since Cheetah, a black drag queen, and one of the longest tavern brawls ever filmed.

59   *The Conqueror*

A Howard Hughes Production
R.K.O. (1956) 110 min.
CinemaScope/Technicolor
   P/D–Dick Powell/W–Oscar Millard/M–Victor Young/C–Joseph La Shelle, Leo Tover, Harry J. Wild, William Snyder/E–Robert Gilmorek, Kenneth Marstella/AD–Albert D' Agostino, Carroll Clark/CD–Michael Woolfe, Yvonne Wood
   Cast–John Wayne (Temujin), Susan Hayward (Bortei), Pedro Armendariz (Jamuga), Agnes

Moorehead (Hunlun), Thomas Gomez (Wang Khan), John Hoyt (Shaman), William Conrad (Kasar), Ted de Corsia (Kumlek), Leslie Bradley (Targutai), Lee Van Cleef (Chepei), Peter Mamakos (Bogurchi) with Leo Gordon, Richard Loo, Sylvia Lewis, Jarma Lewis, Fred Graham, Jeanne Gerson

The Conqueror is one of the most maligned films of all time, and not without some good reason. What modern film buffs fail to realize is that, at the time of its original release, the picture did receive a number of favorable reviews and was one of the higher grossing films of 1956. Among its virtues are the sumptuous sets and costumes and the breathtaking scenery. Unfortunately, the visual splendors are all but forgotten the moment John Wayne opens his mouth to utter another line of inane dialogue. Although he does cut an imposing figure as Genghis Khan, his delivery of the lines is laughable, to say the least. Susan Hayward, as a redhaired Tarter princess, never looked lovelier. Since she was already an old hand at delivering the stylized dialogue often used in epics, she fares far better than her leading man in the acting department. Oscar Milland's screenplay recounts the early life of Temujin, later to be know as Genghis Khan, and his capture of Bortei, the fiery daughter of Kumlek, leader of the enemy Tarters. The location filming in St. George, Utah, proved lethal for several members of the cast and crew. A-Bomb testing in 1951 in nearby Yucca Flats, Nevada, resulted in the company of *The Conqueror* being exposed to considerable doses of radiation. In later years many of the people involved in the filming developed cancer, including director Dick Powell and stars John Wayne and Susan Hayward, who all died of the disease. *The Conqueror* was Howard Hughes' favorite of all his personal productions. To ensure that the film would not suffer the indignity of cutting for television, Hughes bought back the rights to the film after R.K.O. had been sold and refused to allow it to be shown. Following a brief theatrical re-release in 1960, *The Conqueror* remained unseen until after the death of Hughes in 1976.

Silver Screen: Loaded with sweeping spectacle and colorful violence. Wayne has a little trouble with the highfalutin' dialogue; but Pedro Armendariz tosses off imposing lines with real dignity.

Motion Picture: The story, rich in adventure and barbaric thrills, is frankly not based on historic fact. This Technicolor spectacle set the studio back a fast $6,000,000 and, believe me, it's worth every last cent.

60   *The Conquest of Mycenae*

(Ercole Contro Moloch; Hercules Against Moloch/ Hercules Attacks)
Explorer Film, Rome–C.F.F.P., Paris (1963) 100 min.
Euroscope/Eastman Color
U.S.–A Walter Manley Presentation
Embassy (1964)
P–Bruno Turchetto/D–Giorgio Ferroni/W–Arrigo Equini, Remigio Del Grosso, Giorgio Ferroni/M–Carlo Rustichelli/C–Augusto Tozzi/E–Antonietta Zita/AD–Arrigo Equini/CD–Elio Micheli
Cast–Gordon Scott (Glaucus/Hercules), Rosalba Neri (Demetra), Jany Clair (Deianira), Alessandra Panaro (Medea), Michel Lemoine (Oineo), Arturo Dominici (Penteo) with Nerio Bernardi, Pietro Maraschichi, Gaetano Scala, Giovanni Pazzafini, Mario Lodolini

When Demetra, the widow of the King of Mycenae, gives birth to a deformed baby boy, she and the high priest of Moloch declare that the child is the earthly reincarnation of their god. When the boy grows to manhood his cruelty knows no bounds. Mycenae has become the most powerful city in Greece and Moloch requires human sacrifices to appease his bloodlust. Forced to wear a mask to hide his hideously deformed features, Moloch takes sadistic pleasure in destroying the beauty of the young girls who are sacrificed to him. Tired of the oppression inflicted on them, some of the Greek cities unite and send the mighty warrior Glaucus to Mycenae with the hope of starting a revolt against Moloch. Glaucus, using the name Hercules, allows himself to be captured and taken to the palace as a slave. Queen Demetra is impressed with his strength and appoints him to the palace guard. He is able to use this position to organize the uprising. As the united Greek armies descend on Mycenae, Glaucus faces the monstrous Moloch in his underground cavern and destroys him. All of the large scale action sequences are stock footage from other films, including Giorgio Ferroni's *The Trojan Horse*. The scenes in the caverns of Moloch featuring his hoard of drum beating slave girls are

Constantine (Cornel Wilde) and his beautiful wife Fausta (Belinda Lee): *Constantine and the Cross* (1962).

totally over-the-top and the masked Moloch is an interesting touch. Unfortunately, when his features are finally revealed, the makeup looks as if a child molded it out of clay.

61   *Constantine and the Cross*

(Costantino il Grande; Constantine the Great)
A Jonia Film (1961) 120 min.
Totalscope/Eastman Color
U.S.–A Beaver-Champion Picture/A Joseph E. Levine Presentation
Embassy (1962)
   P–Ferdinando Felicioni/D–Lionello De Felice/ W–Ennio De Concini, Lionello De Felice, Ernesto Guida, Franco Rossitti, Guglielmo Santangelo/ M–Mario Nascimbene/C–Massimo Dallamano/ E–Mario Serandrei/AD–Franco Lolli/CD–Giancarlo Bartolini Salimbeni
   Cast–Cornel Wilde (Constantine), Belinda Lee (Fausta), Christine Kaufmann (Livia), Elisa Cegani (Elena), Massimo Serato (Maxentius), Fausto Tozzi (Hadrian), Tino Carraro (Maximianus), Carlo Ninchi (Constantius Chlorus), Vittorio Sanipoli

(Apuleius) with Franco Fantasia, Lauro Gazzolo, Enrico Glori, Carlo Tamberlani

Constantine and the Cross is a long and slow moving account of Constantine's rise to power and eventual conversion to Christianity. The film is memorable for its impressive battle scenes (reused in countless peplum films for years to come) and because of the striking presence of Belinda Lee as Constantine's wife Fausta. Lee had her first featured role in *The Runaway Bus* in 1954. The Rank Organisation groomed her for stardom but failed to provide her with roles that showcased her considerable beauty and ability. After leaving her native England, she found her niche in a series of European costume pictures, most notably *Messalina* (Vittorio Cottafavi; 1960) and *The Nights of Lucretia Borgia* (Sergio Grieco; 1960). As a temptress there were few who could equal her. Her career was cut short when she died in an automobile accident near

Las Vegas, Nevada, in 1961 at the age of twenty-six. *Constantine and the Cross* did not have its American release until the year after her death. The secondary female role is played by Christine Kaufmann, whose innocent looks never fail to elicit sympathy. Cornel Wilde is seldom able to rise above the one dimensional character that is provided by the screenwriters. In A.D. 303 Constantine and his friend Hadrian are returning to Rome from the wars in Gaul when they are ambushed. Hadrian is injured and left in the care of a Christian family while Constantine returns to Rome. Constantine is betrothed to Fausta, the daughter of Emperor Maximianus. The emperor's son, Maxentius, is jealous of his father's affection for Constantine and plots to disgrace him. This becomes the basis for intense palace intrigue culminating in Christian persecution, clashing armies and Constantine's famous vision of a glowing cross in the sky.

62   *Coriolanus, Hero Without a Country*

(Coriolano, Eroe Senza Patria / Thunder of Battle / Terror of the Gladiators)
Dorica–Explorer Film 58, Rome–C.F.F.P., Paris (1964) 96 min.
Euroscope / Eastman Color
  P–Bruno Turchetto / D–Giorgio Ferroni / W–Remigio Del Grosso / M–Carlo Rustichelli / C–Augusto Tiezzi
  Cast–Gordon Scott (Caius Marcius Coriolanus), Alberto Lupo, (Sizinius), Lilla Brignone (Volumnia), Philippe Hersent (Cominius), Rosalba Neri (Virginia), Pierre Cressoy (Aufidius), Nerio Bernardi (Menenius) with Angela Minervini, Aldo Bufi Landi, Valerio Tordi

Coriolanus is the most revered commander in the Roman empire but he is opposed by the Tribune Sicinius, who plots to dishonor the popular officer. After winning a major battle against the Volshi, Coriolanus returns to Rome in triumph and the Senate appoints him

Gordon Scott (center) as *Coriolanus, Hero Without a Country* (1964).

Consul. Sicinius accuses him of planning a dictatorship and Coriolanus is banished from Rome. The exiled soldier goes to the leader of the Volshi and convinces him to plan another assault on Rome. This time Coriolanus plans to lead the attack against his former countrymen. The story of Coriolanus is the basis of a play by William Shakespeare, but the screenplay draws little from this source for its inspiration.

63   Creatures the World Forgot

A Hammer Film Production (1971) 95 min.
Technicolor
U.S.–Columbia
  P/W–Michael Carreras/D–Don Chaffey/M– Mario Nascimbene/C–Vincent Cox/E–Chris Barnes/ PD–John Stoll/AD–Roy Taylor, Jose MacAvin
  Cast–Julie Ege (Nala), Brian O'Shaughnessy (Mak), Tony Bonner (Toomak), Robert John (Rool), Marcia Fox (Dumb Girl), Rosalie Crutchley (Old Crone) with Don Leonard, Beverly Blake, Doon Baide, Ken Hare, Sue Wilson, Derek Ward, Fred Swart, Josie Kiesouw, Hans Kiesouw, Gerard Nonthuis

Creatures the World Forgot is the final film of Hammer's prehistoric trilogy; it is also the least memorable. Columbia Pictures and Hammer gained much publicity in their worldwide talent hunt to find the screen's "new sex symbol for the Seventies." Lovely Julie Ege, a former Miss Norway, was the lucky winner but the film does little to showcase her talent or beauty. Her naturally blonde hair was dyed black, in a curious reversal of what Hammer had previously done to Raquel Welch and Victoria Vetri, the leading ladies in their other prehistoric films. In addition to this, Ege's character, Nala, doesn't even appear until the film is half over. Nevertheless, she did manage to use *Creatures the World Forgot* as a springboard for her film career. For several years thereafter Julie Ege was a familiar name in British cinema, including Frankie Howerd's spoof of epic films, *Up Pompeii*. *Creatures the World Forgot* relates the violent history of a tribe of Stone Age people through two generations. It achieves a more realistic approach than either *One Million Years B.C.* or *When Dinosaurs Ruled the Earth*, by eliminating the anachronistic presence of dinosaurs with cavemen. Unfortunately, this was due to budgetary restrictions and not a desire for authenticity. The addition of a few dinosaurs would certainly have helped to add some much needed excitement. As it is, the most exciting scene occurs early in the film with the eruption of twin volcanoes, but even this sequence relies heavily on stock footage from *One Million Years B.C.* The extensive location photography at Lone Creek Falls in Southwest Africa is the film's greatest asset. Mario Nascimbene, who composed the highly inventive scores for the two previous films, this time around reuses his main theme from *Solomon and Sheba*.

Cue Magazine: Michael Carreras, who wrote and produced this adventure story, has little innovative to say about the stone-age set. The best that can be noted about the actors is that they look tan and the men are hirsute while the women are not.

Los Angeles Herald-Examiner: One prays for the entrance, stage right, of a dinosaur gnashing its mammoth teeth and stamping its special effects department feet. But, alas, no dinosaur.

64   The Crusades

Paramount (1935) 123 min.
  P/D–Cecil B. DeMille/W–Harold Lamb, Waldemar Young, Dudley Nichols/M–Rudolph Kopp/ C–Victor Milner/E–Anne Bauchens/CD–Travis Banton
  Cast–Loretta Young (Berengaria), Henry Wilcoxon (Richard), Kathrine DeMille (Alice), Alan Hale (Blondel), Joseph Schildkraut (Conrad), C. Henry Gordon (Philip), George Barbier (Sancho), Montagu Love (Blacksmith), Lumsden Hare (Robert), William Farnum (Hugo), Ian Keith (Saladin) with Hobart Bosworth, Pedro de Cordoba, Ramsey Hill, Mischa Auer, Maurice Murphy, Jason Robards, Oscar Rudolph, J. Carrol Naish, Albert Conti

Following the tremendous box office success of his version of *Cleopatra* in 1934, and with the faith of the Paramount executives restored, Cecil B. DeMille embarked on one of his most elaborate and expensive excursions into the distant past. *The Crusades* relates the story of King Richard the Lion-Hearted of England and his fight to reclaim the Holy Land from the Moslems. Initially, Richard embarks on the Crusade to escape his obligation to marry Alice of France. Soon the love of the beautiful Barengaria helps to bring more noble motivations to the fore and rekindles Richard's belief in God. The scenario is confused and without a doubt DeMille's most flagrant distortion of historical facts. When DeMille attempts to translate two hundred years' worth of events into two hours of screen time, the results are disastrous. The script reduces the battle of faiths to a conventional love triangle between Richard, Barengaria and Saladin, the ruler of Islam. Henry Wilcoxon plays Richard as a vulgar and boorish oaf, displaying little of the charm he brought to the part of Marc Antony the previous year. Quite the opposite is Ian Keith. After giving rather overdrawn performances in both *The Sign of the Cross* and *Cleopatra*, Keith brings dignity and subtlety to the role of Saladin. Loretta Young is lovely as the gentle Barengaria and does not say, "You've just gotta save Christianity, Richard! You gotta!" despite erroneous reports to the contrary. Joseph Schildkraut reprises his dreadful performance as King Herod in *Cleopatra*, this time as the treacherous Conrad of Montferrat. The production is lavish in the extreme. Each scene is filled with so many extras milling around that the central characters are all but lost. The film turned out to be a box office failure and for more than a decade DeMille concerned himself with elaborate versions of American history.

AA Nomination: Best Cinematography

New York Times: The Crusades possess the true quality of a screen epic. It is rich in the kind of excitement that pulls an audience irresistibly to the edge of its seat.

Time: As a picture it is historically worthless, didactically treacherous, artistically absurd. None of these defects impairs its entertainment value.

65 *Damon and Pythias*

(Il Tirano di Siracusa; The Tyrant of Syracuse)
International Motion Picture Enterprises (1962) 99 min.
Eastman Color
U.S.–Metro-Goldwyn-Mayer
  P–Sam Jaffe/D–Curtis Bernhardt/W–Bridget Boland, Barry Oringer, Samuel Marx, Franco Rig-

anti/M–Angelo Francesco Lavagnino/C–Alto Toni/E–Niccolo Lazzari/AD–Alberto Boccianti/CD–Andriana Berseli
  Cast–Guy Williams (Damon), Don Burnett (Pythias), Ilaria Occhini (Nerissa), Liana Orfei (Adriana), Marina Berti (Mereka), Arnoldo Foa (Dionysius), Carlo Giustini (Cariso), Andrea Bosic (Arcanos), Osvaldo Ruggeri (Demetrius) with Maurizio Baldoni, Franco Fantasia, Larry Montaigne, Carlo Rizzo, Gianni Bonagura, Aldo Silvani, Giovana Maculani, Carolyn Fonseca

In 400 B.C. Pythagoras' doctrines of brotherhood have begun to spread throughout Greece. Dionysius, the tyrannical ruler of Syracuse, hopes to stamp out these beliefs which he thinks may threaten his rule. Pythias is sent from Athens to rescue the philosopher Arcanos but he set upon by robbers led by the notorious scoundrel Damon. When Damon and Pythias are forced to flee for their lives from Dionysius' guards, a friendship begins to develop between them. As time passes, Damon gains ever-increasing respect for the idealistic Pythias. Pythias is captured by Dionysius and Damon offers himself instead so that his friend may return to his pregnant wife in Athens. Dionysius accepts the proposal and Damon is imprisoned to await execution. On the day the sentence is to be carried out, Pythias returns to Syracuse to save the life of his friend. This interesting, and often exciting, film is marred by several poor performances. Don Burnett is hopelessly modern despite his antiquated garb. Guy Williams tries hard to bring off the part of a good-natured rogue but often seems merely churlish. Worst of all is Ilaria Occhini as Pythias' wife Nerrisa. Her overwrought performance is an embarrassment to behold. Marina Berti is wasted in the minor role of Pythia's sister.

66 *David and Bathsheba*

20th Century–Fox (1951) 116 min.
Technicolor
  P–Darryl F. Zanuck/D–Henry King/W–Philip Dunne/M–Alfred Newman/C–Leon Shamroy/E–Barbara Mclean/AD–Lyle Wheeler, George W. Davis/CD–Edward Stevenson
  Cast–Gregory Peck (David), Susan Hayward (Bathsheba), Raymond Massey (Nathan), Kieron Moore (Uriah), James Robertson Justice (Abishai), Jayne Meadows (Michal), John Sutton (Ira), Dennis Hoey (Joab), Walter Talun (Goliath), Francis X.

Guy Madison (left) and Don Burnett as *Damon and Pythias* (1962), devoted friends with very different temperaments.

Bushman (Saul) with Paul Morgan, Teddy Infuhr, Leo Pessin, John Burton, Gwyneth Verdon, Gilbert Barnett, Lumsden Hare, George Zucco, Allan Stone

Originally conceived as Fox's answer to *Samson and Delilah*, *David and Bathsheba* is that rarest of Hollywood Epics—a film done with taste and sincerity. The production is lavish without being grandiose or gaudy, with the emphasis on characterization instead of spectacle. Philip Dunne's literate screenplay focuses on the troubled years of David's reign when he was a disillusioned monarch who had begun to doubt his faith. He falls in love with Bathsheba, the wife of Uriah the Hittite, a captain in his army. When Bathsheba becomes pregnant by David, he contrives to have Uriah killed in battle so that he can marry her. Overcome with guilt, David rejects his people and his beliefs. Famine strikes the land of Israel and the people rise up against their er-

rant ruler. David eventually reaffirms his covenant with God and regains the love of the Israelites. Though sometimes slow moving, *David and Bathsheba* relies on emotion and not action for its impact. Gregory Peck is outstanding as David, equally adept at portraying passion and guilt. Susan Hayward is given less to do as Bathsheba but she is beautiful enough to make David's adoration believable. As originally filmed, her famous bath took place behind a semi-transparent screen but this proved too racy for the censors and the scene was refilmed using a more discreet wooden one. Jayne Meadows deserves mention as David's bitter first wife, Michal. Those familiar only with her television commercial and game show appearances will be surprised at the depth and ability of her performance. Famed Broadway star Gwen Verdon appears as a palace dancing girl. Alfred Newman's exquisite background music effectively underscores the drama.

AA Nominations: Best Screenplay, Color Cinematography, Color Art Direction, Musical Score, Color Costume Design

Picturegoer: Beneath the impressive weight employed in the telling of the Biblical story of King David and Bathsheba there runs a contrasting simplicity that reduces the principals involved to plain human beings.

Motion Picture: Gregory Peck is very handsome and well cast as the chosen king who sins for love. Susan Hayward is beautiful but not too believable as the woman for whom a king almost loses his kingdom.

Life: While the movie is full of authentic detail, the producers had to draw the line somewhere; and Bathsheba, who has been represented stark naked in classic paintings, is discreetly shielded by a translucent screen.

67 *David and Goliath*

(David e Golia)
An Ansa Production (1960) 95 min.
Totalscope/Eastman Color
U.S.–A Beaver-Champion Attractions Presentation
Allied Artists (1961)

P–Emimmo Salvi/D–Richard Pottier, Ferndinando Baldi/W–Umberto Scarpelli, Gino Mangini, Ambrogio Molteni, Emimmo Salvi/M–Carlo Innocenzi/C–Carlo Fiore/E–Franco Fraticelli/AD–Oscar D'Amico/CD–Ditta Peruzzi

Cast–Orson Welles (King Saul), Ivo Payer (David), Eleonora Rossi Drago (Merab), Edward Hilton (Samuel), Massimo Serato (Abner), Giulia Rubini (Michal), Pierre Cressoy (Jonathan), Furio Meniconi (Asrod), Kronos (Goliath), Dante Maggio (Creth), Luigi Tosi (Benjamin), Umberto Fiz (Lazar), Ugo Sasso (Huro)

Although more widely released than most, *David and Goliath* is no better or worse than the bulk of action-oriented Biblical films which poured out of Europe during the early sixties. The plot covers some of the same ground as other films about David, but concentrates on the early portion of his relationship with King Saul. It also elaborates on the character of Goliath to a greater extent. When David's beloved Elga is killed by a bolt of lightning, he questions the wisdom of a god who could allow such a tragedy. Shortly thereafter, the prophet Samuel pronounces David to be the one who has been chosen by God to rule over Israel. David sets off to Jerusalem to try and seek out the meaning of

King David (Gregory Peck) takes Bathsheba (Susan Hayward) for his wife in *David and Bathsheba* (1951).

God's design. The wisdom of David quickly comes to the attention of King Saul and he entreats the shepherd to come to the palace and council him. This is an unwelcome occurrence for the court counselor Abner, who has been planning with Saul's daughter Merab to steal the throne of her father. The Philistine army attacks Israel and David goes out to meet with their king. It is agreed that if David can defeat the mighty Goliath the Philistines will retreat. David conquers Goliath and returns to Jerusalem in triumph. Saul declares David a hero and presents him with the hand of his daughter Michal in marriage. The film ends on an optimistic note, barely hinting at the dark days ahead for Saul and David. Orson Welles is particularly hammy in his portrayal of a brooding King Saul gone to seed. Obviously this was one of his "take the money and run" roles. Ivo Payer is far more of a hunk than most of the other cinematic Davids. In the early scenes he is closer to the beefcake stars of the peplum films than the shepherd boy seen in other versions of this story. Kronos, a European circus performer, plays the

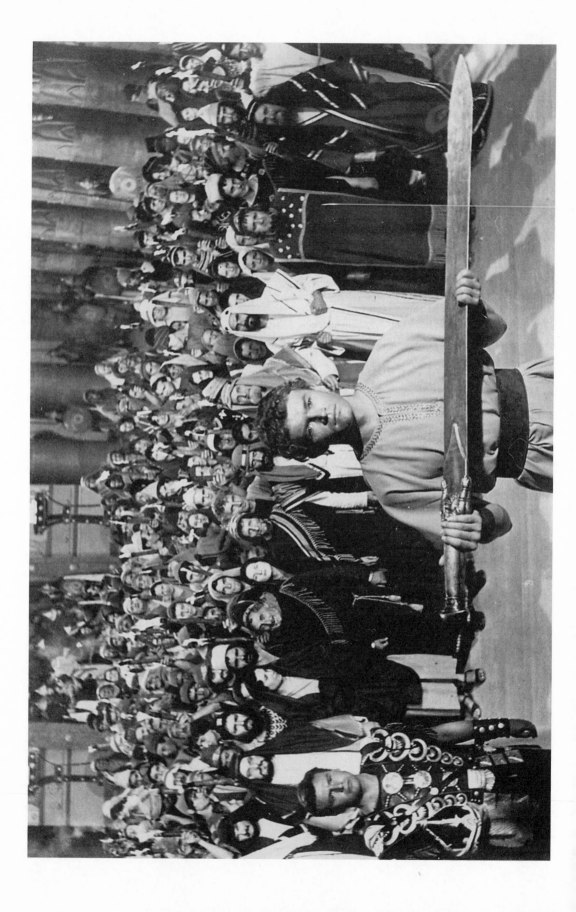

giant Goliath. In long shots he wears a padded body suit to give his figure a more massive appearance. Otherwise, the illusion of his great size is accomplished by skillful camera placement. The location filming in Yugoslavia and Israel enhances the overall impact of the production which, with its flashy sets and costumes, is the most colorful version of this oft-told tale.

68   *Day of Triumph*

A Century Films Production
Select Pictures Corp. (1954) 110 min.
Eastman Color
     P–James K. Friedrich / D–Irving Pichel, John T. Coyle / W–Arthur T. Horman / M–Daniel Amfitheatrof / C–Ray June / E–Thomas Neff / PD–John T. Coyle / CD–Paul McCardle
     Cast–Lee J. Cobb (Zadok), Robert Wilson (Jesus), Richard Freud (Caiaphas), Joanne Dru (Mary Magdalene), Tyler McVey (Peter), Touch Connors (Andrew), Toni Gerry (Cloas), James Griffith (Judas), Everett Glass (Annas), Lowell Gilmore (Pilate), Anthony Warde (Barabbas), Peter Whitney (Nikator), John Stephenson (John the Baptist) with Lawrence Dobkin, Keith Richards, Rick Vallin, Robert Cornthwaite, Dean Cromer, Robert Sherman, Mel Marshall, George Sawaya, Burt Kaiser, Renny McEvoy

Day of Triumph was the Rev. James K. Friedrich's reverent addition to the biblical boom of the early fifties. Friedrich was an Episcopal priest who had produced fifty-three films for church and television. *Day of Triumph* was his second theatrical motion picture (see *The Great Commandment*). Filmed on a limited budget, the production often resembles many of the studio-bound television dramas of the period. One factor which sets it apart from these is the dazzling Eastman Color photography by Ray June. However, the extremely bright colors are often at odds with the sober tone of the presentation. The screenplay displays very little originality in relating the circumstances leading up to the crucifixion of Christ. These events are told mainly in flashback by the religious zealot Zadok, a character who also appears in *The Great Commandment*. Zadok hopes to enlist the aid of Jesus in the

fight against the unjust Roman rule. Robert Wilson, a relatively unknown actor, was chosen to portray Jesus. His interpretation has a far tougher edge than most, but his dialogue is limited to pious recitations of scripture. *Day of Triumph*'s one concession to the typical Hollywood style representation of the Bible occurs in the introduction of Mary Magdalene. As in DeMille's version of *The King of Kings*, she is shown as an elegant courtesan rather than a lowly prostitute. Her conversion to a life of godliness is sudden and unconvincing as played by Joanne Dru.

69   *The Defeat of Hannibal*

(Scipione l'Africano; Scipio Africanus)
Ente Nazionale Industrie Cinematografiche (1937) 102 min.
U.S.–A Walter Manley Enterprises Presentation
Medallion (1963) 85 min.
     P–Federico Curioni / D–Carmine Gallone / W–Carmine Gallone, Camillo Mariani dell'Anguillara, Sebastiano Luciani, Silvio Maurano / M–Ildebrando Pizzetti / C–Anchise Brizzi, Ubaldo Arata, Massimo Terzano / E–Osvaldo Hafenrichter / AD/CD–Pietro Aschieri
     Cast–Annibale Ninchi (Scipio), Camillo Pilotto (Hannibal), Isa Miranda (Velia), Carlo Lombardi (Lucio), Carlo Ninchi (Leilo), Memo Benassi (Cato), Francesca Braggiotti (Sofonisba), Fosco Giachetti (Massinissa), Marcello Giorda (Siface), Lamberto Picasso (Hasdrubal)

Scipio Africanus was the first motion picture to be produced at Benito Mussolini's newly constructed Cinecitta studios near Rome, the largest complex of its type in Europe. The production was supervised by Mussolini's son, Vittorio. The plot tells of the great Roman hero Scipio and his battle against the invading Carthaginian general Hannibal during the Second Punic War. As Hannibal is about to descend upon Rome, Scipio takes the Roman army to Africa to attack Carthage in the hope that Hannibal will abandon his assault and return to defend his homeland. Produced on a grand scale at a great cost (reportedly over $2 million), the film received scant distribution outside of Italy due, in part, to the heavy-handed inclusion of Fascist propaganda. A

Opposite: **David (Ivo Payer) presents the sword of Goliath to King Saul in *David and Goliath* (1961).**

shorter version eventually appeared on U.S. television under the title *The Defeat of Hannibal*. It is a grand spectacle with its immense sets and cast of 30,000 extras. The battle sequences are some of the most authentic looking ever put on film, but the cruelty inflicted on the elephants during these scenes was not faked and is extremely disturbing. Isa Miranda gives a good performance as a Roman girl taken captive by the lecherous Hannibal but Francesca Braggiotti just about steals the show. As the doomed temptress Sofonisba she looks like a cross between Claudette Colbert in *The Sign of the Cross* and Patricia Laffan in *Devil Girl from Mars*, but plays it more like the latter.

70   *Demetrius and the Gladiators*

20th Century–Fox (1954) 101 min.
CinemaScope / Technicolor
   P–Frank Ross / D–Delmer Daves / W–Philip
Dunne / Based on a character created by Lloyd C. Douglas / M–Franz Waxman / C–Milton Krasner / E–Dorothy Spencer, Robert Fritch / AD–Lyle Wheeler, George W. Davis / CD–Charles Le Maire
   Cast–Victor Mature (Demetrius), Susan Hayward (Messalina), Michael Rennie (Peter), Debra Paget (Lucia), Anne Bancroft (Paula), Jay Robinson (Caligula), Barry Jones (Claudius), William Marshall (Glycon), Richard Egan (Dardanius), Ernest Borgnine (Strabo) with Charles Evans, Everett Glass, Karl Davis, Jeff York, John Cliff, Dayton Lummis, Carmen de Lavallade

First announced as *The Story of Demetrius* and later as *The Gladiators*, this film went into production before *The Robe* had even been released to theatres. Most of the sets from the first film were reused, with one very notable exception. Caligula's private arena was built especially for *Demetrius and the Gladiators*, as it was finally titled. CinemaScope prints of *The Robe* open with a quick shot of the arena. This was added at the last minute and is miss-

The mad emperor Caligula (Jay Robinson) rants as Messalina (Susan Hayward) and his courtiers look on: *Demetrius and the Gladiators* **(1954).**

ing from the standard 35mm flat prints of the film. The sequel lacks the piety of its predecessor but makes up for this in excitement and intrigue. Victor Mature, Michael Rennie and Jay Robinson repeat their roles from *The Robe*. Robinson gives an even more maniacal performance as the demented emperor Caligula and most of the film's memorable moments belong to him. After the execution of Marcellus and Diana, Caligula remembers the robe of Jesus and mistakenly believes that it possesses magical powers. When he sends his soldiers to the Christian sector of the city to find it, a fight ensues and Demetrius is arrested. He is sentenced to be trained as a gladiator. At the gladiator school Demetrius is noticed by Messalina, wife of the emperor's uncle Claudius. Messalina uses her considerable wiles to corrupt Demetrius and they soon become lovers. Several reels later Demetrius regains his faith and the insane Caligula is assassinated by his own guards. The Philip Dunne screenplay tends to whitewash some of the historical personages. Claudius is spared all of his infirmities and Messalina's final curtain vow of fidelity is utter nonsense. Despite this, the production is a handsome one populated with good performers, which all adds up to a very high entertainment quota.

Newsweek: Demetrius is a CinemaScope, Technicolored behemoth of a film. As Victor Mature remarks at one point: "To be a Christian these days is anything but dull."

Photoplay: Begins where *The Robe* ends, but for all its widescreen pagan pageantry, conflict, and vocal reverence, the continuation does not rank with the original in strength or conviction.

Motion Picture: The sequel to *The Robe* has all the spectacular qualities of its predecessor, but the theme of Jesus' garment here loses much of its strength. Scenes in the arena are full of excitement.

71   *Desert Desperadoes*

(La Peccatrice del Deserto / The Sinner)
A Venturini-Express Production (1955) 81 min.
U.S.–A John Nasht Presentation
R.K.O. (1959)

P–John Nasht / D–Steve Sekely, Gianni Vernuccio (uncredited) / W–Victor Stolloff, Robert Hill / M–Renzo Rossellini / C–Massimo Dallamano

Cast–Ruth Roman (The Woman), Akim Tamiroff (The Merchant), Othelo Toso (Verrus), Gianni Glori (Fabius), Arnoldo Foa (The Chaldean), Alan Furlan (Rais), Nino Marchetti (Metullus)

A wanton Babylonian woman is tied to a stake and left in the desert to die. The caravan of a wealthy merchant finds her and the Roman captain Verrus insists on taking her with them. Later, the caravan comes upon a group of Judeans fleeing the cruel rule of King Herod. Varrus is sympathetic to their plight and offers to protect them. The Woman and the Merchant enter into a pact to betray the Judeans in exchange for the money offered by King Herod for their return. The Roman soldier Fabius is put on guard but he is seduced away from his post by the beautiful Babylonian so that the Merchant can send a message to Herod. Fabius is whipped for deserting his post and the Woman, who has fallen in love with the young soldier, begins to regret her actions. To atone for her treachery, the Woman tries to help the Judeans escape before Herod's men arrive but she is too late. Herod's soldiers attack the caravan, killing the Judeans, most of the Romans and the Woman. Filmed in Italy and on location in Egypt the curious U.S. retitling would suggest that the movie is a Western. Picked up for release by R.K.O. shortly before the studio went under, *Desert Desperadoes* received very scant distribution in America and is now all but forgotten. Alan Furian, who plays the role of Rais the Arab, doubled as assistant director on the film.

72   *Druids*

TFI International–Eiffel Productions–Transfilm (2000) 115 min.
Color
U.S.–Columbia / TriStar Video (2001)

P–Claude Leger / D–Jacques Dorfmann / W–Rospo Pallenberg, Norman Spinrad, Jacques Dorfmann, Anne De Leseleuc / M–Pierre Charvet / C–Stefan Ivanov / E–Marie Castro / PD–Didier Naert / AD–Anastas Yanakiev / CD–Edith Vesperini

Cast–Christopher Lambert (Vercingetorix), Klaus Maria Brandauer (Julius Caesar), Bernard-Pierre Donnadieu (Dumnorix) with Max Von Sydow, Ines Sastre, Maria Kavardjiknova, Yannis Baraban, Denis Charvet, Jean-Pierre Rives, Vincent Moscato, Youri Angelov, Valentin Ganev, Stefan Danailov, Marin Yanev

This is a "Bad Hair Epic." This particular aberration was popularized by *Braveheart*, which was a good film with bad hair. *Druids* is a bad film with bad hair. This French-Canadian co-production was filmed in Bulgaria and stars former Tarzan/Highlander Christopher Lambert. His hair is the worst of all. He also has a peculiar speaking voice which is a cross between Harvey Fierstein and Elmer Fudd. Other than that, his performance consists mainly of a smoldering gaze. The story begins in 60 B.C. when the King of the Gauls is assassinated by one of his tribal leaders. His young son Vercingetorix escapes, vowing vengeance. Years later, with Julius Caesar's army invading his homeland, Vercingetorix hopes to ally his people with the Romans. Caesar betrays him and Vercingetorix unites the Gauls to fight the Romans. He is crowned their king and leads them in battle against the mighty Roman army. The Battle of Alesia is the decisive victory for Caesar, and the Gauls are slaughtered. Vercingetorix gives himself up to Caesar so that his remaining people may be spared. Max Von Sydow is the chief Druid who wanders in and out of the story contributing nothing to the plot. Fortunately, this at least gave the distributors an excuse to change the title of the movie from *Vercingetorix* to the more tolerable (and pronounceable) *Druids*. A comic highlight of the film occurs when the Romans are laying siege to the walled city of the Gauls. First the Gauls hurl live chickens at the Romans and then, as if flinging fowl wasn't enough, the women taunt the soldiers by exposing their breasts and shaking them. The Romans' wild reaction brings to mind that infamous Mardi Gras taunt "Show us your boobs!"

73   *Duel of Champions*

(Orazi e Curiazi; Horatii and Curiatii)
A Lux-Tiberia-Terence Young Production (1961) 105 min.
Techniscope/Technicolor
U.S.–Medallion (1964)

P–Domenico Fazzari/D–Terence Young, Ferdinando Baldi/W–Ennio De Concini, Carlo Lizzani, Giuliano Montaldo/M–Angelo Francesco Lavagnino/C–Amerigo Gengarelli/E–Renzo Lucidi/AD–Giulio Bongini/CD–Mario Giorsi

Cast–Alan Ladd (Horatio), Jacques Sernas (Marcus), Robert Keith (Tulius Hostilius), Franco Fabrizi (Curazio), Franca Bettoja (Marcia), Luciano Marin (Eli) with Mino Doro, Jacqueline Derval, Osvaldo Ruggeri, Andrea Aureli, Piero Palermini, Evi Marandi, Alana Ladd, Violette Marceau, Umberto Raho, Alfredo Varelli, Nando Angelini, Franca Pasut

In the early days of Rome, the courageous Roman warrior Horatio is taken prisoner by the enemy Albans and the troops under his command are slaughtered. The Romans mistakenly think that he has willingly joined the Albans rather than risk death. When he escapes his captors and returns to Rome he is disgraced and dishonored for his supposed cowardice. Horatio also learns that his younger brother Marcus has been made heir to the throne of Rome in his place. After years of continuous war between Rome and the Albans a seer tells the opposing kings that the dispute can only be settled by conflict between three brothers from each city. The Horatii brothers, including Horatio and Marcus, are chosen to represent Rome and the Curiatii brothers to represent Alba. To further complicate matters, the Horatiis' sister has fallen in love with one of the Curiatii brothers. Alan Ladd, nearing the end of his career, is miscast as Horatio and seems disinterested and weary. Jacques Sernas would have been far better in the lead role but, as it is, his part is a relatively minor one.

74   *Duel of the Titans*

(Romolo e Remo; Romulus and Remus)
A Titanus-Ajace Cinematografica Production (1962) 108 min.
CinemaScope/Eastman Color
U.S.–Paramount (1963) 90 min.

P–Alessandro Jacovoini/D–Sergio Corbucci/W–Sergio Corbucci, Luciano Martino, Sergio Leone, Franco Rossetti, Ennio De Concini, Duccio Tessari/M–Piero Piccioni/C–Enzo Barboni, Dario Di Palma/E–Gabriele Varriale/AD–Giancarlo Simi/CD–Cesare Rovatti

Cast–Steve Reeves (Romulus), Gordon Scott (Remus), Virna Lisi (Julia), Ornella Vanoni (Tarpeja), Jacques Sernas (Curzio), Laura Solari (Rea Silvia) with Massimo Girotti, Franco Volpi, Jose Greci, Piero Lulli, Andrea Bosic, Enrico Glori, Bruno Tocci, Germano Longo, Enzo Cerusico, Franco Balducci, Nando Angelini, Giuliano Dall'Ovo

The peplum genre's most popular leading men in their only film together: Gordon Scott (left) and Steve Reeves in *Duel of the Titans* (1963).

Duel of the Titans features the peplum genre's two most famous musclemen in their only appearance together. Steve Reeves and Gordon Scott star, respectively, as the twin brothers Romulus and Remus. Abandoned in their infancy and suckled by a she-wolf, the brothers are adopted by a former soldier who teaches them the art of battle. They grow up to become men of very different temperaments. Romulus is peace loving and gentle, while Remus is hot-headed and believes only in the power of force. They become rivals for supremacy and for the love of the beautiful Sabine princess Julia. To Remus' chagrin, Romulus is elected leader with Julia as his consort. Remus departs with his followers but many are killed in a volcanic eruption. Remus eventually returns to challenge his brother. Their climactic duel results in the death of Remus, leaving Romulus to establish the city of Rome on the spot where his brother died.

In addition to seeing "Hercules against Tarzan," *Duel of the Titans* presents Virna Lisi in one of her early steps toward international stardom. The cast also includes those two spectacle stalwarts Massimo Girotti and Jacques Sernas as villains. Lots of action, a better than average script and an interesting cast make *Duel of the Titans* one of the best of its kind. Although cut by Paramount for the theatrical release, the longer version has since been shown on television.

75   *The Egyptian*

20th Century–Fox (1954) 139 min.
CinemaScope/Color by DeLuxe
   P–Darryl F. Zanuck/D–Michael Curtiz/W–Philip Dunne, Casey Robinson/Based on the novel by Mika Waltari/M–Bernard Herrmann, Alfred Newman/C–Leon Shamroy/E–Barbara Mclean/Ad–Lyle Wheeler, George W. Davis/CD–Charles Le Maire

Michael Curtiz directs Edmund Purdom and Bella Darvi in a scene from *The Egyptian* (1954).

Cast–Edmund Purdom (Sinuhe), Jean Simmons (Merit), Victor Mature (Horemheb), Gene Tierney (Baketamon), Michael Wilding (Akhnaton), Bella Darvi (Nefer), Peter Ustinov (Kaptah), Judith Evelyn (Taia), Henry Daniell (Mikere), John Carradine (Grave Robber), Anitra Stevens (Nefertiti), Carl Benton Reid (Senmut), Tommy Rettig (Toth) with Donna Martell, Mimi Gibson, Carmen de Lavallade, Henry Thompson, Mike Mazurki

The discovery of a solar boat in Egypt in the early fifties prompted a revival of interest in ancient Egypt. It didn't take Hollywood long to jump on the bandwagon with most of the major studios announcing their productions set in the land of the Nile. MGM had the "non-ancient" *Valley of the Kings*, Warner Bros. had *Land of the Pharaohs*, Paramount had DeMille's remake of *The Ten Commandments* and Fox had *The Egyptian*. *The Egyptian* had its beginnings in 1938 with the produc-

tion of a play called *Akhnaton* by Finnish author Mika Waltari. Waltari's research for this play led him to write the novel *The Egyptian* which was published in Finland in 1945. The book was a tremendous success, translated into eight languages and selling over a million copies in Europe. The English translation by Naomi Walford appeared in 1949 and eventually came to the attention of Fox studio head, Darryl F. Zanuck. In 1954, Zanuck was searching for a suitable property as a follow-up to *The Robe*. Like *The Robe*, *The Egyptian* was a best selling novel which combined history and religion. *The Egyptian* had the added bonus of containing an ample amount of sex as well. Zanuck bought the movie rights and set his reliable screenwriters Philip Dunne and Casey Robinson to the task of adapting the novel's 500 plus pages into a workable script. The story chronicles the life and times of a man and his search for truth during the fourteenth century B.C. An infant, set adrift on the Nile in a reed boat, is rescued and adopted by a physician and his wife, who name him Sinuhe. Sinuhe grows to manhood and, like his foster father, becomes a physician. When he and his friend Horem-heb save the life of the young pharaoh Akhnaton, Sinuhe is appointed physician to the royal family. An obsessive love affair with a mercenary harlot named Nefer causes Sinuhe to become disillusioned with life. He leaves Egypt and wanders for many years in foreign countries. Eventually returning to his homeland, he finds himself a pawn in the Holy War caused by Akhnaton's belief in one true God. The sincere love of the tavern maid Merit and the secret to spiritual peace he learns from a dying Akhnaton, restore Sinuhe's faith in humanity before he exiled by the new pharaoh, Horemheb. Original casting for the film included Marlon Brando as Sinuhe, Kirk Douglas as Akhnaton and Faith Domergue as Merit. Although Marlene Dietrich had been mentioned for the role of Nefer, Zanuck opted to cast his current mistress Bella Darvi instead. In protest, Brando bowed out, claiming that he was suffering from "personal and professional" difficulties. When Fox threatened to sue him for two million dollars he agreed to return to the studio to play Napoleon in *Desiree* (1954). Kirk Douglas backed up Brando's decision by also leaving the cast but he ended up starring with Bella Darvi anyway in *The Racers* the following year. Faith Domergue was passed over by Zanuck when Jean Simmons became available. Edmund Purdom was borrowed from MGM to replace Brando as Sinuhe and he gives an effectively understated performance. Purdom's Hollywood career was jettisoned when he ran afoul of the powerful gossip columnist, Louella Parsons. He left the U.S. and went to Europe where he became a frequent star of many of the European epics that were made during the sixties. Despite the endless ridicule heaped on her brief American film career, Bella Darvi is convincing as the heartless whore Nefer. Darvi, who had been a model in Paris, returned to Europe where she continued a sporadic acting career until her death by suicide in 1971. Filmed at a cost of $5 million, *The Egyptian* was Fox's most expensive production since *Forever Amber* in 1947. Unlike some of the other Egyptian films produced at this time, *The Egyptian* could not boast the use of authentic location photography (except for a brief prologue) and yet it is one of the most visually authentic of all the movies dealing with ancient Egypt. Zanuck hired an Egyptologist to ensure this authenticity. Sixty-seven sets were constructed on the Fox backlot. Countless props and costumes were designed with great attention paid to historical accuracy. The musical score of *The Egyptian* prompted the union of two of Hollywood's greatest composers, Bernard Herrmann and Alfred Newman. Herrmann had been contracted to score the film but when the release date was advanced three weeks, Newman stepped in to collaborate on the task. The result is one of the truly great background scores for a motion picture. The original running time of *The Egyptian* was to have been two hours and thirty minutes with an intermission at the 75 minute point. Shortly before the film's August 24, 1954, premiere, Zanuck decided to cut the picture to its present length and dispense with the intermission.

AA Nomination: Best Color Cinematography

Time: *The Egyptian* has a kind of blurby, big-adjective poetry about it. Authenticity is rampant in every scene.

Life: As a spectacle, the result is lavishly successful.

Variety: *The Egyptian* is a big and important film in every respect. It's big and splashy and sometimes breathtaking in its CinemaScoped dramatics.

Motion Picture: Against brilliant settings that re-create ancient Egypt in fascinating detail, Edmund Purdom dominates a big cast with his dignified portrayal and fine appearance.

76   *El Cid*

A Samuel Bronston Production in association with
  Dear Film Productions
Allied Artists (1961) 184 min.
Super Technirama 70 / Technicolor
  P–Samuel Bronston / D–Anthony Mann / W–Fredric M. Frank, Philip Yordan / M–Miklos Rozsa / C–Robert Krasker / E–Robert Lawernce / AD / CD–Veniero Colasanti, John Moore

Charlton Heston as *El Cid* (1961).

Cast–Charlton Heston (El Cid), Sophia Loren (Chimene), Raf Vallone (Ordonez), Genevieve Page (Urraca), John Fraser (Alfonso), Gary Raymond (Sancho), Hurd Hatfield (Arias), Massimo Serato (Fanez), Herbert Lom (Ben Youssef), Frank Thring (Al Kadir), Douglas Wilmer (Moutamin), Michael Hordern (Don Diego), Andrew Cruiksank (Count Gormaz)

El Cid is producer Samuel Bronston's masterpiece and one of the finest films in the entire epic genre. The story of the heroic eleventh century knight who leads the defense of Spain against the invading Moors is told grandly and with style. Bronston first thought of filming *El Cid* in 1958 prior to beginning work on his version of *King of Kings*. The Christ story proved to be such a tremendous undertaking that *El Cid* was put on a back burner until *King of Kings* neared completion. Charlton Heston and Sophia Loren were Bronston's first choices for the leading roles but Loren had prior commitments and could not be secured for the part of Chimene. Jeanne Moreau was briefly considered as a re-

placement but Loren suddenly became available for a twelve week period. This limited availability posed further problems for what was already shaping up to be a complicated production. When Loren asked that her dialogue be simplified, Ben Barzman was brought in to do an uncredited rewrite on the screenplay. In the meantime, Orson Welles was replaced by Herbert Lom in the role of Ben Youssef. Despite the fact that the story takes placed over a period of some twenty years, Sophia Loren refused any aging makeup and remains her youthful self throughout. Charlton Heston, in the title role, give the performance of his career. As Rodrigo Diaz de Bivar, later know as "El Cid," Heston is able to take this unfailingly noble and stalwart character, who was also loyal to a fault, and make him completely believable. Massimo Serato, veteran villain of dozens of low budget European spectaculars, is cast against type as El Cid's faithful companion Fanez. Director Anthony Mann deserves credit for pulling off one of the more potentially absurd scenes in screen history. The dead Cid is strapped upright to his horse and sent out to lead his troops into the final battle. Mann's excellent direction makes this sequence inspiring, but never the least bit corny. Heston was less enthusiastic about Mann's direction and feels that if *El Cid* had been directed by either David Lean or William Wyler it would have been the greatest epic film ever made.

AA nominations: Best Color Art Direction, Original Song, Musical Score

77 *The Emperor Caligula*

(Caligola ... La Storia Mai Raccontata; Caligula ... the Untold Story)
Metaxa Corporation S.A.–Cinema 80 (1983) 100 min
Panoramica/Telecolor
U.S.–Trans World Entertainment
   P–Eduard Jones, Alexander Sussman/D–David Hills/W–Richard Franks, Victoria J. Newton, David Hills/M–Carlo Maria Corde/C–Frederico Slonisco/E–George Morley/PD–Linda Mann/AD–Lucius Pearl/CD–Helen Zimmerman
   Cast–David Cain Haughton (Caligula), Laura Gemser (Miriam), Oliver Finch (Messala), Charles Borromel (Petreio), Fabiola Toledo (Livia), Sasha D'Arc (Ulmer), Alex Freyberger (Enzio) with Larry Dolgin, Gabriele Tinti, John Alin, Ulla Luna, Didi

Franks, Donatella Down, Giorgia Williams, Jessica Lopez, Patricia Queen

The Emperor Caligula is little more than a softcore porno film with the trappings of an Epic. Obviously inspired by the Penthouse production of *Caligula* (1979), this film lacks a well known cast but the performances are nevertheless competent. David Cain Haughton, in particular, is quite acceptable as the mad emperor. There are very few of the historical facts about Caligula in evidence. Instead the audience is given a continual parade of bare bosoms and bottoms with some graphic violence thrown in for good measure. One torture sequence is so sadistic that it fairly beggars description. A great many actual Italian locations were utilized in lieu of building sets.

78   Erik the Conqueror

(Gli Invasori; The Invaders/Fury of the Vikings)
Galatea S.p.A., Rome-S.C. Lyre-Criterion, Paris
  (1962) 88 min.
Dyaliscope/Technicolor
U.S.–American-International (1963) 83 min.
ColorScope
  P–Massimo De Rita/D/C/E–Mario Bava/W–Oreste Biancoli, Piero Pierotti, Mario Bava/ M–Roberto Nicolosi/AD–Giorgio Giovannini/CD–Mario Giorsi
  Cast–Cameron Mitchell (Iron), Giorgio Ardisson (Erik), Alice Kessler (Daja), Ellen Kessler (Rama), Francoise Christophe (Queen Alice) with Andrea Checchi, Jean-Jacques Delbo, Folco Lulli, Enzo Doria, Franco Giacobini, Raffaele Baldassare, Joe Robinson, Gianni Solaro, Franco Fessel, Livia Contardi

Erik the Conqueror is a reworking of the basic plot of Richard Fleischer's *The Vikings*. Once again we have English forces against the Viking hordes, this time with Cameron Mitchell and Giorgio Ardisson as the brothers on opposing sides. The English army destroys a Viking encampment and a small boy is seemingly the sole survivor. The English queen, Alice, adopts him and raises him as her own son. Queen Alice doesn't know that the child is Erik, the offspring of the slain Viking king and that his brother, Iron, has also escaped death. Years later the two brothers must face each other in a fight to the death on the field of battle. The lovely Kessler

Cameron Mitchell (left) and Giorgio Ardisson are Viking brothers in *Erik the Conqueror* (1963).

twins are also on hand as Viking priestesses, each in love with a different brother. *Erik the Conqueror* is a kaleidoscope of brilliant colors and imaginative sets. Mario Bava directs with his customary flair for visual detail. In less talented hands the material could have been unmemorable or, at best, merely repetitive, but Bava infuses the story with vitality and excitement. Bava's cinematography brings many of the same macabre lighting and color techniques to the film that he utilized in his celebrated horror movies. Of the cast, Giorgio Ardisson is especially effective as the younger brother, Erik, who was born a Viking but raised as an Englishman. Cameron Mitchell in his first of several films for Bava, had already appeared with Giorgio Ardisson as Viking brothers in *The Last of the Vikings* (1961). In 1966 he again played a Norseman in Mario Bava's *Knives of the Avenger* but, compared to *Erik the Conqueror*, this is a less impressive work with little of the unbridled imagination of the previous film in evidence.

79   The Erotic Nights of Poppaea

(Les Nuits Erotique de Poppée/Le Calde Notti di
  Poppea; The Hot Nights of Poppaea)
Romana Films (1969) 92 min.
Eastman Color
U.S.–Unreleased
  P–Fortunato Misiano/D–James Reed (Guido

Malatesta)/W–Gianfranco Clerici, Guido Malatesta/M–Angelo Francesco Lavagnino/C–Augusto Tiezzi/E–Jolanda Benvenuti/AD–Pier Vittorio Marchi

   Cast–Olinka Berova (Poppaea), Brad Harris (Valerius), Daniele Vargas (Drusus), Howard Ross (Marcus), Gia Sandri (Lucretia), Femi Benussi (Livia), Tor Altmayer (Seneca), Sandro Dori (Nero), Carla Calo (Calpurnia) with Nello Pazzafini, Albert Balsamo, Silvio Bagolini, Demeter Bitenc, Fortunato Arena

This Italian sex farce charts Poppaea's rise from common prostitute in a Roman bordello to Empress of Rome as the wife of Nero. Titillation is the primary purpose of *The Erotic Nights of Poppaea* and the screen is filled with hordes of bouncing bosoms and bare buttocks. Foremost among these are those of the gorgeous Olinka Berova, who has the biggest bust of all. Czechoslovakian actress Olga Schoberova had been imported to England the previous year by Hammer Films, who changed her name and starred her in *The Vengeance of She*. Touted as the "New Goddess of the Silver Screen," she also starred in *Lucrezia Borgia* prior to her appearance as Poppaea. As the amoral empress she gets plenty of opportunity to display her bountiful figure in a variety of bathtub and bedroom scenes. Brad Harris was so smitten with his beauteous costar that they were married shortly thereafter. Unfortunately, both the marriage and Berova's career were shortlived and she soon faded into obscurity.

80   *Esther*

A Lube/Lux Vide/Beta Film/Quinta/Rai Uno Production (1999) 91 min
Color
U.S.–Syndicated television release

   P–Lorenzo Minoli, Paolo Piria/D–Raffaele Mertes/W–Sandy Niemand/M–Carlo Siliotto/C–Giovanni Galasso/E–Alessandro Lucidi/PD–Paolo Biagetti/CD–Simonetta Leoncini, Giovanni Viti

   Cast–Louise Lombard (Esther), F. Murray Abraham (Mordecai), Jurgen Prochnow (Haman), Thomas Kretschmann (Ahasuerus), Ornella Muti (Vashti) with Frank Baker, John Hollis, Umberto Orsini, Phil Davies, Christopher Ettridge, Natasha Williams

With a running time of 91 minutes, this clocks in as the briefest entry in this chain of made-for-television biblical films. While many

of the other movies in the series seem overlong and padded, the length of *Esther* seems to be just right. The events herein are presented sincerely and with little embellishment, which is a far cry from the colorful histrionics of *Esther and the King*. Unfortunately, this is not always a good thing. There is little dramatic hook and even less romance. Often, the potentially moving story comes across as a bit pedestrian. To its credit, *Esther* is a stunningly designed production. There is a great attention to detail evident in the sets and costumes which successfully replicate the splendor of the Persian empire of 475 B.C. Louise Lombard is quite and thoughtful as Esther while Thomas Kretschmann plays Ahasuerus as weak-willed and childish. Raffaele Mertes, who was the cinematographer on the previous movies in this series, graduated to director with this film.

81   *Esther and the King*

(Ester e il Re)
A Raoul Walsh/Galatea S.p.A., Rome Production (1960) 109 min.
CinemaScope/Technicolor
U.S.–20th Century–Fox

   P/D–Raoul Walsh/W–Raoul Walsh, Michael Elkins/M–Angelo Francesco Lavagnino, Roberto Nicolosi/C–Mario Bava/E–Jerome Webb/AD–Giorgio Giovannini/CD–Anna Maria Fea

   Cast–Joan Collins (Esther), Richard Egan (Ahasuerus), Denis O'Dea (Mordecai), Sergio Fantoni (Haman), Rik Battaglia (Simon), Renato Baldini (Klidrates), Folco Lulli (Tobia), Gabriele Tinti (Samuel), Rosalba Neri (Keresh), Daniela Rocca (Vashti)

The story of the Old Testament heroine Esther was a proposed project of Cecil B. DeMille that was never realized. This Italian-American coproduction has the usual emphasis on action but it is also a fairly faithful adaptation of the biblical narrative of the Hebrew woman who wed a Persian king to prevent the persecution of her people. When King Ahasuerus returns from the wars he discovers that Queen Vashti has been unfaithful to him. Her attempts to regain his favor fail and she is banished. Custom demands that all the virgins in the land come before the king so that he may choose another bride from among them. Only the beautiful Esther finds

Joan Collins and Richard Egan relax on the set of *Esther and the King* (1960).

favor in his eyes, and, not knowing that she is a Jew, he makes her his queen. The king's evil prime minister, Haman, resents Esther's influence over Ahasuerus and plots the destruction of both her and her people. Fortunately, the faith and purity of Esther prevail. Joan Collins and Richard Egan are adequate in the title roles, but, as written, their parts don't call for any incredible feats of acting ability. Given her propensity for portraying bitches, it is rather refreshing to see that Joan Collins was capable of playing another type of character. Daniela Rocca is especially good in her brief role. As Queen Vashti she does an exotic dance in hope of winning back the affection of her estranged husband. In the European version of the film she ends up topless but American audiences see her only from behind. The great Mario Bava was responsible for the dazzling color photography.

Time: Readers of the Bible will be surprised to learn that this brassy extravaganza is based on the Book of Esther. As the King said: "What court idiot decided to bore me with this sorry spectacle?"

82 *Excalibur*

Orion Pictures/Warner Bros. (1981) 140 min. Technicolor

P/D–John Boorman/W–Rospo Pallenberg, John Boorman/Based on *Le Morte d'Arthur* by Sir Thomas Malory/M–Trevor Jones/C–Alex Thomson/E–John Merritt/PD–Anthony Pratt/AD–Tom Hutchinson/CD–Bob Ringwood

Cast–Nicol Williamson (Merlin), Nigel Terry (Arthur), Cherie Lunghi (Guinevere), Nicholas Clay (Lancelot), Helen Mirren (Morgana), Paul Geoffrey (Percival), Liam Neeson (Gawain), Gabriel Byrne (Ulher), Robert Addie (Mordred), Corin Redgrave (Cornwall) with Patrick Stewart, Niall O'Brien, Keith Buckley

John Boorman began writing his vision of Arthurian legend in the sixties but it wasn't

Henri Vidal and Michele Morgan were lovers on screen and off during the filming of *Fabiola* (1951).

produced until the Sword and Sorcery film boom of the early eighties. Unlike its cinematic predecessors, the emphasis in *Excalibur* is not on knights in armor. Instead, the focus is on magic and mysticism. Ulher Pendragon rapes the wife of his enemy Cornwall and the result of their union is Arthur. The sorcerer Merlin takes the child and raises him. As a young man, Arthur is the only person able to withdraw the sword Excalibur from the stone which holds it and, because of this, he is hailed as king. All of the famous elements of the story of Arthur are present but the plot often takes a backseat to the production design. Like other John Boorman films, *Excalibur* is beautiful to watch but dramatically confused. Sometimes so much is going on in

a scene that it is difficult to decide what to center your attention on. The characters, with the exception of Helen Mirren's Morgana, are underdeveloped and uninvolving. In the end, *Excalibur* is a visually rewarding but ultimately frustrating and empty experience.

AA Nomination: Best Cinematography

83 *Fabiola*

Salvo D'Angelo Produzioni Universalia (1949) 165 min.
U.S.–A Jules Levy Presentation
United Artists (1951) 96 min.

P–Salvo D'Angelo/D–Alessandro Blasetti/W–Alessandro Blasetti, Jean Georges Auriol, Vitaliano Brancati/Based on the novel by Cardinal Nicholas Wiseman/M–Enzo Masetti/C–Mario Craveri/E–

Mario Serandrei/AD–Arnaldo Foschini/CD–Veniero Colasanti

Cast–Michele Morgan (Fabiola), Henri Vidal
(Rhual), Massimo Girotti (Sebastian), Michel
Simon (Fabius), Elisa Cigani (Sira), Gabriele Fer-
zetti (Claudius) with Gino Cervi, Louis Salou,
Carlo Ninchi, Paolo Stoppa, Sergio Tofano, Aldo
Silvani

Filmed in Italy in 1948, *Fabiola* was the first
of the post–World War II European epics.
When the film was picked up for distribution
in the United States it was dubbed into English and over an hour was cut from the original running time. What remains is a fragmented, but nevertheless spectacular, motion
picture. Immensely successful in Europe, *Fabiola* did for the Italian film industry exactly
what *Samson and Delilah* would do in Hollywood. These two films started the epic ball
rolling that continued throughout the fifties
and sixties. The roots of the entire genre of
peplum films can be traced directly to the homoerotic images which dominate *Fabiola*.
Popular French actress Michele Morgan is the
beautiful Fabiola, a Roman noblewoman who
becomes a Christian in the difficult days before the rise of Constantine. Her lover, Rhual,
is a gladiator who must overcome many ob-
stacles before they can be together. Morgan
and Vidal became real-life lovers and were
wed soon after filming *Fabiola*. Henry Vidal
had a promising career which ended when he
died of a heart attack in 1959 at the age of 40.
Massimo Girotti, in his first epic role, portrays
the Roman officer Sebastian who is crucified
by his own soldiers when they discover that he
is a Christian. The arena sequences are some
of the most realistic and harrowing ever
shown on the screen. Some 7,000 extras, including 200 French and Italian athletes, took
part in these scenes. The United Artists release of *Fabiola* was adapted by Marc Connelly
and Fred Pressburger and edited by Frank W.
Madden.

Motion Picture: Ancient paganistic Rome is
shown with all its gaudiness, debauchery, intrigue and resentment to Constantine's desire
to free the slaves and accept Christianity.
Henri Vidal, Michele Morgan, Michel Simon
are on the Christian side in effective leading
roles.

84   *The Face That Launched a Thousand Ships*

(*L'Amante di Paride*)
Gino Del Duca Productions (1953) 67 min.
Technicolor
U.S.–Four Star

P–Victor Phalen, Hedy Lamarr/D–Marc Alle-
gret, Edgar G. Ulmer/W–Salka Viertel, Vadim Pe-
nianikoy, Aeneas MacKenzie/M–Alessandro Ci-
cognini/C–Desmond Dickinson/E–Thomas Pratt,
Manuel Del Campo/AD–Virgilio Marchi/CD–Vittorio Nino Novarese

Cast–Hedy Lamarr (Helen), Massimo Serato
(Paris), Cathy O'Donnell (Anonae), Robert Beatty
(Menelaus), Serena Michelotti (Cassandra), Guido
Celano (Jupiter), Alba Arnova (Venus), Enrico
Glori (Priam)

Despite the success of *Samson and Delilah*,
the film career of Hedy Lamarr was on the
wane in the early fifties. She went to Europe,
reportedly to star in a movie as Queen Esther
but nothing ever came of this project. Plans
for a spectacular version of Helen of Troy
were then announced with Hedy Lamarr as
co-producer and star. Prince Paris of Troy
journeys to Sparta to offer a peace treaty but
the Spartan king, Menelaus, already has plans
for a war on Troy. He asks his beautiful wife
Helen to detain the prince while he attempts
to convince the other Greek nations to join
him. Menelaus' plan goes awry when Helen
and Paris fall in love and run off to Troy together. In Troy, Paris and Helen are confronted by Anonae, who is also in love with
the prince. The Greeks sail their armada of a
thousand ships on Troy and the war wages
ten years. Paris dies of battle wounds and
Anonae commits suicide so that they can be
together. The Greeks invade the city with the
help of the Trojan Horse and an unhappy
Helen is taken back to Sparta. As filming pro-
gressed the money began to run out so the
final result was somewhat less than antici-
pated. A semblance of plot was constructed
from the existing footage and released in Europe in 1953. Hedy Lamarr began to work on
a new production called *Femmina* in which she
would portray Empress Josephine, Genevieve
of Brabant, and Mary Queen of Scots. The
Genevieve and Josephine segments were completed when, once again, funds ran out. Rather
than scrap the entire project, the Helen of

Troy feature was edited down to approximately thirty minutes and incorporated into *Femmina*, which was released as a 96 minute feature called *The Love of Three Queens* in 1955. Lamarr's co-stars in the new sequences were Terence Morgan, Cesare Danova and Gerald Oury. The "Helen of Troy" section remains the most interesting part of *The Love of Three Queens* with Lamarr as a very Delilah-like Helen and Massimo Serato in an uncharacteristic romantic role. The dialogue is incredibly stilted with delivery to match but the visuals are some compensation, despite the restricted budget.

85   *The Fall of Rome*

(Il Crollo di Roma)
Atlantica Cinematografica (1963) 89 min.
Totalscope/Eastman Color
U.S.–Medallion
   P–Marco Vicario/D–Anthony Dawson (Antonio Margheriti)/W–Antonio Margheriti, Gianni Astolfi, Mario Mancini/M–Riz Ortolani/C–Riccardo Pallottini/E–Renato Cinquini/AD–Riccardo Domenici
   Cast–Carl Mohner (Marcus), Lorendana Nusciak (Svetla), Jim Dolan (Caius), Andrea Aureli (Rako), Ida Galli (Licia), Maria Grazia Bucella (Xenia), Piero Palermini (Valerius), Giancarlo Sbragia (Giunio) with Nando Poggi, Joe Pollini, Claudio Scarchilli, Renato Terra, Roberto Bettoni, Mimmo Maggio, Carlo Tamberlani, Laura Rocca

   With the death of Constantine, the persecution of the Christians begins again. The new ruler of Rome is the Proconsul Giunio who is aided by his henchman Valerius in seeking out the Christians for slaughter. Marcus, a Centurion, sympathizes with the Christians and ends up fighting in the arena to defend them. Just when the plight of the Christians seems utterly hopeless, an earthquake destroys the arena and surrounding buildings. Marcus and the Christians escape to start a new life away from Rome. A standard Romans vs. Christians storyline is enlivened somewhat by Margheriti's direction.

Gladitorial combat in the arena during *The Fall of Rome* (1963).

86   The Fall of the Roman Empire

A Bronston-Roma Production
Paramount (1964) 188 min.
Ultra Panavision 70/Technicolor
  P–Samuel Bronston/D–Anthony Mann/W–Ben
Barzman, Basilio Franchina, Philip Yordan/M–
Dimitri Tiomkin/C–Robert Krasker/E–Robert
Lawrence/PD/CD–Veniero Colasanti, John Moore
  Cast–Sophia Loren (Lucilla), Stephen Boyd
(Livius), Alec Guinness (Marcus Aurelius), James
Mason (Timonides), Christopher Plummer (Commodus), John Ireland (Ballomar), Anthony Quayle
(Verulus), Mel Ferrer (Cleander), Omar Sharif (Sohamus), Eric Porter (Julianus), Douglas Wilmer
(Niger), Peter Damon (Claudius), Andrew Keir
(Polybius), Finlay Currie (Caecina) with George
Murcell, Lena Von Martens, Gabriella Licudi, Norman Wooland, Michael Gwynn, Rafael Calvo , Virgilio Teixeira

Sophia Loren and Stephen Boyd are caught up in the chain of events which led to *The Fall of the Roman Empire* (1964).

The Fall of the Roman Empire, though filmed in Europe, was the last of the grand style Hollywood epics. Following in the wake of Mankiewicz's *Cleopatra*, the film failed to make much of an impression on a spectacle weary public and therefore fared badly at the box office. This hastened the downfall of Samuel Bronston Productions, which made only one more film, *Circus World* (1964). In 1967 another project, to be called Isabella of Spain, never got beyond the planning stage. Thus the motion picture industry was deprived of one of its most colorful and extravagant figures, producer Samuel Bronston. Bronston began his career as an independent producer in Hollywood during the forties and produced his first large-scale historical film, *John Paul Jones*, in 1959. He later moved his operation to Madrid where he oversaw the production of such colossal undertakings as *King of Kings* and *El Cid*. Bronston was so pleased with his association with Charlton Heston on *El Cid* that he asked him to star as Livius in *The Fall of the Roman Empire*. Heston disliked the script and opted instead to appear in Bronston's film about the Boxer Rebellion, *55 Days at Peking* (1963). Kirk Douglas was approached to play Livius but, having similar reservations about the screenplay, he also declined. As it turned out, the film's greatest flaw is a weak performance by Stephen Boyd in this role. He and Sophia Loren fail to generate excitement as a romantic duo and this damages the film considerably. Despite this, *The Fall of the Roman Empire* did not deserve the audience neglect and critical pans it suffered. The strong supporting cast does much to compensate for any deficiencies in the two lead players, with Alec Guinness a standout as Emperor Marcus Aurelius. When focusing on the dying ruler and his attempts to prevent his mad son Commodus from inheriting the throne, the plot is absorbing. As soon as the emphasis shifts to the nominal love story, interest wanes. Technically the film is superior, with lavish sets and costumes. The Roman Forum set alone is surely one of the most impressive ever constructed for a motion picture, outdoing even *Cleopatra* for sheer opulence. Fortunately the passing years have strengthened the reputation of this film and it is now regarded as a high point of epic cinema. The original 188 minute running time of *The Fall of the Roman Empire* was hastily cut to 172 minutes for the road show presentations. Later, when the film went into general release, it was edited down to 152 minutes.

AA Nomination: Best Musical Score

San Diego Evening Tribune: An onlooker's attempt to become immersed in the historical drama is constantly hampered by a vapid, limping story that carries little intellectual light and less emotional voltage.

Cosmopolitan: Despite its flaws—some performances are wooden, some sequences confusing—the picture is a stunning production that generates many moments of excitement.

Movie: To be real or not to be real, is the question that seems to have puzzled director Anthony Mann. The inability to decide which way to go causes the film's early collapse.

87   *Fellini Satyricon*

United Artists (1970) 136 min.
Panavision/Color by DeLuxe
   P–Alberto Grimaldi/D–Federico Fellini/W–Bernardo Zapponi, Federico Fellini/M–Nino Rota/C–Guiseppe Rotunno/E–Ruggero Mastroianni/AD–Luigi Scaccianoce, Giorgio Giovannini/PD/CD–Danilo Donati
   Cast–Martin Potter (Encolpius), Hiram Keller (Ascyltus), Max Born (Giton), Capucine (Tryphaena), Salvo Randon (Eumolpus), Magali Noel

Martin Potter as the handsome Encolpius in
Fellini Satyricon **(1970).**

(Fortunata), Mario Romagnoli (Trimalchio), Fanfulla (Vernacchio), Tanya Lopert (Caesar) with Gordon Mitchell, Alain Cuny, Lucia Bose, Donyale Luna, Giuseppe Sanvitale, Hylette Adolphe, Joseph Wheeler, Danica La Loggia, Antonia Pietrosi, Wolfgang Hillinger

Federico Fellini's highly publicized but ultimately unsatisfying version of Petronius' satire of life in ancient Rome is one of the great cinematic curiosities. Notorious at the time of its release due to graphic depictions of sex and sadism and a casual attitude toward homosexuality, *Satyricon* took the newly liberated cinema to its limits. The fragmented story line tells of the student Encolpius and his obsession for his young lover Giton. When Giton runs away with their friend Ascyltus, Encolpius follows in hot pursuit. Along the way the three youths encounter a variety of typical Fellini grotesques. In choosing his cast, Fellini used amateur actors Martin Potter, Hiram Keller and Max Born in the leads and professionals like Capucine, Alain Cuny and Gordon Mitchell in character parts. The design of the production is closer to futuristic science fiction fantasy than it is to any of the previous depictions of ancient Rome. This concept adds to the uniqueness and accounts for much of the film's reptilian attraction. A rival Italian film company rushed their pornographic version of *Satyricon* into theaters prior to Fellini's in order to capitalize on the vast amount of publicity being given to the title. This production was judged obscene by the Italian government and quickly vanished but, to avoid confusion, the title of the Fellini version was changed to *Fellini Satyricon*.

Entertainment World: Visually *Satyricon* is the *2001* of the historic past. Each frame is lit and composed like a masterpiece of glowing classic art.

88   *Fire Monsters Against the Son of Hercules*

(Maciste Contro i Montri; Maciste Against the Monsters/Colossus of the Stone Age/Land of the Monsters)
E.U.R. Cinematografica, Rome (1962) 80 min.
Totalscope/Eastman Color
U.S.–Embassy (1964)
   P–Giorgio Martelli/D–Guido Malatesta/W–Arpad De Riso, Guido Malatesta/M–Gian Stellari,

Margaret Lee and Reg Lewis gasp at the approach of another tacky monster in *Fire Monsters Against the Son of Hercules* (1964).

Guido Robuschi/C–Giuseppe La Torre/E–Enzo Alfonsi
  Cast–Reg Lewis (Maciste), Margaret Lee (Moab), Andrea Aureli (Fuan), Luciano Marin (Aidar), Birgit Bergen (Raja) with Nello Pazzafini, Miria Kent, Fulvia Gasser, Rocco Spataro, Tania Snidersic, Ivan Pengow, Demeter Bitenc, Mimmo Maggio

This prehistoric peplum film is known by a variety of titles but no matter what it's called, it is still one of the silliest films in the entire genre. The filmmakers should be given some measure of credit for at least attempting something different by setting the story in the

Stone Age rather than ancient Greece or Italy; however, the uniqueness of the setting is small compensation for the utter inanity of the rest of the film. Reg Lewis, in his only peplum role, plays Maciste (in some prints he is called Maxis, yet another son of Hercules). The standard plotline has Maciste appear out of nowhere to aid the peaceable Sun People when they are set upon by the aggressive Moon Tribe. During the course of the film, Maciste is called upon to battle a variety of ludicrous monsters. The monsters are so absurd looking that the actors involved should be given full marks for being able to keep a straight face when threatened by them. Worse even than the monsters are the hysterical hairstyles worn by the leads. Lewis sports a blond ducktail and Margaret Lee wears a wig so bad that it seems to be constantly on the verge of slipping off her head. Reg Lewis had been set to star as a Tarzan-type in Antonio Leonviola's *Taur, il Re Della Forza Brutale*, but he was replaced by Joe Robinson shortly after filming commenced.

89 *First Knight*

A Zucker Bros. Production (1995) 134 min.
Columbia/Sony Pictures
Technicolor
   P–Jerry Zucker, Hunt Lowry/D–Jerry Zucker/W–Lorne Cameron, David Hoselton, William Nicholson/M–Jerry Goldsmith/C–Adam Greenberg/E–Walter Murch/PD–John Box/CD–Nana Cecchi
   Cast–Sean Connery (Arthur), Richard Gere (Lancelot), Julia Ormond (Guinevere), Ben Cross (Malagant), Liam Cunningham (Agravaine), John Gielgud (Oswald) with Christopher Villiers, Valentine Pelka, Ralph Ineson, Colin McCormack, Stuart Bunce, Tom Lucy

There is little of Arthurian legend on view in this new take on the story of King Arthur. The prologue tells us that "Times were hard. A man made his living any way he could. And Lancelot had always been good with a sword." The powerful knight Malagant has left the service of King Arthur and now fights against his sovereign for control of the kingdom of Camelot. The caravan of Arthur's bride-to-be, Guinevere, is attacked by Malagant's men but she is rescued by Lancelot, a wandering swordsman. They are attracted to each other

immediately but Guinevere chooses to honor her commitment to Arthur. When another attempt to kidnap Guinevere succeeds, Lancelot goes to Malagant's stronghold to rescue her. As a reward, Arthur makes Lancelot one of his Knights of the Round Table. Guinevere's homeland of Leonesse is laid siege by Malagant and she, Arthur and Lancelot ride off with their army to save her people. Malagant is temporarily thwarted and the victors return to Camelot in triumph. Lancelot decides to resist temptation by leaving the city but Guinevere finally gives into her love for him. They are locked in a passionate embrace when Arthur enters the room and sees the lovers. He decides to subject them to a public trial but it is interrupted by the arrival of Malagant and his army. Arthur is mortally wounded and Lancelot avenges him by killing Malagant. The dying Arthur asks Lancelot to look after Guinevere. *First Knight* is a fairly entertaining movie with some fine technical credits to bolster the deficiencies in the script and the miscasting of Richard Gere. As a shaggy Lancelot, Gere has the sole American accent in the cast. He is also a bit too long of tooth to make his sword swinging convincing. Sean Connery tends to overplay his part but Julia Ormond is near perfect as Guinevere.

90 *The Fourth King*

(Il Quarto Re)
A Titanus Production (1996) 90 min.
Color
U.S.–Unreleased
   P–Guido Lombardo/D–Stefano Reali/W–Enrico Medioli/M–Ennio and Andrea Morricone/C–Gianni Mammolotti/E–Paolo Benassi/AD–Francesco Bronzi/CD–Lina Taviani
   Cast–Maria Grazia Cucinotta (Izhira), Raoul Bova (Alazar), Billy Dee Williams (Caspar), Daniel Ceccaldi (Melchior), Joachim Fuchsberger (Baldassar), Wilfred Baasner (Bakir)

In this movie made for Italian television, Alazhar, a young farmer and bee-keeper, leaves his wife and reluctantly joins the Three Magi on their journey to find the newborn Messiah. Alazhar's wife Izhira is pregnant with their first child and, although he attempts to leave the Magi and return to her, they prevent him by using their magic. Alazhar is captured by bandits and Caspar, one of the Magi, rescues him. During the remainder of their quest Alazhar is of continual help to the three kings, so much so that they offer to make him a king as well. Upon their arrival in Bethlehem, Alazhar gives his gift to the Christ child—a jar of honey.

91   *Francis of Assisi*

A Perseus Production
20th Century–Fox (1961) 106 min.
CinemaScope/Color by DeLuxe
   P–Plato A. Skouras/D–Michael Curtiz/W–Eugene Vale, James Forsythe, Jack Thomas/Based on the novel *The Joyful Beggar* by Louis de Wohl/M–Mario Nascimbene/C–Piero Portalupi/E–Louis R. Loeffler/AD–Edward Carrere/CD–Vittorio Nino Novarese
   Cast–Bradford Dillman (Francis), Dolores Hart (Clare), Stuart Whitman (Paolo), Pedro Armendariz (The Sultan), Cecil Kellaway (Cardinal Hugolino), Eduard Franz (Pietro), Finlay Currie (The Pope) with Mervyn Johns, Russell Napier, John Welsh, Harold Goldblatt, Edith Sharpe, Jack Lambert, Oliver Johnston, Malcolm Keen, Brendon Fitzgerald, Ferndinand Hilbeck

In Assisi during the early 13th century, Francis Bernadoni, the son of a wealthy merchant, joins the army struggling to liberate Sicily. He becomes friends with Paolo, a young nobleman who has also joined the fight. During the battle Francis fights bravely, but a mysterious voice compels him to leave the army and return home. Accused of being a deserter, Francis is imprisoned. He is released at the intervention of Paolo but Francis once again hears the voice, which he now recognizes as God speaking to him. He is told to rebuild a ruined church, which he does despite opposition from his family. Vowing to lead a life of poverty, Francis founds a new religious order with the blessing of the Pope. When the woman Paolo loves becomes a nun, he blames Francis and renounces their friendship. Francis travels to the Holy Land to intervene in the warfare between the Christian Crusaders and the Moslems. Upon returning home, Francis discovers that the rules of his Franciscan order have been abandoned by most of the other brothers. Francis refuses to conform to their new principles and, sick and blind, he moves into a cave to live apart from the others. The Lord blesses the dying Francis with stigmata. Bradford Dillman, a fine actor usually confined to supporting roles, makes the most of his star turn as Francis. His performance is sincere and touching. To research her role, Dolores Hart spent several weeks in a convent prior to the filming. She was so impressed by this way of life that in 1963 she left behind her Hollywood career and became a nun at the Benedictine Laudis Monastery in Bethlehem, Connecticut. Technical advisor on the film was Vincenzo Labella, who later produced the epic TV mini-series *Jesus of Nazareth*, *A.D.* and *Moses*. *Francis of Assisi* had its world premiere on July 12, 1961, in San Francisco, the city named for St. Francis. 20th Century–Fox, obviously doubtful about trying to sell the picture on its own merits, devised an advertising campaign using the catchline "How a lusty, fighting 'Rebel with a Cause' exchanged his sword for a cross!"

Bradford Dillman suffers stoically as *Francis of Assisi*.

92   *From the Manger to the Cross*

Vitograph Inc. (1913) 70 min.

P–Kalem Company/D–Sidney Olcott/W–Gene Gauntier/C–George Hollister/AD–Henry Allen Farnham

Cast–Robert Henderson-Bland (Jesus), Percy Dyer (Jesus as a Youth), Gene Gauntier (Mary), Alice Hollister (Mary Magdalene), Sam Morgan (Pilate), James Ainsley (John the Baptist)

From the Manger to the Cross is one of the earliest feature length motion pictures dealing with the life of Christ. Filmed on location in Egypt and the Holy Land, it is surprisingly sophisticated in its execution. The scenes are not merely a series of static tableaus, which is often the case with of many films of this vintage. The subtitles are quotes directly taken from scripture and the performances are effectively subdued. Overall it is a very impressive production.

93   *A Funny Thing Happened on the Way to the Forum*

A Melvin Frank–Quadrangle Films S.A. Production

United Artists (1966) 99 min.

Color by DeLuxe

P–Melvin Frank/D–Richard Lester/W–Melvin Frank, Michael Pertwee/Based on the play by Harold Prince, Burt Shevelove, Larry Gelbart/ Songs: Music and Lyrics by Stephen Sondheim/Incidental Music by Ken Thorne/C–Nicholas Roeg/E–John Victor Smith/AD–Syd Cain/PD/ CD–Tony Walton

Cast–Zero Mostel (Pseudolus), Phil Silvers (Lycus), Buster Keaton (Erronius), Michael Crawford (Hero), Jack Gilford (Hysterium), Annette Andre (Philia), Michael Hordern (Senex), Leon Greene (Miles Glorious), Patricia Jessel (Domina) with Roy Kinnear, Alfie Bass, Pamela Brown, Andrew Faulds, Inga Neilsen, Jon Pertwee, Beatrix Lehmann, John Bluthal

A Funny Thing Happened on the Way to the Forum but this wasn't it. This adaptation of the Broadway musical is a labored affair full of pratfalls and mugging. Directed with Richard Lester's typically frenetic touch (jump cuts, speeded up action, quick zooms) the film seems to be desperately seeking laughs but

everything comes off as a bit stale and forced. Zero Mostel is, at best, an acquired taste and he plays every scene as if he is still on stage playing to the balcony. The rest of the cast isn't much better when it comes to subtlety, but then this isn't exactly subtle material. The musical is loosely adapted from Plautus' play *Miles Glorius* and involves many incidents of mistaken identity. Pseudolus, a slave in the household of Senex and his harridan wife Domina, continually plots and schemes to gain his freedom. The close proximity of Lycus' brothel creates endless diversion for most of the characters, particularly Senex' young son Hero. Hero is played by a pre-Phantom Michael Crawford, obviously gearing up for his terrible turn in the film version of *Hello Dolly* a few years later. *Forum* was filmed at the Samuel Bronston Studios in Madrid on many of the sets left over from *The Fall of the Roman Empire*. Reportedly, Richard Lester went to great lengths to create an authentic vision of ancient Rome. This seems an unusual ambition for a movie in which the characters suddenly break into song and behave in a most contemporary fashion. The best thing about the film are the wonderful end titles by Richard Williams.

AA Nomination: Musical Score

94   *The Fury of Achilles*

(L'Ira di Achille)

Uneurop-Film, Rome (1962) 116 min.

Ultrascope/Eastman Color

U.S.–American-International (1965)

P/D–Marino Girolami/W–Gino de Santis/M–Carlo Savina/C–Mario Fioretti/E–Mirella Casini/ AD–Savirio D'Eugenio/CD–Luciana Marinucci

Cast–Gordon Mitchell (Achilles), Jacques Bergerac (Hector), Cristina Gajoni (Xenia), Gloria Milland (Briseis), Enio Girolami (Patroclus), Piero Lulli (Odysseus), Mario Petri (Agamemnon), Roberto Risso (Paris), Fosco Ciachetti (Priam) with Pietro Tordi, Edith Peters, Laura Rocca

The Fury of Achilles makes the great Greek hero its focal point and is surprisingly faithful to *The Iliad*. In the tenth year of the Trojan War, the warrior Achilles and King Agamemnon quarrel over the fate of a female captive. Achilles refuses to honor the commands of Agamemnon any longer and withdraws from

The Greek general Achilles (Gordon Mitchell, center) makes plans for the downfall of Troy in *The Fury of Achilles* (1965).

the battle. It isn't until his dearest friend, Patroclus, is killed by Hector, the son of the Trojan king, that Achilles returns to action. In a bloody single combat to the death, Achilles fights Hector to avenge the murder of Patroclus. Gordon Mitchell plays Achilles as a fierce warrior, but ultimately compassionate man. He does a commendable job in what is probably his best role.

95   *The Fury of Hercules*

(La Furia di Ercole)
Cineproduzioni Associate, Rome—Comptoir Français, Paris (1961) 97 min.
Supertotalscope/Eastman Color
U.S.—Medallion (1962)
   P—Mario Maggi/D—Gianfranco Parolini/W—Gianfranco Parolini, Giovanni Simonelli, Arpad De Riso, Sergio Sollima, M. D'Amien/M—Carlo Innocenzi/C—Francesco Izzarelli/E—Mario Sansoni/AD—Oscar D'Amico/CD—Vittorio Rossi

Cast—Brad Harris (Hercules), Brigitte Corey (Jasmine), Mara Berni (Comida), Serge Gainsbourg (Manisthos) with Alan Steel, Elke Arendt, Carlo Tamberlani, Gianfranco Gasparri, Irena Prosen, Ivan Dobric, Romano Ghini, Nick Stefanini

   Yet another Hercules entry, but this one lacks the more imaginative touches present in the Steve Reeves and Reg Park films. *The Fury of Hercules* is a straightforward sword and sandal movie without any of the usual fantasy elements. Brad Harris is suitably muscular as Hercules but the weak script provides no opportunity for him to display any amount of acting ability. He also lacks the charisma of many of the other peplum stars who have assayed the same role. The plot has Hercules journey to the city of Arpad (could this be an in joke perpetrated by one of the screenwriters?). When he arrives, he learns that his friend, the king, has died and that his weak-willed daughter Comida now sits upon the throne. The new queen's evil prime minister Manisthos convinces her that Hercules is her enemy, despite the fact that she has loved him since childhood. To prove his loyalty, Hercules must endure many tests of strength, including fights with elephants, lions, and a man in the same unconvincing ape costume used in *Terror of Rome Against the Son of Hercules*. Direction is, for the most part, indifferent. Alan Steel portrays the corrupt captain of the queen's guard and spends most of his time attempting to kill Hercules. Steel is one of the few peplum stars who could vacillate between heroic and villainous roles with equal effect.

96   *Fury of the Pagans*

(La Furia dei Barbari; The Fury of the Barbarians)
Arion Film (1960) 102 min.
Dyaliscope/Eastman Color
U.S.–Columbia (1962) 86 min.

P–Mario Bartolini, Guiliano Simonetti/D–Guido Malatesta/W–Gino Mangini, Umberto Scarpelli/M–Gian Stellari, Guido Robuschi/C–Vincenzo Seratrice/E–Roberto Giandalla, Mario Sansoni/AD–Pier Vittorio Marchi

Cast–Edmund Purdom (Toryok), Rossana Podesta (Leonora), Livio Lorenzon (Korvo) with Carla Calo, Daniele Vargas, Andrea Fantasia, Ljubica Jovic, Amedeo Novelli, Nick Stefanini, Guilio Massimi, Simoneta Simsoni, Raffaela Pelloni, Luciano Marin, Vittoria Febi

Fury of the Pagans features three of the peplum genre's most prolific stars in a story of rape, death and revenge. When the betrothed of Toryok, chief of the village of Nyssia, is raped and murdered by the barbaric Lombard warrior Korvo, Toryok vows vengeance. Two years later, Korvo returns from Italy with the beautiful hostage Leonora and Toryok sees his chance for revenge. Toryok helps Leonora escape and then leads an attack on Korvo and his warriors. Despite the casting of Edmund Purdom, Rossana Podesta and Livio Lorenzon, *Fury of the Pagans* emerges as standard screen fare with more than its share of burning, pillaging and murder. *Fury of the Pagans* also suffered from Columbia's decision to distribute the picture in black and white instead of color for its U.S. theatrical release. This became an unfortunate, but common, practice for Columbia imports during the early sixties.

Genre icon Rossana Podesta is a beautiful barbarian in *Fury of the Pagans* (1962).

Many of these films were later shown on television in their original color format.

97   *Genghis Khan*

Columbia (1965) 124 min.
Panavision/Technicolor

P–Irving Allen/D–Henry Levin/W–Clarke Reynolds, Beverly Cross/Based on a story by Berkely Mather/M–Dusin Radic/C–Geoffrey Unsworth/E–Geoffrey Foot/AD–Maurice Carter, Heino Weidemann, Mile Nickolic/CD–Cynthia Tingey

Cast–Omar Sharif (Temujin), Stephen Boyd (Jamuga), James Mason (Kam Ling), Eli Wallach (Shah of Khwarezm), Francoise Dorleac (Bortei), Telly Savalas (Shan), Robert Morley (Emperor of China), Michael Hordern (Geen), Yvonne Mitchell (Katke), Woody Strode (Sengal), Kenneth Cope (Subodai), Roger Croucher (Kassar) with Don Borisenko, Patrick Holt, Suzanne Hsaio, George Savalas, Carlo Cura, Gustavo Rojo, Dusan Vujsic, Jovan Tesic, Andreja Marcic, Thomas Margulies, Yamata Pauli, Linda Loncar

There is something about the character of Genghis Khan that seems to inspire filmmakers to gross feats of miscasting and inane dialogue. Following in the footsteps of Howard Hughes' *The Conqueror*, this version of the life

Steeve Reeves receives the award for "Best Looking Man in a Skimpy Costume" in *The Giant of Marathon* **(1960).**

of Genghis Khan features some truly awful performances by such oriental types as James Mason and Robert Morley. As usual, Morley is playing Morley but Mason's concept of his character seems to consist mainly of an over-bite and squinting. The result is a racial stereotype on a par with Mickey Rooney in *Breakfast at Tiffany's* and Marlon Brando in *Teahouse of the August Moon*. The young Mongol, Temujin, is held in slavery by Jamuga, the chief of the Merkits. When Temujin escapes his captors he becomes the leader of a band of fugitives who help him raid the Merkit camp and abduct Bortei, the fiancée of Jamuga. Winning the love of Bortei, Temujin and his cohorts go to China to ally themselves with the emperor against Jamuga. Unlike *The Conqueror*, *Genghis Khan* is far more concerned with the animosity between Temujin and Jamuga than it is with the romance between Temujin and Bortei. As Bortei, the late Francoise Dorleac, sister of Catherine Deneuve, made her English language film debut. Omar Sharif as Genghis Khan is certainly an improvement over John Wayne in the same role.

San Diego Union: Usually spectacles are dreadful ("The Fall of the Roman Empire") or inspiring ("Ben-Hur"). There seemed to be no in-between until this Columbia color epic came along.

Films and Filming: It is an American success story with the necessary dressing of love, female beauty, parenthood, pride and fortitude.

98   *The Giant of Marathon*

(La Battaglia di Maratona; The Battle of Marathon)
Titanus-Galatea, Rome-Lux-Lyre, Paris (1960) 92 min.
Dyaliscope / Eastman Color
U.S.–Metro-Goldwyn-Mayer

P–Bruno Vailati/D–Jacques Tourneur/W–Ennio De Concini, Augusto Frassinetti, Bruno Vailati/M–Roberto Nicolosi/C–Mario Bava/E–Mario Serandrei/AD–Marcello Del Prato/CD–Marisa Crimi

Cast–Steve Reeves (Philippides), Mylene Demongeot (Andromeda), Ivo Garraini (Creuso), Daniela Rocca (Karis), Sergio Fantoni (Teocrito), Alberto Lupo (Milziade), Daniele Vargas (Dario), Gianni Loti (Teucro) with Philippe Hersent, Miranda Campa, Anita Todesco

The Giant of Marathon, although a distortion of historical fact, is a handsome production filled with action and romance. Steve Reeves has one of his best roles as the famous Olympic hero Philippides, who was instrumental in staving off an invasion of Greece by the Persians. Mylene Demongeot and Daniela Rocca are the women who compete for his amorous attentions. Rocca is especially effective as the wanton who sacrifices her life to save the man she loves, even though she knows he has never loved her. The action highlight of the film is a well-staged sea battle which features some excellent underwater photography. Jacques Tourneur directed the main dialogue sequences but the film was completed by Mario Bava. Future "Hercules" Alan Steel can be spotted in an unbilled supporting role as one of the Olympian athletes.

99   *The Giants of Rome*

(I Giganti de Roma/Fort Alesia)
N.C. Devon Film, Rome–Radius Productions, Paris
   (1964) 98 min.
Widescope/Eastman Color
U.S.–Walter Manley Enterprises
   P–Mino Loy, Luciano Martino/D–Anthony Dawson (Antonio Margheriti)/W–Ernesto Gastaldi, Luciano Martino, Arlette Combret/M–Carlo Rustichelli/C–Fausto Zuccoli/AD–Jean Paul Coutan-Laboureur/CD–Riccardo Domenici
   Cast–Richard Harrison (Claudius), Wandisa Guida (Livia), Ettore Manni (Castor) with Ralph Hudson, Nicole Tessier, Goffredo Unger, Renato Baldini, Piero Lulli, Alessandro Sperli, Philippe Hersent, Maurizio Conti, Alberto Dell'Acqua, Jean Claude Madal, Renato Montalbano, Claudio Scarchilli

In 52 B.C. during the Roman conquest of Gaul, the legions of Julius Caesar are encamped at Fort Alesia. Caesar receives word that the Gauls have a secret weapon capable of destroying the Roman forces. Caesar chooses five of his bravest soldiers, led by the valiant Claudius, who are charged with the task of learning the whereabouts of this new weapon and destroying it. The small band of legionaries are soon captured by the Druids, who have also taken captive a beautiful Roman woman named Livia. The Romans escape from the Druid caves, but one of them dies in the process. After many close calls, the Romans find the stronghold of the Gauls and discover that the weapon is a giant catapult. Claudius succeeds in destroying the catapult but only he and Livia escape alive. A grateful Caesar sends them back to Rome to be married in the Temple of Venus. This inexpensive actioner has a good cast and a reasonably exciting story. Richard Harrison as Claudius may be prone to slapping women and yelling "shut up" when he's angry but he turns out to have a tender heart in the end.

100   *The Giants of Thessaly*

(Il Giganti della Tessaglia/The Argonauts/Jason
   and the Golden Fleece)
Alexandra P.C., Rome–S.C. Lyre, Paris (1960) 95
   min.
Supertotalscope/Eastman Color
U.S.–Medallion (1961) 86 min.
   D–Riccardo Freda/W–Giuseppe Masini, Mario Rossetti, Riccardo Freda/M–Carlo Rustichelli/C–Vich Vaclav, Raffaele Masciocchi/E–Otello Colangeli/AD–Franco Lolli/CD–Mario Giorsi
   Cast–Roland Carey (Jason), Ziva Rodann (Creusa), Massimo Girotti (Orpheus), Luciano Marin (Eurystheus) with Alberto Farnese, Nandine Duca, Cathia Caro, Alfredo Varelli, Gil Delmare, Maria Theresa Vianello, Nando Tamberlani, Alberto Sorrentino, Massimo Pianforini, Raffaele Baldassarre, Paolo Gozlino, Nando Angelini,

The Giants of Thessaly is a total bastardization of the story of Jason and his search for the Golden Fleece. All of the events from mythology are abandoned in favor of a script which bears more resemblance to *The Odyssey* of Homer than it does to Apollonius' *Quest for the Golden Fleece*. Movies like this undermined the success of the excellent *Jason and the Argonauts*, released two years later. in 1250 B.C., the Golden Fleece, a present from Zeus to the kingdom of Jolco in Thessaly, is stolen. In anger Zeus declares that volcanoes will rain

Jason takes a mighty leap to retrieve the Golden Fleece in *The Giants of Thessaly* (1961).

fire upon Jolco until the fleece is returned. King Jason and his men set sail on the Argo to the far-off land of Colchis, where the fleece has been taken. On the way they encounter a violent storm which carries them to an island populated solely by beautiful women. The ruler is Gaea, a sorceress who turns men into sheep. When Jason spurns her advances she reverts to her actual hideous countenance. Meanwhile back in Jolco, Jason's wife Creusa is fending off the advances of a would-be usurper to the throne. The Argonauts land on another island and encounter a giant cyclopean monster, which they slay. Arriving at last in Colchis, Jason climbs a colossal statue to reclaim the fleece. He arrives back in Jolco just in time to prevent the forced marriage of his wife to the villainous pretender. Massimo Girotti as Orpheus gives the only semblance of a performance. His death scene, when he imagines the approach of Eurydice to take him to the Underworld, is actually quite affecting. Roland Carey is, if nothing else, an energetic Jason. It is odd, in a film so liberally sprinkled with mythological personages, that the character of Hercules is absent from the crew of the Argo. Peplum films were generally trying to find an excuse to include Hercules rather than exclude him and, for once, the presence of his character would have been accurate. Director Riccardo Freda helmed a number of memorable horror films and was also responsible for the peplum horror movie *The Witch's Curse* (aka *Maciste in Hell*) starring Kirk Morris.

101 *Gladiator*

A Douglas Wick Production
Dreamworks/Universal (2000) 154 min.
Panavision/Technicolor

P–Douglas Wick, David Franzoni, Branko Lustig/D–Ridley Scott/W–David Franzoni, John Logan, William Nicholson/M–Hans Zimmer, Lisa Gerrard/C–John Mathison/E–Pietro Scalia/PD–

Gladiator **Russell Crowe defends himself in mortal combat (2000).**

Arthur Max/AD–John King, David Allday, Benjamin Fernandez, Peter Russell, Keith Pain/CD–Janty Yates

Cast–Russell Crowe (Maximus), Joaquin Phoenix (Commodus), Connie Nielsen (Lucilla), Oliver Reed (Proximo), Derek Jacobi (Gracchus), Djimon Hounsou (Juba), Richard Harris (Marcus Aurelius), David Schofield (Falco), Tomas Arana (Quintus), Ralf Moeller (Hagen), David Hemmings (Cassius), Spencer Treat Clark (Lucius)

The aged emperor Marcus Aurelius decides to pass the rule of Rome on to his faithful general Maximus, rather than his dissolute son Commodus. When Commodus learns of this, he murders his father and orders the execution of Maximus and his wife and son. Maximus escapes death but is captured and sold as a slave to Proximo, a supplier of gladiators for the Roman arena. In the Colosseum, Maximus becomes a favorite of the crowds and sees his chance for revenge on Commodus for the death of his family. Lucilla, the crazed emperor's sister, and Gracchus, a dissident Roman senator, attempt to involve Maximus in their plot to overthrow Commodus. Detractors of the film have said that

Gladiator is just a standard revenge movie in Roman drag. This is selling the merits of this outstanding motion picture extremely short. Chief among its virtues are Ridley Scott's exciting direction and a collection of fine performances. The brutal yet moving portrayal of Maximus by Russell Crowe is particularly impressive. Surprisingly, he was second choice for the role. Mel Gibson was approached to star but declined, feeling the part was too reminiscent of *Braveheart*. The story of *Gladiator* covers much the same ground as *The Fall of the Roman Empire*, but now it has been tarted up with today's state-of-the-art technical effects. The producers took an extreme risk in sinking over $100 million into a genre which had its heyday over thirty years before. Fortunately, the moviegoing public responded enthusiastically and made the film a tremendous commercial success. Many critics were also impressed and the Academy of Motion Picture Arts and Sciences awarded the Oscar to *Gladiator* as Best Picture of the Year. Special mention should be made of Oliver Reed, whose performance as Proximo turned out to be his last. While on location in Malta, Reed died suddenly. With two of his major scenes left to film, the script had to be rewritten to accommodate his absence. Computer generated images of Reed were also employed to help tie up loose ends. The film is dedicated to his memory.

AA Nominations: Best Picture*, Actor (Russell Crowe)*, Supporting Actor (Joaquin Phoenix), Director, Original Screenplay, Art Direction, Costume Design*, Cinematography, Film Editing, Original Score, Sound*, Visual Effects*

Variety: A muscular and bloody combat picture, a compelling revenge drama and a truly transporting trip back nearly 2,000 years. Crowe is simply splendid.

New Yorker: The simplicity of the plot feels right; whenever the movie strays into complexity it founders and slows. What you want is the games, and Scott delivers them avidly, complete with unfed tigers.

Los Angeles Times: A supremely atmospheric film that shrewdly mixes traditional Roman movie elements with the latest computer generated wonders.

102 *Gladiator of Rome*

(Il Gladitore di Roma/Battles of the Gladiators)
C.I.R.A.C.–Giorgio Agliani Cinematografica, Rome
(1962) 100 min.
Euroscope/Eastman Color
U.S.–Medallion (1962)

P–Adriano Merkel/D–Mario Costa/W–Gian
Paolo Callegari, Giuseppe Mariano/M–Carlo
Franci/C–Pier Ludovico Pavoni/E–Antonietta
Zita/CD–Giorgio Desideri

Cast–Gordon Scott (Marcus), Wandisa Guida
(Nisa), Ombretta Colli (Aglae), Roberto Risso (Va-
lerius), Eleonora Vargas (Prisca), Alberto Farnese
(Rufo), Piero Lulli (Astarte) with Charles Bor-
romel, Nando Tamberlani, Mirko Ellis, Pietro De
Veco, Andrea Aureli, Miranda Campa

This story is set during the reign of the Emperor Caracalla. Nisa, the daughter of conquered nobility, is a Roman hostage living under
the protection of a benevolent Patrician family on a provincial Roman estate. She is loved
by the son of the family, Valerius. By her side
is Marcus, who has guarded her since birth, a
giant of a man with nearly superhuman strength.
When the family is suspected of being Christians, they are slaughtered and Nisa and Marcus are taken as slaves. Valerius, returning home
to find death and destruction, sets out to rescue Nisa from slavery. Marcus and Nisa eventually end up at a gladiator school where he
is trained to fight in the arena. Nisa is made a
house slave to the owner of the school and
his wife. Valerius discovers Nisa's whereabouts
and attempts to buy her, but her jealous mistress refuses. With the help of Valerius, the
slaves escape from the gladiator school but,
after a bloody battle, they are recaptured and
condemned to be crucified. Only an unexpected
twist of fate finally frees them. *Gladiator of Rome*
has a slow moving plot and is not one of Gordon Scott's better vehicles. Scott was one of the
few peplum stars who could act, an attribute
all too often wasted on the roles he was offered. The Marcus-Nisa relationship is a direct
copy of Ursus and Lygia in *Quo Vadis*. Despite
the title, the action never moves into Rome itself and remains confined to the provinces.

103 *Gladiators Seven*

(I Sette Gladiatori)
Columbus Film S.p.A., Rome–Atenea Films,
Madrid (1962) 93 min.
Techniscope/Eastman Color
U.S.–Metro-Goldwyn-Mayer (1963)

P–Cleto Fontini, Italo Zingarelli/D–Pedro La-
zaga, Alberto De Martino (uncredited)/W–Alessandro Continenza, Bruno Corbucci, Alberto De
Martino, Giovanni Grimaldi/M–Marcello Giom-
bini/C–Adalberto Albertini, Eloy Mella/ E–Otello
Colangeli/AD–Piero Poletto, Antonio Simont/
CD–Mario Giorsi

Cast–Richard Harrison (Darius), Lorendana
Nusciak (Aglaia), Livio Lorenzon (Panurgus), Ger-
ard Tichy (Hiarba), Edoardo Toniolo (Milon),
Emilia Wolkowca (Ismere), Enrique Avila (Livius),
Joseph Marco (Xeno), Antonio Rubio (Mados), An-
tonio Molino Rojo (Macrobius), Barta Berry (Flac-
cus), Tony Zamperla (Vargas), Franca Badeschi
(Licia)

Gladiators Seven opens with an exciting
gladiatorial combat in the arena of Rome.
Darius, once a member of the Spartan nobility but now a Roman slave, must fight for his
life against overwhelming odds. When he defeats all of the warriors set against him, the
spectators demand his freedom. Darius returns home to Sparta to discover that his father has been murdered. He vows vengeance
on the killers and assembles a group of former gladiators to help him in his cause. Despite an action packed opening, the remainder
of the film is a conventional revenge story
with a rather tepid climax. Richard Harrison
gives his usual reliable performance as the
stalwart hero Darius, leader of the Spartan
gladiators. The rest of the cast is adequate,
but not outstanding. From a technical standpoint, *Gladiators Seven* is one of the most visually impressive of all the peplum films. The
widescreen color photography elevates the
film beyond the limitations of its tired plot.
The background score by Marcello Giombini
is another major attribute and helps give the
action sequences a heightened sense of excitement.

104 *The Goddess of Love*

(La Venere di Cheronea; The Venus of Chero-
nea/Aphrodite, déesse de l'amour/Aphrodite,
Goddess of Love)
Faro Film, Rome–Rialto Film, Paris (1958) 85 min.
Totalscope/Ferrania Color
U.S.–20th Century–Fox (1960) 68 min.
CinemaScope/Color by DeLuxe

P–Gian Paolo Bigazzi/D–Victor Tourjansky,
Fernando Cerchio (uncredited)/W–Diamiano

Richard Harrison (center) is one of the *Gladiators Seven* (1963).

Damiani/M–Michel Michelet/C–Arturo Gallea/
CD–Giancarlo Bartonini Salimbeni

Cast–Jacques Sernas (Lucian), Belinda Lee (Helen), Massimo Girotti (Praxiteles), Maria Frau (Iris) with Luigi Tosi, Claudio Gora, Elli Parvo, Enzo Fiermonte, Camillo Pilotto

In this French-Italian coproduction Lucian, a Macedonian soldier, collapses on a beach and awakens to see a beautiful girl rising out of the waves like a vision of Aphrodite. He learns that she is Helen, a Greek shepherdess who has been chosen by the sculptor Praxite-

Belinda Lee nurses Jacques Sernas back to health in *The Goddess of Love* (1960).

les to pose for a statue of the Goddess of Love. Although Laertes becomes friends with Praxiteles, they are both rivals for the love of Helen. The film bears some superficial resemblance to Robert Wise's *Helen of Troy*, not the least of which is Jacques Sernas as the leading man. Massimo Girotti gives a strong performance as the famed sculptor who falls in love with his beautiful model. Victor Tourjansky was assisted in his direction by Fernando Cerchio, although some sources list Giorgio Rivalta as the director of this film.

105 *Gold for the Caesars*

(Oro per i Cesari)
Adelphia Films, Rome–C.I.C.C. Films, Paris (1963)
  90 min.
Technicolor
U.S.–Metro-Goldwyn-Mayer
  P–Joseph Fryd/D–Andre de Toth/W–Arnold Perl/Based on the novel by Florence A. Seward/M–Franco Mannino/C–Raffaele Masciocchi/AD–Ottavio Scotti/CD–Mario Giorsi

Cast–Jeffrey Hunter (Lacer), Mylene Demongeot (Penelope), Ron Randell (Rufus), Massimo Girotti (Maximus), Giulio Bosetti (Scipio), Ettore Manni (Luna), Georges Lycan (Malendi), Furio Meniconi (Dax)

Florence A. Seward's prizewinning historical novel *Gold for the Caesars* had been planned for filming by MGM as early as 1961. When *King of Kings* failed to perform up to MGM's expectations at the box office, the project was given over to Joseph Fryd to be filmed as an economical European production. The plot was altered considerably in adapting it for the screen. The strong characterization of the original novel was abandoned and the action sequences were emphasized. Ironically, two of the stars of *King of Kings*, Jeffrey Hunter and Ron Randell, were reunited in *Gold for the Caesars*. Hunter is Lacer, an architect slave who is sent to Northern Spain to oversee the building of a Roman bridge. Upon completion of this task the proconsul Maximus offers

The Roman general Maximus (Massimo Girotti, right) warns his mistress (Mylene Demongeot) that she must remain true to him as Giulio Bosetti looks on in this scene from *Gold for the Caesars* (1963).

Lacer freedom if he will supervise a gold mining operation. Lacer falls in love with Penelope, the beautiful mistress of Maximus, incurring the Roman's wrath. Unfortunately, he needs Lacer to find the gold needed in his bid to become Emperor of Rome. The architect must also contend with an avalanche, the cruel centurion Rufus and the threat of attacking Celts. In the exciting finale, a bursting dam destroys the army of the Celtic invaders and the greedy Maximus. Riccardo Freda was the second unit director on the impressive action scenes. Although it was relegated to B movie statis by MGM, *Gold for the Caesars* is superior to many of the Euro-epics by virtue of its fine cast and outstanding production values.

106   *The Golden Horde*

Universal-International (1951) 77 min. Technicolor

P–Howard Christie, Robert Arthur/D–George Sherman/W–Gerald Dryson Adams/M–Hans J. Salter/C–Russell Metty/E–Frank Gross/AD–Bernard Herzbrun, Alexander Golitzen/CD–Leah Rhodes

Cast–Ann Blyth (Princess Shalimar), David Farrar (Sir Guy), George Macready (Shaman), Henry Brandon (Juchi), Howard Petrie (Tugluk), Richard Egan (Gill), Marvin Miller (Genghis Khan), Peggie Castle (Lailee), Poodles Hanneford (Friar John)

The Golden Horde is just one of many costume pictures cranked out by Universal-International in the early fifties. The studio termed these "Easterns" as opposed to "Westerns" but the basic plots often seemed interchangeable for either genre. *The Golden Horde* is worth mentioning primarily because, unlike the majority of Universal's other costumers, it does not feature an Arabian Nights setting. The barbarian armies of Genghis Khan are sweeping across Asia toward Samarkand, the gateway to Persia. A band of Crusaders, led by Sir Guy of Devon, proposes to defend Samarkand from the invaders but the offer is rebuffed by Princess Shalimar, the ruler of the city. Shalimar plans to use her considerable beauty to seduce Juchi, the son of Genghis Khan, and thus save her kingdom without bloodshed. Sir Guy falls in love with Shalimar and, when her plan goes awry, he and his men defeat the invaders and save the city. Despite some attempt at historical detail, *The Golden Horde* is indistinguishable from the rest of Universal's similar output featuring stunning Technicolor photography and elaborate costuming. Worth noting is Richard Egan in a supporting role. He would soon become a full-fledged star at 20th Century–Fox.

Motion Picture: There's plenty of savage sword-play, much leaping over parapets. Fairly exciting if you like swashbucklers.

107   *Goliath Against the Giants*

(Goliath Contro i Giganti)
Cineproduzioni Associate, Rome–Procusa P.C.U., Madrid (1961) 90 min.
Supertotalscope/Eastman Color
U.S.–Medallion
    P–Cesare Seccia, Manuel Perez/D–Guido Malatesta/W–Gianfranco Parolini, Giovanni Simonelli, Cesare Secca, Arpad De Riso, Sergio Sollima/M–Carlo Innocenzi/C–Alessandro Ulloa/E–Mario Sansoni, Edmondo Lozzi/AD–Ramiro Gomez, Carlo Santono Cito/CD–Vittorio Rossi
    Cast–Brad Harris (Goliath), Fernando Rey (Bokan), Gloria Milland (Elea), Barbara Carroll (Daina), Jose Rubio (Briseos), Carmen De Lirio (Diamira), Fernando Sancho (Namathos) with Lina Rosales, Francisco Bernal, Ray Martino, Ignazio Dolce, Luigi Marturano, Angel Ortiz, Manuel Arbo, Nello Pazzafini, Gianfranco Gasparri

Typical muscleman film with all the trappings of the peplum genre, i.e., gladiators, monsters, Amazons and lions. When he learns that an evil tyrant has seized the throne of his homeland, Goliath sets sail to right this wrong. Along the way a sea monster wrecks the ship and the survivors are washed ashore in the land of the Amazons. Goliath eventually reaches his destination and leads the populace in revolt against the despicable ruler. Before he can ride off into the sunset, Goliath must first rescue his beloved from the dread Valley of the Giants. The giants are actually a group of hairy caveman types who live in a valley filled with mist and prehistoric monsters. Goliath defeats the giants with ease and decides to leave the monsters, who are shown only fleetingly, to their own devices. *Goliath Against the Giants* is an undistinguished effort enlivened by Fernando Rey's hysterical performance as Bokan, the tyrant. Gianfranco Parolini co-directed the film and is listed in the credits as "Artistic Director."

108   *Goliath and the Barbarians*

(Il Terrore dei Barbari; The Terror of the Barbarians)
A Standard S.r.l. Production (1959) 88 min.
Totalscope/Eastman Color
U.S.–American-International (1959)
ColorScope
    P–Emimmo Salvi/D–Carlo Campogalliani/W–Emimmo Salvi, Gino Mangini, Nino Stresa, Giuseppe Tafarel, Carlo Campogalliani/M–Carlo Innocenzi/Les Baxter (U.S. version)/C–Adelberto Albertini/E–Franco Fraticelli/AD–Camillo Del Signore, Emilio D'Andria/CD–Giovanna Matili
    Cast–Steve Reeves (Emiliano/Goliath), Chelo Alonso (Londo), Bruce Cabot (Alboino), Giula Rubini (Sabina), Livio Lorenzon (Igor), Luciano Marin (Marco), Arturo Dominici (Delfo), Furio Meniconi (Svevo), Fabrizio Capucci (Bruno), Andrea Checchi (Agnese), Tino Scotti (Count Danjele) with Ugo Sasso, Cesare Fantoni, Carla Calo, Paul Muller, Eleonora Vargas, Luigi Tosi

This was the first motion picture starring Steve Reeves to be released following the tremendous box office success of Pietro Francisci's *Hercules.* American-International Pictures originally announced this film as *Colossus and the Golden Horde* co-starring Chelsea (!) Alonso. The title was eventually changed to *Goliath and the Barbarians* and AIP was able to reap a considerable harvest in ticket sales, spurred, no doubt, by the extensive advertising campaign. The prologue tells us that in the year A.D. 568 "if you didn't love or fight ...

Chelo Alonso and Steve Reeves happily ride off into the sunset at the conclusion of *Goliath and the Barbarians* (1959).

life was a very short and dull affair." Alboino, King of the Lombards, leads his barbarian hordes into northern Italy where they pillage villages and kill the inhabitants without mercy. When his father is victim of such a massacre, Emiliano vows vengeance. Disguised as a hideous monster, he avenges his people and becomes known as the "Goliath" to the barbarians. Of course, along the way he falls in love with a tempestuous barbarian beauty. Chelo Alonso, as the Lombard princess loved by Goliath, gets the opportunity to perform several exotic dance routines.

109   *Goliath and the Dragon*

(La Vendetta di Ercole; The Vengeance of Hercules/Goliath's Revenge)
Piazzi Produzione, Rome–Comptoir Français, Paris (1960) 83 min.
Totalscope/Eastman Color
U.S.–An Omnia Production

American-International (1960) 90 min.
ColorScope
P–Achille Piazzi, Gianni Fuchs/D–Vittorio Cottafavi/W–Ennio De Concini, Achille Piazzi, Gianni Fuchs, Marco Piccolo, Archibald Zounds, Jr./M–Alexandre Derevitsky/Les Baxter (U.S. version)/C–Mario Montuori/E–Maurizio Lucidi/AD–Franco Lolli/CD–Ditta Peruzzi
Cast–Mark Forest (Goliath), Broderick Crawford (Eurystheus), Eleonora Ruffo (Deianira), Philippe Hersent (Illus), Sandro Maretti (Ismene), Federica Ranchi (Thea), Gaby Andre (Alcinoe) with Wandisa Guida, Giancarlo Sbragia, Carlo Cara, Piero Pastore, Renato Terra, Ugo Sasso, Salvatore Furnari, Stefano Valle, Corrado Sonni, Nino Milano

This was the first of the Hercules films to be made without the stalwart presence of Steve Reeves as the mythical hero, despite advance publicity announcing him as the star. Preferring to go on to more diverse endeavors, Reeves declined to appear again as Her-

Goliath (Mark Forest) saves a captive maiden from a terrible fate in *Goliath and the Dragon* (1960).

cules. Instead, we have Mark Forest in his film debut. Brooklyn-born bodybuilder Lou Degni was dubbed by physical culture enthusiasts as "The Adonis with the Perfect Physique." As Mark Forest, he was an able replacement for Reeves and carved out a respectable career for himself as a major peplum star. In Europe the film was entitled *The Vengeance of Hercules*, but when AIP bought the U.S. distribution rights, they decided to change the title, and some of the content as well. The name of the main character was changed to Emilius the Mighty, more commonly known as Goliath of Thebes. A background score by Les Baxter, which reuses his themes from *Goliath and the Barbarians*, was also added. To provide further exploitation possibilities, newly filmed sequences with a dragon were inserted into the plotline. The effective, though regrettably brief, distance shots of the dragon are the work of stop-mo-

tion animator Jim Danforth. The closeups are a rather tacky full-sized mock-up of the dragon's head. Goliath goes to the Cave of Horrors to retrieve the Blood Diamond and restore it to its rightful place in the temple of the gods. On his journey he is attacked by the three-headed dog Cerberus, and a particularly unconvincing giant bat. With the Blood Diamond restored, Goliath goes home to enjoy a quite life with his wife Deianira, but his brother Illus (in the European version Illus is his son) believes that Goliath is trying to steal away the woman he loves. All of this is part of a plot by the dastardly King Eurystheus to get rid of Goliath. During the coarse of the story, Goliath fights a ferocious bear to rescue a beautiful woman, confronts an evil centaur who has kidnapped Deianira, and battles an elephant to save the life of Illus. As if these trials weren't enough, the AIP version has him return to the Cave of Horrors

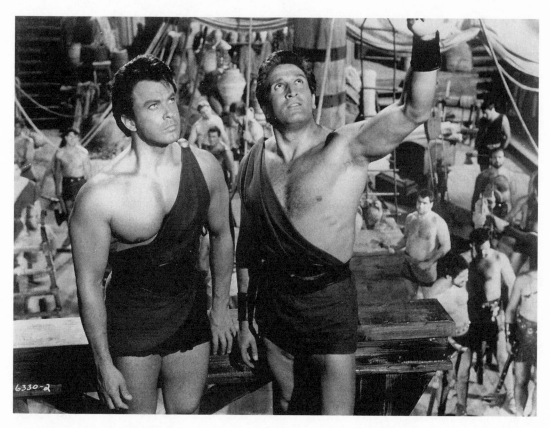

Mark Forest and Mimmo Palmara are rebels fighting against oppression in *Goliath and the Sins of Babylon* (1964).

to battle the dragon of the title. Actually, the inclusion of the dragon was a wise move and punches up the climax considerably. As a whole, the movie lacks the sure touch of director Pietro Francisi, who was responsible for the two previous Hercules films. Vittorio Cottafavi would achieve far greater success with his next Hercules effort, *Hercules and the Captive Women.* Broderick Crawford is very much out of place as the villain of the piece. He blusters through the part of King Eurystheus as if he were still in the television series *Highway Patrol.*

110   *Goliath and the Sins of Babylon*

(Maciste, l'Eroe Piu Grande del Mondo; Maciste, the Greatest Hero in the World)
Leone Film (1963) 80 min.
Techniscope/Technicolor
U.S.–American-International (1964)

P–Elio Scardamaglia/D–Michele Lupo/W–Roberto Gianviti, Francesco Scardamaglia, Francesco Ardamaglia, Lionello De Felice/M–Francesco De Masi/Les Baxter (U.S. version)/C–Guglielmo Mancori, Mario Sbrenna/E–Alberto Gallitti/AD–Pier Vittoria Marchi

Cast–Mark Forest (Goliath), Eleanora Bianchi (Resia), Giuliano Gemma (Xandros), Jose Greci (Alceo), John Chevron (Evandro), Erno Crisa (Pergaso), Piero Lulli (Meneos), Arnaldo Fabrizio (Morakeb) with Mimmo Palmara, Livio Lorenzon, Ugo Sasso, Nello Pazzafini

Each year the village of Nefer is required to pay tribute to the ruler of Babylon by handing over twenty-four virgins for sacrifice. A group of men, led by the brave Xandros, decides to go against this edict and free the captive maidens. They are joined in this endeavor by the powerful warrior Goliath. What follows is one of the glossier action spectaculars, filled with excitement but short on plot. As always, Mark Forest is an impressive presence

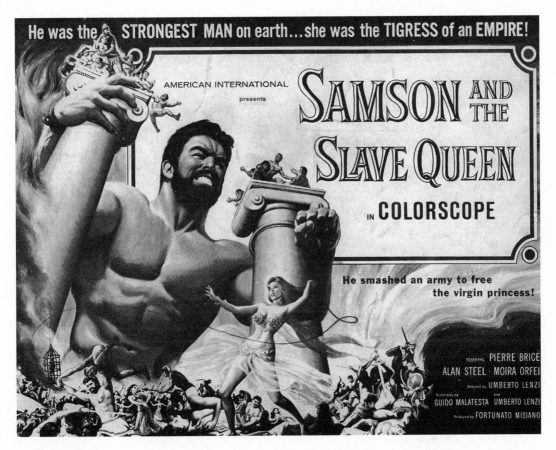

On the same bill with *Goliath and the Sins of Babylon* was *Samson and the Slave Queen* (1964). Ads suggested it was another spectacular set in ancient times, but ads lied.

as the title character. The romantic chores are handled by Giuliano Gemma and Eleanora Bianchi. Mimmo Palmara and Livio Lorenzon are also on hand in rare "good guy" roles. The film is well directed, although the comedy relief (the inevitable midget sidekick which plagues so many of these films) is heavy-handed and irritating. The photography is outstanding and utilizes the widescreen Techniscope process with many interesting effects. Several actions scenes highlight the film, including a sea battle and a chariot race. The latter sequence incorporates footage from *Theodora, Slave Empress* (1953). *Goliath and the Sins of Babylon* was yet another Maciste film bought and retitled for domestic release by AIP. On the same double bill was *Samson and the Slave Queen* starring Alan Steel. The advertisements for this film indicate another spectacular set in ancient times but it is actu-

ally *Zorro Against Maciste* and has nothing at all to do with antiquity. This was typical of the misleading and exploitative promotion techniques used by AIP at the time ... but they sure sold tickets!

111   *Goliath and the Vampires*

(Maciste Contro il Vampiro; Maciste Against the
  Vampire / The Vampires)
Societe Ambrosiana Cinematografica, Rome (1961)
  97 min.
Totalscope / Technicolor
U.S.–A Dino De Laurentiis Presentation
American-International (1964) 91 min.
ColorScope
  P–Paolo Moffa / D–Giacomo Gentilomo, Sergio Corbucci (uncredited) / W–Sergio Corbucci, Duccio Tessari / M–Angelo Francesco Lavagnino / C–Alvaro Mancori / E–Eraldo Da Roma / AD–Gianni Polidori / CD–Vittorio Rossi
  Cast–Gordon Scott (Goliath), Jacques Sernas

Jacques Sernas shows Gordon Scott the latest wonder drug in *Goliath and the Vampires* (1964).

(Kurtik), Gianna Maria Canale (Astra), Eleonora Ruffo (Giulia), Annabella Incontrera (Magda), Rocco Vitolazzi (Ciro), Mario Feliciani, Renato Terra, Van Aikens, Emma Baron, Guido Celano

This peplum fantasy has so many plot elements that it almost defies description. Goliath's village is attacked by masked warriors and the women are taken on a ship to the island kingdom of Salmanak. Somehow Goliath manages to get there by horseback and finds the women are being sold as slaves. He uses his great strength to set them free but discovers that his bride-to-be, Giulia, is not among them. With the help of Kurtik, the ruler of the underground city of the Blue Men, he learns that Giulia is a captive in the sultan's palace. The hand of the sultan is being forced by his concubine Astra who is a follower of the vampiric entity Kobrak. The evil Kobrak plans to capture Goliath and duplicate his physique and strength to create an army of unstoppable robots. For the climax, Kobrak

takes on the form of Goliath and the twin strongmen fight a battle to the death. Also thrown into the mix are faceless warriors, a pit of insect-like monsters, mummified men, virgins drained of their blood to feed the vampire ... a real gallery of horrors! Imaginative production design and a cast of familiar peplum faces help to make this an above average entry in the muscleman genre.

112 *Goliath at the Conquest of Damascus*

(Golia alla Conquista di Bagdad; Goliath at the Conquest of Baghdad)
A Titanus Production (1964) 95 min.
Giant Panoramic/Eastman Color
U.S.–American-International (1965) 87 min.

P–Fortunato Misiano/D–Domenico Paolella/W–Luciano Martino, Domenico Paolella/M–Angelo Francesco Lavagnino/C–Augusto Tiezzi/E–Jolando Benvenuti

Cast–Rock Stevens (Goliath), Mario Petri (Yssur), Helga Line (Fatma), Arturo Dominici (Kaicew),

Rock Stevens (aka Peter Lupus) starred in *Goliath at the Conquest of Damascus* **prior to baring it all for** *Playgirl* **magazine.**

Piero Lulli (Thor), Anna Maria Polani (Miriam), Daniele Vargas

The Kurds capture the city of Baghdad, forcing King Selim and his daughter, Miriam, into exile. Miriam is in love with the son of the Caliph of Nisibi and attempts to go there to be married to him. While en route, her caravan is raided by the Karigitis, a group of bandits who have been hired by Thor, the chief of the Kurds, to prevent the marriage. Thor believes that such a union could give King Selim enough support to retake Baghdad. A servant escapes from the Karigitis' attack and convinces the powerful Goliath to intervene on Miriam's behalf. Goliath pretends to join the Karigitis, but does his best to undermine Thor's plans. A final battle between the Kurds and the combined forces of Goliath, King Selim and the Caliph of Nisibi regains the throne of Baghdad for the rightful ruler. Rock Stevens had been chosen from several hundred contestants for the part of "Mr. Galaxy" in AIP's *Muscle Beach Party*. He then went to Europe to star in several peplum films, of which this was the last.

113   Great Bible Adventures
"Seven Rich and Seven Lean Years"
An MGM TV Production
ABC TV Network (1966) 50 min.
Color
   P–Stanley Niss/D–Boris Sagal
   Cast–Hugh O'Brian (Joseph), Joseph Wiseman (Pharaoh), Katharine Ross (Asenath), Eduardo Ciannelli (Aton), Torin Thatcher (Potiphar), Ilka Windish (Potiphar's Wife) with John Abbott, Paul Mantee, Anthony Caruso, Sorrell Booke, Leonard Mudie

Hugh O'Brian as Joseph in the television pilot *Great Bible Adventures* (1966).

The story of Joseph has had several television incarnations. This one was the pilot episode for a proposed series which was created and executive produced by Henry Denker. Denker had an extensive background in biblical subjects. He had written a popular radio series based on Fulton Oursler's *The Greatest Story Ever Told* which aired Sunday nights from 1947 to 1949. His novel *Salome, Princess of Galilee* was published in 1952. Despite this impressive pedigree and an interesting cast, the series was not picked up by the network. During the seventies two more TV versions of Joseph surfaced. The first was the 1974 TV movie *The Story of Jacob and Joseph* with Tony Lo Bianco as Joseph. In 1978 a TV series called *Greatest Heroes of the Bible* featured an episode called "Joseph in Egypt" which starred Sam Bottoms in the title role. A definitive version of *Joseph* aired on Ted

Turner's TNT network in 1995. Later that same year, Showtime aired yet another version of the story entitled *Slave of Dreams*, which did not approach the quality of the Turner version.

114   *The Great Commandment*

A Cathedral Films Production (1939) 85 min.
20th Century–Fox (1942)
   P–John T. Coyle, James K. Friedrich/D–Irving Pichel/W–Dana Burnet/M–Hans J. Salter, Walter Jurman/C–Charles Boyle/E–Ralph Dixon/AD–Edward Jewell
   Cast–John Beal (Joel), Maurice Moscovich (Lamech), Albert Dekker (Longinus), Marjorie Cooley (Tamar), Warren McCullum (Zadok), Lloyd Corrigan (Jamuel), Olaf Hytten (Nathan) with Ian Wolfe, Albert Spehr, Lester Schareff, Harold Minjir, Anthony Marlowe, Marc Loebell, Earl Gunn

The Great Commandment was the first offering of Cathedral Films, a production company specifically organized by the Rev. James K. Friedrich for the purpose of producing quality Christian entertainment. The plot incorporates the coming of the Messiah and the story of the Good Samaritan with a love triangle involving two dissimilar brothers and the girl betrothed to one of them. Joel and Zadok are the sons of Lamech. Joel loves the village girl Tamar but she is betrothed to his older brother. Zadok is a zealot who violently opposes the Roman rule. Their personal drama is played out against the broader canvas of the last days of Christ prior to the crucifixion. *The Great Commandment* was made without the benefit of a prearranged distribution outlet. The film was previewed for the press in October 1939. *Variety* praised its "finely etched characterizations and high production standards" and the *Hollywood Reporter* stated that "the picture has frequent touches of greatness." Despite the praise, no distributor was immediately forthcoming. In 1940 20th Century–Fox purchased the film outright for $170,000. The scheduled national release date was set for June 1940 but, following two advance preview showings, the picture was shelved. Fox then planned to use portions of the film in a biblical production to star Tyrone Power and Linda Darnell. After spending another $340,000 to develop this project, Fox decided to release the film in its original form in October 1942. The release was minimal and in 1948 Cathedral Films attempted, unsuccessfully, to buy back the movie from Fox. The film languished in the vaults until 1966 when Cathedral finally repurchased *The Great Commandment* from Fox for a proposed theatrical rerelease that never materialized.

115   *The Great Leaders*

(I Grandi Condottieri/Samson and Gideon)
San Paolo Films, Rome–San Pablo Films, Madrid
  (1965) 105 min.
Eastman Color
U.S–No theatrical release
  P–Tonio Di Carlo/D–Marcello Baldi, Francisco Perez Dolz/W–Ottavio Jemma, Flavio Nicolini, Marcello Baldi, Tonino Guerra/M–Teo Usuelli/C–Marcello Masciocchi/E–Giuliana Attenni/AD–Ot-

tavio Scotti, Sigfrido Burman/CD–Giorgio Desideri
  Cast–Anton Geesink (Samson), Rosalba Neri (Delilah), Ivo Garrani (Gideon), Fernando Rey (Messenger of God) with Giorgio Cerioni, Luz Marquez, Paolo Gozlino, Ana Maria Noe, Maruchi Fresno, Piero Gerlini, Lucio De Santis, Sergio Ammirata, Barta Berry, Jose Jaspes, Consalvo Dell'Arti

This is one of several films produced by the Paulus Brothers, a religious order of the Catholic Church. These films were authorized by the Vatican as part of a proposed series which would depict the entire Old Testament. The first film in the series, *Patriarchs of the Bible* (Marcello Baldi; 1963), relates the stories of the Book of Genesis from Adam and Eve to Joseph. *The Great Leaders* deals with Gideon and Samson from the Book of Judges. Since the budgets of these films are generally somewhat modest, the screenplay usually sticks to the basics with little elaboration on the original texts. The Gideon portion is told with restraint and a fair amount of humor. Fernando Rey, who is often the villain in peplum films, portrays an envoy of Jehovah to good effect. The Samson story begins promisingly enough with a Samson who is imposing but not musclebound. Halfway through this sequence, the script resorts to imitation DeMille, complete with midgets and a sympathetic Delilah. The destruction of the Temple of Dagon is rather impressive, given the obvious budgetary restrictions.

116   *The Greatest Story Ever Told*

United Artists (1965) 197 min.
Ultra Panavision 70/Technicolor
  P/D–George Stevens/W–James Lee Barrett, George Stevens/Based on the book by Fulton Ousler/M–Alfred Newman/C–WIlliam C. Mellor, Loyal Griggs/E–Argyle Nelson, Frank O'Neill/AD–Richard Day, William Creber/CD–Vittorio Nino Novarese
  Cast–Max Von Sydow (Jesus), Carroll Baker (Veronica), Van Heflin (Bar Amand), Charlton Heston (John the Baptist), Dorothy McGuire (Mary), Sidney Poitier (Simon), Claude Rains (Herod), John Wayne (The Centurion), Ed Wynn (Aram), David McCallum (Judas) with Shelley Winters, Telly Savalas, Martin Landau, Angela Lansbury, Roddy McDowall, Pat Boone, Victor Buono, Richard Conte, Jose Ferrer, Sal Mineo

The crucifixion scene from *The Greatest Story Ever Told* (1965) with Max Von Sydow (center) as Jesus.

Fulton Ousler's popular book *The Greatest Story Ever Told* was purchased by 20th Century–Fox shortly after its publication in 1951. It was first announced for production in 1955 to debut the newly developed widescreen CinemaScope 55 process. It took ten more years for the film version to finally appear. In October 1960 Fox advertised that John Wayne had been signed to play the important role of "The Roman." In January 1961 Fox stated that the George Stevens production of *The Greatest Story Ever Told* would now be filmed in Todd-AO. Six months later, Spencer Tracy, Sidney Poitier, Max Von Sydow and Elizabeth Taylor (as Mary Magdalene) were added to the cast. Within three months' time Fox had removed the title from its production schedule because of the tremendous costs being incurred by their runaway production of *Cleopatra*. That same year George Stevens moved the project to United Artists and the film was eventually completed for release in 1965. The

finished product certainly wasn't worth the effort and the wait. *The Greatest Story Ever Told* is reverent and well intentioned but it is hampered by a very dull script and a collection of annoying cameo performances. The Arizona, Utah and Nevada location photography, while beautiful, never conveys an illusion of the Holy Land. George Stevens' desire to shoot the picture entirely in the United States with a mainly American cast and crew was commendable, but why use landscapes so patently American? It often looks as if the characters have stumbled into a John Ford Western. In its favor, the film does have a wonderful portrayal of Jesus by Max Von Sydow, and Alfred Newman's score, despite some heavy tampering by director Stevens, is one of his finest. Poet Carl Sandburg had a hand in writing the screenplay and remained a creative associate throughout the filming. *The Greatest Story Ever Told* is another epic that suffered through extensive re-editing. When it was originally reviewed by *Variety*, the running time was 225 minutes. Director Stevens was requested by United Artists to trim the picture by a half-hour for the roadshow engagements. Later, when the movie went into general release it was cut down to 141 minutes.

AA Nominations: Best Color Cinematography, Art Color Direction, Color Costume Design, Special Effects, Musical Score

McCalls: The Greatest Story Ever Told has been brought stunningly to the screen. Although the events have often been depicted upon the screen, they have never been treated with greater historical accuracy nor with such discernment and grace.

Variety: Striding amid the extras, bit players and miscast celebrities, [Max Von Sydow] conveys calm, anger, authority and a blessed apartness in equal measure.

117   *Hannibal*

(Annibale)
Liber Films (1960) 103 min.
Supercinescope/Technicolor
U.S.–Warner Bros.
   P–Ottavio Poggi/D–Edgar G. Ulmer/W–Mortimer Braus, Alessandro Continenza/M–Carlo Rustichelli/C–Marcello Masciocchi/E–Renato Cinquini/AD–Ernest Kromberg/CD–Giancarlo Bartolini Salimbeni
   Cast–Victor Mature (Hannibal), Rita Gam (Sylvia), Gabriele Ferzetti (Fabius Massimus), Milly Vitale (Danila), Rik Battaglia (Hasdrubal), Franco Silva (Maharbal), Mario Girotti (Quintilius), Mirko Ellis (Mago), Andrea Aureli (Varro)

This film, which is a fictionalized account of Hannibal's invasion of Italy via the Alps, is notable mainly for its well-staged battle scenes. As the Carthaginian general is marching his troops toward Rome, he takes captive Sylvia, the niece of a Roman senator. After showing her the strength of his army, he sets her free in the hope that she will tell her people of the futility of resistance against such a tremendous force. Sylvia, who has fallen in love with Hannibal, does not tell the Romans what she has seen until her country suffers a great defeat at the battle of Trebbia. Her uncle admonishes her for consorting with the enemy and sends her to live in the Temple of Vesta as punishment. She escapes to rendezvous with Hannibal at his encampment, but

the unexpected arrival of Hannibal's wife causes Sylvia to flee back to Rome in despair. She is captured by the Romans, tried for her treason and sentenced to be buried alive. With the death of Sylvia and the beheading of his brother Hasdrubal by the Romans, Hannibal begins to realize that his campaign will not succeed. Victor Mature added another epic role to his roster with his effective portrayal of Hannibal. Rita Gam, whose film career at this point was on a downward spiral, was suggested for her part by no less than Princess Grace of Monaco. The two actresses had been friends in Hollywood and, when the part of Sylvia was being cast, Princess Grace contacted the producer to recommend Gam for the role. The real stars of the show are the forty-five elephants who comprise the bulk of Hannibal's army. With little effort they manage to upstage the human performers in the film. Edgar G. Ulmer, director of several notable "B" pictures in the United States, handled the complexities of the production with the uncredited assistance of Carlo Ludovico Bragaglia.

118   *Head of a Tyrant*

(Giuditta e Oloferne; Judith and Holophernes)
Vic Films, Rome–C.E.C., Paris (1960) 94 min.
Totalscope/Technicolor
U.S.–Universal-International
   P–Gian Paolo Bigazzi/D–Fernando Cerchio/W–Fernando Cerchio, Damiano Damiani, Guido Malatesta, Gian Paolo Callegari/M–Carlo Savina/C–Pier Ludovico Pavoni/PD–Giorgio Scalco/CD–Vittorio Nino Novarese
   Cast–Massimo Girotti (Holophernes), Isabelle Corey (Judith), Renato Baldini (Arbar), Yvette Masson (Rispa), Gianni Rizzo (Ozia), Camillo Pilotto (Belial), Daniela Rocca (Naomi), Ricardo Valle (Isaac), Leonardo Botta (Galaad), Luigi Tosi (Iras) with Gabriele Antonini, Lucia Banti, Enzo Doria

It had been nearly fifty years since D.W. Griffith's film version of *Judith of Bethulia*. The story of an innocent girl who gives herself to a cruel general to save her people seems to be surefire motion picture material. Therefore, it is surprising that a sound version was not produced earlier than 1960. *Head of a Tyrant* is a fine film and, although it was give a full theatrical release in the United States, it has seldom been seen since. It deserves to be

Judith (Isabelle Corey) prepares to behead the man she loves (Massimo Girotti) in *Head of a Tyrant* (1960).

taken out of limbo and made available once again. One reason for its inaccessibility and lack of reputation may be the fact that none of the performers are easily recognizable to American audiences. Massimo Girotti has appeared in countless European costume spectaculars but he never achieved fame in the United States. The part of Holophernes was a real departure for Girotti as he was generally cast as a heroic leading man. His excellent performance is the highlight of *Head of a Tyrant*. When the army of the Assyrian general Holophernes conquers the city of Bethulie, he abolishes the worship of Jehovah and orders the populace to revere the Assyrian god of war, Azzur. When the people refuse his demands, Holophernes stages a massacre. A young girl named Judith plans to go to the palace and kill the tyrant. She dances before the general and he is captivated by her beauty. Unfortunately, Judith also finds herself overcome by love for Holophernes and is unable to carry out her plan. Despite his love for Judith, Holophernes resolves to destroy the city of Bethulie. Before he can give the order, Judith finds the courage to kill him. As the Assyrian army approaches the palace she appears on the steps holding the head of their leader in her hands. Spurred on by her actions, the people rise up against their oppressors. Isabelle Corey was only eighteen years old at the time *Head of a Tyrant* was made and she gives a commendable performance as Judith. Technical credits are above average and the supporting cast is quite good. The Book of Judith is one of the Apocryphal books of the Old Testament. It is found in Catholic versions of the Bible but not in Hebrew or Protestant editions.

119   *Helen of Troy*

Warner Bros. (1956) 118 min.
CinemaScope/WarnerColor

P–G.L. Blattner (uncredited)/D–Robert Wise/ W–John Twist, Hugh Gray, N. Richard Nash/Based on *The Iliad* by Homer/M–Max Steiner/C–Harry Stradling/E–Thomas Reilly/AD–Edward Carrere, Ken Adam/CD–Robert Furse

Cast–Rossana Podesta (Helen), Jack/ Jacques Sernas (Paris), Robert Douglas (Agamemnon), Sir Cedric Hardwicke (King Priam), Stanley Baker (Achilles), Niall MacGinnis (Menelaus), Nora Swinburne (Hecuba), Torin Thatcher (Ulysses), Brigitte Bardot (Andraste), Janette Scott (Cassandra), Ronald Lewis (Aeneas), Harry Andrews (Hector) with Eduardo Ciannelli, Marc Lawrence, Maxwell Reed, Robert Brown, Barbara Cavan, Terence Longden, Guido Notari, Patricia Marmont, Tonio Selwart, Georges Zoritch, Edmund Knight

Helen of Troy is one of the most enjoyable and romantic of the fifties epics and time has only increased its reputation as such. In 1952 three separate productions of the story of Helen of Troy were in the planning stages. Cecil B. DeMille abandoned his in favor of a new

Jack (Jacques) Sernas and Rossana Podesta as Paris and Helen, the doomed lovers of *Helen of Troy* (1956).

version of *The Ten Commandments*. Hedy Lamarr produced and starred in *The Face That Launched a Thousand Ships*, and a truncated version of this appears in *The Love of Three Queens*, released in 1955. The third and only fully realized production was made by Warner Bros., but not without its share of problems. Announced in 1953 as a Widescreen 3D production directed by Gordon Douglas, *Helen of Troy* went through several changes of cast and crew before filming finally got under way. Warners wanted their contract star Virginia Mayo to play Helen and Tyrone Power as Paris but Robert Wise, the final choice for director, thought unfamiliar faces would have more impact. A worldwide talent hunt resulted in the selection of twenty-year-old Rossana Podesta to portray the title role. She had already appeared in several European films, including *Ulysses*, but it was the part of Helen that established her as an enduring icon of the epic genre. Jack (Jacques) Sernas had tested for the part of Aeneas but Warner executives were so impressed with his handsome face and form that they elevated him to the starring role of Paris. Although physically perfect for their roles, both Podesta and Sernas had to have their dialogue dubbed so that their accents would not clash with those of the primarily British supporting cast. Once filming got under way, a fire at Cinecitta studios destroyed 80 percent of the $95,000 reproduction of the city of Troy. Robert Wise hastily assembled his crew to film the conflagration, hoping the footage could be used for the fall of Troy. Shooting ran overtime and over budget and eventually Raoul Walsh was sent to Italy to assist Wise in completing the picture. The screenplay takes some liberties with Homer's version. While sailing to Sparta on a mission of goodwill, Paris, Prince of Troy, is shipwrecked. He is found on the beach and nursed back to health by a beautiful woman whom he mistakes for the goddess Aphrodite. They fall in love but Paris soon learns that she is Helen, wife of Menelaus, King of Sparta. He also discovers that the Greeks are planning a war to loot the riches of Troy. Helen is caught in an attempt to help Paris escape and she must flee to Troy with her lover. The ensuing assault on Troy by the Greeks lasts ten long years. The war is finally brought to a tragic conclusion for the Trojans with Ulysses' plan to use a gigantic wooden horse to breach the insurmountable walls of Troy. Paris dies in the final battle and Helen is unwillingly taken home to Sparta by her husband. The finished film cost $6 million and had its global premiere on January 26, 1956, in fifty-six countries simultaneously. In 1959 *Helen of Troy* was reissued on a double bill with *Land of the Pharaohs*. Brigitte Bardot, who plays the relatively minor role of Helen's handmaiden, was suddenly given top billing in the new advertising campaign to capitalize on her current worldwide popularity.

Time: The film is most successful when it transforms Homeric epithet into moving picture.

Variety: Spectacular and lavish retelling of Homeric legend. Like many tales of antiquity, the story is occasionally stilted.

Films in Review: There are things about this film worth commending—one of them is the use of new faces in the leads.

Motion Picture: Ancient battles set off by a classic love rage across the screen in this imposing spectacle.

120   *Helen of Troy*

A Fuel Entertainment Production
USA TV Network (2003) 180 min.
Color
    P–Ted Kurdyla, Ronni Kern / W–John Kent Harrison / W–Ronni Kern / M–Joel Goldsmith / C–Edward J. Pei / E–Michael Ornstein / PD–James Allen / CD–Van Broughton
    Cast–Sienna Guillory (Helen), Matthew Marsden (Paris), James Callis (Menelaus), Rufus Sewell (Agamemnon), John Rhys-Davies (Priam), Stellan Skarsgard (Theseus), Maryam D'Abo (Hecuba), Daniel Lapine (Hector), Emilia Fox (Cassandra), Nigel Whitmey (Odysseus), Joe Montana (Achilles), Katie Blake (Clytemnestra) with Edward Mercieca, Kristina Paris, Craig Kelly, Manuel Cauchi

    This TV mini-series is all tricked out with modern effects (computer generated images, stop-shutter photography, etc.) but it lacks the sweep and high romance of the 1956 version. It also lacks a credible "Helen." Sienna Guillory is a decent actress but she does not possess the beauty or charm to make you believe her face could launch a thousand ships or cause a ten year war. Most of the acting honors go to Rufus Sewell as the treacherous Agamemnon. His powerful presence dominates every scene he is in. James Callis is also memorable as an uncharacteristically sympathetic Menelaus. The most effective sequence in the movie belongs to him when, in the thick of battle, he glimpses Helen watching from the walls of Troy. For a moment, all around him is frozen in time. The fighting soldiers freeze and even arrows halt their flight. The script ignores Homer and takes a cue from the 1956 version by presenting Helen and Paris in a sympathetic light, with the Greeks being motivated by greed rather than honor. Although Ronni Kern's teleplay includes elements which were missing from the earlier film, such as the death of Agamemnon at the hand of his wife Clytemnestra, important characters like Patroclus and Polydorus are strangely absent.

Los Angeles Times: This "Helen of Troy" is so tragically bad it's good. TV's new Helen hits gurgling lows that will be hard to match, affirming that first-rate trash always trumps second-rate art.

Variety: A stiff portrait of mythology ... somber and stifled in places that call for more user-friendly storytelling.

121   *Hercules*

(Le Fatiche di Ercole; The Labors of Hercules)
O.S.C.A.R. Film S.p.A.–Galatea Production (1958)
    107 min.
Dyaliscope / Eastman Color
U.S.–A Joseph E. Levine-Embassy Pictures Presentation
Warner Bros. (1959)
    P–Frederico Teti / D–Pietro Francisci / W–Pietro Francisci, Ennio De Concini, Gaio Frattini / M–Enzo Masetti / C–Mario Bava / E–Mario Serandrei / AD–Flavio Mogherini / CD–Giulio Coltellacci, Corrado Bartolini
    Cast–Steve Reeves (Hercules), Sylva Koscina (Iole), Gianna Maria Canale (Antea), Fabrizio Mioni (Jason), Ivo Garrani (Pelias), Arturo Dominici (Eurysteus), Mimmo Palmara (Iphitus), Andrea Fantasia (Laertes), Gabriele Antonini (Ulysses), Aldo Fiorelli (Argus), Walter Grant (Aesculapius) with Lydia Alfonsi, Gina Rovere, Afro Poli, Gino Mattera, Gian Paolo Rosmino

The epitome of "beefcake": Steve Reeves as *Hercules* (1959).

In 1957 Italian director Pietro Francisci was searching for an actor to play the leading role in a film about Hercules. Actors were tested from all over Europe but the "right" person could not be found. One day Francisci's daughter saw the MGM musical *Athena* (1954), which featured champion bodybuilder Steve Reeves in a supporting role. Reeves, who had been Mr. America in 1947 and Mr. Universe in 1950, had just the look the director wanted. He was brought to Italy for a screen test and quickly got the part. Reeves told *Newsweek*

"Of course my muscles helped, but my face was important, too. It had to be a typical American-boy face, a sympathetic one, like me." *Hercules* is a loose adaptation of the legend of Jason and the Golden Fleece, with the emphasis on the Hercules character instead of Jason. Only the bare bones of the original myth remain and, instead, the action focuses on Hercules' tremendous feats of strength. Hercules sets sail with Jason and his crew in search of the Golden Fleece which will help Jason to regain the throne of Jolco from his evil uncle, Pelias. Along the way they put ashore on the island of the Amazons. The queen, Antea, falls in love with Jason although she realizes that he must be put to death in accordance with the laws of her people. Hercules rescues him and together they resume their quest, which ends in the land of Colchis. After fighting a tribe of gorilla men, the fleece is finally found in a tree guarded by a dragon. Jason slays the beast and returns to Jolco with his prize. The treacherous Pelias is not so quick to give up his throne and sends his soldiers against Jason and his followers. Eventually right triumphs; Jason gets the throne of Jolco and Hercules gets the woman he loves. In 1959 American promoter Joseph E. Levine bought the U.S. distribution rights to the completed film for a mere $120,000. Although the film had already been dubbed into English, Levine was unhappy with the voices used and had it redubbed. He also spent $1.2 million on publicity. *Hercules* took in over $18 million and made Steve Reeves a star. Reeves' salary rose from the $12,000 he got for *Hercules* to $150,000 per picture. The film also gave birth to the peplum genre. Within months, both *Samson and Delilah* and *David and Bathsheba* were reissued with new advertising campaigns highly reminiscent of the one for *Hercules*. As *Variety* stated at the time, "Italo Beefcake tops Cheesecake." Future "Bond Girl" Luciana Paluzzi can be glimpsed briefly as a handmaiden.

Modern Screen: Steve Reeves, the huskiest hunk of he-male this side of Stillman's Gym, is a natural as Hercules. He's periodically distracted by a succession of curvy Italian actresses in roles ranging from young princesses to Amazon warriors. Matter of fact, Steve's aren't the only biceps displayed in this musclebound adventure spectacle.

122　*Hercules*

A Golan-Globus Production
Cannon Films (1983) 98 min.
Technicolor
U.S.–MGM/UA

P–Menahem Golan, Yoram Globus/D/W– Lewis Coates (Luigi Cozzi)/M–Pino Donaggio/C–Alberto Spagnoli/E–James Beshears/PD– Antonello Geleng/CD–Adriana Spadaro/SVE–Armando Valcauda

Cast–Lou Ferrigno (Hercules), Sybil Danning (Andriana), Brad Harris (King Augeias), Ingrid Anderson (Cassiopea), Rossana Podesta (Hera), Mirella D'Angelo (Circe), Delia Boccardo (Athena), Claudio Cassinelli (Zeus), William Berger (King Minos), Yehuda Efroni (Dorcon), Gianni Garko (Valcheus), Bobby Rhodes (Xenodama) with Roger Larry, Gabriella George, Frank Garland, Steven Candell, Eva Robbins

Lewis Coates always seems to have ambitions loftier than the budgets he has to work with (i.e.: *Star Crash*). Consequently, his films have a look of desperation about them. *Hercules* is Coates' attempt to fuse the peplum genre with science fiction. The end result is a curious hybrid which succeeds on neither level. Contrary to Greek mythology, Hercules is presented as the orphaned son of the murdered king of Thebes. The story does include some mythological elements such as the infant Hercules strangling two serpents and the cleaning of the Augean stables by diverting the course of a river. It also includes several unconvincing, and unmythological, mechanical monsters for our hero to battle. Much footage is devoted to the Greek gods, on the Moon rather than Mount Olympus, manipulating the lives of mortals as in *Jason and the Argonauts*. The film also borrows ideas from *Star Wars*, *The Colossus of Rhodes* and *Atlantis, the Lost Continent*. The production design is imaginative, considering the limitations of the budget, but the visuals are often marred by the poor quality of the special effects. At 6'5" and 262 pounds, Lou Ferrigno is a massive and thoroughly convincing Hercules. Rossana Podesta, as Hera the Queen of the Gods, retains her beauty and star presence despite her outrageous costuming. Two other peplum regulars, Brad Harris and Gianni Garko, are featured in supporting roles.

123   *Hercules*

A Walt Disney Pictures Production
Buena Vista (1997) 93 min.
Color
  P–Alice Dewey, John Musker, Ron Clements/
D–John Musker, Ron Clements/W–Ron Clements,
John Musker, Bob Shaw, Donald McEnery, Irene
Mecchi/Songs: Music by Alan Menken, Lyrics by
David Zippel/E–Tom Finan/PD–Gerarld Scarfe/
AD–Andy Gaskill
  Voices–Tate Donovan (Hercules), Susan Egan
(Meg), Danny DeVito (Phil), James Woods
(Hades), Rip Torn (Zeus), Samantha Eggar (Hera),
Joshua Keaton (Young Hercules) with Bobcat
Goldthwait, Hal Holbrook, Amanda Plummer

  With *Hercules*, the Disney studio's 35th animated feature, the animation department
chose to depart from the dramatic and serious
tone of their two previous animated movies
Pocahontas (1995) and *The Hunchback of Notre
Dame* (1996). In the words of one *Hercules*
character, instead of "making the story sound
like some Greek tragedy" they decided to
"lighten up, dude." The result is a combination of Greek mythology and Sylvester Stal-
lone's *Rocky*. On Mount Olympus, Zeus and
Hera celebrate the birth of their son Hercules.
Meanwhile, Hades, the king of the Underworld, is planning to unleash the Titans and
take over Mount Olympus. Seeing Hercules as
a potential threat, Hades has the baby abducted and uses a powerful potion to deprive
him of most of his godly powers. Abandoned
on earth, Hercules is adopted by a kindly
farmer and his wife who soon discover the
child's amazing strength. As a young man,
Hercules learns from his real father Zeus that
he can once again become a god if he proves
himself as a hero. The remainder of the story
consists of Hercules attempts to go from
"Zero to Hero," with musical commentary by
a group of gospel-singing Muses. Though not
in a league with Disney's best animated features, *Hercules* is an entertaining enough diversion. The animation is more stylized than
usual and the story moves along at a brisk
pace. Less positive elements are James Woods'
fast talking Hades and dialogue peppered with
contemporary "hip" expressions which dated
the movie almost immediately.

124   *Hercules Against Rome*

(Ercole Contro Roma/Samson Against All)
Romana Film, Rome–S.F.F. Alfred Rode, Paris
  (1964) 87 min.

In *Hercules Against Rome* (1964) Alan Steel defends the peasants from Roman cruelty.

Totalscope/Eastman Color
U.S.–American-International
P–Fortunato Misiano/D–Piero Pierotti/W–Arpad De Riso, Piero Pierotti, Nino Scolaro/M–Angelo Francesco Lavagnino/C–Augusto Tiezzi/E–Jolanda Benvenuti/AD–Salvatore Giancotti
Cast–Alan Steel (Hercules), Wandisa Guida (Ulpia), Anna Arena (Fenicia) with Daniele Vargas, Mimmo Palmara, Livio Lorenzon, Andrea Aureli, Walter Licastro, Dina De Santis

In A.D. 244 Marcus Philippus (known to history as Philip the Arab), the Prefect of the Praetorian Guards, engineers the assassination of the emperor Gordian and sets himself up in his place. Ulpia, the daughter of Gordian is in love with the young consul Trajan Decius, but Philippus attempts to force her into marriage. Fortunately, Trajan's good friend is none other than Hercules. Together they convince the Roman army to march against the usurper. The tyrant is defeated and Trajan becomes the new emperor with Ulpia at his side. For once, a bit more historical fact is incorporated into the script, which makes this fairly unique for a peplum film.

125 *Hercules Against the Barbarians*

(Maciste nell'Inferno di Genghis Khan; Maciste in the Hell of Genghis Khan)
Jonia Film S.r.L. , Rome (1964) 91 min.
Totalscope/Eastman Color
U.S.–American-International
P–Jacopo Comin, Ferdinando Felicioni/D–Domenico Paolella/W–Domenico Paolella, Alessandro Ferrau, Luciano Martino/M–Giuseppe Piccillo/C–Raffaele Masciocchi/E–Otello Colangeli/AD–Alfredo Montori/CD–Vera
Cast–Mark Forest (Hercules), Ken Clark (Kubilai), Gloria Milland (Armina), Jose Greci (Arias), Renato Rossini (Gasan), Mirko Ellis (Vladimir), Roldano Lupi (Genghis Khan) with Tullio Altamura, Harold Bradley, Mirko Valentin, Elisabeth Wu, Daniela Igliozzi, Renato Navarrini, Ugo Sasso, Bruno Scipioni, Renato Terra

In the twelfth century, the Mongol forces of Genghis Khan invade Poland but are defeated at Kracow by a giant of a man they call "The Hurricane." This is actually Hercules, once again come to aid the oppressed. Genghis Khan orders his son Kubilai to conquer Poland or suffer the consequences. Kubilai learns that twenty years before the Polish princess Ar-

mina was hidden away in a small village to protect her from the Mongol invasion. Armina, who is in love with Hercules, does not know of her royal heritage. Kubilai and his men capture Armina and take her to the Khan's stronghold. The Polish prince reveals to Hercules that Armina is his sister. Hercules vows to rescue her from Genghis Khan, but he must renounce his love for her when she ascends the throne. After defeating a Polish boa constrictor and crocodile, Hercules joins a troop of entertainers who are going to the Khan's court. Bored with the Chinese plate spinners, the Mongol ruler is easily impressed with the strongman's abilities. Kubilai, on the other hand, thinks that the stranger is really Hercules and has him imprisoned. The treacherous Kubilai has his father murdered and then fights against his brother to become ruler of the Mongols. With all of this dissension within, the Mongols are defeated by Hercules and the Poles. Armina turns the rule of Poland over to her brother and rides off with Hercules into the sunset.

126 *Hercules Against the Mongols*

(Maciste Contro i Mongoli; Maciste Against the Mongols)
A Jonia Film S.r.L., Rome (1964) 90 min.
Totalscope/Eastman Color
U.S.–American-International
P–Jacopo Comin/D–Domenico Paolella/W–Alessandro Ferrau, Luciano Martino, Domenico Paolella/M–Carlo Savina/C–Raffaele Masciocchi/E–Otello Colangeli/AD–Alfredo Montori/CD–Vera
Cast–Mark Forest (Hercules), Maria Grazia Spina (Bianca) with Ken Clark, Jose Greci, Renato Rossini, Nadir Baltimore, John McDouglas, Bruno Scipioni, Renato Terra, Tullio Altamura

In A.D. 1227 Genghis Khan dies and his three brawny sons, ignoring his final wish for peace, embark on a reign of terror. They invade a European city and take captive Princess Bianca because they believe she knows where her father has hidden the royal treasure. Hercules comes to the rescue and defeats the Mongols by trapping their army between a flood and a fire, which drives them into quicksand. There is very little story here but the movie makes up for this by giving the audience plenty of action. The highlight is a contest between Hercules and the three hunky sons of Genghis Khan (played by Ken Clark, Renato Rossini and Nadir Baltimore). There is so much beef on display during this scene, you might think you are watching a cattle drive. Most of the same cast and crew returned for *Hercules Against the Barbarians*. Although this film is also about the Mongols it is neither a sequel nor prequel to *Hercules Against the Mongols*.

127   Hercules Against the Moon Men

(Maciste Contro gli Uomini della Luna/Maciste e
  la Regina di Samar; Maciste and the Queen of
  Samar)
Nike Cinematografica, Rome–Comptoir Français,
  Paris (1964) 92 min.
Cromoscope/Eastman Color
U.S.–Governor Films (1965) 88 min.
Lunarscope/Cosmicolor
  P–Luigi Mondello/D–Giacomo Gentilomo/W–
Arpad De Riso, Nino Scolaro, Giacomo Gentilomo,
Angelo Sangermano/M–Carlo Franci/C–Oberdan
Trojani/AD–Amedeo Mellone
  Cast–Alan Steel (Hercules), Jany Clair (Agar),
Anna Maria Polani (Selena) with Nando Tamberlani, Jean-Pierre Honore, Delia D'Alberti, Goffredo
Unger, Anna Maria Dionisio, Paola Piretti

In this combination of peplum and science fiction, Hercules attempts to free the people of the kingdom of Samar from the rule of their evil queen, who is under the spell of invading Moon Men. This silly, but diverting, entry has the indomitable Alan Steel (real name: Sergio Ciani) fight a collection of Moon monsters before the inevitable cataclysm destroys the invaders. In the film's one inventive touch, the sequences which take place in the mountain kingdom of the Moon Men are filmed in sepia tone, rather than full color ... or Cosmicolor, as stated in the American publicity material.

128   Hercules Against the Sons of the Sun

(Ercole Contro i Figli del Sole)
Wonder Films, Rome–Explorer Films, Madrid
  (1964) 89 min.
Totalscope/Eastman Color
U.S.–Walter Manley Enterprises

P/D–Osvaldo Civirani/W–Franco Tannozzini,
Osvaldo Civirani/M–Lallo Gori/C–Julio Ortaz
Plaza/E–Nella Nannuzzi/AD–Pier Vittorio Marchi/CD–Mario Giorsi
  Cast–Mark Forest (Hercules), Giuliano Gemma
(Mytha) Anna Maria Pace (Yamara) with Franco
Fantasia, Angela Rhu, Giulio Donnini, German
Grechi, Carlo Latimer

A terrible storm shipwrecks Hercules on the shores of the "New World" and he is soon befriended by the Inca prince, Mytha. Mytha is the leader of a group of rebels who wish to restore their imprisoned king to his rightful place on the throne. To do this they must overthrow the king's evil brother Atahualpa. This all-too-familiar peplum plotline is enhanced by the novelty of the setting. The opening shot of a huge Inca gateway is impressive as are the colorful and elaborate costumes. These are a welcome change from the usual Roman, Greek and Egyptian sets and costumes which were reused in film after film. *Hercules Against the Sons of the Sun* has more than its share of silly dance routines, courtesy of choreographers Gino Landi and Archie Savage. The was Mark Forest's final peplum film.

129   Hercules and the Captive Women

(Ercole alla Conquista di Atlantide; Hercules and
  the Conquest of Atlantis)
S.p.A. Cinematografica, Rome–Comptoir Français,
  Paris (1961) 101 min.
Super Technirama 70/Technicolor
U.S.–Woolner Bros. (1963) 93 min.
  P–Achille Piazzi/D–Vittorio Cottafavi/W–
Alessandro Continenza, Vittorio Cottafavi, Duccio
Tessari, Archibald Zounds, Jr./M–Gino Marinuzzi,
Armando Trovajoli/Gordon Zahler (U.S. version)/
C–Carlo Carlini/E–Maurizio Lucidi/ Hugo Grimaldi (U.S. version)/AD–Franco Lolli/CD–Vittorio Rossi
  Cast–Reg Park (Hercules), Fay Spain (Queen Antinea), Laura Altan (Ismene), Ettore Manni (Androcles), Luciano Marin (Illus) with Mimmo Palmara, Mario Petri, Ivo Garrani, Mario Valdemarin, Enrico Maria Salerno, Salvatore Funari, Maurizio Caffarelli, Gianmaria Volante, Mino Doro, Alessandro Sperili

Hercules and the Captive Women is one of the most imaginative of all the Hercules films and the only one to be shot in 70mm. British bodybuilder Reg Park is excellent as Hercules. He abandons Steve Reeves' stoic interpretation and portrays the character as a rather lazy and reluctant hero, with a sense of humor as well developed as his muscles. Park, who was living in South Africa, had been contacted by producer Achille Piazzi and asked to come to Rome for a screen test. Once there, Park was coached by New York method actor Burt Nelson, who also played the Ettore Manni part in the screen test. The plot has Hercules taking leave of his faithful wife Deianira to set sail with his sovereign Androcles, the King of Thebes, to the island kingdom of Atlantis. There, the evil queen Antinea is breeding a race of superhuman warriors to use in her plans for world domination. On the way to Atlantis, Hercules stops at the island of Proteus to rescue Ismene, the daughter of Queen Antinea, who has been left there as a sacrifice to the monster. To save her he defeats Proteus, who is able to change form at will, but proves to be no match for Hercules. Upon arriving in Atlantis, Hercules is met with hostility for having offended the god Proteus. Androcles is put under a spell and Hercules must do battle with the bizarre mutant soldiers of the queen in order to free him. Of course, Hercules triumphs and the kingdom of Atlantis sinks into the sea. For the U.S. release of *Hercules and the Captive Women* the film was only shown in standard 35mm widescreen and sections of Hans J. Salter's music for *The Creature from the Black Lagoon* were incorporated into the background score by Gordon Zahler.

130   *Hercules and the Princess of Troy*

(The Mighty Hercules)
Embassy (1965) 50 min.
ABC TV Network
Color
 P–Joseph E. Levine, Albert Band / D–Albert Band (Alfredo Atonini) / W–Larry Forrester, Ugo Liberatore / M–Fred Steiner / C–Enzo Barboni / E–John Woodcock, Russell Wiles
 Cast–Gordon Scott (Hercules), Diana Hyland (Princess Diana), Paul Stevens (Diogenes), Mart Hulswit (Ulysses), Steve Garrett (Petra), Gordon Mitchell (Pirate Captain), Giorgio Ardisson (Leander), Roger Browne (Ortag), Jacques Stanislavski (Argus), Mario Novelli (Bortus) with Dan Christian

Hercules and the Princess of Troy was another unsuccessful attempt by Joseph E. Levine and Embassy Pictures to turn the Hercules films into a television series (see *Hercules in the Land of Darkness*). Unlike the previous venture, this time no expense was spared in creating an original pilot film. The Italian-American co-production had its premier on the ABC television network in 1965. Despite the fact that it did not launch a television series as hoped, *Hercules and the Princess of Troy* is a high quality endeavor in every respect. It is actually far superior to many of the Hercules films produced for theatrical release at the time. The premise of the series was to have been the various adventures that Hercules and his crew encounter on their long voyage home to Thebes. In the first of these, Hercules' ship is attacked by pirates who are raiding the ships sailing out of Troy. Hercules defeats the pirates and liberates the captives that are being held on board. From them he learns that each month Troy must sacrifice a maiden to a sea monster which lives in the waters surrounding the city. Hercules and his men go to Troy in hope of defeating the monster and preventing further sacrifices. The monster itself is an imposing, and expensive, creation by Carlo Rambaldi, who later created special effects for the 1976 remake of *King Kong* and *Alien*. The cost of this mechanical monster was $25,000. Joseph E. Levine assembled an impressive cast headed by Gordon Scott, more hirsute than usual as Hercules. Also, peppered throughout the cast are familiar peplumites Roger Browne, Gordon Mitchell and Giorgio Ardisson. The narration is spoken by actor Everett Sloane.

131   *Hercules and the Tyrants of Babylon*

(Ercole Contro i Tiranni di Babilonia)
Romana Films (1964) 87 min.
Totalscope / Eastman Color
U.S.–American-International
 P–Fortunato Misiano / D–Domenico Paolella / W–Luciano Martino, Domenico Paolella / M–Angelo Francesco Lavagnino / C–Augusto Tiezzi / E–Jolanda Benvenuti
 Cast–Rock Stevens (Hercules), Helga Line (Tanit), Mario Petri (Phaleg), Anna Maria Polani (Esperia), Livio Lorenzon (Salmanassar), Tullio Al-

tamura (Assur) with Mirko Valentin, Eugenio Bottari, Franco Balducci, Diego Pozzetto

Babylon is ruled by the tyrants Salmanassar, Assur and their sister Tanit. During a raid, the Babylonian army unknowingly captures Esperia, the Queen of Helledes. When Phaleg, King of Assyria, discovers that Esperia is enslaved he goes to Babylon with the intention of buying her. He then plans to force her into marrying him so that he can rule Helledes. The Babylonian rulers learn the identity of their captive and they plan to use her as a tool to conquer Helledes for Babylon. Phaleg, vowing the best intentions, convinces Hercules to help him save Esperia. Hercules soon realizes that he has been duped by the conniving Phaleg. Hercules organizes a slave army which brings about the destruction of Babylon, defeats Phaleg and his soldiers, and restores Esperia to her rightful place on the throne. Rock Stevens was a bodybuilder and former titleholder who went to Europe to appear in a trio of films directed by Domenico Paolella, including *Challenge of the Gladiator* and *Goliath at the Conquest of Damascus* (both 1964). He later returned to the United States where, as Peter Lupus, he became a featured player on the original *Mission Impossible* television series.

132   Hercules in New York

(Hercules Goes Bananas)
RAF-United (1970) 91 min.
Eastman Color
    P/W–Aubrey Wiseberg/D–Arthur A. Seidelman/M–John Balamos/C–Leo Lebowitz/E–Donald Finamore/AD–Perry Watkins/CD–Charles D. Tomlinson
    Cast–Arnold Schwarzenegger (Hercules), Arnold Stang (Pretzie), Tania Elg (Nemesis), Michael Lipton (Pluto) with Deborah Loomis, James Karen, Ernest Graves, Tanny McDonald, Howard Burstein, Merwin Goldsmith, George Bartenteff

Bored with life on Mount Olympus, Hercules defies the will of his father Zeus and goes to Earth—modern-day New York City to be precise. He befriends a half-pint pretzel salesman and, together they invade the world of professional wrestling. They become involved with some crooked promoters who bet big bucks on the seemingly undefeatable strongman. When the goddess Juno deprives Hercules of his great strength and he loses an important competition, the crooks decide to get even. Everybody has to start somewhere and this is the beginning of Arnold Schwarzenegger's film career (herein billed as "Arnold Strong"). After this, there was nowhere to go but up. "Filmed entirely in New York City" (as it is proudly stated in the opening credits) the movie is a sorry, amateurish mess from start to finish. Young

A young Arnold Schwarzenegger flexes his muscles as *Hercules in New York* **(1970).**

Reg Park, Giorgio Ardisson and Mino Doro set sail for the Underworld in *Hercules and the Haunted World* (1964).

Arnold, looking for all the world like some innocent, musclebound puppy, is required to do little except doff his shirt and flex his muscles. In some prints his voice has been dubbed but you must see the version with his original audio track to experience the full horror. And how on Earth did Tania Elg become involved with this poor excuse for a movie?

133   *Hercules in the Haunted World*

(Ercole al Centro della Terra; Hercules at the Center of the Earth)
S.p.A. Cinematographica, Rome (1962) 91 min.
Totalscope Super 100/Technicolor
U.S.–Woolner Bros. (1964) 89 min.
    P–Achille Piazzi/D/C–Mario Bava/W–Mario Bava, Duccio Tessari, Alessandro Continenza, Franco Prosperi/M–Armando Trovajoli/E–Mario Serandrei/AD–Franco Lolli/CD–Mario Giorsi
    Cast–Reg Park (Hercules), Christopher Lee (Lico), Leonora Ruffo (Deianira), Giorgio Ardis-

son (Theseus), Franco Giacobini (Telemachus) Marisa Belli (Aretusa), Ely Draco (Giocasta), Ida Galli (Persephone) with Grazia Collodi, Mino Doro, Monica Neri, Raffaele Baldassarre, Aldo Pedinotti, Gaia Germani

    This is one of the very best of the Hercules films thanks to Mario Bava's direction and cinematography. Reg Park delivers a very different interpretation of the character from the one he gave the previous year in *Hercules and the Captive Women*. This time he is far closer in spirit to the Steve Reeves version of the mythical strongman. British horror star Christopher Lee is the villainous Lico, a practitioner of black magic who puts a spell on Hercules' beloved Deianira. An oracle tells Hercules that the spell can only be broken by obtaining the Golden Apple which grows on a tree in Hades. Hercules sets out with his friend Theseus to the kingdom of the Underworld where they endure a bizarre series of adventures. Theseus is rescued from certain death by Persephone, the daughter of Pluto, God of the Underworld. They fall in love and he takes her back to Earth with him. This brings the wrath of her father down on both Theseus and Hercules. Hercules eventually returns to save Deianira but Lico uses his black arts once again to prevent her rescue. In a sequence worthy of the best of Mario Bava's horror films, the dead rise from their graves to attack Hercules. *Hercules in the Haunted World* is full of typical Bava touches such as brilliant color schemes, atmospheric lighting effects and weird set pieces. A thoroughly fascinating film which successfully incorporates the best of two distinctly dissimilar genres. Giorgio Ardisson, a former Vatican Guard, is dashing and likeable as Theseus. His slim, blond image makes for an interesting contrast to the dark and muscular Park. For the U.S. release, Woolner Bros. altered the background score and added a prologue which was not in European versions of the film.

134   *Hercules in the Vale of Woe*

(Maciste Contro Ercole nella Valle dei Guai;
  Maciste Against Hercules in the Valley of Woe)
Cinescolo (1962) 95 min.
Totalscope/Eastman Color
U.S.–Embassy (1964)
  P–Cavevari and Colombo/D–Mario Mattoli/ W–Vittorio Metz, Marcello Marchesi/M–Gianni Ferrio/C–Enzo Oddone/E–Roberto Cinquini
  Cast–Kirk Morris (Maciste), Frank Gordon (Hercules), Liana Orfei (Deianira) with Franco Franchi, Ciccio Ingrassia, Raimondo Vianello, Mario Carotenuto, Bice Valori, Gino Bramieri, Francesco Mule, Ave Ninchi, Gianna Cobelli, Gino Buzzanca, Fanfulla

The popular Italian comedy team of Franco Franchi and Ciccio Ingrassia portray two twentieth-century small time wrestling promoters who are transported via time machine to ancient Mycenae, where the inhabitants believe they are a punishment sent by Zeus. Be-

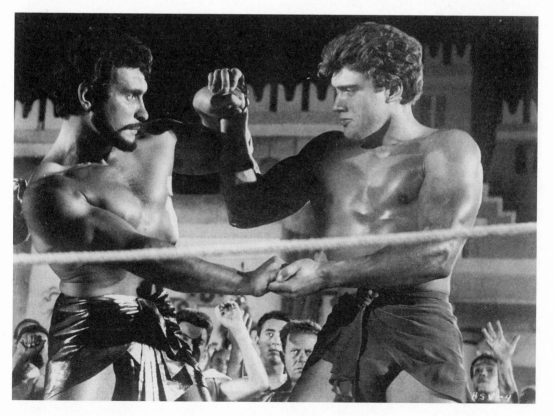

Frank Gordon and Kirk Morris were wrestling long before the WWF in *Hercules in the Vale of Woe* (1964).

fore this film is over the audience may agree with them. When Hercules appropriates the time machine, the two con men enlist the aid of Maciste to help get it back. Through an idiotic chain of events, Maciste's strength is transferred to one of the time travelers and he engages in a wrestling match with Hercules. As with other peplum spoofs, *Hercules in the Vale of Woe* features lowbrow humor, a terrible music score and absolutely no laughs. The two mythical strongmen have very little screen time, most of it being devoted to the antics of the irritating Franchi and Ingrassia. The puerile plot manages to include the mythological personages of the Cyclops, Minotaur and Circe. The film was also released in Italy under the title *I Due Pretoriani*, the emphasis being on the comedians rather than the strongmen. Frank Gordon is impressive as Hercules in his only peplum role.

135   Hercules, Prisoner of Evil

(Ursus, il Terror dei Kirghisi; Ursus, the Terror of Kirghizia)
Adelphia Compagnia-Societa Ambrosiana Cinematografica, Rome
(1964) 90 min.
Totalscope/Eastman Color
U.S.–American-International

   P–Luciano Cattania/D–Anthony Dawson (Antonio Margheriti), Ruggero Deodato (uncredited)/ W–Marcello Sartarelli/M–Franco Trinacria/C– Gabor Pogany/E–Otello Colangeli/AD–Riccardo Domenici

   Cast–Reg Park (Hercules), Ettore Manni (Ilo), Mireille Granelli (Aniko), Furio Meniconi (Zara), Maria Teresa Orsini (Katia) with Lilly Mantovani, Serafino Fuscagni, Ugo Carboni, Giulio Maculani, Claudio Scarchilli, Piero Pastore, Gaetano Quartararo

   A horrible shrieking monster is terrorizing the forests of Kirghizia, causing all manner of murder and mayhem. Prince Zara, ruler of the city of Sura, is fearful that Hercules is plotting to steal his throne. Zara's cousin Aniko, the daughter of the late Khan, is in love with Hercules and plans to marry him. As the battle for power escalates, the monster continues to indiscriminately attack the opposing sides. Hercules' brother Ilo eventually discovers that Aniko is an impostor. In reality she

is an evil sorceress whose magic potion can turn a man into a monster. She has seduced Hercules for the sole purpose of using him to destroy all opposition to her claim on the throne. Director Antonio Margheriti made his reputation in the Euro-horror genre, to which this film is closely related with its Jekyll/Hyde theme featuring Hercules as both hero and monster. Reg Park is as imposing as ever in the Hercules role but he isn't given all that much to do until the final scenes. Most of the action revolves around Ettore Manni as Ilo and his efforts to learn the truth about the monster's attacks. A French version entitled *La Vie Erotique d'Hercules* was later released with soft core sex footage added.

136   Hercules, Samson and Ulysses

(Ercole Sfida Sansone; Hercules Challenges Samson)
Internazionale Cinematografica (1964) 90 min.
Eastman Color
U.S.–Metro-Goldwyn-Mayer (1965) 85 min.
   P–Joseph Fryd/D/W–Pietro Francisci/M–Angelo Francesco Lavagnino/C–Silvano Ippoliti/AD –Giovanni Giovannini/CD–Gaia Romanini

   Cast–Kirk Morris (Hercules), Richard Lloyd (Samson), Liana Orfei (Delilah), Enzo Cerusico (Ulysses), Aldo Guiffre (Saran of Gaza), Andrea Fantasia (Laertes), Walter Grant (Aesculapius) with Fulvia Franco, Diletta D'Andrea, Nando Mariani, Pietro Tordi, Ugo Sasso, Alina Zalewska, Aldo Pini

   This is an interesting and entertaining attempt to combine characters from Greek mythology with characters from the Bible. Conceived as a sequel to the two Steve Reeves– Pietro Francisci "Hercules" films, it also serves as a prequel, of sorts, to the story of Samson and Delilah. Hercules, his wife Iole and their young son are living peacefully in the kingdom of Ithaca. When a marauding sea monster destroys several ships, Hercules and Ulysses, the teenage son of King Laertes, get together a ship and crew to go in search of the beast. A storm shipwrecks them in Judea where the Philistines mistake Hercules for the Danite rebel Samson. The Saran of Gaza enlists the aid of the beautiful Delilah in an attempt to seduce the strongman. In the meantime, the real Samson thinks that Hercules is an ally of his enemies. Following a powerful

Delilah (Liana Orfei) begs Samson (Richard Lloyd) to spare her life in *Hercules, Samson and Ulysses* (1965).

confrontation in which Hercules and Samson make rubble of some temple ruins, the two musclemen decide to join forces to battle the Philistines. Samson spares the life of Delilah, despite Hercules' warning that one day he may regret this decision. The title of the film would more accurately have been *Hercules, Samson and Deiliah*, as they are the focus of the story. Ulysses is a minor character who has little part in the proceedings. Kirk Morris, once known as "The Young Steve Reeves," is an able Hercules, Richard Lloyd (aka Rod Flash Ilush) is also quite appropriate as Samson. Liana Orfei has one of her better roles as Delilah and makes the most of the opportunity. Andrea Fantasia, Walter Grant and Aldo Pini reprise their roles from Francisci's previous Hercules films. *Hercules, Samson and Ulysses* has a gloss that many of the other peplum films lack and the production values are

above average. A curious bit of costuming has the Philistine soldiers wearing what appear to be Nazi storm trooper helmets. For performance, plot and production this film ranks much higher than most peplum movies.

Films and Filming: The Italian spectaculars with the muscle men heroes are still being made: but now in a bid to stop their waning popularity producers are presenting us with two or more heroes in each film.

137   *Hercules the Avenger*

(La Sfida dei Giganti; Challenge of the Giants)
Plaza Film S.p.A.–Schermi Riuniti S.p.A., Rome (1966)
Techniscope / Technicolor
U.S–No theatrical release
  D / E–Maurice Bright (Maurizio Lucidi) / W–Enzo Gicca / M–Ugo Filippini / C–Alvaro Mancori / AD–Giorgio Giovannini

Sylvia Lopez is the dazzling temptress Orphale in *Hercules Unchained* (1960).

Cast–Reg Park (Hercules), Audrey Amber (Deianira), Gia Sandri (Queen of Syracuse), Giovanni Cianfriglia (Antaeus) with Franco Ressel, Luigi Barbini, Gianni Solaro, Luigi Donato, Corrado Sonni, Giulio Maculani, Mimmo Poli

When his son is mauled by a lion, Hercules goes to Hades to try and free his spirit and restore his health. During Hercules' absence Antaeus, the evil son of the Earth Goddess, convinces the Queen of Syracuse that he is Hercules and forces her to share her throne with him. Antaeus kills a priestess of Jove who accuses him of being an impostor. Jove helps Hercules rescue the spirit of his son so the hero can avenge the murder of the priestess. Hercules battles Antaeus and eventually destroys him while holding him in the air, thereby depriving him of contact with Mother Earth. *Hercules the Avenger* was the brainchild of Maurizio Lucidi, who had been the editor on *Hercules and the Captive Women*. This patchwork movie liberally borrows sequences from that film as well as *Hercules in the Haunted World*. Lucidi used this film to break into directing. The highlight of *Hercules the Avenger* is the battle between Reg Park and Giovanni Cianfriglia, who had been a stunt double for Steve Reeves. This was Reg Park's final peplum film.

138   *Hercules Unchained*

(*Ercole e la Regina di Lidia*; *Hercules and the Queen of Lydia*)
A Lux Film–Galatea, Italy–Lux Compagne Cinematographique de France Production (1959) 101 min.
Dyaliscope/Eastman Color
U.S.–A Joseph E. Levine–Embassy Pictures Presentation
Warner Bros. (1960)
    P–Bruno Vailati/D–Pietro Francisci/W–Pietro Francisci, Ennio De Concini/M–Enzo Masetti/C–Mario Bava/E–Mario Serandrei/AD–Massimo Tavazzi/CD–Maria Baroni
    Cast–Steve Reeves (Hercules), Sylva Koscina (Iole), Silvia Lopez (Omphale), Primo Carnera (Antaeus), Carlo D'Angelo (Creon), Sergio Fantoni

(Eteocles), Gabriele Antonini (Ulysses), Cesare Fantoni (Oedipus), Andrea Fantasia (Laertes), Mimmo Palmara (Polynices), Walter Grant (Aesculapius), Fulvo Carrara (Castor) with Patrizia Della Rovere, Aldo Fiorelli, Willy Columbini, Gino Mattera, Aldo Pini, Elda Tattoli, Marisa Valenti, Gianni Loti, Nino Marchetti

Originally announced as *Hercules Against the Gods*, this sequel was filmed back-to-back with *Hercules* and is a definite improvement over the original. It has all of the previous film's virtues and few of its faults. Many of the original cast members return, headed by Steve Reeves and Sylva Koscina. Once again Pietro Francisci directs and coauthors the screenplay which cleverly incorporates elements from myths relating to Antaeus, Oedipus and Omphale. Following the events which took place in *Hercules*, the strongman is returning to his home in Thebes, accompanied by his new wife Iole and their friend, the youthful Ulysses. Along the way they are challenged by Antaeus (champion boxer and wrestler, Primo Carnera). Antaeus is the offspring of the Earth Goddess and, as long as he can stay in contact with the ground, no one can defeat him. Hercules holds Antaeus in the air until he is drained of his strength and the trio can pass in safety. Nearing the city, they discover that King Oedipus has abdicated and that his two sons now rule Thebes alternately for six-month periods. Eteocles refuses to give up the throne to Polynices when his turn to rule has come so a war between the rival brothers in imminent. Hercules sets out a journey to try and establish peace, but along the way he stops at a spring for a drink of water. He doesn't know that these are the "Waters of Forgetfulness." He loses consciousness and is taken to Omphale, Queen of Lydia. The sequences involving Omphale are the most memorable part of *Hercules Unchained*, reaching new heights in camp entertainment. Omphale is a flame-haired temptress in chiffon and spike heels who has her lovers executed when she tires of them. Her kingdom is a riot of brilliant colors (courtesy of Mario Bava) and fanciful set designs. Especially effective is the cavern where she has her former lovers embalmed and put on display. Fortunately, Hercules escapes their fate. The story becomes less interesting when it again focuses

on the rivalry between the sons of Oedipus and their battle to rule Thebes. Joseph E. Levine was again able to publicize this into a blockbuster at the box office and *Hercules Unchained* made even more money than its predecessor.

139   *Hero of Rome*
(Il Colosso di Roma; The Colossus of Rome/Arm of Fire)
Dorica Films, Rome–Les Filmes Jacques Letienne and Unicite, Paris
(1964) 90 min.
Spesvision/Eastman Color
U.S.–Embassy (1965)
   P–Bruno Turchetto/D–Giorgio Ferroni/W–Alberto Montanari, Remigio Del Grosso/M–Angelo Francesco Lavagnino/C–Augusto Tiezzi/E–Antonietta Zita/CD–Elio Micheli
   Cast–Gordon Scott (Caius Mucius Scaevola), Gabriella Pallotta (Cloelia), Massimo Serato (Tarquin), Maria Pia Conte (Valeria) with Gabriele Antonini, Franco Fantasia, Bernard Farber, Nando Angelini, Arena Fortunato, Tullio Altamura, Valerio Tordi, Attilio Dottesio, Roldano Lupi, Philippe Hersent

In 510 B.C. the ruler Tarquin was banished from Rome by the will of the people. He then joined the Etruscan leader Lars Porsena in waging war on Rome. This minor Gordon Scott vehicle combines the stories of two Romans who were instrumental in winning this war, the warrior Caius Musius and the virgin Cloelia. The film involves them in a fictitious romance with the emphasis on the character of Caius Mucius. When Musicus is captured by the Etruscans he burns his right hand in order to prove the courage of Rome. Afterwards, he is known by the name of Scaevola, which means "left handed." Cloelia and nine other Roman maidens are given over to Lars Porsena as a token of goodwill but the treachery of Tarquin forces the ten women to flee by swimming the River Tiber back to Rome. Realizing that the peace treaty has been violated, Cloelia returns to the camp of Porsena. When Tarquin threatens the life of Cloelia, Scaevola and his army attack to save her. Gordon Scott is typically heroic in the title role. Gabriele Antonini, who appeared as the young Ulysses in both of the Steve Reeves "Hercules" films, plays the son of Porsena, incongruously dubbed with a very proper British accent.

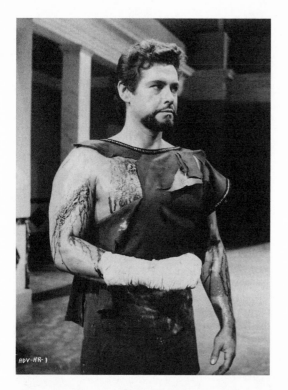

ADV-HR-1

140   *Herod the Great*

(Erode il Grande/Le Roi Cruel; The Cruel King)
Vic-Faro-Explorer Film, Rome–C.F.P.C., Paris
 (1959) 90 min.
Totalscope/Eastman Color
U.S.–A Samuel Schneider Presentation
Allied Artists (1960)
   P–Victor Tourjansky/D–Arnaldo Genoino/W–
Damiano Damiani, Tullio Pinelli, Frederico Zardi,
Fernando Cerchio, Victor Tourjansky M–Carlo
Savina/C–Massimo   Dallamano/E–Antonietta
Zita/AD–Giorgio Scalco/CD–Vittorio Nino No-
varese
   Cast–Edmund Purdom (Herod), Sylvia Lopez
(Miriam), Massimo Girotti (Octavian), Sandra Milo
(Sarah), Alberto Lupo (Aaron) with Renato Bal-
dini, Corrado Pani, Enrico Glori, Elena Zareschi,
Camillo Pilotto, Carlo D'Angelo, Adolfo Geri,
Fedele Gentile, Enzo Fiermonte, Fiodor Schaliapin

Left: Gordon Scott plays the courageous soldier Caius mucius who leads the Romans
against the Etruscans in *Hero of Rome* (1965).
Below: Edmund Purdom is the troubled monarch of Judea and Sylvia Lopez is his beautiful wife in *Herod the Great* (1960).

H-41A

Edmund Purdom tackles one of his meatiest roles as Herod, the mad King of Judea. He approaches it with much of the same gusto he brought to the part of Rasputin in *Nights of Rasputin*, filmed a year later. Octavian defeats the forces of Mark Antony at the battle of Actium and Herod realizes that he must go to the victor to form an alliance. Upon returning to Judea, he wrongly suspects his faithful wife Miriam of committing adultery with the captain of his guards. Suspicion and jealousy cause Herod to descend further into madness until he eventually condemns his innocent wife to death by stoning. When a child is born in Bethlehem, it is prophesied that he will one day become the King of the Jews. Herod, in a fit of jealous rage, orders the murder of all the newborn male children in Bethlehem. With the blood of so many innocent victims on his conscience, King Herod dies alone and consumed by guilt. *Herod the Great* is a handsome production in every respect with grandiose sets, colorful costumes and a compelling cast. Sylvia Lopez looks too flashy for the part of the innocent Miriam but she is effective as the tragic queen nevertheless. With a typical Euro-epic disregard for facts, Herod kills his son Antipas, thereby depriving history of the man who would behead John the Baptist.

141　*The Huns*

(La Regina dei Tartari; The Queen of the Tarters)
Columbus S.p.A., Rome–Comptoir Français, Paris (1960) 85 min.
Totalscope / Eastman Color
U.S.–A William Hunter Presentation for Producers International (1962)
ColorScope
　P–Jacques Isken, Carlo Lombardi / D–Sergio Grieco / W–Eric Klauss, Marcello Giorcioli, Rate Furlan / M–Bruno Ganfora / C–Alfio Contini / E–

Chelo Alonso as the Queen of the Tarters in *The Huns* (1962).

Enzo Alfonsi/AD–Alberto Boccianti/CD–Mario Giorsi

Cast–Chelo Alonso (Tanja), Jacques Sernas (Malok), Folco Lulli (Igor), Mario Petri (Timur) with Philippe Hersent, Ciquita Caffelli, Piero Lulli, Andrea Scotti, Pietro Tordi

Former cabaret dancer turned peplum star, Chelo Alonso, is the Tarter queen who is opposed, but loved, by a Hun warrior (Jacques Sernas). When the Huns raid her village, Tanja is taken prisoner. Although the creed of the fierce Huns is "take no prisoners," Tanja's life is spared by the Hun's leader, Igor. Years pass and Tanja, who is like a daughter to Igor, becomes an accepted member of the tribe. When Igor is dies in battle, Tanja is proclaimed Queen of the Tarters. The young warrior Malok is attracted to Tanja but this does not prevent him devising a plan to overthrow her rule. This is a routine action picture with the added advantage of two attractive and capable leading players in the persons of Alonso and Sernas. Folco Lulli, however, gives

the film's most memorable performance as the Hun chieftain, Igor the Great.

142   *I, Claudius*

A London Film Production (1937) Not Completed

P–Alexander Korda/D–Josef von Sternberg/W–Josef von Sternberg, Lajos Biro, Carl Zuckmayer, Arthur Wimperis, Lester Cohen, Robert Graves/Based on the novels by Robert Graves/C–Georges Perinal/AD–Vincent Korda/CD–John Armstrong

Cast–Charles Laughton (Claudius), Merle Oberon (Messalina), Flora Robson (Livia), Emlyn Williams (Caligula), Robert Newton (Cassius), John Clements (Valenz) with Basil Gill, Everley Gregg

Alexander Korda's *I, Claudius* is probably the most famous unfinished film and one of the most intriguing legends in the history of motion pictures. On February 15, 1937, *I, Claudius* began filming at Denham Studios near London. The entire lot was given over to the filming of this monumental production

Emlyn Williams (on throne) as Caligula in the unfinished film, *I Claudius* (1937).

with enormous sets filling every available sound stage. The famous art director, William Cameron Menzies, was set to direct the impressive cast, which included Charles Laughton and Merle Oberon. Complications arose and Korda was prevailed upon to hire Joseph von Sternberg to direct as part of a financial agreement with Marlene Dietrich, who was owed back salary for her work in Korda's film *Knight Without Armour*. Von Sternberg was well known as a "woman's director," so the choice was an advantageous one for up-and-coming star Merle Oberon, whose beauty and talent Korda hoped to showcase in this important production. Charles Laughton, however, was terribly unhappy with von Sternberg's direction. Always a problematic actor who needed a great deal of nurturing, Laughton was miserable over von Sternberg's aloof attitude and neglect. Laughton's inability to find the key to the character of Claudius was a major factor in the film's eventual collapse. When Merle Oberon suffered an automobile accident and had to be hospitalized, Korda called a halt to the production. Filming stopped on March 16, one month after it had begun. The superlative BBC documentary, *The Epic That Never Was* (Bill Duncalf; 1965), chronicles the brief history of *I, Claudius* in great detail. Through the use of interviews and the existing footage that was shot, Duncalf not only shows that a classic film was in the making but creates a moving portrait of Charles Laughton. The demise of *I, Claudius* deprived the world of what might have been Laughton's finest performance. In 1976, BBC Television in association with London Film Productions produced the TV series *I, Claudius* which consisted of 13 one hour episodes. Written by Jack Pullman and starring Derek Jacobi as Claudius, this became one of the most acclaimed television programs of its time. John Hurt gives an especially memorable performance as the demented Caligula. Others in the large cast include Sian Phillips as Livia, Brian Blessed as Augustus and Sheila White as Messalina.

143   *In the Beginning*

Hallmark Entertainment/Babelsberg International Film

NBC TV Network (2000) 140 min.
Color

P–Paul Lowin, David V. Picker, Robert Halmi, Jr./D–Kevin Connor/W–John Goldsmith/M–Ken Thorne/C–Elemer Ragalyi/E–Barry Peters, Bill Blunden/PD–Keith Wilson/CD–Maria Hruby

Cast–Martin Landau (Abraham), Jacqueline Bisset (Sarah), Billy Campbell (Moses), Eddie Cibrian (Joseph), Christopher Lee (Ramses I), Amanda Donohoe (Zuleika), Geraldine Chaplin (Yocheved), Fred Weller (Jacob), Diana Rigg (Rebeccah), David Warner (Eliezer), Alan Bates (Jethro), Steven Berkoff (Potiphar), Art Malik (Ramses II), David Threlfall (Aaron), Victor Spinetti (Pharaoh's Magician)

Hallmark Entertainment temporarily abandoned classical fantasy literature (*The Odyssey*, *Gulliver's Travels*) and turned their attention to the Bible. Their previous biblical endeavor was the dreadful *Noah's Ark* but this time they came up with a winner. *In the Beginning* relates stories from the books of Genesis and Exodus or, as the ads said, "From Creation to the Commandments." This is a lot to attempt in the relatively brief running time, but one of the great virtues of this film is that it does not overstay its welcome. It is also amazingly thorough, including everything from Adam and Eve (effectively told in flashback by Abraham) to the Hebrews' arrival in the promised land. The stories of Noah's Ark and Sodom and Gomorrah are absent, presumably since they had just been given the full treatment in *Noah's Ark* a year earlier. The cast is generally quite good, although Eddie Cibrian looks and acts a bit too modern as Joseph. The style of the production is half Turner and half DeMille. The opening sequences are reminiscent of the Turner television biblical series complete with the overused Morocco location filming. When the story of Joseph moves into Egypt it recalls the gaudier Hollywood epics. The final sequence dealing with Moses is like a *Reader's Digest* condensation of DeMille's 1956 version of *The Ten Commandments*. Some scenes are almost identical to ones in that film, the notable difference being the absence of Anne Baxter. Instead we have Victor Spinetti hardening Pharaoh's heart. With all of the material it covers, the pace of *In the Beginning* is understandably faster than most movies of its type. When compared to the often plodding Turner biblical films, it fairly races along. All in all, it is an entertaining and painless Sunday school lesson which is well worth watching.

144   The Inquiry

(L'inchiesta)
Italian International Film–Clesi Cinematografica (1986) 107 min.
Color
U.S.–HBO Video (2001)
  P–Fulvio Lucisano, Silvio and Anna Maria Clementelli/D–Damiano Damiani/W–Ennio Flajano, Suso Cecchi D'Amico, Damiano Damiani, Vittorio Bonicelli/M–Riz Ortolani/C–Franco Di Giacomo/AD–Enrico Fiorentini/CD–Giulia Mafai
  Cast–Keith Carradine (Taurus), Harvey Keitel (Pilate), Phyllis Logan (Claudia), Angelo Infanti (Trifone), Lina Sastri (Mary Magdalene), John Forgeham (Marcus), Luciano Bartoli (Criside), Erik Schumann (Flavius) with Silvan, Paola Molina, Angelo D'Angelo, Laura De Marchi, Jean Francois Poron, Sal Borgese, Stefano Da Vanzati, Manuel De Blas

Disturbed by the rumors surrounding the crucifixion of Jesus, the emperor Tiberius sends the Roman official Taurus to Palestine to investigate. Taurus' arrival is met with suspicion by the governor Pontius Pilate who questions the motivations of the inquiry. Pilate's wife Claudia is still captivated by the memory of Jesus and agrees to help Taurus in his search for the whereabouts of Jesus' body. Despite growing evidence to the contrary, Taurus still believes that Jesus was a fraud. As the investigation escalates Taurus is forced to face facts that defy his well ordered Roman logic. Disguised as a Jew, he goes out among the people to try and find Mary Magdalene in the hope that she can provide him with the answers he is seeking. The Inquiry is an interesting and well acted drama which never had a theatrical release in the U.S. The lack of commercial potential is the obvious reason but this doesn't change the fact that it is still worth watching. Keith Carradine is particularly good in a very complex role.

145   Intolerance

Wark Productions Company (1916) 220 min.
  P/D/W/E–D.W. Griffith/C–G.W. Bitzer, Karl Brown
  Cast–Lillian Gish (The Woman Who Rocks the Cradle), Modern Story–Mae Marsh (Dear One),

Robert Herron (Boy), Fred Turner (Father), Sam de Grasse (Jenkins), Vera Lewis (Mary) with Monte Blue; Babylonian Story–Constance Talmadge (Mountain Girl), Elmer Clifton (Rhapsode), Alfred Paget (Belshazzar), Seena Owen (Princess Beloved), Carl Stockdale (Nabonidus) with Tully Marshall, George Siegmann, Elmo Lincoln; French Story–Margery Wilson (Brown Eyes), Eugene Pallette (Prosper Latour), Frank Bennett (Charles IX), Josephine Crowell (Catherine de Medici) with Maxfield Stanley; Nazarene Story–Howard Gaye (Jesus), Lillian Langdon (Mary Magdalene), Erich von Stroheim (Pharisee) with Bessie Love, Gunther von Rittau

Prior to the release of Birth of a Nation in 1915, D.W. Griffith had already begun work on a new film to be called The Mother and the Law which would deal with the exploitation of factory workers by their employers. Griffith eventually decided to make this just one story in a film focusing on various examples of intolerance throughout the history of mankind. The four stories are told simultaneously, cutting from one to another in increasingly rapid succession. In addition to "The Mother and the Law Sequence," there is a story about the massacre of the French Huguenots, a life of Christ, and "The Fall of Babylon." It is this latter sequence that is best remembered, due in part to Griffith's attempt to outdo even Cabiria in magnificence. The set of Belshazzar's palace, which rose over ninety feet high, was designed by Griffith and set builder Frank Wortman. Some 2,000 extras were hired to appear in the scenes featuring the Feast of Belshazzar and the subsequent invasion by Cyrus the Persian. As the filming went over schedule and over budget, Griffith lost the faith of his backers and was forced to use his personal finances in order to complete the picture. When Intolerance was released it was met with a cool reception from the public. Two years later, in an attempt recoup some of his losses, Griffith edited out "The Fall of Babylon" sequence and released it as a separate feature with additional footage and a newly filmed happy ending.

146   The Invincible Brothers Maciste

(Gli Invincibili Fratelli Maciste/The Invincible Gladiators)
An I.F.E.S.A. Production (1965) 87 min.

Richard Lloyd is one of *The Invisible Brothers Maciste* (1965).

Eastman Color
U.S.–ABC Films

P–Vincenzo Musolino / D–Roberto Mauri / W–Edoardo Mulargia, Roberto Mauri / M–Felice di Stefano / C–Romolo Garroni / E–Enzo Alabiso / CD–Sergio Selli

Cast–Richard Lloyd and Tony Freeman (The Maciste Brothers), Antonio de Teffe (Akim), Ursula Davis (Jhana), Gia Sandri (Nice) with Claudie Lange, Franco Visconti, Ruth von Hagen

The Invincible Brothers Maciste is a minor film which appeared late in the peplum cycle. The Maciste brothers (which sounds like a circus act) are called upon to aid a young prince in rescuing his betrothed from the clutches of a tribe of Leopard Men. The underground kingdom of the Leopard Men is ruled by a malevolent queen (Claudie Lange) who wants the handsome prince for her consort. The climactic earthquake, which destroys the city and its queen, had by this time become a convention of the genre. Indeed, the entire film has an all too familiar feel to it. Richard Lloyd

(formerly known as Rod Flash Ilush) is imposing as the older Maciste brother. He is also give far more to do in the film than his younger, and nearly mute, sibling (Tony Freeman, aka Mario Novelli). The sets and costume designs are particularly ludicrous this time around. Antonio de Teffe is billed as Anthony Steffen in English language prints of this film.

147 *The Invincible Gladiator*

(Il Gladiatore Invincibile)
Columbus Film S.p.A., Rome–Atenea Film, Madrid (1962) 92 min.
Techniscope / Eastman Color
U.S.–Seven Arts (1963)

P–Alberto De Martino, Italo Zingarelli, Cleto Fontini / D–Anthony Momplet, Alberto De Martino / W–Francesco De Feo, Francesco Thellung, Alberto De Martino / M–Carlo Franci / C–Eloy Mella / E–Otello Colangeli / AD–Piero Poletto / CD–Mario Giorsi

Cast–Richard Harrison (Rizius), Isabelle Corey

(Sira), Leo Anchoriz (Rabirius), Joseph Marco (Vibius), Livio Lorenzon (Itus) with Riccardo Canale, Antonio Molino Rojo, Edoardo Nevola, Jole Mauro, Giorgio Ubaldi

In the third century A.D. the king of the city of Acastus dies, leaving his twelve-year-old son Darius as heir to the throne. The prime minister, Rabirius, is to rule the kingdom until the boy comes of age. Rabirius secretly plans to kill Darius. He will then marry the king's daughter Sira to make sure that his place on the throne is secured. Rezius, a noble gladiator, unwittingly becomes a pawn of the would-be usurper. When he realizes he is fighting on the wrong side, he switches his allegiance and helps the young king regain his throne. *The Invincible Gladiator* is a fairly standard entry with such conventions of the peplum genre as a chariot race and the ever-popular gang of spear-wielding midgets in the arena. Although production values are only average, Richard Harrison's agreeable presence gives the film considerable appeal and the action sequences are well staged. Harrison had played bit parts in Hollywood films such as *Jeanne Eagles* and *South Pacific* before landing a somewhat larger role in *Master of the World* (1961) for American-International Pictures. While making this movie, Harrison met and married the daughter of AIP executive James H. Nicholson. Not wanting to rely on his father-in-law for acting roles, Harrison accepted producer Italo Zingarelli's invitation to appear in the Italian production *The Invincible Gladiator*. This was the first of many European epics to feature Richard Harrison in the lead. After the peplum craze ended he went on to even greater success as a Spaghetti Western star.

San Diego Evening Tribune: "The Invincible Gladiator" is Richard Harrison, faced with the challenge of defeating all sorts of nasty characters. This comic strip Italian production is complete with the usual array of muscular men and shapely handmaidens, all conventionally undressed.

148   *Jacob*

A Turner/Lube/Lux Vide/Beta Film/Rai Uno Production
U.S.–TNT Network (1994) 94 min.
Color

P–Gerald Rafshoon, Lorenzo Minoli/D–Peter Hall/W–Lionel Chetwind/M–Marco Frisina/C–Ennio Guarnieri/E–Bill Blunden/PD–Enrico Sabbitini, Paolo Biagetti/CD–Enrico Sabbitini
Cast–Matthew Modine (Jacob), Lara Flynn Boyle (Rachel), Giancarlo Giannini (Laban), Irene Papas (Rebekah), Joss Ackland (Isaac), Sean Bean (Esau), Juliet Aubrey (Leah) with Christoph Waltz, Philip Locke, Christoph Ohrt, Daniel Newman, Cecilla Dazzi

The sons of Isaac and Rebekah have two very different personalities. While the elder, Esau, is out hunting for game, the younger, Jacob, is helping to heal the sick. Knowing that Jacob is the chosen of God, Rebekah convinces Jacob to wrongly obtain the blessing of the first born from his elderly father. This is only the beginning of the familial treacheries which abound in *Jacob*. When his wife Leah asks Jacob "Have you ever wanted something so badly that you would deceive even the people you love to get it?," she sums up the entire foundation that this story is built upon. Although this is one of the shortest entries in the Turner Bible series, it still suffers from the snail's crawl pacing which afflicts the series as a whole.

149   *Jacob, the Man Who Fought with God*

(Giacobbe ed Esau; Jacob and Esau)
San Paolo Films, Rome–San Pablo Films, Madrid (1964) 98 min.
Eastman Color
U.S.–No theatrical release
P–Emilio Cordero/D–Marcello Baldi/W–Ottavio Jemma, Giuseppe Mangione/M–Teo Usuelli, Gino Marinuzzi/C–Marcello Masciocchi/E–Giuliana Attenni, Lina Coterini/AD–Piero Poletto/CD–Vittorio Bettini
Cast–Fosco Giachetti, Luisa Della Noce, Jean Morcier, John Douglas, Giorgio Cerioni, Alfredo Rizzo, Roberto Paoletti, Sergio Ammirata, Piero Bugli, Dario Dolci, Massimo Giuliano, Rosalia Maggio, Paolo Pieri

This Paulus Brothers production is the least satisfying film in a series which includes *The Great Leaders* and *Saul and David*. The first half of *Jacob, the Man Who Fought with God* is devoted to the story of Abraham. The treatment is very similar to that given the same material in John Huston's *The Bible ... In the Beginning*, but lacks the powerful star presences of

Talos the Bronze Giant threatens *Jason and the Argonauts* (1963).

George C. Scott and Ava Gardner. The major drawback of this film is an unfamiliar European cast giving uniformly mediocre performances. The story also needs more focus. The remainder of the movie centers on the sons of Isaac and Rebecca. Encouraged by his mother, the younger son Jacob tricks his aged father into bestowing his blessings on him rather than his older brother Esau. An infuriated Esau drives Jacob away and he must seek refuge with his uncle Laban. Laban tricks Jacob into years of servitude. When he finally leaves and returns to his homeland, Jacob is forgiven and welcomed by Esau. The dramatic conflicts are minimal and the characters, as presented, are uninteresting.

150   *Jason and the Argonauts*

A Morningside Worldwide Film / A Charles H. Schneer Production
Columbia (1963) 104 min.
Dynamation 90 / Eastman Color

P–Charles H. Schneer / D–Don Chaffey / W–Jan Read, Beverly Cross / M–Bernard Herrmann / C–Wilkie Cooper / E–Maurice Rootes / PD–Geoffrey Drake / AD–Herbert Smith, Jack Maxsted, Tony Sarzi Braga / SVE–Ray Harryhausen

Cast–Todd Armstrong (Jason), Nancy Kovack (Medea), Gary Raymond (Acastus), Laurence Naismith (Argus), Niall MacGinnis (Zeus), Michael Gwynn (Hermes), Douglas Wilmer (Pelias), Jack Gwillim (King Aeetes), Honor Blackman (Hera), John Cairney (Hylas), Nigel Green (Hercules) with Patrick Troughton, Andrew Faulds, John Crawford, Douglas Robinson

Jason and the Argonauts is so well thought of today that it is difficult to realize that it was not a critical or financial success at the time of its release in 1963. For several years Ray Harryhausen had wanted to do a film based on Greek mythology. The success of previous pictures which featured his special effects animation convinced Columbia Pictures to invest an unheard of $3.5 million in a fantasy project based on the legend of Jason and the

Golden Fleece. The same story had been filmed a few years earlier as *Hercules* but that adaptation of the myth was liberal, to say the least. Harryhausen and producer Charles H. Schneer hoped that their production would be the definitive film version of this tale. The end result does take some liberties with the original myths but it is a far more faithful adaptation than either *Hercules* or *The Giants of Thessaly*. Jason returns to the kingdom of Thessaly to reclaim the throne that was taken from his murdered father by the evil Pelias. Pelias agrees to give up the throne if Jason can procure the mythical Golden Fleece, which is in the land of Colchis. Jason, with the help of the gods of Mount Olympus, acquires a ship and crew to assist him in his quest. Before they can reach Colchis they are faced with a variety of trials and tribulations. On the Isle of Bronze they encounter the bronze giant Talos who wrecks their ship, the *Argo*. In Phrygia they must fight the winged Harpies. While sailing through the Clashing Rocks the ship is nearly destroyed again but the sea god Triton intervenes and saves them. Arriving in Colchis, King Aeetes opposes Jason's attempt to take the Fleece. Medea, a priestess, agrees to help Jason and together they go to the lair of the Hydra, the seven-headed monster that guards the Golden Fleece. Jason kills the beast but before he can escape with his prize, King Aeetes uses magic to transform the Hydra's teeth into an army of skeleton soldiers. Jason and his men manage to defeat the skeletons and set sail, with Medea, back to Thessaly. *Jason and the Argonauts* features some of Ray Harryhausen's finest special effects work. Talos and the skeleton army are especially memorable. Todd Armstrong and Nancy Kovack are a trifle weak in the lead roles of Jason and Medea but the supporting cast is superlative. Nigel Green in particularly good as Hercules. The decision to eschew the standard muscleman interpretation of the character was an inspired one. Bernard Herrmann's score is as exciting as the images it accompanies. Despite these virtues, *Jason and the Argonauts* enjoyed slim success at the American box office. Audiences, saturated with European-filmed mythological epics, failed to take notice of what they must have thought was more of the same. Negative critical response only aggravated the situation. Time has proved both audiences and critics wrong, and *Jason and the Argonauts* has become an enduring classic fantasy film and Ray Harryhausen's masterpiece.

151 *Jason and the Argonauts*

Hallmark Entertainment
NBC TV Network (2000) 139 min.
Color
  P–Robert Halmi, Sr., Robert Halmi, Jr., Dyson Lovell / D–Nick Willing / W–Matthew Faulk, Mark Skeet / M–Simon Boswell / C–Sergi Kozlov / E–Sean Barton / PD–Roger Hall / CD–Carlo Poggioli
  Cast–Jason London (Jason), Dennis Hopper (Pelias), Frank Langella (Aeetes), Natasha Henstridge (Hypsipyle), Derek Jacobi (Phineas), Angus MacFayden (Zeus), Olivia Williams (Hera), Jolene Blalock (Medea), Brian Thompson (Hercules), David Calder (Argos), Adrian Lester (Orpheus) with Tom Harper, Mark Lewis Jones, Diana Kent, James Callis

This lavish television version of the story of Jason and his search for the Golden Fleece is yet another production from the prolific company Hallmark Entertainment. Although it will not dispel memories of the 1963 version it does stand on its own as good entertainment. As a child, Jason sees his treacherous uncle Pelias murder his father and seize his kingdom. With the help of his father's loyal bodyguard, Jason is spirited away to safety. Twenty years later Jason returns to confront Pelias and demand his birthright. Pelias agrees to honor Jason's claim if he can find the legendary Golden Fleece. Jason and his crew set sail on the *Argo* for the land of Colchis where the fleece is the prized possession of the ruler, King Aeetes. The voyage is fraught with dangers including encounters with the sea god Neptune, murderous Amazons, Harpies, a giant mechanical bull and a dragon. Unlike the original version, the story is not built around the effects sequences and thus they have far less impact. These scenes also seem to stop the forward momentum of the plot rather than move it along. The computer generated special effects are impressive but fail to provide the sense of wonder inspired by Ray Harryhausen's creations. The quality of the cast varies greatly. Derek Jacobi and Frank Langella give their usual excellent perfor-

Brian Deacon as *Jesus* is crucified (1979).

mances but Dennis Hopper seems as out of place in this as he does in *Samson and Delilah* (1996). Jason London's main contributions as Jason are bedroom eyes and a mullet haircut.

152 *Jesus*

A Genesis Project Production/An Inspirational
  Films Presentation

Warner Bros. (1979) 117 min.
Color
  P–John Heyman, Richard Dalton/D–Peter Sykes, John Krish/W–Barnet Fishbein/M–Riga (aka Nachum Heiman)/CD–Rochelle Zactzman
  Cast–Brian Deacon (Jesus), Rivka Noiman (Mary), Yossef Shiloah (Joseph), Niko Nitai (Simon Peter), Peter Frye (Pontius Pilate), Eli Danker (Judas Iscariot), Talia Shapira (Mary Magdalene),

Richard Peterson (Herod) with Mosko Alkalai, Kobi Assaf, Eli Cohen, Nisim Gerama, David Goldberg, Miki Mfir, Milo Rafi, Gad Roll

Filmed in Israel and financed by Campus Crusade for Christ International to the tune of $6 million, *Jesus* is described in the opening as "A documentary taken entirely from the Gospel of Luke, Chapters 3–24." While one might quibble about the term "documentary" you could not argue that the film isn't slavishly faithful to its source. As such, it presents the story without elaboration in a totally nonexploitive way but this helps to rob it of the dramatic momentum you usually associate with a motion picture. Instead you have, quite simply, a sermon. After testing 263 Israeli actors for the part of Jesus, producer John Heyman decided to use British actor Brian Deacon, one time husband of celebrity non-entity Rula Lenska. Deacon gives the part as good as he gets but his particular cross to bear is a terrible wig. The remainder of the cast was chosen from the local talent. One of the directors was Peter Sykes who had already made his reputation as a director of British horror films. Surprisingly, this very uncommercial film was given a theatrical release by Warner Bros. Now it is owned by a company called "The Jesus Film Project" and one of their goals is to make *Jesus* the most translated and widely viewed film in history. An 83 minute version of the film is extensively distributed by Christian organizations as a teaching tool.

153 *Jesus*

A Five Mile River Films Ltd/Lube/Lux Vide Production
U.S.–CBS TV Network (2000) 174 min.
Color
   P–Lorenzo Minoli, Judd Parkin, Russell Kagan, Paolo Piria/D–Robert E. Young/W–Suzette Couture/M–Patrick Williams/C–Raffaele Mertes/E–Benjamin Weissman/AD–Paolo Biagetti/CD–Simonetta Leoncini, Giovanni Viti
   Cast–Jeremy Sisto (Jesus), Gary Oldman (Pontius Pilate), Jacqueline Bisset (Mary), Debra Messing (Mary Magdalene), Jeroen Krabbe (Satan), Armin Mueller Stahl (Joseph), David O'Hara (John the Baptist), G.W. Bailey (Livio), Claudio Amendola (Barabbas), Christian Kohlund (Caiaphas), Luca Zingaretti (Peter) with Stefania Rocca, Ian Duncan, Tom Lockyer, Luca Barbareschi, Gilly Gilchrist

With their series of Bible films abandoned by Turner Broadcasting, Lorenzo Minoli and Lube/Lux Vide Productions moved on to greener pastures, and the major networks, with *Jesus: The Epic Mini-Series*. It is always interesting to see the latest "take" on the life of Christ and this one is certainly a mixed bag. Technically it is superior, although much of the color photography has that "golden glow" which permeates these TV biblical movies. The performances range from the excellent (Jacqueline Bisset as Mary) to the awful (G.W. Bailey as Livio). Jeremy Sisto is somewhere in between. His Jesus is a laid back, fun loving guy who just happens to be the Son of God. However, when things start to get serious, he is definitely not one to suffer in silence. The main problem with *Jesus: The Epic Mini-Series* is the laughable quality of some of the dialogue. Here are a few prime examples:

1. PONTIUS PILATE TO A SYCOPHANT: "I love the way you kiss up to me, Livio."

2. JESUS TO THE MULTITUDES: "I need to rest for awhile so please go home."

3. MARY MAGDALENE TO MARY: "Pretty funny, huh? A prostitute afraid of a man."

4. MARY TO JESUS: "Your father would be so proud."
   JESUS: "Which one?"

In addition to these gems some of the scenes are badly conceived. When Jesus chooses his twelve disciples it brings to mind choosing a team for volleyball in high school gym class. Weirdest of all are the sequences with Jeroen Krabbe as Satan dressed in what looks like a black Armani suit. While showing Jesus bleak glimpses of the future he tells him, "Killing for Christ will be a big business through the centuries." Patrick Williams' background score seems to be constantly trying to convince the audience of the importance of what we are watching. It is nevertheless jarring when the score is suddenly replaced by Andrew Lloyd Webber's *Pie Jesu* as Jesus is taken from the cross and put into the tomb. It's as if the producers couldn't decide whether or not to take the subject seriously or make it a pop culture event. The original ending, which was cut for American television, had Jesus in modern dress leading a group of smiling children down a street in present day Rome. The production is dedicated to the memory of Enrico Sabbatini, a frequent collaborator on this series of biblical films.

Washington Post: Quite wonderful ... a golden, flowing work of tremendous power and beauty.

154   *Jesus Christ Superstar*

A Norman Jewison Film (1973) 103 min.
A Universal Pictures and Robert Stigwood Presentation
Todd–AO 35 / Technicolor
P–Norman Jewison, Robert Stigwood / D–Norman Jewison / W–Melvyn Bragg, Norman Jewison / Based on the rock opera by Andrew Lloyd Webber and Tim Rice / Songs: Music by Andrew Lloyd Webber, Lyrics by Tim Rice / C–Douglas Slocombe / E–Antony Gibbs / PD–Richard MacDonald / AD–John Clark / CD–Yvonne Blake

Cast–Ted Neeley (Jesus), Carl Anderson (Judas), Yvonne Elliman (Mary Magdalene), Barry Dennen (Pontius Pilate), Joshua Mostel (Herod), Philip Toubus (Peter), Bob Bingham (Caiaphas), Larry Marshall (Simon Zealotes) with Kurt Yaghjian, Paul Douglas, Robert LuPone, Jonathan Wynne, Richard Molinare, Jeff Hyslop

The original 1969 concept album of *Jesus Christ Superstar* was the first major success for Andrew Lloyd Webber and Tim Rice. It led to stage productions in London's West End and on Broadway. A film version was inevitable but, rather than attempt to copy the stylized vision of antiquity employed in the stage versions, director Norman Jewison chose a different approach. In the film, a busload of hippies arrive in the Holy Land and proceed to enact their version of the last days of Christ. Played out in ancient ruins, the costuming includes both traditional and con-

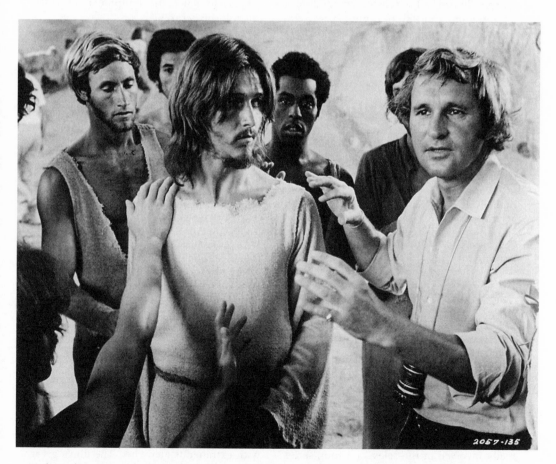

Ted Neeley as Jesus and director Norman Jewison on the set of *Jesus Christ Superstar* (1973).

temporary styles. While Jesus is dressed in the expected white robes, the Roman soldiers wear tank tops, camouflage pants and construction helmets. Some of this works but some of it doesn't. You have to give Norman Jewison credit for trying something different but the concept seems very dated when viewed now. Despite this drawback, the film version of *Jesus Christ Superstar* does have impact, chiefly because of the Webber and Rice songs. Also in 1973 there was a film version of that other contemporary musical about Jesus, *Godspell*. It was directed by David Greene with songs by Stephen Schwartz. While *Jesus Christ Superstar* has merely dated, *Godspell* is virtually unwatchable today. Although Ted Neeley and Carl Anderson continued to play Jesus and Judas in stage productions of *Jesus Christ Superstar* for nearly two decades, some of the other cast members had more diverse careers. Yvonne Elliman had several hit records during the disco era and Philip Toubus, using the name Paul Thomas, became a star and director of hardcore adult films.

AA Nomination: Best Score Adaptation

155   *Jesus of Nazareth*

(Gesu di Nazareth)
An ITC/RAI Co-Production (1977) 371 min.
A Sir Lew Grade Presentation
Color
U.S.–NBC TV Network
   P–Vincenzo Labella/D–Franco Zeffirelli/W–Anthony Burgess, Suso Checchi D'Amico/M–Maurice Jarre/C–Armando Nannuzzi, David Watkin/E–Reginald Mills/PD–Gianni Quaranta/AD–Francesco Fedeli/CD–Marcel Escoffier, Enrico Sabatini
   Cast–Robert Powell (Jesus), Olivia Hussey (Mary), Anthony Quinn (Caiaphas), Michael York (John the Baptist), Anne Bancroft (Mary Magdalene), Ian McShane (Judas), Rod Steiger (Pontius Pilate), James Mason (Joseph of Arimathea), Laurence Olivier (Nicodemus), James Earl Jones (Balthasar) with Ernest Borgnine, Claudia Cardinale, Valentina Cortese, James Farentino, Donald Pleasence, Ralph Richardson, Fernando Rey, Peter Ustinov, Christopher Plummer, Stacy Keach, Ian Holm, Marina Berti, Tony Lo Bianco, Simon MacCorkindale, Oliver Tobias

British entrepreneur Sir Lew Grade was already involved in the television mini-series *Moses the Lawgiver*, starring Burt Lancaster,

when he and producer Vincenzo Labella decided on *Jesus of Nazareth* as a follow-up project. Filmed on location in Morocco and Tunisia, the finished product is the closest anyone has come, so far, to a definitive movie version of the life of Christ. The film's humanized depiction of Jesus was criticized by some at the time of its original release but now it is difficult to understand what the controversy was all about. *Jesus of Nazareth* was first presented as a six-hour event on the NBC television network in April 1977. It was later rerun on NBC, with additional footage, as an eight-hour mini-series. In the United Kingdom it was released as a 180 minute theatrical feature. The movie is filled with interesting performances by an all-star cast but it is actor Robert Powell as Jesus and director Franco Zeffirelli who deserve most of the praise. Together they have succeeded, where so many others have failed, in attempting to bring this difficult subject to life.

156   *Joseph*

A Turner/Lube/Lux Vide/Beta Film/Rai Uno Production
U.S.–TNT Network (1995) 185 min
Color
   P–Gerald Rafshoon, Lorenzo Minoli/D–Roger Young/W–Lionel Chetwynd, James Carrington/M–Marco Frisina/C–Raffaele Mertes/E–Benjamin Weissman/PD–Enrico Sabbatini, Paolo Biagetti/CD–Enrico Sabbatini
   Cast–Paul Mercurio (Joseph), Ben Kingsley (Potiphar), Martin Landau (Jacob), Leslie Anne Warren (Potiphar's Wife), Alice Krige (Rachel), Jamie Glover (Benjamin), Valeria Cavalli (Asenath), Mike Atwell (Judah), Kelly Miller (Tamar), Stefano Dionisi (Pharaoh) with Dominique Sanda, Warren Clarke, Monica Bellucci, Gloria Carlin, Michael Angelis, Vincenzo Nicoli, Colin Bruce, Davide Cincis, Rodolfo Corsato, Pete Lee-Wilson

This entry in the series of Turner TV biblical films won an Emmy for Best Mini-Series. One reason it stands out from the rest of the cycle may be that, unlike the others, there is no classic movie version for comparison. But this is not meant to sell the merits of this production short. The story of Joseph as told in the Bible is an especially detailed one and, for once, the running time does not seem padded with extraneous elements. The film's greatest asset is the presence of Paul Mercurio in the title role. Mercurio had been an Australian dancer and choreographer who starred in the popular film *Strictly Ballroom*. His performance as Joseph is an appealing mixture of innocence and sincerity. The supporting cast is excellent with the exception of Leslie Anne Warren who gives an extremely overwrought performance as Potiphar's unfaithful wife.

The New York Post: A great miniseries! *Joseph* may be the best Bible film ever made.

Variety: The rich Genesis story of Joseph has been turned into an impressively straightforward, persuasive two-night event that may lack bugles and bells, extravagant palaces and armies of extras, but makes up for it with sincerity and restraint.

157   *Joseph and His Brethren*

Columbia (1955) Not Completed
CinemaScope/Technicolor
P–Jerry Wald/D–William Dieterle/W–Louis N. Parker, Clifford Odets, John Lee Mahin/CD–Jean Louis
Cast–Rita Hayworth (Zuleika), Kerwin Mathews (Joseph) with Lee J. Cobb, Joseph Schildkraut

A film version of the biblical account of Joseph had been a pet project of Columbia studio head Harry Cohn for many years. It was touted in the trades as "The most important and costly production in Columbia history." A variety of actors, including Tony Curtis, Frank Sinatra and Jack Lemmon, were under consideration for the lead role but the honor finally fell to Columbia's young contract player Kerwin Mathews. Mathews had recently made his film debut opposite Kim Novak in *Five Against the House*. Rita Hayworth, Columbia's reigning glamour queen, was to play Potiphar's faithless wife Zulieka, with a black wig concealing her famous red tresses. According to studio publicity, director William Dieterle was sent to Egypt with a full production crew where he shot three hours of Technicolor location background footage with 17,500 Egyptian extras. Back in Hollywood, the script was being finished while vast sets were built, using every available space of the Columbia lot. Before principal photography could begin, Cohn and Hayworth had one of their legendary disputes. According to Kerwin Mathews, Hayworth's current hus-

band, Dick Haymes, had designed a diamond necklace for his wife and she insisted on wearing it in the film. Cohen argued that the ancient Egyptians did not have diamond jewelry and that he wanted *Joseph and His Brethren* to be as authentic as possible. Hayworth was also upset that Haymes had not been considered for the part of Joseph and that her request to include former husband Orson Welles in the cast had been denied. As a result, the leading lady walked off the picture and flew to Paris to meet her daughter. Cohn sued for breach of contract. The production was halted and, for the next eighteen months, Harry Cohn and Rita Hayworth battled it out in court. Both Maureen O'Hara and Hedy Lamarr were briefly mentioned as possible replacements for Hayworth but Cohn soon announced that his up and coming new sex goddess, Kim Novak, had been chosen for the part. In 1958, Frank Capra was asked by Cohn to work on script revisions for *Joseph* but, when Cohn died soon afterwards, the project was shelved permanently. It is a pity that the film was never made. Kerwin Mathews has stated that the screenplay was brilliant and the location footage was spectacular. Mathews, an actor whose talent matched his good looks, would have made an ideal Joseph. All in all, the end result was a dreadful waste of some potentially fine elements.

Rita Hayworth makeup test for the unfinished *Joseph and His Brethren* **(1955).**

158 *Joseph and His Brethren*

(Giuseppe Venduto dai Fratelli/Sold into Egypt)
Jolly Films (1961) 103 min
Cinescope/Eastman Color
U.S.–Colorama Features (1963)

P–Ermanno Donati, Luigi Carpentieri/D–Irving Rapper, Luciano Ricci (uncredited)/W–Oreste Biancoli, Ennio De Concini, Guglielmo Santangelo/M–Mario Nascimbene/C–Riccardo Pallottini/E–Mario Serandrei/AD–Oscar D'Amico/CD–Maria De Matteis

Cast–Geoffrey Horne (Joseph), Robert Morley (Potiphar), Belinda Lee (Henet), Carlo Giustini (Reuben), Finlay Currie (Jacob), Arturo Dominici (Rekmira), Robert Rietty (Pharaoh), Marietto (Benjamin–child), Mario Girotti (Benjamin–adult), Vira Silenti (Asenath) with Julian Brooks, Mimo Billi, Marco Guglielmi, Dante De Paolo, Charles Borromel, Helmuth Schneider, Loris Bazzocchi, Antonio Segurini

A silent version of the saga of Joseph entitled *Joseph in the Land of Egypt* was filmed by Thanhouser in 1914. It was directed by Eugene Moore and starred James Cruze and Marguerite Snow. A later attempt by Columbia studios to film a sound version of the story proved to be a costly disaster. It was not until 1961 that a new version was finally completed in Italy. Joseph is the favorite son of his father Jacob. The jealousy of his older brothers is so great that they sell him to a slave trader and tell Jacob that he has been killed by a wild beast. Joseph is taken to Egypt and sold to Potiphar, an official in the court of the pharaoh. Potiphar's young wife, Henet, attempts to seduce Joseph but he rejects her advances. In a fury of frustration, Henet tells her husband that the handsome slave has attempted to rape her. Joseph is thrown into prison where he gains notoriety as an interpreter of dreams. When Pharaoh is troubled by strange dreams, Joseph is asked to decipher the meaning of them. Pharaoh is so impressed by the wisdom and honesty of Joseph that he frees him from prison and names him Viceroy of Egypt. This position of authority eventually enables Joseph to be reunited with his family. Although the production is Italian, the principal stars of *Joseph and His Brethren* are British and the director is an American. Geoffrey Horne is adequate as Joseph and Finlay Currie lends his usual authority as his father Jacob. Belinda Lee plays the type of temptress role she perfected in her all-too-brief screen career. As Potiphar's conniving wife she fairly seethes with pent-up sexuality. Robert Morley as Potiphar is one of the stranger bits of casting within memory. He is wildly out of place and seems to be wondering how he ever got into this picture to begin with. Mario Girotti, who plays Joseph's younger brother Benjamin as an adult, later achieved international fame under the name of Terence Hill. Although the episodic screenplay lacks depth and characterization, it does manage to convey the dramatic highlights of Joseph's life with some degree of success. Far less successful is the quality of the set and costume design. A bit more authenticity in these departments would have elevated *Joseph and His Brethren* into a higher category of motion picture.

Belinda Lee attempts to seduce Geoffrey Horne in *Joseph and His Brethren* (1961).

159 *Judith of Bethulia*

Biograph (1914) 60 min.

P/D–D.W. Griffith/W–Frank Woods/Adapted from the poetical tragedy by Thomas Bailey Aldrich/C–G.W. Bitzer

Cast–Blanche Sweet (Judith), Henry B. Walthall (Holofernes), Mae Marsh (Naomi), Robert Harron (Nathan) with Lillian Gish, Dorothy Gish, Kate Bruce, Alfred Paget, Christy Cabanne, Harry Carey, Gertrude Robinson, Eddy Dillon, C.H. Mailes

The roots of the American epic can be found in this early silent movie made by film pioneer D.W. Griffith. It contains all of the elements that would eventually come to define the epic genre. There are mighty armies, dancing girls, sex, sacrifice and redemption. Made in Chatsworth, California, and Bronx Park, New York, in 1913 for the Biograph Company, the film broke precedent by running four reels instead of the usual two. It also cost the unheard of sum of $36,000. Judith is a wealthy widow who lives in the city of Bethulia. The Assyrian army lead by the great general Holofernes assaults the city walls but cannot penetrate them. Although the people remain safe inside the city, they suffer from thirst and famine. Judith leaves the city and goes to the camp of Holofernes, where she plans to seduce and kill the general. She gains the favor of Holofernes but loses sight of her objective by falling in love with him. She prays to God for guidance and is given a vision of her people slaughtered by the Assyrians. Judith drugs Holofernes' wine and cuts off his head. Distraught over the death of their commander, the Assyrian troops are easily routed and the city is saved. Judith is hailed as the savior of her people but, for her, the praise comes with great personal loss.

160   *Julius Caesar*

Metro-Goldwyn-Mayer (1953) 121 min.
P–John Houseman/D–Joseph L. Mankiewicz/ Based on the play by William Shakespeare/M–Miklos Rozsa/C–Joseph Ruttenberg/E–John Dunning/AD–Cedric Gibbons, Edward Carfagno/CD–Herschel McCoy

Cast–Marlon Brando (Mark Antony), James Mason (Brutus), John Gielgud (Cassius), Louis Calhern (Julius Caesar), Edmond O'Brien (Casca), Greer Garson (Calburnia), Deborah Kerr (Portia), Richard Hale (Soothsayer), Alan Napier (Cicero), John Hoyt (Decius Brutus) with John Doucette, George Macready, Michael Pate, William Cottrell, Douglas Watson, John Hardy, Tom Powers, Ian Wolfe, Lumsden Hare, Michael Ansara, Jack Raine, Douglas Dumbrille, Edmund Purdom

MGM's version of *Julius Caesar* is one of the greatest critical and box office successes ever produced from a Shakespearean source. The play reached the screen with little alteration to the original text and is performed by a high powered cast of very talented players. John Gielgud, in his first American film, is the standout cast member. As Cassius, he brings all the subtlety and nuance to the character that Shakespeare must have intended. At first Marlon Brando may seem an odd choice for Shakespearean tragedy, but he effortless manages to dispel any negative preconceived notions and makes his Mark Antony a memorable characterization. Director Joseph L. Mankiewicz and producer John Houseman decided to dispense with Technicolor and unnecessary spectacle so as not to detract from the drama. The higher aspirations of the producer and director were somewhat tarnished by MGM's exploitative advertising campaign

Poster art for the 1953 version of *Julius Caesar*.

The 1970 version of *Julius Caesar* featured an all-star cast.

which luridly proclaimed, "Thrill to blood feuds ... spectacle ... golden-haired beauties in a pagan land ... ruthless men and their goddess like women in a sin-swept era."

AA Nominations—Best Picture, Best Actor (Marlon Brando), Musical Score, B/W CInematography, B/W Art Direction*

Time: The best Shakespeare that Hollywood has yet produced. Deserves three rousing cheers.

Motion Picture: Though it may be a bit premature to shout Academy Award, still one has an irresistible urge to say it in connection with the superior acting, expert and detailed production of Shakespeare's *Julius Caesar.*

161   *Julius Caesar*

Commonwealth United/American-International (1970) 117 min.
Panavision/Technicolor

P–Peter Snell/D–Stuart Burge/Based on the play by William Shakespeare Adapted by Robert Furnival/M–Michael Lewis/C–Ken Higgins/E–Eric Boyd-Perkins/PD–Julia Trevelyan Oman/AD–Maurice Pelling/CD–Robin Archer

Cast–Charlton Heston (Mark Antony), Jason Robards, Jr. (Brutus), John Gielgud (Julius Caesar), Richard Chamberlain (Octavius), Robert Vaughn (Casca), Richard Johnson (Cassius), Diana Rigg (Portia), Christopher Lee (Artemidorus), Jill Bennett (Calpurnia) with Alan Browning, Norman Bowler, Andrew Crawford, Peter Eyre, Michael Gough, Derek Godfrey

Charlton Heston has had a lengthy professional association with the character of Mark Antony. In 1947 he had a minor part in a stage production of *Antony and Cleopatra*, starring Catherine Cornell. Heston next played the part of Cinna in an early television adaptation of *Julius Caesar* on "Studio One" for CBS. In 1950 he graduated to the starring role of Antony in a 16mm version of *Julius Caesar*, directed by David Bradley in Chicago for $11,000. When he undertook the role of Antony in a new motion picture adaptation of the play in 1970 he was obviously no stranger to the part. John Gielgud, who had played Cassius in the 1953 film version, was now given the opportunity to assay the title role. The supporting cast was made up of a competent array of stars, but after an impressive credit sequence it soon becomes apparent that an all-star cast can do little to save this version of Shakespeare's tragedy. No one could compete with Jason Robards' dreadful portrayal of Brutus. It is certainly one of the worst renditions of a Shakespearean character ever foisted on an unsuspecting public. Orson Welles had been the first choice for the role but was passed over in favor of Robards. The company soon had reason to regret this decision as Robards continually missed rehearsals, refused to mount a horse, and held up production due to illness. Robards' performance aside, the film is interesting but not in the same league as the earlier MGM version. Several of the performances are worth noting. Richard Johnson is outstanding as Cassius and Richard Chamberlain gets one of his first opportunities to show off his acting abilities as something other than Dr. Kildare. A considerable amount of male and female nudity was filmed and highly publicized prior to the film's release but this was not included in the version released in America.

162 *Jupiter's Darling*

Metro-Goldwyn-Mayer (1955) 96 min.
CinemaScope/Eastman Color

P–George Wells/D–George Sydney/W–Dorothy Kingsley/Based on the play *Road to Rome* by Robert E. Sherwood/Songs: Music by Burton Lane, Lyrics by Harold Adamson/C–Paul C. Vogel, Charles Rosher/E–Ralph E. Winters/AD–Cedric Gibbons, Urie McCleary/CD–Helen Rose, Walter Plunkett

Cast–Esther Williams (Amytis), Howard Keel (Hannibal), Marge Champion (Meta), Gower Champion (Varius), George Sanders (Fabius Maximus), William Demarest (Mago), Richard Hayden (Horatio), Michael Ansara (Marharbal), Douglas Dumbrille (Scipio), Norma Varden (Fabia), with Henry Corden, Martha Wentworth, John Olszewski

Jupiter's Darling was MGM's attempt to fuse the type of film the studio did best (the musical) with the type of film currently in vogue (the epic). Unfortunately, the picture doesn't really work as either and must be considered a curiosity, at best, or a disaster, at worst. The plot reduces Hannibal's invasion of Rome to comic highjinks, punctuated with a few musical numbers. On the plus side, Howard Keel makes a splendid Hannibal and Marge and Gower Champion contribute some energetic dance routines. Typically, for MGM, the production is a sumptuous one. The sets and costumes are as stunning as one would expect, given the talent involved. On the negative side, the songs are totally unmemorable; a real problem for a musical. Excuses for Esther Williams to show off her swimming abilities seem even more contrived than usual. The film was such a resounding flop that it finished Williams' career at MGM. George Sanders' musical numbers were cut from the finished film. When viewing these outtakes, Sanders looks extremely uncomfortable while singing, but valiantly carries on with his usual degree of professionalism.

Screen Stories: Sprawling, lavish musical presents Howard Keel as the conqueror Hannibal.

David (Richard Gere) makes love to Bathsheba (Alice Krige) in *King David* (1985).

163 *King David*

Paramount (1985) 113 min.
Panavision/Technicolor
P–Martin Elfand/D–Bruce Beresford/W–Andrew Birkin, James Costigan/Based on the books of Samuel I and II, Chronicles I, and the Psalms of David/M–Carl Davis/C–Donald McAlpine/E–William Anderson/PD–Ken Adam/AD–Terry Auckland-Snow/CD–John Mollo
Cast–Richard Gere (David), Edward Woodward (Saul), Alice Krige (Bathsheba), Cherie Lunghi (Michal), Jack Klaff (Jonathan), Gina Bellman (Tamar), James Combs (Ammon), Dennis Quilley (Samuel), Niall Buggy (Nathan), Hurd Hatfield (Ahimelech), Tim Woodward (Joab), John Castle (Abner), Luigi Montefiore (Goliath) with Christo-

pher Malcolm, Simon Dutton, Jean Marc-Barr

Bruce Beresford and Edward Woodward, director and star respectively of the successful Australian film *Breaker Morant* (1979), reteamed for this version of the Old Testament account of the life of David, the shepherd boy who became the king of the Israelites. The first half of the film is a nearly scene-for-scene recapitulation of Marcello Baldi's *Saul and David*. This is no doubt unintentional and due to the fact that both films adhere very closely to the books of Samuel on which they are based. This is also the best developed portion of *King David*. The screenplay provides excellent character conflict and motivation and Edward Woodward is outstanding in his complex portrayal of the tormented King Saul. With the death of Saul the story loses momentum. A good cast, capable direction and excellent production values simply cannot compete with the miscasting of Richard Gere in the title role. Gere approaches the part as if he were appearing in a film set in contemporary times and not in the Israel of 975 B.C. When the focus becomes his reign as the troubled monarch, the film flounders badly and the narrative becomes confused. Even David's love for Bathsheba is given short shrift and seems to be a passionless affair. Alice Krige's considerable talent and unusual beauty are totally wasted in the brief footage devoted to Bathsheba. Despite these pitfalls, director Beresford successfully depicts the barbarity and violence of these ancient times, avoiding the whitewashed treatment often accorded to biblical personages. Assistant director Victor Tourjansky was involved in a number of European epics during the early sixties.

164 The King of Kings

Pathé Exchange Inc. (1927) 115 min.

P/D–Cecil B. DeMille/W–Jeanie Macpherson/ M–Hugh Riesenfeld/C–J. Peverell Marley/E–Anne Bauchens, Harold McLernon

Cast–H. B. Warner (Jesus), Dorothy Cumming (Mary), Jacqueline Logan (Mary Magdalene), Joseph Schildkraut (Judas), Ernest Torrance (Peter), Rudolph Schildkraut (Caiaphas), James Neill (James), Joseph Stiker (John), Victor Varconi (Pontius Pilate), Julia Faye (Martha), Robert Edeson (Matthew), Sidney D'Albrook (Thomas), David Imboden (Andrew), Charles Belcher (Philip) with Clayton Packard, Robert Ellsworth, Charles Requa, John T. Prince, Casson Ferguson, Sam De-Grasse, Mabel Coleman, Montague Love, William Boyd, George Seigmann, Theodore Kosloff

In 1924 Adolph Zukor attempted to renegotiate Cecil B. DeMille's contract with Paramount Pictures, hoping to curb the extravagant spending of the profligate director. The result was the cancellation of his contract entirely. DeMille wasted no time in purchasing the Thomas Ince Studios and was soon producing and directing films under the moniker of DeMille Studios. His third venture as an independent producer became what many consider to be his finest film, *The King of Kings*. It is certainly the most subdued of his religious subjects, although he is unable to completely divest himself of his usual tendencies toward exaggeration. *The King of Kings* opens with an elaborate party at the home of Mary Magdalene who is portrayed as an exotic courtesan in love with Judas. When she learns of her lover's devotion to Jesus she sets out, in her zebra-drawn chariot, to see for herself what has inspired his adoration. With the exception of these opening sequences, the film is reverent and seldom subject to the typical DeMille excesses. The remainder of the movie offers a fairly straightforward representation of the four Gospels, ending with the Resurrection, in two-strip Technicolor. H.B. Warner is everything DeMille had hoped his cinematic Christ would be, compassionate and tender but also exuding a powerful feeling of strength and wisdom. Warner's interpretation of Jesus has seldom been equaled in subsequent motion pictures. Although it became one of his most widely viewed films, DeMille never earned a monetary profit from *The King of Kings*. All of his proceeds were donated to charity. DeMille gained his reward from the thousands of letters he received throughout the next thirty years from people who loved *The King of Kings*.

Variety: The King Of Kings will live forever, on the screen and in memory.

New York Times: This production is entitled *The King of Kings*, and it is, in fact, the most impressive of all motion pictures.

165 King of Kings

Metro-Goldwyn-Mayer (1961) 168 min.
Super Technirama 70/Technicolor

P–Samuel Bronston/D–Nicholas Ray/W–Philip Yordan/M–Miklos Rozsa/C–Frank F. Planer, Milton Krasner, Manuel Berenguer/E–Harold Kress/ AD/CD–Georges Wakhevitch

Cast–Jeffrey Hunter (Jesus), Siobhan McKenna (Mary), Hurd Hatfield (Pontius Pilate), Ron Randell (Lucius), Viveca Lindfors (Claudia), Rita Gam (Herodias), Carmen Sevilla (Mary Magdalene), Brigid Bazlen (Salome), Rip Torn (Judas), Robert Ryan (John the Baptist), Harry Gardino (Barabbas), Frank Thring (Herod Antipas), Guy Rolfe (Caiaphas), Royal Dano (Peter) with Gregoire Aslan, Maurice Marsac, Eric Connor, George Coulouris, Conrado San Martin, Gerard Tichy, Luis Prendes, Jose Antonio, Jose Nieto

When Samuel Bronston first announced his intentions to produce a film about the life of Christ it was to be directed and written by John Farrow and entitled *The Son of Man*. The final result, *King of Kings*, was made without Farrow and became the first of Samuel Bronston's mega spectaculars. For a time it seemed that Bronston might assume the mantle of "Master Showman" that had been worn by Cecil B. DeMille, but Bronston's films never proved to be the tremendous crowd pleasers that DeMille's had been. Apart from the title, the 1961 version of *King of Kings* bears little resemblance to the 1927 DeMille film. DeMille chose to focus on the final episodes in the life of Christ. This version presents an overall view of the political climate at the time of Christ and the effect that his life and death had on the people, from peasant to potentate. Director Nicholas Ray, best known for his hard hitting studies in realism, succeeds in creating an uncompromising representation of the conflicts between the Jews and the Romans. At the time of its release, the film was derisively referred to by critics as "I Was a

Nicholas Ray directs Brigid Bazlen (as Salome) on the set of *King of Kings* (1961).

Teenage Jesus" due to the casting of Jeffrey Hunter. When viewed today it is difficult to imagine what all the complaints were about as Hunter gives a fine performance in what is generally considered an unplayable role. Who could ever attempt to portray Jesus and realize everyone's expectations? Other outstanding cast members are Siobhan McKenna as the gentle Mary, and Robert Ryan, who gives the screen's best portrayal of John the Baptist thus far. Harry Guardino, as Barabbas, is the weakest member of the cast. Perhaps the film's greatest casting coup is Brigid Bazlen as Salome. Admittedly, her acting leaves much to be desired but, at 16, she is the perfect age for the role, and her infamous dance is convincingly wanton. The dance was choreographed by Nicholas Ray's wife Betty Utey. All of the sequences involving the sybaritic court of Herod are quite memorable. Georges Wakhevitch's set and costume designs help to reinforce the suffocating atmosphere that permeates these scenes. The dissolute nobility seems trapped in their palace just as the birds are trapped in the golden cages which decorate the sets. Spoiled and jaded to the point of boredom, Bazlen's Salome personifies the results of this corrupt society. One of the dramatic highlights of *King of Kings* is the Sermon on the Mount which took 21 days to film and employed over 7,000 extras. Upon completion of filming, MGM thought the finished picture was slow moving and excessively long. Against the wishes of both the producer and the director, the studio cut the film. The incoherent result forced MGM to enlist the services of writer Ray Bradbury to write a narration (spoken by Orson Welles) to bridge some of the gaps left by the editing. *King of Kings* was only moderately successful at the box office and a disappointed MGM refused to participate in future Bronson projects. As an independent producer, Samuel Bronston went on to become a major force in the production of epic films, creating two masterpieces of the genre, *El Cid* and *The Fall of the Roman Empire*.

Silver Screen: Already this picture has been much criticized for certain omissions and additions, but the average moviegoer should certainly find this well worthwhile despite the slowness and occasional stiffening by the starch of misdirected piety.

Cosmopolitan: A mammoth spectacle of biblical times. The large cast plays with varying distinction in a series of visually striking, frequently stilted tableaux.

Show Business Illustrated: An erratically directed but beautifully staged story of Christ, played by a wooden faced Jeffrey Hunter.

166   *King Richard and the Crusaders*

Warner Bros. (1954) 114 min.
CinemaScope / WarnerColor
P–Henry Blake / D–David Butler / W–John Twist / Based on *The Talisman* by Sir Walter Scott / M–Max Steiner / C–J. Peverell Marley / E–Irene Morra / AD–Bertram Tuttle / CD–Marjorie Best

Cast–Rex Harrison (Ilderim / Saladin), Virginia Mayo (Lady Edith), George Sanders (King Richard), Laurence Harvey (Sir Kenneth), Robert Douglas (Sir Giles), Michael Pate (Conrad), Paula Raymond (Queen Berengaria) with Lester Matthews, Anthony Eustrel, Henry Corden, Wilton Graff, Nejla Ates, Nick Cravat, Leslie Bradley, Bruce Lester, Mark Dana, Peter Ortiz

King Richard and the Crusaders was the first (and worst!) of Warner Bros. early CinemaScope epics. Following in the hoofprints of MGM's *Knights of the Round Table* and Fox's *Prince Valiant*, Warner's entry was a poor imitation. King Richard of England goes to the Holy Land to drive out the heathen Saracens led by Saladin. Dissent leads to treachery among his allies and only the valiant Sir Kenneth of Scotland proves to be a loyal subject. Saladin falls in love with a beautiful infidel, but, unlike DeMille's version, it is not Queen Berengaria. Instead, her companion, Lady Edith, is the object of his affections, despite the fact that she and Sir Kenneth are in love. Once again, the battle of faiths is reduced to a love triangle. The film is very studio bound and the few exteriors are all too obviously filmed in California. George Sanders, Laurence Harvey and Virginia Mayo, generally competent actors, give perfectly dreadful performances. Rex Harrison survives by not seeming to take himself, or the film, too seriously. George Sanders, as Richard the Lion-Hearted, is a far cry from Henry Wilcoxon in *The Crusades* and, for all its flaws, the DeMille film is superior in almost every respect. This should indicated the quality of *King Richard and the Crusaders* since *The Crusades* is one of DeMille's weakest efforts. Max Steiner contributes a score reminiscent of the many he composed for Errol Flynn films and it is one of the best things about this movie.

Hollywood Reporter: Fills the breadth of the CinemaScope screen with a wealth of pagentry—an ace entertainment!

Lady Edith (Virginia Mayo) is loved by Saladin (Rex Harrison) in *King Richard and the Crusaders* (1954).

Motion Picture Daily: A very big picture, a very fast and fascinating picture, with one of the most exciting final sequences ever contrived.

167   *Kings of the Sun*

A Mirisch Company Presentation
United Artists (1964) 108 min.
Panavision/Color by DeLuxe
  P–Lewis J. Rachmill/D–J. Lee Thompson/W–Elliott Arnold, James R. Webb/M–Elmer Bernstein/C–Joseph MacDonald/E–William Reynolds/AD–Alfred Ybarra/CD–Norma Koch
  Cast–Yul Brynner (Black Eagle), George Chakiris (Balam), Shirley Anne Field (Ixchel), Richard Basehart (Ah Min), Brad Dexter (Ah Haleb), Barry Morse (Ah Zok), Armando Silvestre (Isatai), Leo Gordon (Hunac Ceel), Victoria Vetri (Ixzubin) with Rudy Solari, Ford Rainey, Angel Di Steffano, Jose Moreno

The great Mayan empire at Chichen Iza is attacked by the fierce army of Hunac Ceel.

The Mayan king is killed and his young son, Balam, must lead his people to safety. They go to the sea where a coastal tribe joins them in their flight. Balam and the Mayans sail north across the Gulf of Mexico and eventually land on the shore of a new world. In this land they build a village and begin construction of a pyramid, under the watchful eyes of a local Indian tribe led by their chief, Black Eagle. Believing that his land is being invaded, Black Eagle goes to Balam and challenges him to a fight. Black Eagle is badly wounded and taken captive by the Mayans. Ixchel, a beautiful young woman whom Balam loves, nurses Black Eagle back to health and falls in love with him. The Mayan priests want to sacrifice Black Eagle to their gods but Balam intervenes and sets the Indian free. The two tribes live in peace until Balam's jealousy over Ixchel causes a rift between them. Hunac Ceel and his army attack the new Mayan village

George Chakiris is an unlikely Mayan prince in *Kings of the Sun* (1964).

and Black Eagle and his tribe help the Mayans to defeat the invaders. During the battle Black Eagle is mortally wounded and Balam and Ixchel are reunited. *Kings of the Sun* is unique in its choice of subject matter. Obviously the producers were trying to do something different but the screenwriters were not up to the task. While the visuals are often compelling the story is not and poor Yul Brynner is given some of the most unspeakable dialogue of his career. One line in particular about Indian babies leading buffalos around by their noses is awful once but the script has him repeat it again! When watching *Kings of the Sun* it's best just to close your ears and take in the scenery, which is often spectacular.

168 *Knights of the Round Table*

Metro-Goldwyn-Mayer (1954) 115 min.
CinemaScope / Technicolor

P–Pandro S. Berman / D–Richard Thorpe / W–Talbot Jennings, Jan Lustig, Noel Langley / Based on *Le Morte d'Arthur* by Sir Thomas Malory / M–Miklos Rozsa / C–F.A. Young, Stephen Dade / E–Frank Clarke / AD–Alfred Junge, Hans Peters / CD–Robert Furse

Cast–Robert Taylor (Lancelot), Ava Gardner (Guinevere), Mel Ferrer (King Arthur), Anne Crawford (Morgan Le Fay), Stanley Baker (Modred), Felix Aylmer (Merlin), Maureen Swanson (Elaine), Gabriel Woolf (Percival), Anthony Forwood (Gareth), Robert Urquhart (Gawain), with Ann Hanslip, Niall MacGinnis, Jill Clifford, Stephen Vercoe

MGM's first CinemaScope motion picture was a follow-up to their enormously successful version of *Ivanhoe* (1952), which also starred Robert Taylor. Like its predecessor, *Knights of the Round Table* was produced in the United Kingdom to utilize some of MGM's British funds. The film was given the lavish production usually associated with MGM's product, with the added bonus of some breathtaking location photography in England and Ireland but, unfortunately, the quality of the script was not equal to the quality of the scenery. The potential for romance and passion inherent in the legend of King Arthur is almost completely lacking. Robert Taylor

The legendary lovers Guinevere and Lancelot as played by Ava Gardner and Robert Taylor in *Knights of the Round Table* (1954).

and Ava Gardner are more polite than passionate as the famous lovers Lancelot and Guinevere. Taylor looks too old for the part of the dashing young knight. The role might better have gone to Stewart Granger, another member of the MGM talent stable. Ava Gardner is gorgeous as Guinevere but she seems uncomfortable in the medieval costuming. *Knights of the Round Table* best succeeds as a storybook spectacle. The battles and jousting matches are given far more footage than the love affair and, consequently, it is these scenes you come away remembering. Maureen Swanson, as the tragic Elaine, is responsible for whatever pathos the film possesses.

AA Nomination: Best Sound

Motion Picture: Pageantry at its best is the word for this CinemaScope spectacle. Rousing battle scenes and arresting jousts add excitement to the film.

169   *Knives of the Avenger*

(I Coltelli del Vendicatore / Viking Massacre)
Sider Films (1966) 85 min.
Techniscope / Technicolor
U.S.–World Entertainment Corp. (1967)

P–P. Tagliferri / D–John Hold (Mario Bava) / W–Mario Bava, Alberto Liberati, Giorgio Simonelli, Giovanni Simonelli / M–Marcello Giombini / C–Antonio Rinaldi / E–Otello Colangeli / AD–Alberto Tavazzi / CD–Giorgio Desideri

Cast–Cameron Mitchell (Rurik), Elissa Pichelli (Karin), Fausto Tozzi (Aghen), Giacomo Rossi Stuart (Harald), Luciano Polletin (Moki) with Renato Terra, Amedeo Trilli

A band of vengeful Vikings returns to the village from which they have been exiled. Their leader is Aghen, who is seeking Karin, the wife of King Harald. Three years before, Harald sailed off to war and has not returned. Heeding the advice of a soothsayer, Karin and

Cameron Mitchell shows Luciano Polletin how to throw a dagger in *Knives of the Avenger* (1967).

Joan Collins is a scheming princess out to seduce the pharaoh (Jack Hawkins) in *Land of the Pharaohs* (1955).

her son Moki are living in hiding away from the village. A lone rider on horseback befriends the mother and son and fights to protect them from the evil Aghen. The stranger is Rurik, once leader of a rival tribe who invaded Harald's village. During that raid, Rurik wounded Harald and raped Karin. Repentant, he has returned to try and right this wrong and see the boy who may be his son. Mario Bava's second Viking movie isn't nearly as inventive or exciting as his first. The atmospheric sets and colorful lighting effects of *Erik the Conqueror* are replaced by location filming in all-too-familiar Italian locales. The plot of *Knives of the Avenger* has sometimes been compared to *Shane*. The film does seem like a Western in Viking garb. The background score has a Western flavor and there is even a showdown, with knives instead of six-shooters. Not the best Bava film but of more than passing interest to his legion of admirers.

170   *Land of the Pharaohs*

A Continental Company Production
Warner Bros. (1955) 104 min.
CinemaScope/WarnerColor
   P/D–Howard Hawks/W–William Faulkner, Harry Kurnitz, Harold Jack Bloom/M–Dimitri Tiomkin/C–Lee Garmes, Russell Harlan/E–V. Sagovsky/AD–Alexander Trauner/CD–Mayo
   Cast–Jack Hawkins (Khufu), Joan Collins (Nellifer), Dewey Martin (Senta), Alexis Minotis (Hamar), James Robertson Justice (Vashtar), Luisa Boni (Kyra), Sydney Chaplin (Treneh), Kerima (Nailla) with James Hayter, Piero Giagnoni

   Howard Hawks confessed he had little affection for this mammoth production about the building of the Great Pyramid. Despite three screenwriters, including famed novelist William Faulkner, Hawks complained that he "didn't know how a Pharaoh talks." Actually in the person of Jack Hawkins, he talks very well indeed. *Land of the Pharaohs* is a largely fictitious account of the reign of the pharaoh

Khufu (also known as Cheops) and his betrayal by a treacherous concubine. The filming of this story was one of the largest endeavors attempted by a motion picture studio up to that time. Sixteen CinemaScope cameras were sent to Egypt, accompanied by "the largest location crew ever sent abroad from Hollywood." The end result is an entertaining and eye-filling motion picture. By dealing with an earlier period in Egyptian history than most films of this type, *Land of the Pharaohs* has a unique look and atmosphere. Howard Hawks takes full advantage of the Cinema-Scope screen and at every opportunity fills it with marvelous images and spectacular vistas. One scene alone employed over 9,000 extras. The principal players are good with the exception of Hawks' regular, Dewey Martin, who looks and acts like a fifties matinee idol. Joan Collins foreshadows her later role in the television series *Dynasty*. In the part of Nellifer, an evil princess from the island of Cyprus, she gains the Pharaoh's favor and then plots to take over his throne. To obtain her objective she lies, cheats and murders. The justly famous climax finds her entombed alive within the pyramid in payment for her perfidy. Dimitri Tiomkin provides an appropriately exotic background score. Interiors were filmed at Cinecitta Studios in Rome.

Motion Picture: A marvelous opening spectacle catches the whole sense of the strange, magnificent splendor that was Egypt. The story's dramatic enough, but it can't compare to the magic of an ancient time so well recreated.

171   The Last Days of Pompeii

(Gli Ultimi Giorni di Pompei)
Film d'Arte Italiano (1913) 87 min.
    P–Ernesto Maria Pasquali/D–Mario Caserini/W–Arrigo Frusta/Based on the novel by Edward Bulwer-Lytton/CD–Samperoni and Gentil
    Cast–Fernanda Negri Pouget (Nydia), Eugenia Tettoni Fior (Ione), Ubaldo Stefani (Glaucus), Antonio Grisanti (Arbaces), Cesare Giani-Carini (Apoecides), Vitale Di Stefano (Claudius)

The blind slave girl Nydia is hopelessly in love with the Roman patrician Glaucus. Glaucus, however, only has eyes for the beautiful Ione. Abraces, the High Priest of Isis, also covets Ione. He uses the jealousy of Nydia to concoct a plot to get rid of Glaucus and take Ione for his own. It all comes to a climax in the arena of Pompeii where Glaucus is to be sacrificed to the lions. The convenient eruption of Mount Vesuvius saves Glaucus. Nydia sacrifices herself to help Glaucus and Ione escape from the doomed city. The first feature length version of Edward Bulwer-Lytton's novel is notable for its impressive sets and costumes. The direction in the early part of the film is fairly static but the action sequences at the end are quite sophisticated for the time. The story was filmed again in Italy in 1926 starring Maria Corda as Nydia and Victor Varkoni as Glaucus. This version was directed by Carmine Gallone and Amleto Palmeri.

172   The Last Days of Pompeii

A Merian C. Cooper Production
R.K.O. (1935) 100 min.
    P–Merian C. Cooper/D–Ernest B. Schoedsack/W–Ruth Rose, Boris Ingster/M–Roy Webb/C–J. Roy Hunt/E–Archie F. Marshek/AD–Van Nest Polglase/CD–Aline Bernstein/SVE–Willis O'Brien
    Cast–Preston Foster (Marcus), Alan Hale (Burbix), Basil Rathbone (Pontius Pilate), John Wood (Flavius as a man), Louis Calhern (Prefect), David Holt (Flavius as a boy), Dorothy Wilson (Clodia), Wyrley Birch (Leaster), Gloria Shea (Julia), Frank Conroy (Gaius), Edward Van Sloan (Clavus), William V. Mong (Cleon) with Murray Kinnell, Henry Kolker, John Davidson, Ziffie Tilbury

Following the tremendous success of his production of *King Kong* (1933), Merian C. Cooper began to plan his next motion picture. Having recently visited the ruined city of Pompeii on his honeymoon, Cooper decided to produce a film which would climax with the eruption of Mount Vesuvius. R.K.O. gave him the go-ahead and a budget of $1 million— a general budget that would enable him to use the newly developed three-strip Technicolor process. Borrowing the title of the famous Bulwer-Lytton novel *The Last Days of Pompeii*, but not the plot, Ruth Rose, wife of director Ernest B. Schoedsack, fashioned an original screenplay. Before filming could commence the R.K.O. executives informed Cooper that the budget had been cut in half. Consequently, several proposed sequences were scrapped and Cooper was forced to use black and white photography instead of color. Preston Foster portrays Marcus, an honest blacksmith who becomes an embittered and ruthless gladiator after his wife and child are killed in an accident. His adopted son Flavius finally shows Marcus that the way to truth and salvation is through Jesus. Unfortunately, to get to this point is a rather long and tedious haul enlivened considerably by Basil Rathbone's wonderful performance as Pontius Pilate. The climactic eruption of Mount Vesuvius makes the wait worthwhile as it provides an excellent opportunity for special effects genius Willis O'Brien to show his stuff. The collapse of the gigantic colossus in the arena is especially impressive but even more complex, from a technical standpoint, was the destruction of the Temple of Jupiter. Twenty effects technicians

operated the wires and rods which brought the temple down as the action was captured by four high speed cameras. Weeks of preparation paid off and the difficult effect was accomplished without a hitch.

173   The Last Days of Pompeii

(Gli Ultimi Giorni di Pompei)
Cineproduzione, Rome–Procusa, Madrid–Transocean, Monaco
(1959) 103 min.
Supertotalscope / Eastman Color
U.S.–United Artists (1960)
   P–Paolo Moffa / D–Mario Bonnard / W–Ennio De Concini, Sergio Leone, Duccio Tessari, Sergio Corbucci / Based on the novel by Edward Bulwer-Lytton / M–Angelo Francesco Lavagnino / C–Antonio Ballesteros / E–Eraldo Da Roma / AD–Ramiro Gomez / CD–Vittorio Rossi

Angel Aranda and Steve Reeves are involved in a dispute during *The Last Days of Pompeii* (1960).

Cast–Steve Reeves (Glaucus), Christine Kaufmann (Ione), Barbara Carroll (Nydia), Anne-Marie Baumann (Julia), Fernando Rey (Arbaces), Mimmo Palmara (Gallinus), Angel Aranda (Antonius), Guillermo Marin (Askinius), Mino Doro (Consul) with Mario Morales, Angel Ortiz, Lola Torres, Mario Berriatua, Ignazio Dolce

Glaucus, a Roman centurion, returns from the wars to his home in Pompeii and discovers that a marauding gang has burned his home and killed his father. Julia, the beautiful mistress of the Roman consul, has joined forces with the evil High Priest of Isis in an attempt to take control of the city. Together they have organized the terrorist raids and conspired to put the blame on the Christians. Glaucus falls in love with a Christian girl named Ione. When she is sentenced to death in the arena he intervenes to save her life. The eruption of Mount Vesuvius provides an opportunity for their escape, as the dissolute city is destroyed around them. This is one of the better films of its type and the most entertaining version of this oft-filmed story. The screenplay uses some of the characters from the Bulwer-Lytton novel but very little of the plot. Spaghetti Western director Sergio Leone had a hand in the screenplay and was also the Second Unit Director. Leone completed the filming when Mario Bonnard became ill. Unlike many of the peplum films, *The Last Days of Pompeii* makes a definite attempt at authenticity. One-sixteenth of the original city of Pompeii was recreated. Many of the sets are identical to the narrow streets and modest buildings which are still standing there. Only the Temple of Isis is greatly exaggerated, the original being far smaller than the imposing edifice shown in the film. Not forgetting that this is a Steve Reeves movie, much time is spent on physical feats of strength, which include an underwater battle with a crocodile and a gladiatorial combat in the arena.

The volcanic eruption is impressive, but not up to Willis O'Brien's work in the 1935 version. More than twenty years after its original release, *The Last Days of Pompeii* was reissued in Europe, under the title of *Cataclysm*, with Sensurround sound effects.

174   *The Last Days of Pompeii*

A David Gerber/Centerpoint/Rai Radiotelevisione Italiana Production
Columbia Pictures Television
ABC TV network (1984) 329 min.
Color
   P–Richard Irving, William Hill/D–Peter Hunt/W–Carmen Culver/Based on the novel by Edward Bulwer-Lytton/M–Trevor Jones/C–Jack Cardiff/E–Bill Blunden, Richard Marder, Michael Ellis/PD–Michael Stringer/CD–Anthony Mendleson
   Cast–Duncan Regehr (Lydon), Nicholas Clay (Glaucus), Ned Beatty (Diomed), Leslie-Anne Down (Chloe), Linda Purl (Nydia), Olivia Hussey (Ione), Ernest Borgnine (Marcus), Brian Blessed (Olinthus) Franco Nero (Arbaces), Laurence Olivier (Gaius), Anthony Quayle (Quintus), Siobhan McKenna (Fortunata) with Tony Anholt, Joyce Blair, Peter Cellier, Barry Stokes, Marilu Tolo, Stephen Greif, Catriona MacColl, Brian Croucher, Willoughby Goddard, Michael Quill

Publicity artwork for the television mini-series *The Last Days of Pompeii* (1984).

Lydon the gladiator loves the blind slave girl Nydia who loves Glaucus the Greek who loves Ione, future priestess in the Temple of Isis. Overshadowing all of their lives is the evil Arbaces, High Priest of Isis. It takes an erupting volcano to sort things out in this unnecessarily prolonged but fairly interesting version of the famous novel. Originally shown as a seven-hour "ABC Novel for Television" a 144 minute version was later released to video. The all-star cast provides several interesting performances, in particular Franco Nero, who is uncharacteristically cast as the villain, and Leslie-Anne Down as a sympathetic prostitute. Ned Beatty, on the other hand, is simply awful as a social climbing fish merchant. Duncan Regehr provides the requisite beefcake as a kindhearted gladiator.

175　*The Last of the Vikings*

(L'Ultimo dei Vichinghi)
A Galatea-Tiberius-Omnia Film (1961) 102 min.

Dyaliscope/Eastman Color
U.S.–A Samuel Schneider Presentation
Medallion (1962)

P–Roberto Capitani, Luigi Mondello/D–Giacomo Gentilomo/W–Luigi Mondello, Arpad De Riso, Guido Zurili/M–Roberto Nicolosi/C–Enzo Serafin/E–Gino Talamo/AD–Saverio D'Eugenio

Cast–Cameron Mitchell (Harald), Edmund Purdom (Sven), Isabelle Corey (Hilde), Helen Remy (Elga), Aldo Bufi Landi (Londborg), Andrea Aureli (Haakon), Giorgio Ardisson (Guntar), Carla Calo (Herta), Nando Tamberlani (Gultred), Corrado Annicelli (Godrun), Piero Lulli (Hardac)

Once again Cameron Mitchell and Giorgio Ardisson are Viking brothers (see *Erik the Conqueror*), but this time they are on the same side. Together they oppose the treacherous Sven who has killed their father and proclaimed himself King of Norway. Only one of the siblings survives to kill Sven and reclaim his father's kingdom. Cameron Mitchell enacts the first of several Viking roles as the elder brother, Harald. This inexpensively produced attempt to cash in on the success of *The*

Giorgio Ardisson, Cameron Mitchell and their friends are *The Last of the Vikings* (1962).

Vikings (1958) is exciting and can hold its own as entertainment but lacks the scope of the Richard Fleischer film or the imagination of Mario Bava's *Erik the Conqueror*. Bava reportedly directed additional sequences for *The Last of the Vikings* but is uncredited.

176 *The Last Roman*

(Kampf um Rom; Struggle for Rome)
C.C.C. Filmkunst, Berlin (1968) 187 min.
Techniscope/Technicolor
U.S.–Allied Artists (1969) 92 min
    P–Artur Brauner/D–Robert Siodmak/W–Ladislas Fodor/Based on the novel *Kampf um Rom* by Felix Dahn/M–Riz Ortolani/C–Richard Angst/E–Alfred Sap/AD–Ernst Schomer, Costel Simionescu/CD–Irms Pauli
    Cast–Laurence Harvey (Sethicus), Orson Welles (Justinian), Harriet Andersson (Matiswinter), Honor Blackman (Amariswinter), Sylva Koscina (Theodora), Lang Jeffries (Belizarus), Michael Dunn (Narciss), Ingrid Brett (Julia), Robert Hoffman (Totila) with Florin Piersic, Emanoil Petrut, Friedrich Von Ledebur, Dieter Eppler, Ewa Stromberg, Adela Marculescu, Ion Dichiseanu, Fory Etterle

    In the sixth century the power of Rome has been divided and thus severely weakened. When the Goths threaten the city of Rome, the Prefect Sethicus goes to Byzantium to ask the Emperor Justinian for aid. Justinian refuses to help, so the wily Sethicus devises his own plan to undermine the might of the Goths. Rome versus the Goths, the Goths versus Byzantium, Byzantium versus Rome. The tragic outcome finds all but two of the major characters dead. *The Last Roman* was originally shown as two separate features in Germany, the first running 103 minutes and the second 84 minutes. For the American release the running time was cut in half and the film was reduced to a single feature. What remains is a "Reader's Digest" version of the plot in which characters appear briefly and die with alarming regularity. Despite the brevity of the American version, the obvious quality of *The Last Roman* is still evident. The production is lavish and there are several above average performances.

177 *The Last Temptation of Christ*

Universal/Cineplex Odeon Films (1988) 161 min.
Technicolor
    P–Barbara De Fina/D–Martin Scorsese/W–Paul Schrader/Based on the novel by Nikos Kazantzakis/M–Peter Gabriel/C–Michael Ballhaus/E–Thelma Schoomaker/PD–John Beard/AD–Andrew Sanders/CD–Jean-Pierre Belfer
    Cast–Willem Dafoe (Jesus), Harvey Keitel (Judas), Barbara Hershey (Mary Magdalene), David Bowie (Pontius Pilate), Harry Dean Stanton (Paul), Verna Bloom (Mary), Peggy Gormley (Martha), Victor Argo (Peter), Gary Basaraba (Andrew) with Michael Been, Paul Herman, Paul Greco, Steve Shill, Barry Miller, Leo Burmester, Nehemiah Persoff

    Nikos Kazantzakis' controversial 1955 novel *The Last Temptation of Christ* became an equally controversial film in 1988. As the rebel Judas fights against the Roman oppression, the carpenter Jesus builds crosses for the oppressors. For this, Jesus suffers the torments of his own conscience and the scorn of his people. One of those who revile him is the prostitute Mary Magdalene. Before he makes a pilgrimage into the desert in an attempt to commune with his inner spirit, Jesus begs Magdalene to forgive him. Jesus returns from the desert with God's blessing and attempts to educate his people so that they may find the pathway to truth through love. The conventions of the story are present but they are often presented unconventionally. Jesus raises Lazarus from the dead but he is later murdered by zealots because he is the proof of Jesus' greatest miracle. The most extreme departure from the norm occurs when Jesus is on the cross. An angel of God comes to Jesus and declares that he has suffered enough. The angel removes him from the cross and leads him to a life in which he marries Mary Magdalene. When Mary suddenly dies, Jesus remarries and raises a family with his new wife. As an old man on his death bed, he discovers that the angel of God is really Satan and this vision of a "normal" life is a temptation designed to divert him from the path on which he was set by God. Jesus rejects this final temptation and willingly accepts his martyrdom. Willem Dafoe gives an intensely powerful performance. His is not the passive and ethereal depiction of Christ which is often given. Instead his Jesus is a mixture of conflicting emotions with feverish, troubled eyes. He preaches love but also declares "I'm here to set fire to the world!" Martin Scorsese was condemned by various religious sects for making an irreligious film but *The Last Temptation of Christ* is a sincere and heartfelt testament which does not cast doubt on the life of the Messiah, but reaffirms it. The movie was filmed entirely in Morocco and the set decorator was frequent peplum contributor Giorgio Desideri.

Chicago Tribune: The best film of 1988.

178   *Legions of the Nile*

(Le Legioni de Cleopatra; The Legions of Cleopatra)
Alexandra–C.F.C., Rome (1959) 90 min.
Supercinescope / Eastman Color
U.S.–20th Century–Fox (1960)
CinemaScope / Color by DeLuxe
   P–Virgilio De Blasi, Italo Zingarelli / D–Vittorio Cottafavi / W–Vittorio Cottafavi, Ennio De Concini, Giorgio Cristallini, Arnaldo Marrosu / M–Renzo Rossellini / C–Mario Pacheco / E–Sergio Montanari / AD–Antonio Simont / CD–Vittorio Rossi
   Cast–Linda Cristal (Berenice / Cleopatra), Georges Marchal (Mark Antony), Ettore Manni (Curridius), Alfredo Mayo (Octavian) with Jany Clair, Andrea Aureli, Rafael Calvo, Mino Doro, Conrado San Martin, Raphael Duran, Maria Mahor, Daniela Rocca, Juan Majan, Stefano Terra, Salvatore Furnari, Tomas Blanco

The first Egyptian Euro-epic to capitalize on the forthcoming 20th Century–Fox version of *Cleopatra* was *Le Legioni de Cleopatra*. The first announcements of Fox's plan to film *Cleopatra* were made in the autumn of 1958. By December 1959, Fox was shelling out a half-million dollars to buy the rights to *Le Legioni de Cleopatra* to keep it off the market. Obviously, if they had watched the film first they wouldn't have bothered. Apparently somebody did eventually screen the picture and, with a title change to *Legions of the Nile*, Fox released it in 1960 to try and recover some of their impudent investment. The central character in the story is a Roman soldier named Curridius, who comes to Alexandria shortly before Octavian's troops are about to make their final attack on Egypt. He hopes to convince his old friend Mark Antony to leave Cleopatra and rejoin the Romans. Curridius,

Cleopatra (Linda Cristal) attempts to comfort a dying Mark Antony (Georges Marchal) in *Legions of the Nile* (1960).

in the guise of a fun loving vagabond, stays at a local tavern which is periodically visited by a beautiful dancing girl named Berenice. Curridius finally contrives to see Antony, who remains unmoved by the pleas of his friend. When the Egyptian Council of Priests learns of Carriuius' interference, they plot to have him killed. In the meantime Curridius and Berenice are having a torrid love affair. One night he follows her after she leaves the tavern and discovers that she is none other than Cleopatra herself. Believing that the Egyptian queen has merely used him as another plaything, he rejoins the Roman troops as they are about to converge on the city. The remainder of the film adheres to the Cleopatra story more closely. The queen goes to Octavian to beg for Antony's life and is refused. Antony, thinking she has deserted him for the enemy, kills himself. Cleopatra returns and, finding Antony dead, commits suicide (with no asp in sight). *Legions of the Nile* suffers from the schizophrenic mood shifts prevalent in many of the Euro-epics made around this time. It just can't seem to decide what type of film it wants to be. Is it a rollicking gladiator comedy, as the early tavern scenes suggest, or is it a tragic love story? The first part of the movie is filled with much back slapping, raucous laughter and pratfalls. The middle consists of galloping horses and daring deeds. The final third is deadly serious. Perhaps the four credited screenwriters never met to discuss the type of film they were writing. Vittorio Cottafavi directed a number of interesting sword and sandal films with far more style than he exhibits here. On the positive side, the production values are above average for one of these mini-spectaculars. The three leads are appealing, with both Georges Marchal and Ettore Manni giving commendable performances. While Linda Cristal's sultry beauty is perfectly suited for this type of picture, her thesping as the Egyptian queen is the weakest link in the chain.

179　*The Lion of Amalfi*

(Il Leone di Amalfi)
(1950) 89 min.
U.S.–Medallion (1963)
　P–Mario Francisci/D–Pietro Francisci/W–Raul De Sarro, Fiorenzo Fiorentini, Pietro Francisci, Giorgio Graziosi, Ugo Quattrocchi/M–Carlo Rustichelli/C–Guglielmo and Rodolfo Lombardi/AD–Flavio Mogherini
　Cast–Vittorio Gassman (Marco), Milly Vitale (Diana), Elvy Lissiak (Eleanor), Ughetto Bertucci (Luciano), Sergio Fantoni (Ugo), Carlo Ninchi (Massimo) with Achille Mingione, Valerio Tordi, Ugo Sasso, Arnoldo Foa, Umberto Silvestri, Franco Silva

In the eleventh century, the Italian republic of Amalfi is invaded and occupied by the Normans. Marco, the son of the Doge, escapes and joins a band of rebels determined to overthrow the harsh regime imposed by the conquerors. When Marco saves the life of the beautiful Diana and they fall in love, his childhood sweetheart Eleanor is consumed with jealousy and betrays him to the Normans. The rebel forces of Amalfi are able to rescue Marco and he defeats the Norman leader, restoring peace to his homeland. This early Pietro Francisci costumer features a young Vittorio Gassman shortly after his international success in *Bitter Rice* (1948) and prior to his career in Hollywood. Gassman was a

famed stage actor in Italy when producer Sam Zimbalist went to Rome to film *Quo Vadis*. Zimbalist contacted Dore Schary at MGM and Gassman subsequently went to Hollywood where he was tested and won a seven year contract.

180　*The Lion of Thebes*

(Il Leone di Tebe/Helene Reine de Troie; Helen Queen of Troy)
Filmes, Rome–Societe Des Filmes Sirius, Paris (1964) 85 min.
Euroscope/Eastman Color
U.S.–Embassy
　P/D–Giorgio Ferroni/W–Remigio Del Grosso, Giorgio Ferroni, Andrey De Coligny, Jean Kelter/M–Francesco De Masi/C–Angelo Lotti/E–Antonietta Zita/AD–Arrigo Equini/CD–Elio Micheli
　Cast–Mark Forest (Arion), Yvonne Furneaux (Helen), Alberto Lupo (Menelaus), Pierre Cressoy (Rameses) with Massimo Serato, Rosalba Neri, Carlo Tamberlani, Nerio Bernardi, Valerio Tordi, Nello Pazzafini, Diego Michelotti, Pietro Capanna

Suggested by Euripides' tragedy of Helen in Egypt, this story takes place after the defeat of Troy by the Greeks. King Menelaus is sailing back to Sparta with his wife Helen when their ship is caught in a tempest and wrecked on the shores of Africa. Helen and her faithful bodyguard, Arion, survive and cross the desert to the city of Thebes in Egypt. Captured by slave traders, they are taken to the court of the pharaoh Rameses. The Egyptian king is so smitten by the beauty of Helen that he forsakes his intended bride and attempts to woo the former Queen of Sparta. Once again, the beauty of Helen becomes a catalyst for bloodshed. When Rameses is murdered by a treacherous advisor, Helen is blamed and sentenced to death. The intervention of Menelaus, who also survived the shipwreck, and the strength of Arion spare Helen her terrible fate. The concept of Helen in Egypt has great dramatic potential which was used to greater advantage in the Richard Strauss opera and the novel *The World's Desire* by Sir H. Rider Haggard. *The Lion of Thebes* fails to rise above the standard formula for the peplum film and the script soon degenerates into a typical palace intrigue plot. Mark Forest performs the cliché feats of strength which were a requisite of this genre, although the use of a stunt double in many of the action scenes is all too obvious. The title *The Lion of Thebes* refers to the name given to Forest when he defeats the champions of Rameses in hand-to-hand combat. The overall production in very set-bound with the exception of the climactic battle which is lifted from *Queen of the Nile*, evidence that the budget was even less than usual for this type of film. Forest has said that this is his favorite film. It is difficult to understand why. Perhaps it was the opportunity to play opposite the two lovely leading ladies Yvonne Furneaux and Rosalba Neri. Yvonne Furneaux has a striking presence which manages to transcend the meager material on hand. The film's best moment occurs when Furneaux as Helen reflects on the terrible consequences precipitated by her beauty. During this one brief scene, the latent pathos of the material is allowed to shine through.

181 *The Long Ships*

A Warwick-Avala Production
Columbia (1964) 126 min.
Technirama/Technicolor
P–Irving Allen/D–Jack Cardiff/W–Berkely Mather, Beverley Cross/Based on the novel by Frans Bengtsson/M–Dusan Radic/C–Christopher Challis/E–Geoffrey Foot/AD–John Hoesli/CD–Anthony Mendleson
Cast–Richard Widmark (Rolfe), Sidney Poitier (El Mansuh), Rossana Schiaffino (Aminah), Russ Tamblyn (Orm), Oscar Homolka (Krok), Lionel Jeffries (Aziz), Edward Judd (Sven), Beba Loncar (Gerda), Clifford Evans (King Harald) with Colin Blakely, Gordon Jackson, David Lodge, Paul Stassino, Jeanne Moody

Much ado about the Golden Bell of St. James, a legendary giant bell which was cast in the gold taken from Islam by the Crusaders. Rolfe, a Viking vagabond, returns home to tell his father and younger brother Orm that he has discovered the whereabouts of the famous Golden Bell. Rolfe and Orm kidnap Gerda, daughter of King Harald, and steal a newly built Long Ship to go in quest of the Bell. The Vikings are shipwrecked and taken captive by El Mansuh, a Moorish Shiek who is also searching for the golden treasure. El Mansuh is smitten with Gerda and puts her in his harem. The Moor allows the Vikings to repair their ship and bring the Golden Bell

back to him. King Harald and his men, who have been in pursuit of Rolfe and Orm, arrive and defeat El Mansuh, freeing Gerda and claiming the Golden Bell in the name of the king. *The Long Ships* is a rousing adventure which is, at times, a bit too rousing. The comedy aspects are overdone and there is the obligatory Viking feast filled with drunken brawling. This was Sidney Poitier's first film after winning the Oscar for *Lillies of the Field* and he is all but unrecognizable under his Moorish wig.

182 *The Loves of Hercules*

(Gli Amori de Ercole/Hercules vs. the Hydra)
Grandi Schermi Italiani, Rome–Contact Organisation, Paris (1960) 94 min.
CinemaScope/Eastman Color
U.S.–Walter Manley Enterprises (1966)
P–Alberto Manca/D–Carlo Ludovico Bragaglia/W–Alberto Manca, Luciano Doria, Alessandro Continenza/M–Carlo Innocenzi/C–Enzo Serafin/E–Renato Cinquini/AD–Alberto Boccianti/CD–Dario Cecchi, Maria Baroni
Cast–Jayne Mansfield (Deianira/Hippolyta), Mickey Hargitay (Hercules), Massimo Serato (Lico) with Tina Gloriani, Rosella Como, Giulio Donnini, Arturo Bragaglia, Andrea Aureli, Andrea Scotti, Rene Dary, Olga Solbelli, Moira Orfei, Cesare Fantoni, Sandrine, Antonio Gradoli

In 1960 Jayne Mansfield and her husband, bodybuilder Mickey Hargitay, went to Europe to star together in one of the many "Hercules" films that followed in the wake of the Steve Reeves blockbuster. The resulting film, *The Loves of Hercules*, is one of the most curious of all the peplum films, due primarily to the presence of Mansfield. The producers had obviously hoped that the appearance of the famous American sex symbol would ensure a successful release in the United States. Unfortunately, by this time Mansfield's popularity was in decline and the film remained unreleased in the U.S. until 1966. The King of Oechalia causes the wife of his enemy Hercules to be killed and, shortly thereafter, is also murdered. The grieving strongman goes to the kingdom of Oechalia and confronts the king's daughter Deianira. She suspects that Hercules may have been responsible for the recent death of her father. The real culprit is the villainous Lico, who was actually involved in both murders. Deianira agrees to submit to a trial by ordeal at the hands of Hercules to prove her innocence. She is exonerated from the crime by virtue of her great courage and Hercules quickly falls in love with the beautiful queen. When her betrothed is assassinated, Hercules is assumed to be the guilty party. Hercules goes off in search of the one man who can prove his innocence but finds him in the powerful jaws of the three-headed Hydra, a gigantic fire-breathing dragon. Hercules slays the monster but is badly wounded in the process. A group of Amazons find Hercules and take him to their city to nurse him back to health. Hippolyta, Queen of the Amazons, lusts after Hercules but, realizing that he is in love with Deianira, she magically takes on the face and form of his beloved to gain his devotion. Hercules falls under the spell of Hippolyta but he is brought to his senses by a friendly Amazon who tells him of her queen's deception. Hercules leaves to rescue Deianira, who has been imprisoned by the evil Lico. The climax takes place in the cave of a monstrous ape man who kills Lico and has obvious designs on Deianira. Hercules clobbers the ape man with a huge boulder and rides off into the sunset with Deianira. Although Jayne Mansfield, in a black wig, is fairly effective as Deianira (she swoons a lot), she is ludicrous as the red-wigged Hippolyta. Her performance as the Amazon queen takes "camp" to new heights and, quite simply, must be seen to be believed. Even more unusual is the fact that the filmmakers found it necessary to pad the bosom of the already preternaturally buxom actress. At times she seems in danger of toppling over. Mickey Hargitay, also no slouch in the chest department, is fine as Hercules, although his dialogue is dubbed by an actor with a British accent. Despite his muscular qualifications Mickey Hargitay's only other peplum film was *Vengeance of the Gladiators* (Luigi Capuano; 1964). Later, he became a frequent actor in Euro-horror films.

183   *The Loves of Pharaoh*

(Das Weib des Pharao; The Pharaoh's Wife)
Paramount (1922)
   P/D–Ernst Lubitsch/W–Norbert Falk, Hanns Kraly
   Cast–Emil Jannings (Amenes), Dagny Servaes

(Theonis), Paul Wegener (Samalak), Harry Liedtke (Ramphis) with Lyda Salmonova, Paul Biensfeldt, Albert Bassermann, Friedrich Kuhne

German director Ernst Lubitsch had already established himself in his own country as a specialist in costumes dramas. Many of these had starred his discovery Pola Negri who, as a result of these colorful roles, was imported to Hollywood by Paramount. With his favorite leading lady gone Lubitsch set about finding a new actress he could cultivate into stardom. The result of his search was Dagny Servaes, a Viennese actress whom he felt could have even greater international appeal than Pola Negri. To showcase his new discovery, Lubitsch mounted a lavish spectacular set in ancient Egypt. Servaes portrays a beautiful slave girl who is loved by the pharaoh Amenes and the handsome young slave Ramphis. Although his leading lady was not the audience pleaser he had hoped, the movie did bring Lubitsch to the attention of Hollywood. He came to America in 1923 where he gained fame for his direction of sophisticated comedies.

184   *The Loves of Salammbo*

(Salammbo)
A Fides-Stella Production (1960) 72 min.
Totalscope/Eastman Color
U.S.–20th Century–Fox (1962)
CinemaScope/Color by DeLuxe
   P–Luigi Nannerini; D–Sergio Grieco/W– Andre Tabet, Barbara Sohmers, John Berry/Based on the novel *Salammbo* by Gustave Flaubert/M– Alexandre Derevitsky/ C–Piero Portalupe/E–Enzo Alfonsi/AD–Franco Lolli/CD–Beni Montresor
   Cast–Jeanne Valerie (Salammbo), Jacques Sernas (Mathos), Edmund Purdom (Narr Havas), Riccardo Garrone (Hamilcar) with Arnoldo Foa, Kamala Devi, Charles Fawcett, Brunella Bova, Raffaele Baldassarre

Five years after the First Punic War, the army of mercenaries who had been hired to help defend Carthage from the Romans have still not been paid for their services. When the mercenary army threatens to march on Carthage, Salammbo, a priestess and daughter of the great General Hamilcar, promises Mathos, the leader of the mercenaries, that if his army will withdraw they will be paid in full. During their meeting, Salammbo and Mathos fall

Jacques Sernas and Jeanne Valerie are passionate lovers on opposing sides in *The Loves of Salammbo* (1962).

deeply in love. Narr Havas, a powerful Carthaginian nobleman, has the gold payment confiscated and substitutes chests full of stones. When the mercenaries discover that they have been deceived they march on the city. Mathos steals the sacred veil of the goddess Tanit from the temple. It is the symbol of the gods' protection of Carthage. Salammbo, not knowing about the stolen gold, believes that Mathos has gone back on his word. She goes to his

Maciste in King Solomon's Mines **features Reg Park as the mythical strongman in Africa (1964).**

encampment to kill him but succumbs to her desire for him instead. Mathos is captured by the Carthaginians and imprisoned. The evil plot of Narr Havas is finally discovered and he is condemned to death by stoning. Mathos is sentenced to the same fate for stealing the veil of Tanit. As the crowd casts their stones at Mathos, Salammbo runs to his side and publicly declares her love. General Hamilcar entreats his people to forgive Mathos and the two lovers are happily reunited. Gustave Flaubert's novel *Salammbo* had three silent incarnations. The first two versions were made in Italy in 1911 and 1914. The third, a 1924 French film by director Pierre Marodon, was the most spectacular. In 1960 Spyros Skouras planned for 20th Century–Fox to produce a version of the story starring Harry Belafonte and Gina Lollobrigida. This project was abandoned in the wake of the problems surrounding *Cleopatra*. Instead, Fox purchased the rights to this European production. Eighteen-year-old Jeanne Valerie was a protégée of director Roger Vadim. While she is beautiful, her screen presence is not sufficient to carry off the pivotal role of Salammbo. Jacques Sernas and Edmund Purdom, by now old hands at playing in these films, are good in their roles as hero and villain respectively.

185   *Maciste in King Solomon's Mines*

(Maciste nelle Miniere del Re Salomone / Samson in King Solomon's Mines)
Panda Cinimatografica (1963) 93 min.
Techniscope / Technicolor
U.S.–Embassy (1964)
   P–Ermanno Donati, Luigi Carpentieri / D–Martin Andrews / W–Piero Regnoli / M–Francesco De Masi / C–Luciano Trasatti
   Cast–Reg Park (Maciste), Wandisa Guida (Fazira), Dan Harrison (Abukar), Eleonora Bianchi

Gary Lockwood, Anne Helm and a collection of horrors from *The Magic Sword* (1961).

(Samara), Leonard G. Elliot (Riad), Bruno Scipioni (Kadar), Carlo Tamberlani (Zelea) with Giuseppe Addobbati, Nino Persello, Loris Loddi

A temple in the African city of Zimba is built above the mines of King Solomon to protect them from violation. A group of thieves, led by the beautiful but evil Fazira, comes to the city to raid the mines and take over the kingdom from its ruler King Namar. When Maciste learns there is evil afoot he rushes to the rescue but Fazira uses magic to rob him of his will. Reduced to subservience, Maciste is sent to labor in the mines. When his will returns, Maciste escapes and destroys Fazira in a flux of molten gold. Despite some actual African location filming, there is little to set *Maciste in King Solomon's Mines* apart from other films of its type. Although the direction is credited to Mark Andrews, Reg Park has said that it was actually directed by screenwriter Piero Regnoli.

186   *The Magic Sword*

A Bert I. Gordon Production
United Artists (1961) 80 min.
Eastman Color
P/D–Bert I. Gordon/W–Bernard Schoenfeld, Bert I. Gordon/M–Richard Markowitz/C–Paul C. Vogel/E–Harry Gerstad/PD–Franz Bachelin/SVE–Bert I. and Flora Gordon
Cast–Basil Rathbone (Lodac), Estelle Winwood (Sybil), Gary Lockwood (George), Anne Helm (Helene), Liam Sullivan (Sir Branton) with Leroy Johnson, Merritt Stone, Jacques Gallo, David Cross, Angus Duncan

St. George is the patron saint of England. The various exploits of St. George are chronicled in *Acta Sancti Georgh* (Acts of Saint George) which was written sometime prior to A.D. 496. George was a Roman tribune under the rule of Emperor Dioclesian. After vocalizing his disapproval of his emperor's persecution of the Christians, George was imprisoned and eventually beheaded. Later St. George appeared to King Richard during his

Crusade against the Saracens. The most famous of St. George's achievements was his killing of a dragon to save the life of a princess. This is the feat upon which the screenplay of this movie is based. Young George is the adopted son of the dotty sorceress Sybil. When the fair princess Helene is kidnapped by the evil sorcerer Lodac, George and his six faithful companions join the rescue party. The endeavor is led by Sir Branton, a thoroughly bad lot who is secretly in league with Lodac. On their way to Lodac's castle, the valiant knights must face seven curses. These include an ogre and a vampire hag (played by Maila Nurmi, aka Vampira). Only George survives the curses to battle the two headed, fire breathing dragon and save Helene. This silly movie is primarily geared toward children, although there are a number of gruesome touches which could never appear in a children's film today. Producer/director Bert I. Gordon had previously been responsible for a number of low budget science fiction films such as *The Amazing Colossal Man* and *Attack of the Puppet People*. Although this is certainly several notches above his prior films, it still bears the mark of his poor direction and bargain basement special effects. Filmed as *St. George and the Seven Curses*, the title was changed to *The Magic Sword* shortly before its release, presumably to avoid any accusations of blasphemy.

187   The Magnificent Gladiator

(Il Magnifico Gladiatore)
Seven Films S.p.A., Rome (1964) 90 min.
Techniscope/Technicolor
U.S.—No theatrical release
   P–Cleto Fontini/D/W–Alfonso Brescia/M–Marcello Giombini/C–Pier Ludovico Pavoni/E–Nella Nannuzzi/AD–Pier Vittorio Marchi/CD–Mario Giorsi
   Cast–Mark Forest (Hercules), Marilu Tolo (Velida) with Paolo Gozlino, Jolanda Modio, Franco Corbianchi, Oreste Lionello, Nazzareno Zamperla, Giulio Tomei, Fedele Gentile

Hercules, son of the King of Dacio, is taken captive during a battle with the Romans. The emperor Gallieno admires Hercules' prowess in the arena and offers him a position teaching the other prisoners to become gladiators.

The emperor's daughter, Velida, falls in love with Hercules to the dismay of Zuddo, the treacherous commander of the Praetorian guards. Zuddo has found an exact double for the emperor and, taking Gallieno prisoner, replaces him with the impostor. The false emperor starts an argument with Hercules and attempts to have him arrested. Hercules flees with his gladiator friends and goes into hiding, but they are soon captured by the Praetorians and put into prison. With the help of the shepherd Drusio, Hercules and the gladiators escape from their cell and arrive at the palace in time to prevent the forced marriage of Velida to Zuddo. In the ensuing fight, Zuddo is killed and the real emperor is restored to the throne. This low-budget peplum is a colorful actioner which shows off the talents of its handsome star to good advantage.

188   Mary Magdalene

(La Spada e la Croce; The Sword and the Cross)
Liber Films (1958) 93 min.
Supercinescope/Ferraniacolor
U.S.–Amex Pictures (1960)
   P–Ottavio Poggi/D–Carlo Ludovico Bragaglia/W–Ottavio Poggi, Alessandro Continenza/M–Roberto Nicolosi/C–Marcello Masciocchi/E–Renato Cinquini/AD–Ernest Kromberg/CD–Giancarlo Bartolini Salimbeni
   Cast–Yvonne De Carlo (Mary Magdalene), Jorge Mistral (Gaius Marcellus), Rossana Podesta (Martha), Massimo Serato (Anan), Mario Girotti (Lazarus), Andrea Aureli (Barabbas), Rossana Rory (Claudia), Philippe Hersent (Pilate) with Roberto Morgani, Nando Tamberlani, Jonathan Kane, Nadia Brivio, Aldo Pini, Franco Fantasia, Roberto Cesana, Guillo Battiferri

In this above average biblical film, Yvonne De Carlo stars as Mary Magdalene, a high-priced harlot who becomes a faithful follower of Jesus. Kidnapped by Barabbas when his bandits raid her caravan, Mary is rescued by Gaius Marcellus, a Roman officer who falls in love with her. Ashamed of her immoral past, she rebuffs his advances and turns to an even more dissolute lifestyle. She eventually finds salvation when her sister, Martha (played by Rossana Podesta, in a rare supporting role), introduces her to the teachings of Christ. Dramatic license was exercised to the fullest by the screenwriters. In addition to making Mary

The prostitute (Yvonne De Carlo) is loved by a Roman officer (Jorge Mistral) in *Mary Magdalene* (1960).

the mistress of Anan, nephew of the high priest Caiaphas, an even more elaborate fabrication was perpetrated by making Lazarus her younger brother. It all works within the context of the story, if you can allow yourself to forget the source. In addition to Yvonne De Carlo in the title role, the cast is filled with familiar faces from the epic genre. Massimo Serato, as the evil Anan, was the resident villain of the European epic films. He enacted a larger number of dastardly characters than even Livio Lorenzon, that bald-headed barbarian of countless peplum films.

189　*Mary Magdalene*

(Maria Maddalena)
A Lux Vide / Epsilon TV Production (2000) 95 min.
Color
U.S.–Syndicated television release
　　P–Luca Bernabei / D–Raffaele Mertes / W–Gareth Jones, Gianmario Pagano / M–Marco Frisina / C–Giovanni Galasso / E–Elisabetta Marchetti / PD–Paolo Biagetti / CD–Paolo Scalabrino
　　Cast–Maria Grazia Cucinotta (Mary Magdalene), Danny Quinn (Jesus), Massimo Ghini (Vitellious), Giulian De Sio (Herodias), Nathaly Caldonazzo (Susanna), Ambra Angiolini (Salome), Imonol Arias (Amos), Benjamin Sadler (John the Baptist) with Thure Riefenstein, Gottfried John, Roberta Armani, Vittorio Amandola

Poor Mary of Magdala. She is divorced by her conniving husband Amos, who robs her of her home and property. In desperation, she becomes the mistress of a Roman Prefect. When he discovers that she is pregnant, the Roman beats Mary until she looses the baby. After recovering from her injuries, Mary attempts to drown herself in the Sea of Galilee but she is fished out of the water by Jesus and his disciples. Mary is befriended by Queen Herodias, who has heard of Mary's healing powers and seeks a cure for an ailment she is suffering. While in the household of Herod, Mary attracts the attention of the Roman general Vitellious, who takes her as his mistress. Through him, Mary gets revenge on her former husband and the brutal Prefect. Revenge turns out to be a bitter victory for Mary, who is consumed with guilt. She learns the true meanings of love and forgiveness from Jesus and becomes his devoted follower. Not since the heyday of the Hollywood epic has there been such a collection of fabrications and elaboration on the biblical text. You have to go back to *Salome* (1953) and *The Prodigal* (1955) to find the equal of *Mary Magdalene*. Even the glamorous courtesan of DeMille's *The King of Kings* has a more believable background than this Mary. It is interesting to see just how the screenwriters contrive to get Mary involved with the likes of Salome and John the Baptist. Danny Quinn, a son of Anthony Quinn, plays Jesus and his interpretation consists mainly of a dazzling Ultra-White smile. A sequel, *Tomasso*, about the apostle Thomas, was filmed in 2001 by the same company. In it, Danny Quinn and Maria Grazia Cucinotta reprise their roles from *Mary Magdalene*.

190　*Masada*

Arnon Milchan Film Productions Ltd.
Universal (1981) 131 min.
Panavision / Technicolor
　　P–George Eckstein / D–Boris Sagal / W–Joel Oliansky / Based on the novel *The Antagonists* by Ernest K. Gann / M–Jerry Goldsmith, Morton Stevens / C–Paul Lohmann / E–Robert L. Kimble / PD–John H. Senter / AD–George Renne, Kuli Sander / Technical Advisor and Costume Designer–Vittorio Nino Novarese
　　Cast–Peter O'Toole (Cornelius Flavius Silva) , Peter Strauss (Eleazar ben Yair), Barbara Carrera (Sheva), Giulia Pagano (Miriam), David Warner (Falco), Richard Pierson (Ephram) with Anthony Quayle, David Opatoshu, Timothy West, Joseph Wiseman, Alan Feinstein, Dennis Quilley, Anthony Valentine, Paul L. Smith, Nigel Davenport, George Peter Innes, Ray Smith

Barbara Carrera is the Jewish mistress of a Roman general (Peter O'Toole) in *Masada*.

This is a feature length version of the six and one half hour mini-series which aired on the ABC television network in April 1981. It was released theatrically in Britain as *The Antagonists*, the title of the original source material. In A.D. 70, 980 Jewish zealots led by Eleazar ben Yair took refuge in Masada, the abandoned mountain fortress of Herod the Great. For the next three years the legions of Rome laid siege to Masada in order to destroy this last bastion of Jewish rebellion. Finally, when faced with unquestionable defeat, the Jews chose mass suicide over Roman domination. With a price tag of $20 million, *Masada* was the most expensive mini-series of its time. The plot focuses on a battle of wills between the rebel Eleazar (Peter Strauss) and the Roman commander Silva (Peter O'Toole), two very different men who share the common conviction that what they are doing is right. Barbara Carrera provides the love interest as Sheva, the beautiful Jewish captive who becomes the willing mistress of Silva.

While the mini-series sometimes seemed overlong and labored, the feature version is too condensed. A three hour cut might have resulted in a better picture overall. No matter what the length, Peter O'Toole's performance is a standout. He plays Silva as a man of great principal and even greater compassion. In the feature version there is a brief nude scene with Barbara Carrera which did not appear in the mini-series.

191   *The Medusa Against the Son of Hercules*

(Perseo l'Invincibile; Perseus the Invincible/Perseus Against the Monsters/Valley of the Stone Men)
Cineproduzione Bistolfi, Rome–Copercines, Madrid (1962) 93 min.
Totalscope/Eastman Color
U.S.–Embassy (1963)

P–Emo Bistolfi/D–Alberto De Martino/W–Mario Guerra, Luciano Martino, Jose Mallorqui, Eduardo Giorgio Conti, Ernesto Gastaldi, Alberto De Martino, Vittorio Vighi/M–Carlo Franci/C–Eloy Mella, Dario Di Palma/E–Otello Colangeli/AD–Franco Lolli/CD–Angiolina Manichelli
Cast–Richard Harrison (Perseus), Anna Ranalli (Andromeda), Enrico Navarro (Stheno), Elisa Cegani (Danae) with Arturo Dominici, Leo Anchoriz, Roberto Camardiel, Antonio Molino Rojo, Angel Jordan, Rufino Ingles, Jose Sepulveda, Loranzo Robledo,

The Medusa Against the Son of Hercules is a barely recognizable adaptation of the Perseus and Andromeda myth which provides Richard Harrison with one of his better peplum roles. Perseus (in the U.S. version he is an "honorary" son of Hercules) must fight against the cruel king of Argos and his son to save both the woman he loves and her city from destruction. To do this he goes to the Valley of Stone Men and slays the Medusa, a hideous creature that can turn men into stone with a glance. When the Medusa dies, her victims are restored to life and Perseus is able to use them as an army to defeat the forces of Argos. Carlo Rambaldi contributes two rather unconvincing monsters. The "Monster of the Lake" is a larger than life-size mechanical dragon that breathes noxious fumes. "The Medusa" is presented as a sort of walking tree with a cyclopean eye which emits a ray that turns living flesh to stone. Both are a far cry from Ray Harryhausen's splendid animated creatures in *Clash of the Titans*, a later version of the same myth. Despite the variable quality of the special effects the film is fast moving and colorful and Harrison is handsome and heroic as Perseus. Curiously, the Spanish version incorporates more optical effects than the Italian and English language versions of the film.

192   *Messalina*

(Messalina, Venere Imperatrice)
Cineproduzione Bistolfi, Rome (1960) 84 min.
Technirama / Technicolor
U.S.–American-International
  P–Emo Bistolfi / D–Vittorio Cottafavi / W–Ennio De Concini, Mario Guerra, Carlo Romano, Duccio Tessari / M–Angelo Francesco Lavagnino / C–Marco Scarpelli, Luciano Cavalieri / AD–Franco Lolli / CD–Dina Di Bara

Cast–Belinda Lee (Messalina), Spiros Focas (Lucius Massimus), Giulio Donnini (Marcius), Arianna Galli (Silvia), Carlo Giustini (Greta), Arturo Dominici (Caius Silius), Marcello Giorda (Claudius) with Aroldo Tieri, Giancarlo Sbragia

Of the many screen interpretations of Messalina this is probably the most satisfying due to the casting of Belinda Lee in the title role. This is not to suggest that *Messalina* is the most historically accurate or even the best produced version, but Belinda Lee's pagan beauty seems to exude wantonness, and this is just the right quality needed for a successful portrayal of Rome's most dissolute empress. Lee, who played a number of memorable screen temptresses in her brief film career, including Lucretia Borgia in *The Nights of Lucretia Borgia* and Potiphar's wife in *Joseph and His Brethren*, had beauty and charisma. If her life had not been cut short by a tragic au-

Belinda Lee as *Messalina* (1960).

tomobile accident she might have developed into a truly fine actress. Belinda Lee aside, *Messalina* is a fairly average film with the usual historical inaccuracies and an unimpressive roster of male performers who cannot compete with Lee's onscreen persona. A subplot involving a Roman soldier and Christian girl is not only clichéd but unnecessary and detracts from the main action of the story.

193   *Messalina Against the Son of Hercules*

(Gladiatore di Messalina; Gladiator of Messalina/ L'Ultimo Gladiatore/Hercule contre les Mercenaires)
Produzione Prometeo Films, Rome–Les Films Jacques Leitienne and Unicite, Paris (1963) 105 min.
Techniscope/Eastman Color
U.S.–Embassy (1964)
     D–Umberto Lenzi/W–Gian Paolo Callegari, Albert Valentin/M–Carlo Franci/C–Pier Ludovico Pavoni/E–Nella Nannuzzi/AD–Pier Vittorio Marchi/CD–Mario Giorsi
     Cast–Richard Harrison (Glaucus), Lisa Gastoni (Messalina), Marilu Tolo, Philippe Hersent, Livio Lorenzon, Jean Claudio, Gianni Solaro, Enzo Fiermonte, John McDouglas, Laura Rocca, Charles Borromel

Messalina Against the Son of Hercules is another in the series of films retitled and released by Embassy Pictures as part of a TV package. The plot has nothing to do with a "Son of Hercules" and the original title, *Gladiator of Messalina*, is far more appropriate. Glaucus, a young Briton, is captured when Romans invade his village. He is sent to Rome to be trained as a gladiator for Caligula. Once the scene shifts to Rome, the plot incorporates a considerable amount of historical detail. The cruel emperor Caligula is assassinated by his guards who then proclaim Claudius as his successor. The scheming empress, Messalina, attempts to use Glaucus in her plans to seize the throne from her husband. As Messalina, Lisa Gastoni takes full advantage of one of her rare "bad girl" roles. Often seen as the simpering heroine, she does well as the dissolute wife of the emperor Claudius. As usual, Richard Harrison is effective as the courageous gladiator who leads the

people against the malevolent empress. The film is a bit slow moving but at least some credit should be given for its attempts at historical accuracy. Victor Tourjansky, who often helmed these projects, served as the assistant director here.

194   *Messalina, Messalina*

(Mesalina, Mesalina/Messaline, Imperatrice et Putain; Messalina, Empress and Whore)
A Medusa Distribuzione Production (1977) 90 min.
Telecolor
U.S.–United Artists
     P–Renato Jaboni, Ennio Onorati/D–Bruno Corbucci/W–Mario Amendola, Bruno Corbucci/M–Guido and Maurizio De Angelis/C–Marcello Masciocchi/E–Daniele Alabiso/CD–Alberto Verso/ Adaptation of Sets–Claudio Cinini
     Cast–Anneka Di Lorenzo (Messalina), Lory Kay Wagner (Agrippina), Vittorio Caprioli (Claudius), Tomas Milian (Baba), Giancarlo Prete (Silius), Alessandra Cardini (Calpurnia), Bombolo (Narcissus) with Raf Luca, Pino Ferrara, Luca Sportelli, Sal Borgese, Ombretta Di Carlo, Primo Marcotulli, Viviana Larice, Lino Toffolo

If there were a contest for the "Worst Movie" included in this book *Messalina, Messalina* would be one of the top contenders for that dubious distinction. The list of adjectives which could be used to describe this film is limitless. A few examples are vulgar, tasteless, disgusting, puerile, crude and just plain awful. It also boasts one of the oddest credits ever listed in a motion picture:

> "Certain elements of the sets and decorations created for the film 'Caligula' by Danilo Donati have been used in the production of this film without his consent."

Although *Messalina, Messalina* was released while *Caligula* was still enmeshed in post production difficulties, it was filmed on sets left over from that infamous opus. Watching *Caligula* maybe akin to watching an automobile accident but *Messalina, Messalina* is totally unwatchable. The producers decided to take one of the grimmest eras of Roman history and turn it into a rollicking soft core sex comedy with plenty of gratuitous full frontal female nudity. The climax is an incredible over-the-top bloodbath which out-gores any horror film. The plot is summed up by a character early on: "Messalina screws everyone in sight." 'Nuff said.

195   *The Mighty Crusaders*

(La Gerusalemme Liberata; The Liberators of Jerusalem)
Max Productions (1960) 87 min.
Supercinescope/Color
U.S.–Falcon Productions Inc.
　　P–Ottavio Poggi/D–Carlo Ludovico Bragaglia/W–Alessandro Continenza/M–Roberto Nicolosi/C–Rodolfo Lomardi/E–Renato Cinquini/PD–Ernest Kromberg/CD–Giancarlo Bartolini Salimbeni
　　Cast–Francisco Rabal (Tancrid), Sylva Koscina (Clorinda), Gianna Maria Canale (Armida), Rik Battaglia (Renaldo), Philippe Hersent (Godfrey) with Livia Contardi, Andrea Aureli, Carlo Tamberlani

This story of Crusaders versus Saracens focuses on two Christian warriors who fall in love with Saracen princesses, with disastrous results. The warrior, Tancrid, is smitten with Clorinda, a fiery beauty who rides with the heathen army into battle. The valiant leader, Renaldo, is seduced by the charms of Armida, the daughter of the King of Damascus. Armida betrays him and he is taken prisoner. Tancrid frees Renaldo, but in a violent aftermath Clorinda is mortally wounded. *The Mighty Crusaders* is a routine action picture with strong performances by Sylva Koscina and Gianna Maria Canale.

196   *Mighty Ursus*

(Ursus)
Cine Italia S.p.A, Rome–Antena S.L., Madrid (1961) 92 min.
Totalscope/Eastman Color
U.S.–United Artists (1962)
　　P–Italo Zingarelli D–Carlo Campogalliani/W–Giuliano Carmineo, Giuseppe Mangione, Sergio Sollima/M–Roman Vlad/C–Eloy Mella/E–Franco Fraticelli/AD–Piero Poletto/CD–Antonio Cortes
　　Cast–Ed Fury (Ursus), Mary Marlon (Doreide), Moira Orfei (Attea), Mario Scaccia (Setas), Luis Prendes (Mok), Cristina Gajoni (Magali) with Manuel Arbo, Rafael Calvo, Soledad Miranda, Kriss Huerta

Having already utilized the names of other famous strongmen such as Hercules, Samson, Atlas and Goliath, Italian moviemakers decided to borrow the name of a character from

Ed Fury and Mary Marlon in *Mighty Ursus* **(1962).**

Quo Vadis for yet another musclebound hero. Ursus returns from the wars to discover his beloved Attea has been abducted and is about to be sacrificed to a pagan goddess. With the help of a blind shepherdess named Doreide, Ursus sets out to the island where Attea has been taken. Ursus is unaware that the wicked high priest has transformed Attea into a priestess of evil. When Ursus arrives on the island, he and Doreide are taken captive. Attea attempts to enlist Ursus' great strength for her own vile purposes but he rebukes her advances. In a scene reminiscent of the climax of *Quo Vadis*, Ursus is sentenced to fight a bull in the arena to save Doreide. Ursus defeats the bull with his bare hands and then leads the slaves in revolt. Attea and the high priest are killed, leaving Ursus to return home with Doreide, whose sight has been miraculously restored. Despite a fairly standard peplum storyline, *Mighty Ursus* is a better than average film with some excellent production values. The spectacular sets were left over from Samuel Bronston's *King of Kings*, which was filmed in Spain at the same time as *Mighty Ursus*. Ed Fury had appeared in minor roles in several Hollywood films, including *Hell and High Water*, *Female on the Beach* and *Bus Stop*. It was the latter which brought him to the attention of director Joshua Logan, who asked Fury to appear in the Broadway production of *Fanny*. During his stint in *Fanny*, Fury was spotted by an Italian producer who asked him to come to Europe to appear in *Colossus and the Amazon Queen*. *Mighty Ursus* was his next film. He later appeared as Ursus in *Ursus in the Valley of the Lions* (Carlo Ludovico Bragaglia; 1962) and *Son of Hercules in the Land of Fire* (Giorgio Simonelli; 1963). Ed Fury is ably supported in *Mighty Ursus* by Moira Orfei as the malevolent Attea and Mary Marlon (real name: Maria Luisa Merlo) as the gentle Doreide.

197   *The Minotaur*

(Teseo Contro il Minotauro: Theseus Against the Minotaur/Warlord of Crete)
Agliani-Mordini-Illiria Films (1960) 92 min.
Totalscope/Technicolor
U.S.–United Artists (1961)
   P–Dino Mordini, Giorgio Agliani, Rudolph Solmsen/D–Silvio Amadio/W–Alessandro Continenza, Gian Paolo Callegari, Daniel Mainwaring/M–Carlo Rustichelli/C–Aldo Giordani/E–Nella Nannuzzi/AD–Piero Poletto/CD–Enzo Bulgarelli
   Cast–Bob Mathias (Theseus), Rosanna Schiaffino (Ariadne/Phaedra), Alberto Lupo (Chryone), Rik Battaglia (Demetrios), Nico Pepe (Gerione), Carlo Tamberlani (King Minos) with Nerio Bernardi, Susanne Loret, Emma Baron, Elena Zareschi, Maria Maleff, Paul Muller, Adriano Micantoni, Alberto Barberito, Tiziana Cassetti

Olympic and decathlon champion Bob Mathias stars as Theseus in this loose adaptation of the famous Greek myth of Theseus and the Minotaur. The evil Princess Phaedra attempts to murder her twin sister Ariadne but the plan is thwarted by Theseus, Prince of Athens. Theseus leaves Ariadne in the care of his father and goes to Crete to help rescue his friend Demetrios' family from imprisonment. Demetrios is killed in the attempt and Theseus is wounded while evading capture. Amphitrite, a sea goddess, tends his wounds and restores him to health. In the meantime, the army of Crete has invaded Athens and taken Ariadne prisoner. Theseus rescues Ariadne from prison and Phaedra is killed in the fracas. Theseus and Ariadne enter the labyrinth

Theseus (Bob Mathias) rescues his beloved (Rosanna Schiaffino) from *The Minotaur* (1961).

to slay the monstrous Minotaur, a half-bull, half-human creature who devours the youths that are ritually sacrificed to it. The Minotaur itself is a big disappointment; more bear than bull and totally unconvincing. After the big build-up, it is a major letdown. Fortunately, the film, as a whole, is lively and entertaining and Rosanna Schiaffino is quite good in her duel role.

198   *Mole Men Against the Son of Hercules*

(Maciste, l'Uomo Più Forte del Mondo; Maciste the Strongest Man in the World)
Leone Film (1961) 98 min
Totalscope / Techincolor
U.S.–Embassy (1963)

P–Elio Scardamaglia / D–Antonio Leonviola / W–Antonio Leonviola, Marcello Baldi, Giuseppe Mangione / M–Armando Travajoli / C–Alvaro Mancori / E–Otello Colangeli / AD–Franco Lolli / CD– Gaia Romanini

Cast–Mark Forest (Maciste), Paul Wynter (Bangor), Moira Orfei (Queen), Gianni Garko (Katan) with Raffaella Carra, Enrico Glori, Roberto Miali, Nando Tamberlani, Cinzia Cam, Carla De Foscari, Rosalia Gavo, Graziella Granata, Janine Hendy, Bruna Mori, Anna di Martino, Franca Posesello, Gloria Hendy, Luciana Vivaldi

One morning, just before dawn, Maciste is hauling a whale out of the ocean when he sees some horsemen being pursued by strangely garbed riders. He defends the horsemen and, when the sun rises, the one surviving pursuer is destroyed by the sun's rays. Maciste learns that he was a member of a tribe of Mole Men who live in caverns beneath the surface of the earth. At night they come out and raid the neighboring villages, taking the people as captives to work in their underground diamond mines. Maciste rescues one of the Mole Men's prisoners, Bangor, and together they descend into the subterranean caverns to try and liberate the captives. The kingdom of the Mole Men is ruled by their malefic queen, Alismoyab, who is so turned on by the strength of Maciste that she is willing to forego her evil ways if he will marry her. The real villain of the piece is the High Priest who wants his son to marry the queen and will stop at nothing to achieve this end. With the presence of both Mark Forest and Paul Wynter, this is a real beefcake fest filled with plenty of oiled muscles and lots of sadistic torture sequences designed to show them off.

199   *The Mongols*

(I Mongoli)
Produzione Cinematografica, Rome–Royal Film, France (1961) 120 min.
Euroscope / Eastman Color
U.S.–Colorama Features (1962) 105 min.

P–Guido Giambartolomei / D–Andre De Toth, Leopoldo Savona (uncredited) / W–Ottavio Alessi, Alessandro Ferrau, Ugo Guerra, Luciano Martino / M–Mario Nascimbene / C– Aldo Giordani / E–Otello Colangeli / AD–Ottavio Scotti / CD– Enzo Bulgarelli

Cast–Jack Palance (Ogatai), Anita Ekberg (Hulina), Antonella Lualdi (Amina), Franco Silva (Stephen of Krakow), Roldano Lupi (Genghis Khan), Gianni Garko (Henry de Valois), Gabriella Pallotta (Lutezia), Pierre Cressoy (Igor) with Tuen Wang, Gabriele Antonini, Vittorio Sanipoli

A lengthy account of the Mongol invasion of Poland with the benefits of a handsome production and an in-

Maciste in chains: Mark Forest in *Mole Men Against the Son of Hercules* (1963).

teresting cast. The Mongol hordes of Genghis Khan descend on Europe and a delegation, led by Stephen of Kracow, is sent from Poland in the hope of establishing a peace treaty. Ogatai, the cruel son of Genghis Khan, pretends friendship but later imprisons and tortures the noble knights. With the arrival of Genghis Khan peace is assured by the aging warrior but he is assassinated by Hulina, the ambitious mistress of Ogatai. Ogatai declares himself emperor and announces his plans to conquer the rest of Europe. The united armies of Europe, led by Stephen, engage in a bloody battle, which results in the defeat of the Mongols. Jack Palance is his usual villainous self as Ogatai. Anita Ekberg, as his conniving mistress, is even more unlikely as a Mongol than Susan Hayward was as a Tarter in *The Conqueror*. Riccardo Freda directed the action sequences.

200   *Moses*

(Moses the Lawgiver)
An ITC-RAI Co-production (1975)
Technicolor
U.S.–Avco Embassy (1976) 141 min.

   P–Vincenzo Labella/D–Gianfranco De Bosio/ W–Anthony Burgess, Vittorio Bonicelli, Gianfranco De Bosio/M–Ennio Morricone, Dov Seltzer/C–Marcello Gatti/E–Garry Hambling, Peter Boita, John Guthridge, Alberto Gallitti, Freddie Wilson/AD–Pier Luigi Basile/CD–Enrico Sabbatini/SVE–Mario Bava

   Cast–Burt Lancaster (Moses), Anthony Quayle (Aaron), Irene Papas (Zipporah), Ingrid Thulin (Miriam), Laurent Tezieff (Pharaoh Mernefta), Aharon Ipale (Joshua), Mariangela Melato (Bithia), Yossef Shiloah (Dathan), Marina Berti (Eliseba), Samuel Rodensky (Jethro) with Jacques Herlin, William Lancaster, Galia Kohn, Mario Ferrari

Presented by Sir Lew Grade in 1975 as a multimillion-dollar, six-hour television miniseries, *Moses* later surfaced briefly in some countries as a theatrical feature. This treatment abandons DeMille's flamboyant approach and presents the story of Moses in more realistic terms. Unfortunately, it is also extremely dull, enlivened only by Burt Lancaster's bravura performance in the title role. The remainder of the cast is adequate, but not outstanding. The special visual effects by the great Italian horror-meister Mario Bava are surprisingly unimpressive but then this revisionist version goes out of its way to eschew the spectacular.

201   *Moses*

A Turner/Lube/Lux Vide/Beta Film/Rai Uno Production
U.S.–TNT Network (1996) 184 min.
Color

   P–Gerald Rafshoon, Lorenzo Minoli/D–Roger Young/W–Lionel Chetwyn/M–Marco Frisina/C–Raffaele Mertes/E–Benjamin A. Weissman/PD–Paolo Biagetti, Enrico Sabbatini/CD–Enrico Sabbatini

   Cast–Ben Kingsley (Moses), David Suchet (Aaron), Frank Langella (Mernefta), Maurice Roeves (Zerack), Christopher Lee (Ramses), Enrico Lo Verso (Joshua) with Anna Galiena, Anthony Higgins, Geraldine McEwan, Philippe Leroy, Philip Stone, Anton Lesser, Dudley Sutton, Anita Zagaria, Federico Pacifici

As punishment for disobeying him, the Lord caused the Hebrews to wander forty years in the desert before they could enter the promised land. By the time this torturously slow-moving TV movie has run its course, you may feel as if you were with them every step of the way. Part of the problem is the representation of the title character. As played by Ben Kingsley, Moses is a reluctant leader whose persona lacks the dynamic qualities of the previous interpretations of both Charlton Heston and Burt Lancaster. The Hebrews are shown as a whining and complaining people, ill deserved of the attention lavished on them by God. When one of them says "Truly Moses, we should never have doubted you," it is an understatement of major proportions. Immediately thereafter, they doubt him again. Poor Moses; you have to admire his fortitude. Even the usually excellent Frank Langella turns in a lackluster performance as the pharaoh Mernefta. Somehow, the entire production seems drained of life.

   Variety: For all the pic's faults, this timeless story's powerful impact isn't entirely lost.

202   *My Son the Hero*

(Arrivano i Titani; The Titans Are Coming/Sons of Thunder)
Vides, Rome–Les Films Ariane Filmsonor, Paris (1962) 119 min.
Technicolor
U.S.–United Artists (1963) 115 min.

The youngest Titan (Giuliano Gemma) opposes the tyrannical rule of an evil king (Pedro Armendariz) in *My Son the Hero* (1963).

P–Franco Cristaldi, Georges Danciger/D–Duccio Tessari/W–Ennio De Concini, Duccio Tessari/M–Carlo Rustichelli/C–Alfio Contini/E–Maurizio Lucidi/AD–Ottavio Scotti/CD–Vittorio Rossi

Cast–Pedro Armendariz (Cadmus), Giuliano Gemma (Crios), Jacqueline Sassard (Antiope), Serge Nubret (Rator), Antonella Lualdi (Herminoe), Gerard Sety (Hippolytos), Tanya Lopert (Licina), Ingrid Schoeller (Emerate)

Cadmus, the cruel King of Crete, kills his wife and destroys the temple of Jove, setting himself up as a god instead. A seer tells Cadmus that he has incurred the wrath of the gods and when his daughter Antiope falls in love it will bring about his downfall. Because of the grave sacrileges that have been committed by Cadmus, Crios, the youngest of the Titans, is set free from his imprisonment in Hades and sent to earth to deal with the evil ruler of Crete. Crios immediately falls in love with Antiope, who is banished to the island of the Gorgon by her father to prevent her responding in kind. Crios goes back to the underworld and steals the helmet of the god Pluto. This magical helmet renders the wearer invisible. Thus Crios is able to slay the snake-haired Gorgon and rescue the princess. When Cadmus' army arrives on the island, Crios is wounded and Antiope is taken back to her father. At a festival to celebrate his imagined divinity, Cadmus prepares for the sacrificial execution of Crios' friend Rator. Crios and his brother Titans appear and hurl Jove's thunderbolts at the wicked king. The earth opens and Cadmus is swallowed up in the fiery chasm. When United Artists picked up *Arrivano I Titani* for distribution in the U.S. they retitled the film *Sons Of Thunder* and designed a typical spectacle advertising campaign ("They thundered out of Hades to topple a sin-gorged empire!"). Before the film went into theatres, United Artists decided to change tactics and spoof it in the advertising campaign instead ("A gigantic spectacle shot on location for peanuts!"). Artist Frank Frazetta created some clever cartoon style artwork but the cornerstone of this campaign was the outrageous trailer created by Mel Brooks, in which he dubbed over the character's voices with highly exaggerated Yiddish accents. The film does have a definitely lighthearted approach, but it is hardly the rollicking comedy that the new publicity implied. Giuliano Gemma, as Crios, is a departure from the standard musclebound hero so prevalent in European epics at this time. A former acrobat, Gemma performed most of his own stunts, displaying a great deal of agility instead of mere brawn. Gemma appeared in a number of peplum films but achieved his greatest success as the star of numerous Spaghetti Westerns, sometimes using the name "Montgomery Wood."

203   The Nativity

A D'Angelo-Bullock-Allen Production
20th Century–Fox Television (1978) 97 min.
Color by DeLuxe
P–William P. D'Angelo/D–Bernard L. Kowalski/W–Millard Kaufman, Morton S. Fine/M–Lalo Schifrin/C–Gabor Pogany/E–Robert Phillips, Jerry Dronsky/AD–Luciano Spandoni
Cast–Madeleine Stowe (Mary), John Shea (Joseph), Jane Wyatt (Anna), Paul Stewart (Zacharias), Audrey Totter (Elizabeth), George Voskovec (Joachim), Julie Garfield (Zipporah), Jamil Zakkai (Menachem), Freddie Jones (Diomedes), John Rhys-Davies (Nestor), Morgan Shepard (Flavius), Kate O'Mara (Salome), Leo McKern (Herod) with Geoffrey Beevers, Barrie Houghton, Jacob Witkin, Jack Lynn, Michael Balfour

This made-for-television movie was filmed in Spain and focuses on the relationship between Joseph and Mary. Although he is not the most promising of her many suitors, Mary loves Joseph and convinces her parents to accept his proposal of marriage. While Mary and Joseph are planning their future life together, King Herod is faced with the news that soon a Messiah will be born who will be hailed as the King of the Jews. This information drives Herod over the brink into total madness and he sends his three advisors out to discover the whereabouts of this Messiah. In the meantime, Joseph and Mary are attempting to bypass the traditional year long period of betrothal and marry. Shortly after their marriage, Mary has a "visitation" and announces to Joseph that she is pregnant with a baby who will be the Messiah. Joseph is understandably skeptical at first but his love and faith in Mary soon win him over. Joseph and Mary flee Jerusalem and the baby is born in a manger in Bethlehem. This is an interesting movie because it ends where most filmic tales of Christ begin. Unfortunately, Joseph and Mary, are the two least interesting characters in the film. When the focus shifts to the court of Herod or the Roman persecution of the Jews, the story is far more intriguing. Kate O'Mara, who plays Herod's companion Salome, had been a glamour girl in Hammer horror films. Jane Wyatt has what amounts to little more than a cameo role as Mary's mother. Bernard L. Kowalski was a prolific television series director who was also responsible for such esoteric film fare as *The*

Giant Leeches and *Night of the Blood Beast*. These two inexpensive fifties sci-fi movies are memorable for their unnerving atmosphere and unrelentingly sober approach to the material.

204 *Nero's Mistress*

(Mio Figlio Nerone; My Son Nero / Les Week-ends de Neron; Nero's Big Weekend)
Titanus-Lux, Rome–Vides-Marceau, Paris (1956)
104 min.
CinemaScope / Eastman Color
U.S.–Manhattan Films International (1963) 86 min.
P–Franco Cristaldi / D–Steno (Stefano Vanzina) / W–Rodolfo Sonego, Alessandro Continenza, Diego Fabbri, Ugo Guerra, Steno / M–Angelo Francesco Lavagnino / C–Mario Bava / E–Mario Serandrei / AD–Piero Filippone / CD–Veniero Colasanti
Cast–Brigitte Bardot (Poppaea Sabina), Gloria Swanson (Agrippina), Alberto Sordi (Nero), Vittorio De Sica (Seneca), Giorgia Moll (Lydia), Mino Doro (Corbulone) with Mario Carotenuto, Ciccio Barbi, Enzo Furlai, Irene Gay, Augusto Dubbini, Arturo Bragaglia, Carlo Tamberlani

While working for United Press International in Europe, Gloria Swanson took time out to appear in this nonsensical costume farce in 1956. Swanson portrays Nero's disapproving mother Agrippina, who tries to prevent her son from marrying his mistress Poppaea. Mother and son continually attempt to kill each other in a variety of ways but each attempt proves futile. Broad slapstick and puerile humor put this on a par with the majority of the other European epics that were played for laughs. The sets are left over from MGM's *Quo Vadis* and Alberto Sordi bears more than a passing resemblance to Peter Ustinov in that film. *Nero's Mistress* remained unseen in the United States until 1963 when it was given a limited distribution in a shortened version.

205 *A Night in Paradise*

Universal (1945) 84 min.
Technicolor
P–Walter Wanger / D–Arthur Lubin / W–Ernest Pascal / Based on the novel *Peacock's Feather* by George S. Hellman / M–Frank Skinner / C–Hal Mohr, W. Howard Green / E–Milton Carruth / AD–Alexander Golitzen, John B. Goodman / CD–Vera West

Aesop (Turhan Bey) woos the lovely princess Delarai (Merle Oberon) during *A Night in Paradise* (1954).

Cast—Merle Oberon (Princess Delarai), Turhan Bey (Aesop), Thomas Gomez (Croesus), Gale Sondergaard (Attosa), John Litel (Archon), George Dolenz (Ambassador), Paul Cavanagh (Cleomenes) with Ernest Truex, Ray Collins, Douglas Dumbrille, Marvin Miller, Moroni Olson, Richard Bailey, Jerome Cowan

A Night in Paradise has much in common with the series of Jon Hall/Maria Montez Technicolor costume fantasies which were popular in the early forties. In fact, Walter Wanger also produced the first of these, *Arabian Nights*, in 1942. Like *A Night in Paradise*, they were all brightly colored escapist fluff designed to divert the war-weary public. Apparently the formula worked quite well because the films were very successful. This time we have Merle Oberon instead of Maria Montez as the beautiful but haughty princess promised in marriage to the greedy Croesus, King of Lydia. The philospher Aesop is played by Turhan Bey, who was usually featured in supporting roles in the Hall/Montez films. Aesop comes to Croesus in the guise of an old storyteller in an attempt to free the people of his homeland, Samos, from the tyranny of Lydian rule. The message was clear; a powerful nation, under the leadership of a cruel tyrant, oppresses a smaller country. *A Night in Paradise* does not let its message get in the way of romance, however. Without the storyteller disguise, Aesop is actually a dashing and handsome youth who easily wins the love of Princess Delarai. There is also a fantasy element in the person of Gale Sondergaard as Attosa, a sorceress who wishes to revenge herself on Croesus.

206   *Noah's Ark*

Warner Bros.–Vitaphone (1929) 100 min.

P–Darryl F. Zanuck/D–Michael Curtiz/W–Darryl F. Zanuck, Anthony Coldeway/C–Hal Mohr, Barney McGill/E–Harold McCord

Cast—Dolores Costello (Marie/Miriam), George O'Brien (Travis/Japheth), Noah Berry (Nephilim/Nickoloff), Guinn Williams (Ham/Al), Paul McAllistar (Noah/Minister), Malcolm Waite (Shem/Bulkah) with Louise Fazenda, Anders Randolf, Armand Kaliz, William V. Mong, Nigel DeBrulier, Noble Johnson, Otto Hoffman

Director Michael Curtiz had filmed versions of *Sodom and Gomorrah* (1922) and *Samson and Delilah* (1923) in his native Hungary, but it was his story of Egypt at the time of Moses, *Moon of Israel* (1924), that brought him to the attention of Jack Warner, who invited Curtiz to come to America to work at the Warner Bros. studio. With his extensive experience filming spectaculars Curtiz was considered the ideal choice to direct what Jack Warner hoped would be the ultimate motion picture epic. Following in the footsteps of De-Mille's 1923 version to *The Ten Commandments*, *Noah's Ark* employed a modern story set in World War I Europe counterpointed with a lengthy biblical flashback showing the Great Flood. Curtiz proved adept at directing large-scale action but he was ruthless when dealing with his performers. His utter disregard for the safety of his actors is exemplified by the fact that three extras drowned during the flood sequences. Curtiz, is seems, never bothered to find out if anyone could swim before dumping thousands of gallons of water on the unfortunate crowds. *Noah's Ark* was completed and ready for release just as sound films were becoming increasingly popular. The film was withdrawn and several sound sequences were added. The modern story begins after a brief prologue which compares the worship of the Golden Calf to the sins of the Jazz Age. Two Americans (George O'Brien and Guinn Williams) are on the Orient Express just prior to the outbreak of World War I. When the train is derailed, the boys rescue a beautiful German girl (Dolores Costello) from the wreckage. Soon after, war is declared and they join the armed forces to go off and fight in the trenches. When an exploding bomb traps all of the main characters in a cellar, a minister tells them of Noah and the Great Flood. In relating the story of Noah, a young Darryl F. Zanuck incorporated elements from the stories of Moses and Samson into the screenplay as well. Although the same actors play similar characters in both stories, the connection between the two plots is somewhat tenuous. As pure spectacle, the biblical scenes are breathtaking. Gigantic sets and thousands of performers, both human and animal, fill the

Opposite: **Noah builds his ark with the help of some elephants in *Noah's Ark* (1929).**

screen in an overwhelming display of pageantry. Despite the visual splendors, the costly film was lost in the transition from silent to sound movies and became a notorious box office disaster. In 1957 Robert Youngston adapted a seventy-five minute version which was released by Dominant Pictures with modest success.

207 Noah's Ark

Hallmark Entertainment / Babelsberg International
   Film
NBC TV Network (1999) 139 min.
Color
   P–Robert Halmi, Sr., Stephen Jones / D–John Irvin / W–Peter Barnes / M–Paul Grabowsky / C–Mike Molloy / E–Ian Crafford / PD–Leslie Binns / CD–Marion Boyce
   Cast–Jon Voight (Noah), Mary Steenburgen (Naamah), F. Murray Abraham (Lot), Carol Kane (Sarah), James Coburn (The Peddler) with Mark Bazeley, Jonathan Cake, Alexis Denisof, Emily Mortimer, Sonya Walger

This decidedly tongue-in-cheek narrative, which *Variety* accurately dubbed "Noah's Lark," combines the biblical tale of Noah with Sodom and Gomorrah. The scriptwriter seemed determined to re-invent the biblical epic and the end result is filled with jokey, anachronistic dialogue which really doesn't work at all. Intermingling the stories of Noah and Lot is one of the most audacious departures from biblical text since Rita Hayworth's Salome danced to "save" John the Baptist back in 1953. In the Bible, the destruction of Sodom and Gomorrah and the great flood are separated by hundreds of years but in this version Noah and Lot are best friends. Jon Voight's pious portrayal of Noah works against the material. This isn't necessarily a bad thing considering some of the other actors' approach, in particular Carol Kane as Lot's extremely annoying wife. The special effects are impressive but it's hardly worth suffering through the rest of running time to see them.

Los Angeles Times: A laughably bad, stunningly low-burlesque, excruciatingly slow two-parter. And the ark looks less biblical than like an oversized garbage barge.

Variety: Here is that exceedingly rare Bible story that refuses to overstate its case or over-indulge the audience.

208 The Norseman

A Charles B. Pierce / Fawcett-Majors Production
American-International (1978) 90 min.
Panavision / Color by Movielab
   P / D / W–Charles B. Pierce / M–Jamie Mendoza-Nava / C–Robert Bethard / E–Stephen Dunn, Robert Bell / AD–John Ball
   Cast–Lee Majors (Thorvald), Cornel Wilde (Ragnar), Mel Ferrer (Eurich), Susie Coelho (Winetta), Chris Connelly (Rolf), Denny Miller (Rauric) with Jack Elam, Kathleen Freeman, Jimmy Elam, Seamon Glass, Deacon Jones, Chuck Pierce, Jr.

In A.D. 1006 Thorvald the Bold and his band of Viking warriors sail westward from their homeland in search of his father, King Eurich. They eventually land on an unfamiliar shore and name it Vineland (we call it America). Coincidentally, this is the very place that King Eurich and his men landed and met the local Indian tribe. Although the Indians appeared to be friendly they quickly turned on the Vikings, blinding them and forcing them to work in a mill grinding corn. When Thorvald and his pals show up, the Indians don't even pretend to be friendly; it's hatred at first sight. With the help of a sympathetic Indian maiden, Thorvald rescues the captive Vikings and slaughters quite a few Indians before setting sail for home. Lee Majors had scored a big success on television as *The Six Million Dollar Man.* He hoped to use this ill chosen vehicle for his transition to the big screen. Filmed in Florida, this ultra tacky production only proves that Lee Majors was about as adept at playing a Viking as John Wayne was playing Genghis Khan.

209 The Odyssey

Hallmark Entertainment / American Zoetrope
NBC TV Network (1997) 165 min.
Color
   P–Dyson Lovell, Robert Halmi, Sr., Francis Ford Coppola, Fred Fuchs, Nicholas Meyer / D–Andrei Konchalovsky / W–Andrei Konchalovsky, Chris Solimine / Based on *The Odyssey* by Homer / M–Edward Artemyev / C–Sergei Kozlov / E–Michael Ellis / PD–Roger Hall / CD–Charles Knode
   Cast–Armand Assante (Odysseus), Greta Scacchi (Penelope), Isabella Rossellini (Athena), Geraldine Chaplin (Eurycleia), Jeroen Krabbe (Alcinous), Christopher Lee (Tiresias), Irene Papas (Anticlea), Bernadette Peters (Circe), Eric Roberts (Eurymachus), Vanessa Williams (Calypso), Mi-

chael J. Pollard (Aeolus), Nicholas Clay (Meneleus), Alan Stenson (Telemachus) with Alex Cox, Katie Carr, William Houston, Peter Woodthorpe, Stewart Thompson, Ron Cook, Michael Tezcan, Freddy Douglas, Vincenzo Nicoli

This spectacular and exciting version of Homer's *The Odyssey* is one of the best of the made-for-television epics. Shortly after the birth of his son, Odysseus, King of Ithaca, must set sail with the other Greek rulers in a war against the city of Troy. The war lasts for ten years and finally ends with a Greek victory engineered by the intelligence of Odysseus. Odysseus' excessive pride brings about the anger of the sea god Poseidon who prevents the warrior and his crew from returning to Ithaca for another ten years. During the course of his journey home, Odysseus encounters a man-eating Cyclops, horrible sea monsters and two alluring sorceresses. He finally arrives home only to discover that his faithful wife Penelope is being harassed by some very persistent suitors. *The Odyssey* was shot on location in Turkey and Malta at a cost $40 million, making it one of the most expensive TV movies ever. Filled with stunning visuals, including a variety of monsters created by the Jim Henson's Creature Shop, the film is marred only by some glaring bits of miscasting. The most unfortunate of these are Michael J. Pollard as the wind god Aeolus and Bernadette Peters as Circe. The leading players are far better chosen. Armand Assante suffers stoically as Odysseus while Greta Scacchi gives a moving and memorable portrayal of Penelope.

210   *O.K. Nero*

(O.K. Nerone)
A Titanus Production (1951) 90 min.
U.S.–I.F.E. Releasing Corp. (1953)
  P–Niccolo Theodoli/D–Mario Soldati/W–Steno, Alessandro Continenza, Mario Monicelli, Umberto Scarpelli, Lewis E. Ciannelli/M–Mario Nascimbene/C–Mario Montuori/E–Roberto Cinquini/AD–Guido Fiorini
  Cast–Walter Chiari (Fiorello), Carlo Campanini (Jimmy), Silvana Pampanini (Poppaea), Jackie Frost (Licia), Gino Cervi (Nero), Piero Palermini (Marcus), Giulio Donnini (Tigellinus), Alda Mangini (Sophonisba), Rocco D'Assunta (Pannunzio), Alba Arnova

Walter Chiari and Carlo Campanini enact the Italian equivalents of Martin and Lewis in this comedy about two American sailors on leave in Rome. While visiting the Colosseum they are attacked by thieves and knocked unconscious. They awaken to find themselves transported to the time of Nero. When circumstances force them to masquerade as African slave girls, they are bought as gifts for the empress Poppaea. A variety of predictable misadventures ensue. Silvana Pampanini was Italy's reigning glamour queen at the time—a predecessor to Gina Lollobrigida and Sophia Loren. A former Miss Italy, she does manage to fill out her costumes quite nicely as the promiscuous Poppaea. The antics of Chiari and Campanini make this farce all but unwatchable. *O.K. Nero* was filmed at Titanus studios while *Quo Vadis* was being filmed at Cinecitta. It was picked up for American release two years later to capitalize on the growing popularity of historical spectacles.

211   *The Old Testament*

(Il Vecchio Testamento)
Cineproduzioni Associate, Rome–Comptoir Français du Film, Paris (1963) 120 min.
Supertotalscope/Eastman Color
U.S.–Filmar Distribution (1964) 88 min.
  P–Mario Damiani/D–Gianfranco Parolini/W–Giovanni Simonelli, Gianfranco Parolini/M–Angelo Francesco Lavagnino/C–Francesco Izzarelli/E–Edmondo Lozzi/AD–Giuseppe Ranieri, Nico Matul/CD–Vittorio Rossi
  Cast–Brad Harris (Simon), John Heston (Judas), Mara Lane (Diotima), Jacques Berthier (Apollonius), Philippe Hersent (Namele), Margaret Taylor (Miza), Isacaro Ravaioli (Jonathan) Carlo Tamberlani (Mattathias), Enzo Doria (Gionata), Vladimer Leib (Antenone) with Susan Paget, Ivy Stewart, Ignazio Dolce, Sergio Ciani (aka Alan Steel), Giorgio Nenadova, Nick Stefanini, Pino Mattei, Ray Martino

A rather grandly titled film considering that the story encompasses a very small part of the Old Testament, and one of the Apocryphal books at that. During the second century B.C., the Maccabee family led their people in revolt against the tyrannical Syrians who had invaded the city of Jerusalem. Mattathias is the High Priest of the Temple of Jerusalem. When the newly appointed governor, Apollinius, attempts to profane the Temple with the graven image of a false god, Mattathias' son Judas leads the Hebrews in rebellion against their oppressors. Judas represents the use of force, while his brother Simon is a man of peace. Misunderstood Simon is accused of cowardice and of consorting with the enemy. Judas is killed in battle and his younger brother Jonathan takes his place aided by the wise council of Simon. Jonathan is killed in an attack on the Syrian stronghold of Joppa. Simon now becomes the leader of the Hebrews and eventually achieves victory for his people. Simon is played by Brad Harris who forsakes his usual muscleman persona and gives a noteworthy performance in an uncharacteristic role. John Heston (real name: Ivano Staccioli) is also effective as the hotheaded Judas. This story was previously filmed in Italy as *I Maccabei* (Enrico Guazzoni; 1910).

212   *Omar Khayyam*

Paramount (1957) 101 min.
VistaVision/Technicolor
P–Frank Freeman, Jr./D–William Dieterle/W–Barre Lyndon/M–Victor Young/C–Ernest Laszlo/E–Everett Douglas/AD–Hal Pereira, Joseph MacMillan Johnson/CD–Ralph Jester
Cast–Cornel Wilde (Omar Khayyam), Michael Rennie (Hasani), Debra Paget (Sharain), John Derek (Malik), Raymond Massey (The Shah), Yma Sumac (Karina), Margaret Hayes (Zarada), Joan Taylor (Yaffa), Sebastian Cabot (Nizam) with Perry Lopez, Morris Ankrum, Edward Platt, James Griffith, Peter Adams, Henry Brandon, Kem Dibbs, Paul Picerni

Omar Khayyam is appointed as an advisor to the mighty Shah of Persia, a problematic state of affairs since the ruler has just made Omar's beloved Sharain his second wife. The Byzantine army is about to invade the Persian empire and a group of fanatics called the Assassins are attempting to overthrow the Shah within the walls of his own city. Omar discovers the hideout of the Assassins and goes alone to their mountain fortress. There he discovers that his lifelong friend Hasani is the leader of the evil sect. Meanwhile the Shah and his army are able to defeat the Byzantines thanks to Omar's canny calculations, but the Shah is mortally wounded. Omar finds a weakness in the Assassin's stronghold and, in a spectacular fiery finale destroys the last of the Shah's enemies. As a reward for his loyalty he is allowed to marry the recently widowed Sharain. This fictionalized account of the famous 11th century Persian astronomer-poet is an elaborate and colorful affair. Despite its *Arabian Nights* style settings, it never degenerates into the parody so often found in movies from that genre. At times, it has the look and feel of a DeMille film, and some of the dialogue is just as unspeakable. At age 42, Cornel Wilde is a bit old for the part of the young, idealistic astronomer but his performance is effective nevertheless. The score by Victor Young was one of his last and includes an especially beautiful love theme.

213   *One Million B.C.*

(Cave Man)
A Hal Roach Production
United Artists (1940) 80 min.
P/D–Hal Roach, Sr., Hal Roach, Jr./W–Mickell Novak, George Baker, Joseph Frickert/M–Werner R. Heymann/C–Norbert Brodine/E–Ray Snyder/AD–Charles D. Hall/SVE–Roy Seawright
Cast–Victor Mature (Tumak), Carole Landis (Loana), Lon Chaney, Jr. (Akhoba), John Hubbard (Ohtao), Mamo Clark (Nupondi), Edgar Edwards (Sakana), Inez Palange (Tohana), Jacqueline Dalya (Ataf), Mary Gale Fisher (Wandi), Nigel De Brulier (Peytow), Henry Sylvester (Tuta)

This entertaining fantasy was directed, in part, by the great D.W. Griffith and it does bear some superficial resemblance to his 1912 film about the Stone Age, *Man's Genesis*. *One Million B.C.* still maintains his touch, even though he was removed from the picture due to creative differences with Hal Roach, Sr. Griffith's attraction to the project is understandable as it is basically a silent movie, except for a brief narrative prologue. A group of mountain climbers seek refuge from a storm in a cave. Inside they find a scientist who is studying the prehistoric cave paintings located there. To pass the time he interprets the ancient symbols for the gathering. The story which follows is a basic "boy meet girl" plot made unique by the prehistoric setting. The special effects are impressive even though the dinosaurs are modern reptiles enlarged to gigantic size by Roy Seawright's trick photography. These poor creatures would appear again and again throughout the years, courtesy of stock footage from *One Million B.C.*, in countless low budget science fiction films. Although no substitute for the stop-motion animation of the remake, the special effects are some of the best of their type. Victor Mature and Carole Landis are very appealing as the Stone Age Romeo and Juliet. Lon Chaney, Jr., almost unrecognizable in his caveman makeup, is memorable in one of his earliest fantasy film roles.

AA Nominations: Best Special Effects, Musical Score

214   *One Million Years B.C.*

A Hammer–Seven Arts Production (1966) 100 min. Technicolor
U.S.–20th Century–Fox 91 min.
Color by DeLuxe
P/W–Michael Carreras/D–Don Chaffey/Based on a screenplay by Mickell Novak, George Baker, Joseph Frickert/M–Mario Nascimbene/C–Wilkie Cooper/E–James Needs, Tom Simpson/AD–Robert Jones/CD–Carl Toms/SVE–Ray Harryhausen
Cast–Raquel Welch (Loana), John Richardson (Tumak), Percy Herbert (Sakana), Robert Brown (Akhoba), Martine Beswick (Nupondi), Jean Waladon (Ahot), Lisa Thomas (Sura), Malya Nappi (Tohana), Yvonne Horner (Ullah), William Lyon Brown (Payto) with Richard James, Frank Hayden, Terence Maidment, Micky De Rauch

The financial success of their remake of H. Rider Haggard's *She* in 1965 inspired Hammer Films of England to embark on a series of movies with budgets considerably higher than those normally afforded their gothic horror films. Stop-motion animation wizard Ray Harryhausen was approached to do the special effects for a remake of *King Kong* but when Hammer failed to secure the rights to this title, another property was sought out. Hal Roach's 1940 saga of prehistoric life, *One Million B.C.* turned out to be a perfect choice for Hammer and Harryhausen. Touted as Hammer's one-hundredth production, it was also one of their most expensive. Ursula Andress, who had starred to great effect in *She*, was asked to return as the lead, but previous commitments and an inflated salary forced Hammer to search elsewhere. Raquel Welch, a 20th Century–Fox starlet, was chosen and the part elevated her to international stardom, al-

though at the time she thought appearing in the film was "a fate worse than death." Publicity photos of Raquel in her prehistoric bikini created the biggest sensation since Betty Grable looked over her shoulder in her famous forties cheesecake pose. Handsome John Richardson, who had co-starred in *She*, took over the Victor Mature role from the first movie. The simple story tells of the conflicts of the savage Rock Tribe and the more civilized Shell People. Although it retains the basic plot of the original version, the remake benefits from two tremendous advantages. The extensive location filming in the Canary Islands provides a suitably primitive landscape and the special effects are a definite improvement over those in the original. This time the dinosaurs really look like dinosaurs and are not merely lizards and other reptiles blown up to monstrous proportions by effects photography. Ray Harryhausen also provides an impressive volcanic eruption for the climax. Director Don Chaffey and composer Mario Nascimbene would each return to Hammer to work on future projects.

Time: One Million Years B.C. is a gaudier, bawdier copy of a prehistoric (1940) Hollywood epic about life at the yawn of prehistoric mankind. The picture follows a plot line more primitive than its subject.

Newsweek: One Million Years B.C., a remake of the classic caveman clunker, might have been fun if it had been more foolish. Just a bit more stupidity could have turned the trick, but that takes brains.

Los Angeles Times: One Million Years B.C., though lacking the romantic quality of the original, is well-directed by Don Chaffey and the special effects are surprisingly good.

215   *Pharaoh*

(Faron)
Kadr Film–Film Polski (1965) 175 min.
Dyaliscope/Eastman Color
U.S.–Hallmark (1975) 134 min.
P–Ludwik Hager/D–Jerzy Kawalerowicz/W–Tadeusz Konwicki, Jerzy Kawalerowicz/Based on the novel by Boleslaw Prus/M–Adam Walacinski/C–Jerzy Wojcik, W. Zdort/AD–Jerzy Skrzepinski
Cast–Jerzy Zelnik (Rameses XIII), Leszek Herdengen (Pentuer), Barbara Brylska (Kama), Krys-

tyna Mikolajewska (Sarah), Piotr Pawloski (Herhor), Jerzy Buczacki (Thutmosis), with Wieslawa Mazurkiewicz, Stanislaw Milski, Ewa Kriezew

In Ancient Egypt, near the end of the XXth Dynasty, the young prince Rameses resents the power held by the High Priests. In an effort to get him under their influence, the priests use Kama, a seductive temple dancer, to lure Rameses from his Jewish wife, Sarah. The old pharaoh dies and the prince ascends the throne as Rameses XIII. The new pharaoh must now struggle with the priests over the rule of Egypt. This strife comes to a climax when Rameses attempts to use the priests' store of gold to lessen the tax budens of his people. When the opening shot is of two beetles rolling a ball of dung across the screen, you know you're not going to see the conventional Hollywood-style spectacle. Based on a novel by Boleslaw Prus, this fascinating movie is probably the most realistic represen-

tation of ancient Egypt ever produced for the screen. This realism is greatly enhanced by the desert location filming in Egypt and set designer Jerzy Skrzepinski's determination not to guild the lily. Although it was nominated for an Academy Award as Best Foreign Language Film, *Pharaoh* had few U.S. playdates in its original form. It fared only slightly better in a truncated version which surfaced a decade later.

AA Nomination: Best Foreign Language Film

Boxoffice: A definitive work of the 20th dynasty of ancient Egypt ... must be labeled one of the better-grade superspectacles.

216   *The Pharaohs' Woman*
(La Donna dei Faraoni)
Vic Film–Faro Production, Rome (1960) 88 min.
Techniscope/Technicolor
U.S.–Universal-International (1961)

Victor Tourjansky directs John Drew Barrymore and Linda Cristal in *The Pharaoh's Woman* (1961).

P–Giorgio Venturini/D–Victor Tourjansky/W–
Ugo Liberatore, Remigio Del Grosso, Virgilio Tosi,
Massimo Vitali/M–Giovanni Fusco/C–Pier Lu-
dovico Pavoni/E–Antonietta Zita/AD–Arrigo
Equini/CD–Giancarlo Bartolini Salimbeni

Cast–Linda Cristal (Akis), John Drew Barrymore
(Sabaku), Pierre Brice (Amosi), Armando Francioli
(Ramsisu) with Lilly Lembo, Guido Celano, Ugo
Sasso, Nerio Bernardi, Andriena Rossi, Nando
Angelini, Fedele Gentile, Nino Marchetti, Anita To-
desco

In this fictitious tale of royal intrigue, the
Pharaoh of Upper Egypt seizes the throne of
Lower Egypt and unites the country under
one crown. This causes resentment because
Sabaku, Prince of Busbastis, has now been deprived of his birthright. Nevertheless, Sabaku
attempts to maintain a friendly relationship
with his cousin Ramsisu, who is the son of
the reigning pharaoh. The cousins embark on
a hunting trip, accompanied by Amosi, a
young physician who is a friend of Ramsisu.
While on this excursion, the three men meet
a beautiful young woman named Akis. The
trio competes for her affections but she falls
in love with Amosi. When the two princes
gamble for possession of the girl, Amosi helps
her go into hiding to escape them. Word
comes that the pharaoh is dying and Ramsisu
and Amosi must return to Thebes. Believing
that she has been abandoned by Amosi, Akis
gives herself to Sabaku to avoid becoming a
slave. Sabaku soon learns that the old pharaoh
has died and Ramsisu is the new ruler of
Egypt. No longer able to control his jealousy,
Sabaku declares war on his cousin and crowns
himself Pharaoh of Lower Egypt with Akis as
his queen. Eventually, the forces of Ramsisu
defeat those of Sabaku and the young pharaoh enters the city of Bubastis in triumph.
Ramsisu has Sabaku executed and condemns
Akis to a life of slavery. Amosi rescues Akis
and together they flee into the desert. As directed by Victor Tourjansky, who made a career out of such fare, *The Pharaohs' Woman* is
attractive to look at but lacks the dramatic in-
tensity or starpower necessary to bring it off.
John Drew Barrymore gives his usual overwrought performance and Linda Cristal,
whose character should be the focal point of
audience attention, is little more than orna-
mental. She manages to go from peasant girl
to temple dancer to Queen of Lower Egypt
with little change of expression. Technical
credits are of a high caliber but this is merely
the icing on a rather bland cake. *The Pharaohs'
Woman* was the first motion picture to utilize
the Techniscope widescreen process.

217 *Pontius Pilate*

(Ponzio Pilato)
Glomer Film, Rome–Lux C.C.F., Paris (1962) 100
min.
Technirama/Technicolor
U.S.–Z.I.V. International (1964)

P–Enzo Merolle/D–Irving Rapper/W–Gino De
Santis, Gian Paolo Callegari, Ivo Perelli, Oreste
Biancoli, Guy Elmes, Guglielmo Santangelo/M–
Angelo Francesco Lavagnino/C–Massimo Dalla-
mano/E–Renzo Lucidi/PD–Ottavio Scotti/CD–
Ugo Pericoli

Cast–Jean Marais (Pontius Pilate), Jeanne Crain
(Claudia), Basil Rathbone (Caiaphas), Leticia
Roman (Sarah), John Drew Barrymore (Judas),
Livio Lorenzon (Barabbas), Gianni Garko (Jona-
than) with Roger Treville, Massimo Serato, Ric-
cardo Garrone, Carlo Giustini, Paul Muller, Dante
Di Paolo

The Roman emperor Caligula calls Pontius
Pilate before him and demands an account of
Jesus, the supposed King of the Jews. In flashback, Pilate recalls that he was sent by Emperor Tiberius to Palestine to be the military
governor of Jerusalem. His arrival is met with
opposition by the rebel forces led by Barabbas
but the High Priest of the Temple, Caiaphas,
strives to ingratiate himself with the Romans.
One of the rebels is taken prisoner and his
daughter, Sarah, attempts to assassinate Pilate. Pilate is attracted to the girl and sets her
father free. Pilate's wife, Claudia, and their
children arrive unexpectedly in Jerusalem,
curtailing the budding romance between
Sarah and Pilate. Meanwhile, there are rumors in the city that a man named Jesus may
be the Messiah. One day Claudia chances
upon a crowd that has gathered to hear Jesus
speak. Claudia listens and is moved by his
words. Caiaphas soon contrives to have Jesus
arrested for sedition. He is put on trial before
Pilate and, despite Claudia's pleas for his release, Jesus is condemned to be crucified. Following the crucifixion, a tremendous earthquake all but destroys the city and Pilate's wife
and children are killed in the holocaust. Al-

though the story is certainly nothing new, the interesting cast makes *Pontius Pilate* well worth watching. John Drew Barrymore plays both Judas and Jesus but, as the latter, his face is never shown. Leticia Roman is the daughter of famed costume designer Vittorio Nino Novarese. The production values are of a higher caliber than many of the other medium budgeted epics made at Cinecitta Studios during this time.

218   Prehistoric Women

Alliance Productions (1950) 74 min.
Eagle Lion–Pathé Industries
Cinecolor
P–Albert J. Cohen, Sam X. Abarbanel/D–Gregory G. Tallas/W–Sam X. Abarbanel, Gregory G. Tallas/M–Raoul Kraushaar/C–Lionel Lindon/E–James Graham/AD–Jerome Pycha, Jr.
Cast–Laurette Luez (Tigri), Allan Nixon (Ingar), Mara Lynn (Arva), Joan Shawlee (Lotee), Judy Landon (Aras), Kerry Vaughn (Tulle), Tony Devlin (Ruig) with James Summers, Jo Carroll Dennison, Dennis Dengate, Jeanne Sorel, John Merrich, Johann Peturrson, Janet Scott

A Stone Age saga obviously inspired by Hal Roach's *One Million B.C.* but lacking that film's charm and special effects. A tribe of prehistoric Amazons capture a group of male hunters with the idea of subjugating the men into love slaves. Wild-eyed spirfire Laurette Luez is Tigri, the leader of the prehistoric women and Allan Nixon is Ingar, the object of her desires. During the course of the story Ingar invents fire, Tigri invents leverage, and while *Prehistoric Women* may not invent boredom, it certainly induces it. The women engage in seemingly endless tribal dancing while the narrator drones on and on. The one "special effect" is the dread "Flying Dragon" which turns out to be a badly photographed pelican. In the clumsy conclusion the women and men must band together to fight the Guaddi, a terrible nine-foot caveman. They succeed in killing him and go off into the jungle to invent a society based on equal rights for men and women. The generally inferior Cinecolor process is actually quite effective in *Prehistoric Women* with its emphasis on muted brown and green colors.

219   The Prince of Egypt

DreamWorks Pictures (1998) 97 min.
Color
P–Jeffrey Katzenberg, Penney Finkelman Cox, Sandra Rabins/D–Brenda Chapman, Steve Hickner, Simon Wells/W–Philip LaZebnik, Nicholas Meyer M–Hans Zimmer/Songs–Stephen Schwartz/E–Nick Fletcher/PD–Darek Gogel/AD–Kathy Altieri, Richard Chavez
Voices–Val Kilmer (Moses), Ralph Fiennes (Rameses), Michelle Pfeiffer (Tzipporah), Sandra Bullock (Miriam), Jeff Goldblum (Aaron), Danny Glover (Jethro), Patrick Stewart (Seti), Helen Mirren (The Queen), Steve Martin (Hotep), Martin Short (Huy)

Under the leadership of Jeffrey Katzenberg, Walt Disney Studios had managed to take the animated feature in new directions. When he left to join Steven Spielberg and David Geffen in forming DreamWorks SKG, Katzenberg applied his experience to realize an animated movie based on the life of Moses. Four and a half years in production, the finished film is one of the most sensational and dramatic animated features ever made. Refusing to compromise the story by making it a film for children, *The Prince of Egypt* eschews the inclusion of many of the standard devices used in animated movies. The serious tone of the picture, which gained it a PG rating, and Katzenberg's decision to avoid the usual merchandise tie-ins may have hampered its performance at the box office but the film was a prestigious success for DreamWorks. After the two lackluster TV movies about Moses which preceded it, *The Prince of Egypt* is a welcome and exciting change of pace which often recalls the spectacular imagery of DeMille's 1956 version of the story. The relationship between Moses and his step-brother Rameses makes for a very logical dramatic conflict, presenting Rameses as far less of a villain than previous interpretations. The low point of the film is the inclusion of Steve Martin and Martin Short as the voices for the high priests Hotep and Huy, the movie's nominal comedy relief. The high point is the stunning prologue "Deliver Us" which shows the bondage of the Hebrews and instantly establishes the tone of the story to follow.

Variety: Far more than a cartoon rendering of a much-beloved Bible story, "The Prince of

The spectacular prologue to *The Prince of Egypt* (1998).

Egypt" proves an outstanding artistic achievement.

220   *Prince Valiant*

20th Century–Fox (1954) 100 min.
CinemaScope/Technicolor DeLuxe
  P–Robert L. Jacks/D–Henry Hathaway/W–
Dudley Nichols/Based on the comic strip by Harold Foster/M–Franz Waxman/C–Lucian Ballard/
E–Robert Simpson/AD–Lyle Wheeler, Mark-Lee
Kirk/CD–Charles Le Maire
  Cast–Robert Wagner (Valiant), James Mason (Sir
Brack), Janet Leigh (Aleta), Sterling Hayden (Sir
Gawain), Debra Paget (Ilene), Brian Aherne (King
Arthur), Victor McLaglen (Boltar) with Donald
Crisp, Barry Jones, Mary Philips, Howard Wendell,
Tom Conway, Neville Brand, Primo Carnera, John
Dierkes, Don Megowan

  Harold Foster's celebrated comic strip character comes to life in this action-packed
widescreen extravaganza. Valiant, the exiled
Viking prince of Scandia, goes to Camelot in
search of a knighthood. Along the way he
runs afoul of the infamous Black Knight and
barely escapes with his life. Valiant is be-

friended by Sir Gawain and together they uncover a plot against King Arthur. *Prince Valiant*
is beautifully produced but marred by a number of extreme performances, in particular,
Sterling Hayden as Sir Gawain. Despite the
dubious thesping abilities of some of the cast,
Prince Valiant is entertaining and the climactic
assault on a fortress filled with evil Vikings is
very exciting. Franz Waxman contributes a
rousing score which recalls Erich Korngold's
music for the Errol Flynn swashbucklers. A
typically beautiful production from Fox's early
CinemaScope period.

221   *Princess of the Nile*

A Panoramic Production
20th Century–Fox (1954) 71 min.
Technicolor
  P–Robert L. Jacks/D–Harmon Jones/W–Gerald Drayson Adams/M–Lionel Newman/C–Lloyd
Ahern/E–George A. Gittens/AD–Addison Hehr/
CD–Travilla
  Cast–Debra Paget (Taura/Shalimar), Jeffrey
Hunter (Haidi), Michael Rennie (Rama Khan),
Donna Drake (Mirva), Wally Cassell (Goghi),

Prince Valiant (Robert Wagner) is threatened by the Black Knight (James Mason) as Debra Paget, Janet Leigh and Barry Jones look on in the CinemaScope extravaganza *Prince Valiant* (1954).

Edgar Barrier (Shaman), Michael Ansara (Kral), Jack Elam (Basra), Lee Van Cleef (Hakar) with Lester Sharpe, Billy Curtis, Robert Roark, Lisa Daniels, Merry Anders, Honey Harlow, Bobette Bently

In A.D. 1249 Prince Haidi, son of the Caliph of Baghdad, stops at the Egyptian city of Memphis on his way home from battling the Christian Crusaders. The city is currently under siege by the treacherous Bedouin warrior Rama Khan, who plans to kill the ruler, Prince Selim, and wed his daughter, the beautiful Princess Shalimar. Prince Haidi soon discovers that the only opposition to Rama Khan is a band of courageous patriots led by Taura, a dancer at a coffee house called the Tambourine. Haidi joins them in their fight and learns that Taura is none other than Princess Shalimar in disguise. This project was originally announced in 1953 as *Queen of the Nile* to be filmed in 3-D and starring Tyrone Power and

Marilyn Monroe. The script was soon relegated to the 20th Century–Fox "B" picture production unit, Panoramic Pictures, where it was retitled and recast. Hastily filmed on left-over sets from *The Robe*, the final product is closer in spirit to the Maria Montez films of the forties than the Fox epics of the fifties. *Princess of the Nile* is definitely a bargain basement spectacular. Even the musical score is a patchwork of Alfred Newman themes from previous films such as *David and Bathsheba* and *The Mark of Zorro*, reused by musical director Lionel Newman. Most of the publicity for *Princess of the Nile* centered on Debra Paget's daring dance numbers as Taura (supposedly choreographed by Miss Paget herself). Studio press releases stated that the dances were so "steamy" that in the final film the editor was forced to cut to reaction shots of Michael Rennie and Jeffrey Hunter to tone down the effects of Debra's undulations. Viewed today

The Prince of Baghdad (Jeffrey Hunter) loves Taura the dancing girl (Debra Paget), who is really the *Princess of the Nile* (1954).

the film is silly, colorful, and entertaining, but not the least bit erotic.

Photoplay: Most everything here is fluff and nonsense, but quite easy to look at.

Modern Screen: One of the rare 20th Century–Fox pictures not in CinemaScope, this is a melodramatic spectacle in Technicolor which offers the dark-eyed Debra Paget her best screen role to date.

222   *The Private Lives of Adam and Eve*

An Albert Zugsmith Production
Universal-International (1960) 87 min.
Black & White and Spectacolor by Pathé
   P–Red Doff/D–Albert Zugsmith, Mickey Rooney/W–Robert Hill, George Kennett/M–Van Alexander/C–Philip Lathrop/E–Eddie Brossard/ AD–Richard Riedel/CD–Frederick's of Hollywood

Cast–Mickey Rooney (Nick Lewis/The Devil), Mamie Van Doren (Evie Simms/Eve), Marty Milner (Ad Simms/Adam), Fay Spain (Lil Lewis/ Lilith), Mel Torme (Hal Sanders), Cecil Kellaway (Doc Bayles), Tuesday Weld (Vangie Harper), Paul Anka (Pinkie Parker) with June Wilkinson, Ziva Rodann, Theona Bryant, Phillipa Fallon, Barbara Walden, Toni Covington

   In a black and white prologue, eight people are on a bus leaving Paradise, Nevada, and headed for Reno. A storm causes a flash flood which wipes out a bridge just as the bus is crossing it. The passengers escape and seek refuge in a deserted church. Evie and Ad Simms, a quarreling couple, fall asleep and have the same dream. The movie turns to color as Adam awakens in the Garden of Eden. The Devil sends the seductive Lilith to tempt him to eat from the forbidden tree but he resists. So that he will no longer be lonely,

God gives Adam a female companion named Eve. The Devil in the guise of a snake tempts Eve to eat the apple and she convinces Adam to join her. The film turns back to black and white as Adam and Eve are driven from Paradise. The Devil engineers a battle of the sexes between Adam, Eve, and Lilith but good triumphs over evil and God makes Eve pregnant as a reward. For this incredibly bad comedy, Albert Zugsmith assembled an "almost star" cast who mug and overact their way through the story. At the time of its release *The Private Lives of Adam and Eve* was condemned by the then powerful Catholic Legion of Decency, ensuring the film's box office failure. Zugsmith, who had produced some successful films for Universal and MGM, never worked for the major studios again and ended his career directing soft core porn movies.

223   The Prodigal

Metro-Goldwyn-Mayer (1955) 115 min.
CinemaScope / Eastman Color
 P–Charles Schnee / D–Richard Thorpe / W–Maurice Zimm / M–Bronislau Kaper / C–Joseph Ruttenberg / E–Harold Kress / AD–Cedric Gibbons, Randall Duell / CD–Herschel McCoy
 Cast–Lana Turner (Samarra), Edmund Purdom (Micah), Louis Calhern (Nahreeb), Audrey Dalton (Ruth), James Mitchell (Asham), Walter Hampden (Eli), Tania Elg (Elissa), Neville Brand (Rhakim), Frances L. Sullivan (Bosra), Joseph Wiseman (Carmish), Sandra Descher (Yasmin) with John Dehner, Cecil Kellaway, Philip Tonge, David Leonard, Henry Daniell, Paul Cavanagh, Tracy Roberts, Jay Novello, George Robotham, Eugene Mazzola

 The Prodigal is a prime example of the type of kitsch that MGM could turn out when they really put their minds to it. Not that this was the original intent. Studio head, Dore Schary, had hoped to make "a significant spectacle" starring Ava Gardner and Vittorio Gassman but something went wrong along the way. Where the film fails most brutally is in its attempt to translate the brief parable of the Prodigal Son into nearly two hours of screen time. The script elaborates upon the simple story until it is almost beyond recognition. In the film version, Micah, the son of Eli, leaves his family and journeys to Damascus in pursuit of a beautiful priestess of Astarte. While in the sinful city, he squanders his fortune on her and is eventually sold into slavery to pay his debts. In prison he realizes the error of his ways and leads his fellow slaves in revolt against the corrupt high priest of Baal. The priest and priestess are killed in the uprising and Micah returns to the loving arms of his family. Technically *The Prodigal* is magnificent. Filmed entirely in Hollywood at great expense, the sets and costumes are fabulous. Lana Turner wears some particularly eye-popping outfits which were as daring as the times would permit. Turner, who

Lana Turner and Louis Calhern on the set of *The Prodigal* **(1955).**

intensely disliked both the film and her leading man, took credit for altering the costumes to show as much flesh as the censors would allow. Realizing the film was an intellectual wasteland, she decided to at least give audiences some visual stimulation. Ironically, the stills are airbrushed to minimize Turner's exposure but the film reveals her in all of her beaded glory. Turner later said of the film "It should have played Disneyland."

Motion Picture: The film strays somewhat from the spirit of the gospel story, but just as melodrama it carries force.

Variety: Richard Thorpe's direction is hard put to give it any semblance of movement or to get life and warmth into the characters and incidents.

224   *A Queen for Caesar*

(Una Regina per Cesare)
Filmes, Rome–C.F.P.C., Paris (1962) 91 min.
Euroscope/Technicolor
U.S.–Commonwealth United Television
    P–Victor Tourjansky/D–Piero Pierotti/W–Fulvio Gicca/M–Michele Michelet/C–Angelo Lotti/CD–Nadia Vitale
    Cast–Pascale Petit (Cleopatra), Gordon Scott (Julius Caesar), Akim Tamiroff (Pompey), Giorgio Ardisson (Achillas), Rik Battaglia (Lucius), Corrado Pani (Ptolemy) with Franco Volpi, Nando Angelini, Nerio Bernardi, Nino Marchetti, Ennio Balbo, Barbara Loy, Aurora de Alba, Barbara Nardi, Piero Palermini

Another *Cleopatra* imitation, notable only for the vast amount of historical inaccuracies perpetrated by the screenwriter. The events depicted herein occur prior to those usually shown in films dealing with the most famous Queen of Egypt. Cleopatra and her younger brother Ptolemy rule Egypt jointly until Ptolemy's evil advisor Theodotus convinces the king that he need not share the throne with his sister. Cleopatra is imprisoned in the palace dungeon with the handsome captain Achillas as her keeper. It isn't long before Achillas succumbs to the beautiful and wily queen's charms. Together they escape to the desert where Cleopatra hopes to convince the Roman general Pompey to help her regain the throne. When Pompey and Achillas are both killed she decides to throw herself on the mercy of Julius Caesar. She has herself smuggled into Caesar's presence hidden within a carpet and is rolled out at his feet. At this point, the film abruptly ends. *A Queen for Caesar* was another film bought by 20th Century–Fox to protect their multi-million dollar investment starring Elizabeth Taylor. They really needn't have bothered as there is little that the two movies have in common. Pascale Petit is a Continental sex-kitten in the Brigitte Bardot mold and her interpretation of the Cleopatra role is certainly one of the less memorable within memory. Gordon Scott doesn't appear until the film is two-thirds over and then he is given little to do. At age 35, Scott was about twenty years too young to play the aging Julius Caesar, but, as previously mentioned, historical accuracy was obviously not a major concern of the filmmakers. Alternate versions of the final scene were shot. In the European version Ms. Petit is rolled out of the carpet nude but in the U.S. version she modestly covers herself.

225   *The Queen of Babylon*

(La Cortigiana di Babilonia/The Slave Woman)
Pantheon Film, Rome–Rialto Films, Paris (1955) 98 min.
Ferraniacolor
U.S.–20th Century–Fox (1956)
Technicolor
    P–Nat Wachberger/D–Carlo Ludovico Bragaglia/W–Ennio De Concini, Giuseppe Mangione, Carlo Ludovico Bragaglia, Alessandro Continenza, Maria Bory/M–Renzo Rossellini/C–Gabor Pogany/AD–Vittorio Valentini
    Cast–Rhonda Fleming (Semiramis), Ricardo Montalban (Amal), Roldano Lupi (Assur), Carlo Ninchi (Sibari), Tamara Lees (Lysia) with Furio Meniconi, Anna Maria Mori

This early Italian import foreshadows the peplum films of the early sixties by employing second-rate American actors as stars and then dubbing them atrociously. To make matters worse, in the English language version of *The Queen of Babylon* both Rhonda Fleming and Ricardo Montalban don't even dub themselves. This is especially disconcerting in the case of Montalban, as his familiar accent is missing. The production is lavish, but silly. Semiramis, a shepherd girl, finds a wounded Chaldean warrior named Amal and nurses him back to health. Naturally, they fall in love.

Rhonda Fleming is *The Queen of Babylon* (1956).

When the fully recovered Amal leaves, Semiramis is abducted by a band of mercenaries who take her to the city of Babylon to be sold as a slave. Her beauty attracts the attention of the king, who wants her for his wife. She rejects him until she learns that Amal has been captured by the Babylonians and has been sentenced to death. Semiramis agrees to marry the king if he will spare Amal's life. Several plot contrivances later, the king dies and Amal is reunited with his beloved Semiramis, who is proclaimed Queen of Babylon. Another version of the story of Semiramis was made in 1962 starring Yvonne Furneaux as the *Slave Queen of Babylon*.

226   *The Queen of Sheba*

Fox (1921) 92 min.

P–William Fox/D–J. Gordon Edwards/W–J. Gordon Edwards, Virginia Tracy/C–John Boyle

Cast–Betty Blythe (Sheba), Fritz Leiber (Solomon), Claire de Lorez (Amarath), George Siegmann (Armud), Nell Craig (Vashti) with Herbert Hayes, Herschel Mayall, George Nichols

Under the direction of J. Gordon Edwards, who had already guided Theda Bara through the silent historical spectacles *Cleopatra* (1917) and *Salome* (1918), Betty Blythe slinks through this biblical extravaganza in lavish costumes designed by Margaret Whistler. At the time of its release Blythe was quoted as saying, "Twenty-eight costumes and if I put 'em all on at once I couldn't keep warm!" Stills of Ms. Blythe clad in the extravagant but brief costuming are the chief reason the film is remembered. The great set piece of the movie was an elaborate chariot race, staged by Western star Tom Mix. According to studio publicity, the arena built for this scene covered 150 acres and held 5000 extras.

227   The Queen of Sheba

(La Regina de Saba)
An Oro Film (1952) 103 min.
U.S.–A William M. Pizor and Bernard Luber Presentation
Lippert Pictures (1953)

P–Mario Francisci/D–Pietro Francisci/W–Raoul De Sarro, Pietro Francisci, Girogio Graziosi, Vittorio Nino Novarese/M–Nino Rota/C–Mario Montuori/AD–Giulio Bongini/CD–Vittorio Nino Novarese

Cast–Eleonora Ruffo (Balkis), Gino Leurini (Rehoboam), Gino Cervi (Solomon), Marina Berti (Zymira), Franco Silva (Kabael), Isa Pola (Tabuy), Nyta Dover (Kinnor), Umberto Silvestri (Issachar) with Mario Ferrari, Dorian Gray, Franca Tamantini, Fulvia Mammi

Two emissaries from Gad, on their way to a war council in the land of Sheba, are taken prisoner by King Solomon's son, Rehoboam. Rehoboam and his friend Issachar decided to take their place and go to Sheba to can learn what they can about a pending war against Israel. Along the way, they stop at an oasis where Rehoboam meets Balkis, the beautiful daughter of the King of Sheba. Although they are immediately attracted to each other, he does not reveal his true identity to her. Balkis returns to the palace to discover that her father has died and she is now the Queen of Sheba. She is now consecrated to her god Shamash and denied the love of any mortal man. She breaks the law of Shamash by continuing her love affair with the handsome stranger. When the true identity of Rehoboam is finally revealed, Balkis is told that he is betrothed to wed Zymira, Princess of Tyre. In fury, she leads her army in an attack on Jerusalem. Although Rehoboam tells Balkis that he truly loves her, she is convinced by the jealous warrior Kabael to continue the assault. When Zymira intervenes, Balkis finally comes to her senses and publicly declares her love for Rehoboam in the Temple of Solomon. Kabael is killed by an avalanche when he attempts to interfere, a sign that the god of Sheba approves of the lovers' marriage. Like most of the early Italian epics, The Queen of Sheba abandons historical fact in favor of a totally fabricated plot. The costumes and settings are very impressive, although the palace of Balkis seems more like ancient Egypt than the land of Sheba. Marina Berti, fresh from Quo Vadis, is a welcome addition to the cast as Zymira, despite her limited time on screen. This early epic film by Pietro Francisci shows glimpses of the adventurous style of directing he would later perfect in films such as Hercules.

228   Queen of the Nile

(Nefertite, Regina del Nilo; Nefertiti, Queen of the Nile)
Max Productions (1961) 101 min.
Supercinescope (Totalscope)/ Eastman Color
U.S.–Columbia (1962)/ Seven Arts (1964) 90 min.

P–Ottavio Poggi/D–Fernando Cerchio/W– John Byrne, Ottavio Poggi, Fernando Cerchio, Emerico Papp/M–Carlo Rustichelli/C–Massimo Dallamano/ E–Renato Cinquini/AD–Ernest Kromberg/CD–Giancarlo Bartolini Salimbeni

Cast–Jeanne Crain (Tanit/Nefertiti), Edmund Purdom (Tumos), Vincent Price (Benakon), Amedeo Nazzari (Amenophis), Liana Orfei (Merit) with Alberto Farnese, Carlo D'Angelo, Clelia Matania, Piero Palermini, Umberto Raho, Giulio Marchetti, Luigi Marturano, Romano Gio-

Eleonora Ruffo as The Queen of Sheba falls in love with the son of Solomon (1952).

Vincent Price as an evil high priest leads his army against the pharaoh in *Queen of the Nile* (1962).

mini, Raffaele Baldassarre, Adriano Vitale, Gino Talamo

Although it was produced at the time of the *Cleopatra* mania of the early sixties, *Queen of the Nile* owes more to *The Egyptian*, a film it resembles in a number of respects. Once again Edmund Purdom finds himself in ancient Thebes at the time of the pharaoh Akhenaton (herein called Amenophis) and the Holy Wars. Once again he is loved by a selfless woman named Merit. It all must have been déjà vu for Purdom. This time, however, Amenophis is portrayed as more of a madman than a religious visionary. From a historical perspective *Queen of the Nile* is light years away from the painstaking accuracy of *The Egyptian*. The rudimentary facts are presented but most of the plot consists of romantic fiction involving Tanit, daughter of the ambitious High Priest Benakon, who plans to use her as a stepping-stone to the throne of Egypt. She is in love with a young sculptor named Tumos but she has been

promised in marriage to Amenophis. Benakon threatens to have her lover killed if she does not agree to the arranged marriage. Reluctantly, Tanit acquiesces. In a temple ceremony she puts aside her old life and her name is changed to Nefertiti. Tumos and Amenophis have been friends since childhood but the pharaoh knows nothing of the love between the sculptor and the future Queen of Egypt. When Tumos discovers that the pharaoh's new bride is none other than his beloved Tanit, he is convinced that she has callously forsaken him. To the chagrin of the two former lovers, Amenophis asks his friend to sculpt a bust of his beautiful bride. Their romance is soon rekindled but Nefertiti feels that she must stand beside her husband when Benakon attempts to seize the throne from Amenophis. The film is essentially worthless as history but, taken as pure entertainment, it does have a fair amount of action, romance, elaborate sets and costumes, and a trio of interesting performers in the leading roles. Jeanne Crain and Edmund Purdom, with their

Hollywood careers over, followed the example of many other fading actors who found starring roles in European productions. Vincent Price, on the other hand, was about to embark on his greatest era of success. Returning to Hollywood, he would soon become "King of Horror" for the American motion picture industry. In the United States, Columbia Pictures gave *Queen of the Nile* a limited, half-hearted release in 1962. In 1964 it was picked up by Seven Arts who gave it yet another paltry release. Warner Bros. , which had distributed the film in many European countries, finally acquired *Queen of the Nile* and gave the movie its most significant American exposure on television.

Films and Filming: A very respectable spectacle this, but more for the politician who likes to mix romance with affairs of high state.

229   *Quest for Fire*

(La Guerre du Feu)
ICC International Cinema Corporation Production (1981) 97 min.
Color
U.S.–20th Century–Fox
   P–John Kemeny, Denis Heroux/D–Jean-Jacques Annaud/W–Gerard Brach/Special Languages Created by Anthony Burgess/Based on the novel by J.H. Rosney, Sr./M–Philippe Sarde/C–Claude Agostini/E–Yves Langlois/PD–Guy Comtois, Brian Morris/CD–John Hay, Penny Rose
   Cast–Everett McGill (Naoh), Rae Dawn Chong (Rouka), Ron Perlman (Amoukar), Nameer El-Kadi (Ika), Franck-Oliver Bonnet (Aghoo), Jean-Michel Kindt (Lakar) with Kurt Schiegl, Michelle Leduc, Bibi Caspari, Brian Gill, Terry Fitt, Matt Birman, Robert Lavoie

   This Canadian-French coproduction chronicles the travails of a tribe of Stone Age people in their search to regain the fire they have lost. This is a well intentioned depiction of prehistoric life which takes great pains to be scientifically accurate. Unfortunately the end result is slow moving and, for the most part, uninvolving. The impressive location filming was done in Canada, Iceland, Scotland, and Kenya.

   AA Nomination: Best Costume Design*

230   *Quo Vadis?*

Unione Cinematografica Italiana (1924) 102 min.
U.S.–First National (1925)
   P–Giuseppe Brattolo/D/W–Georg Jacoby, Gabriele D'Annunzio/Based on the novel by Henryk Sienkiewicz/C–Curt Courant, Giovanni Bitrotti, Alfredo Donelli
   Cast–Emil Jannings (Nero), Lilian Hall Davis (Lygia), Alphonse Fryland (Marcus Vinicius), Elena di Sangro (Poppaea), Andre Habay (Petronius), Rina De Liguoro (Eunice), Bruto Castellani (Ursus) with Elga Brink, Gino Viotti, Raimondo Van Riel, Gildo Bocci, Lucia Zanussi

   Quo Vadis? had already been filmed in Italy in 1912 by director Enrico Guazzoni as a feature length super spectacle. Imported to the United States the following year, it ran a record twenty-two weeks at New York's Astor Theatre before its profitable general release throughout the rest of the country. Obviously hoping to repeat the international success of this film, executives at U.C.I. decided to do an even more elaborate remake. When Benito Mussolini came into power before filming began, the script was revised to appeal to the new Fascist regime and the character of Nero was softened so as not to offend the new leader of Italy. Arturo Ambrosio had been set to direct the picture but, when the decision was made to seek co-financing from Germany, German director Georg Jacoby was hired to replace him. The famous German star Emil Jannings was also brought in to play Nero. To help insure that the film would be a success in Italy, famed writer Gabriele D'Annunzio was asked to revise the script and co-direct the picture. Millions of lire later the finished film all but sank the Italian movie industry and went on to become an unqualified box office disaster on both sides of the Atlantic. After Emil Jannings won the Academy Award for Best Actor of 1928, *Quo Vadis?* was reissued with a newly recorded musical score to try and capitalize on the fame of its star and recoup some of its losses.

231   *Quo Vadis*

Metro-Goldwyn-Mayer (1951) 171 min.
Technicolor
   P–Sam Zimbalist/D–Mervyn LeRoy/W–John Lee Mahin, S.N. Behrman, Sonya Levin/Based on the novel by Henryk Sienkiewicz/M–Miklos

Mervyn LeRoy directs Robert Taylor in *Quo Vadis* (1951).

Rozsa/C–Robert Surtees, William V. Skall/E–
Ralph E. Winters/AD–William A. Horning, Cedric
Gibbons, Edward Carfagno/CD–Herschel McCoy
    Cast–Robert Taylor (Marcus Vinicius), Debro-
rah Kerr (Lygia), Peter Ustinov (Nero), Leo Genn
(Petronius), Patricia Laffan (Poppaea), Finlay Cur-
rie (Peter), Abraham Sofaer (Paul), Marina Berti
(Eunice), Buddy Baer (Ursus), Felix Aylmer (Plau-
tius), Nora Swinburne (Pomponia), Rosalie

Crutchley (Acte) with Ralph Truman, Norman
Wooland, Peter Miles, Geoffrey Dunn, Nicholas
Hannen, John Ruddock, Arthur Walge, Elspeth
March, Strelsa Brown, Alfredo Varelli, Pietro Tordi

    While Cecil B. DeMille was still putting the
finishing touches on *Samson and Delilah*, other
studios, anticipating the success of his religious epic, began to search for similar prop-

erties. At MGM, both Louis B. Mayer and Dory Schary thought that a remake of Henryk Sienkiewicz's 1895 novel *Quo Vadis* would be ideal subject matter. Schary hired John Huston to direct and Arthur Hornblow, Jr., to produce. Elizabeth Taylor was set to play the Christian girl Lygia and Walter Huston was cast in a supporting role. Stewart Granger was tested for the part of the Roman commander Marcus Vinicius but he was passed over in favor of Gregory Peck. The filming was slated to begin in July 1949 in Rome, where gigantic sets had been constructed at Cinecitta Studios. Unfortunately, Gregory Peck suffered a severe eye infection which delayed filming for several weeks. In the meantime, Mayer and Schary were at odds over what type of movie they were going to make. Schary wanted a socially relevant film which would parallel Nero's persecution of the Christians with Hitler's persecution of the Jews. Mayer wanted a DeMille style spectacle—long on entertainment but short on message. Although over $2 million had already been spent, Mayer won out and filming was postponed until he could assemble a cast and crew more to his liking. Eventually, Sam Zimbalist was signed to produce with Mervyn LeRoy as director and an additional $7 million was poured into the production. The end result went on to become one of the biggest moneymakers in MGM's history. This story of a Roman officer in love with a Christian girl during the time of Nero's persecution of the Christians is spectacular and exciting, if a bit shallow. Robert Taylor and Deborah Kerr, replacing Peck and Taylor in the lead roles, look good but fail to generate much compassion. Far more sympathetic is the subordinate love affair between Leo Genn, as Petronius, and Marina Berti, as his adoring slave girl Eunice. But it is Peter Ustinov, as Nero, who all but steals the show. His performance is more than a match for the film's most striking sequence: the burning of Rome. Thousands of extras fill the screen as one of the greatest conflagrations in motion picture history engulfs them. Miklos Rozsa provided an exceptional score, the first of many he would compose for epic films.

AA Nominations: Best Picture, Supporting Actor (Peter Ustinov and Leo Genn), Color Cinematography, Color Art Direction, Musical Score, Color Costume Design, Editing.

Life: Quo Vadis is the most expensive, most densely populated, most cosmopolitan, in short, the most genuinely colossal movie you are likely to see for the rest of your lives.

Motion Picture: A spectacle-happy production, massive in scale, tremendous in scope. For years to come *Quo Vadis* will remain a marvel of moviedom.

Photoplay: Colossal in its scope, breathtaking in its grandeur, nothing quite like it has ever been seen.

232   *Quo Vadis*

A Rai Uno–Leone Film Co-production (1985) 122 min.
Color
U.S.–Cable television release
P–Lucia Pinnelli, Elio Scardamaglia/D–Franco Rossi/W–Ennio De Concini, Francesco Scardamaglia, Franco Rossi/Based on the novel by Henryk Sienkiewicz/M–Piero Piccioni/C–Luigi Kuveiller/E–Georgio Serrallonga/AD–Luciano Ricceri/CD–Jost Jakob

Cast–Klaus Maria Brandauer (Nero), Max Von Sydow (Peter), Frederic Forrest (Petronius), Cristina Raines (Poppaea), Marie Therese Relin (Lygia), Franciso Quinn (Marcus Vinicius), Barbara De Rossi (Eunice), Gabriele Ferzetti (Piso), Massimo Girotti (Aulus Plastius), Leopoldo Trieste (Chilo), Marko Nikolic (Tigellinus), Françoise Fabian (Pomponia), George Wilson (Pendanius), Angela Molina (Acte)

This 122 minute feature length version is adapted from a 200 minute mini-series made for Italian television. Even at 122 minutes it still seems interminable. Fans of the 1951 MGM version of *Quo Vadis* should do themselves a favor and steer clear of this uninspired remake which manages to drain all of the spectacle, passion and romance from the story. The performances are unmemorable and even the character of Nero comes across as dull, which is no small accomplishment. Some of the production design is interesting in a grotesque way, but it is an all too obvious attempt to emulate *Fellini Satyricon*. This *Quo Vadis* begins with the climax of story which finds Lygia bound in the arena and Ursus fighting a bull to save her life. The main plot is then told in flashback by Petronius. There is scant characterization and the plot lurches from one scene to another with little dramatic cohesion. Franciso Quinn, who plays Marcus Vinicius, is a son of Anthony Quinn. In his first major film role he is given little to do other than appear handsome, which he does admirably.

233   *Rachel's Man*

(Ish Rachel)
A Lonaglade Ltd. Production (1975) 93 min.
Panavision/Technicolor
U.S.–S. J. International Pictures Release
   P-Michael Klinger/D–Moshe Mizrahi/W–Rachel Fabien, Moshe Mizrahi/M–Georges Moustaki/C–Ousama Rawi/E–Dov Hoenig/CD–Tamara Yovtel
   Cast–Leonard Whiting (Jacob), Michal Bat-Adam (Rachel), Mickey Rooney (Laban), Rita Tushingham (Lea), Dalia Cohen (Zilpah) with Yossi Grabber, Avner Hisktyahu, Moshe Ish-Cassit, Rachel Levi, Yair Reubenn, Sari Shapira

   This is a biblical story about deception. Jacob deceives his father Isaac in order to obtain his blessing and the birthright of the first-born. Forced to flee the wrath of his older brother Esau, Jacob seeks refuge with his uncle Laban. Laban uses Jacob's naivety to subjugate him to seven years of servitude. Later Jacob is deceived by his betrothed, Rachel, and is tricked into taking her sister Lea as wife instead. The rest of the story is mostly concerned with Jacob's begetting endless amounts of children by his wives and their bondswomen. This is an obscure British-Israeli co-production which gives new meaning to the term "slow moving." As if the snail's pace at which the story advances weren't enough, the performances are disparate in the extreme. Mickey Rooney hams it up dreadfully and Leonard Whiting speaks every line as if he were still spouting Shakespeare in *Romeo and Juliet*. Poor Rita Tushingham is once again the "ugly duckling," a part she seems to have made a career of playing. The film also suffers from a distinct seventies sensibility, as if the cast were suddenly all going to turn into "flower children" and break into a song from *Hair*.

234   *The Rebel Gladiator*

   (Ursus Gladiatore Ribelle; Ursus the Rebel Gladiator)

Produzione Castor Film, Rome (1962) 98 min.
Techniscope/Eastman Color
U.S.–A Palisade International Presentation
Medallion (1963)
   P–Ferdinando Felicioni/D–Domenico Paolella/W–Alessandro Ferrau, Domenico Paolella, Sergio Sollima/M–Carlo Savina/C–Carlo Bellero/E–Lisetta Urbinati/AD–Alfredo Montori/CD–Elio Micheli
   Cast–Dan Vadis (Ursus), Alan Steel (Marcus Commodus), Carlo Delmi (Septimus), Nando Tamberlani (Marcus Aurelius), Gianni Santuccio (Letus) with Gloria Milland, Jose Greci, Andrea Aureli, Tullio Altamura, Pietro Ceccarelli, Consalvo Dell'Arti, Marco Mariani, Claudio Marzulli, Bruno Scipioni

   Dan Vadis vs. Alan Steel in this battle of the beefcake. In A.D. 180 Marcus Aurelius emperor of Rome dies, leaving his son Marcus Commodus as his heir. Although Commodus promises to honor his father's dying wish for continued peace, he soon plunges Roman into bloody conflict. During a raid on a subjugated village, Commodus and his soldiers are confronted by the strongman Ursus, who defeats the emperor but spares his life. When the woman he loves is kidnapped by the Romans, Ursus must agree to become a gladiator to save her. The brawling and bloodthirsty Commodus goes to the gladiator school in disguise and challenges Ursus to a fight. During the battle, Commodus is wounded and has Ursus imprisoned for attempting to kill the emperor. Ursus escapes from his prison cell and disrupts the emperor's banquet. Furious, Commodus declares that he will fight Ursus in the arena the following day. After a lengthy conflict, Ursus bests Commodus who promises him freedom if he will spare his life. Ursus leaves to join the Roman legions who oppose the unjust rule of Commodus and together they defeat the crazed emperor and his soldiers. Alan Steel has one of his best roles as the musclebound madman Commodus, once again showing that he can be equally effective playing a hero or a villain. The representation of Commodus is probably more accurate here than in either *The Fall of the Roman Empire* or *Gladiator* as the mad emperor often participated in gladiatorial games and fancied himself to be the earthly incarnation of Hercules.

235   The Redeemer

(El Redentor)
A Family Theatre Production
U.S.–Empire Pictures Distributing (1965) 93 min.
Color by DeLuxe
 P–Father Patrick J. Peyton, Father Jerome Lawyer/D–Joseph I. Breen Jr./W–Thomas Blackburn, John Kelly, Robert Gough, James O'Hanlon, Robert Hugh O'Sullivan/M–David Raksin/C–Edwin DuPar/AD–Enrique Alarcon
 Cast–Luis Alvares (Jesus), Antonio Villar (Peter), Maruchi Fresno (Mary), Felix Acaso (Caiaphis) with Manuel Monroy, Alicia Altabella, Manuel Arbo, Carlos Casaravilla, Felix de Pomes, Hebe Donay, Jose Marco Davo, Antonio Casas

 Father Patrick Peyton, head of the Family Rosary Crusade, conceived of a film teatment of the life of Jesus Christ that would not deviate from the gospel narrative. With the sanction of the Catholic Church, he traveled throughout the world seeking contributions to fund the filming of this "inspirational" project. Once adequate funding had been obtained, the production got underway in 1957 at the Sevilla Studios in Madrid. The cast of Spanish performers was directed by Joseph I. Breen, Jr., son of the first Motion Picture Production Code administrator. He was assisted by Spanish director Fernando Palacios. The production, entitled *Los Misterios Del Rosario* (The Mysteries of the Rosary) consisted of three features: *El Amo* (The Master), *El Redentor* (The Redeemer) and *El Salvador* (The Savior). In 1965, Father Peyton decided to prepare the second film in the trilogy for a theatrical release in the United States. For the English language version, the voice of Christ was supplied by actor MacDonald Carey and Sebastian Cabot did the narration. David Raksin, who had previously composed the justly famous background scores for *Laura* and *Forever Amber*, was hired to write a new background score. *The Redeemer* is an account of the last three days of Jesus' life, beginning with his betrayal by Judas. Although the film did receive some playdates in Texas and New Mexico, the overall release was limited and today the movie remains largely unknown.
 The Albuquerque Tribune: Although on wide screen and in color, there is none of the usual Hollywood gaud and embellishment which ruins most Biblical productions.

236   Revenge of the Barbarians

(La Vendetta dei Barbari)
Oriental Film Production (1960) 106 min.
Dyaliscope/Eastman Color
U.S.–American-International (1961) 95 min.
 P/D–Giuseppe Vari/W–Enrico Formai, Gaston Ramazzotti/M–Roberto Nicolosi/C–Sergio Pesce/E–Renato Cinquini
 Cast–Anthony Steel (Olimpius), Daniela Rocca (Galla), Robert Alda (Ataulfo) with Jose Greci, Mario Scaccia, Arturo Dominici, Cesare Fantoni, Giovanni Vari, Sergio Calo, Paolo Reale, Amedeo Trilli, Evi Marandi, Dario Dolce, Anita Todesco, Giulio Maculani

 When the barbaric Visigoths invade Italy during the reign of the emperor Honorius, his cunning and beautiful sister Galla devises a plan to infiltrate the enemy camp. Leading a caravan into enemy territory, Galla allows herself and her retinue to be captured. At a feast in her honor, Galla performs a dance to seduce the Visigoth chieftain, Ataulfo. The ploy works and Ataulfo takes Galla to his tent to make love to her. Later, as Ataulfo sleeps, Galla cannot force herself to slay him. She causes the gates to the Visigoth encampment to be opened and admits the Roman troops led by Olimpius. Galla loves Olimpius and hopes to advance his military career with this victory. Later Galla convinces Olimpius to marry a Roman hostage for political reasons. Her plan backfires when Olimpius falls in love with his new wife. In despair, Galla returns to Ataulfo to offer herself as a hostage to ensure peace. Anthony Steel and Robert Alda are woefully miscast as the Roman officer Olimpius and his enemy Ataulfo. Daniela Rocca, in a rare lead role, virtually carries the film as Galla. She is the sole outstanding element in *Revenge of the Barbarians* and whenever she is onscreen the otherwise leaden plot obediently comes to life.

237   Revenge of the Gladiators

(La Vendetta di Spartaco; Revenge of Spartacus)
Leone Films, S.r.L. (1964) 100 min.
Techniscope/Technicolor
U.S.–Paramount (1965)
 P–Elio Scardamaglia/D–Michele Lupo/W–Lionello De Felice, Ernesto Guida/M–Francesco De

Daniela Rocca is a Roman woman held captive by pagan chieftain Robert Alda in *Revenge of the Barbarians* (1961).

Two familiar peplum faces: Roger Browne and Scilla Gabel in *Revenge of the Gladiators* (1965).

Masi/C–Memmo Mancori/E–Alberto Gallitti/AD–Pier Vittorio Marchi/CD–Walter Patriarca

Cast–Roger Browne (Valerius), Scilla Gabel (Cynthia), Gordon Mitchell (Arminius), Daniele Vargas (Lucius Trasone), Germano Longo (Marcellus), Giacomo Rossi Stuart (Fulvius) with Gianni Solaro, Calisto Calisti, Aldo Pini, Nello Pazzafini, Mary Arden, Franco De Trocchio, Gian Paolo Rosmino

The slave army of Spartacus is defeated and the remaining rebels, including their valiant leader, are condemned to be crucified. When Spartacus disappears from the cross and is rumored to be alive, the slaves are once again inflamed to rebellion. Too late, the rebels discover that Spartacus is indeed dead and that this is a trick perpetrated by the Roman commander Lucius Trasone. A massacre ensues but the few remaining slaves are able to defeat the Romans and escape to freedom. This fast moving action adventure with a good cast of familiar performers benefited from a wider U.S. release than many of its type.

238   *Revolt of the Slaves*

(La Rivolta degli Schiavi)
Ambrosiana Cinematografica S.A.C. (1961) 100 min.
Totalscope / Eastman Color
U.S.–United Artists
   P–Paolo Moffa / D–Nunzio Malasomma / W– Daniel Mainwaring, Duccio Tessari, Stefano Strucchi / Based on the novel *Fabiola* by Cardinal Nicholas Wiseman / M–Angelo Francesco Lavagnino / C– Cecilio Paniagua / E–Eraldo Da Roma / AD–Ramiro Gomez Garcia / CD–Vittorio Rossi
   Cast–Rhonda Fleming (Fabiola / Claudia), Lang Jeffries (Vibio), Dario Moreno (Massimiano), Gino Cervi (Fabio), Ettore Manni (Sebastian), Wandisa Guida (Agnese), Rafael Rivelles (Rutilio), Fernando Rey (Valerio), Serge Gainsbourg (Corvino) with Jose Nieto, Julio Pena, Dolores Francine, Van Aikens, Burt Nelson, Benno Hoffmann, Rainer Penkert, Antonio Casas

   This action-oriented remake of *Fabiola* profits from impressive color widescreen photography. Rhonda Fleming forsakes Michele Morgan's interpretation of Fabiola as an elegant patrician and instead portrays the character as a tempestuous wanton. Fleming and Lang Jeffries were married in the United States and flew to Madrid to spend their honeymoon filming *Revolt of the Slaves*, which was his motion picture debut. The marriage was a short-lived one. Fleming returned to the United States while Jeffries stayed on in Europe to appear in such films as *Alone Against*

Wandisa Guida and Ettore Manni contemplate the *Revolt of the Slaves* (1961).

Rome, *Sword of the Empire* and *Rome in Flames*. Gino Cervi also appeared in the 1947 version of this story and Ettore Manni has one of his best ever roles as the doomed Sebastian. In the English language version Rhonda Fleming's character is called "Claudia."

239   *The Robe*

20th Century–Fox (1953) 135 min.
CinemaScope/Technicolor
P–Frank Ross/D–Henry Koster/W–Philip Dunne, Albert Maltz/Based on the novel by Lloyd C. Douglas/M–Alfred Newman/C–Leon Shamroy/E–Barbara McLean/AD–Lyle Wheeler, George W. Davis/CD–Charles Le Marie
Cast–Richard Burton (Marcellus Gallio), Jean Simmons (Diana) Victor Mature (Demetrius), Michael Rennie (Peter), Jay Robinson (Caligula), Dean Jagger (Justus), Torin Thatcher (Senator Gallio), Richard Boone (Ponitus Pilate), Betta St. John (Miriam), Jeff Morrow (Paulus), Ernest Thesiger

(Tiberius), Dawn Addams (Junia), Leon Askin (Abidor) with Helen Beverly, Frank Pulaski, David Leonard, Michael Ansara, Jay Novello, Nicholas Koster, Harry Shearer, Sally Corner, Frank De Kova, Francis Pierlot, Emmett Lynn

The Robe earned its place in motion picture history as the first feature to be filmed in the anamorphic widescreen process know as CinemaScope. The novel by Lloyd C. Douglas was a best-seller in the early forties and producer Frank Ross has secured the screen rights for $100,000 prior to the book's publication. Between 1943 and 1946 R.K.O. Pictures repeatedly announced their plans to film *The Robe* in Technicolor with Frank Ross producing and Mervyn LeRoy directing from a screenplay by Jane Murfin. When the filming was constantly postponed, MGM showed interest in the project, but once again no movie ever materialized. Near despair, Ross took the property to Darryl F. Zanuck at 20th Century–Fox. Zanuck had been searching for an appropriately grand subject with which to introduce CinemaScope and *The Robe* seemed to be an ideal choice. Tyrone Power was originally considered to play Marcellus, possibly with Jennifer Jones cast opposite him as Diana. Instead Zanuck decided on Richard Burton, who had recently starred in the Fox film *My Cousin Rachel*. Due to the anticipated high cost of production, a standard 35mm "flat" version was filmed simultaneously in the event that CinemaScope proved to be an expensive folly. This would also permit theaters that had not converted to CinemaScope to play the picture. As filming progressed, the studio was so certain of success that a sequel began filming before production on *The Robe* had been completed (see *Demetrius and the Gladiators*). Speculations were accurate and *The Robe* became a tremendous hit, returning close to $20 million for its $4.5 million production cost.

Jean Simmons comforts a tormented Richard Burton in *The Robe* (1953).

CinemaScope revolutionized the motion picture industry, and for over a decade it was the most widely utilized widescreen process. Fortunately, *The Robe* does not depend entirely on the novelty of CinemaScope to create an impact. The film wisely focuses on the human elements, never abandoning this in favor of pageantry. The young tribune, Marcellus Gallio, incurs the displeasure of the emperor's grandson, Caligula, and is sent to Jerusalem as punishment. While there he is given the assignment of crucifying a supposed criminal named Jesus. Throwing dice at the foot of the cross, Marcellus wins Jesus' robe in the game. Later, when he touches the robe a madness, brought on by his guilty conscience, overcomes him. The remainder of the story is concerned with Marcellus' search for the truth about the man he crucified. Marcellus becomes a Christian and is martyred by Caligula, the new emperor. The acting in *The Robe* is uniformly sincere, with Victor Mature, in particular, giving an outstanding performance as the Greek slave, Demetrius. He would most certainly have been nominated for a Best Supporting Actor Academy Award had Zanuck not insisted that the film featured only "stars" and not supporting players. Jay Robinson, twenty-two years old and fresh from the Broadway stage, made his film debut as the crazed Caligula, in one of the most extraordinarily lunatic performances ever captured on film.

AA Nominations: Best Picture, Actor (Richard Burton), Color Costume Design*, Color Cinematography, Color Art Direction*

Photoplay: The long-awaited Technicolor version of Lloyd C. Douglas' famous novel is a movie milestone.

Motion Picture: The much-heralded 20th Century–Fox production of *The Robe* is brought to us in compelling magnificence on the new CinemaScope screen.

240   *Roman Scandals*

A Samuel Goldwyn Production
United Artists (1933) 93 min.
    P–Samuel Goldwyn/D–Frank Tuttle/W–George S. Kaufman, Robert E. Sherwood/Songs: Al Dubin, Harry Warren/M–Alfred Newman/C–Ray June, Gregg Toland/E–Stuart Heisler/AD–Richard Day/CD–John Harkrider

Cast–Eddie Cantor (Eddie), Gloria Stuart (Sylvia), David Manners (Josephus), Edward Arnold (Valerius), Veree Teasdale (Agrippa), Ruth Etting (Olga) with Alan Mowbray, Jack Rutherford, Bonny Bannon

In this musical comedy, Eddie falls asleep in a museum and dreams he has been transported to ancient Rome during the reign of the emperor Valerius. Our hero is put up for sale in the local slave market and bought by the kindly Josephus. Josephus is in love with the captive princess Sylvia and he and Eddie attempt to rescue her from the evil clutches of Valerius. Eddie is enlisted in a plot by the Empress Agrippa to poison the emperor and the mayhem comes to a climax with an exciting chariot race. The musical highlight of the film is "No More Love," sung by Ruth Etting as Olga, the emperor's discarded mistress. Busby Berkeley staged the lavish production numbers which feature the "Goldwyn Girls." One of them is Lucille Ball, all but unrecognizable in a blonde wig.

241   *Romulus and the Sabines*

(Il Ratto delle Sabine; The Rape of the Sabines)
F.I.C.I.T., Rome–C.F.P.I., Paris (1961) 101 min.
CinemaScope/Eastman Color
U.S.–A Walter Manley-Alexander Salkind Presentation
Embassy (1964)
    P–Enrico Bomba/D–Richard Pottier/M–Carlo Rustichelli/C–Adalberto Albertini
    Cast–Roger Moore (Romulus), Mylene Demongeot (Rhea), Scilla Gabel (Drusia), Rossana Schiaffino (Venus), Jean Marais (Mars), Giorgia Moll (Lavinia) with Folco Lulli, Francis Blanche, Claude Conty, Walter Barnes, Mariangela Giordano

The story of the rape of the Sabine women has had several screen incarnations, including a 1945 Italian version starring the comedian Toto and directed by Mario Bonnard. The MGM musical *Seven Brides for Seven Brothers* (1954) relocated the basic plot to the American frontier. *Romulus and the Sabines* is a bit more straightforward in telling the story. It seems that when Romulus founded Rome he neglected to include any women in his master plan. Faced with eventual extinction, he leads his horny men in the kidnapping of the neighboring Sabine women, including the pouty Vestal Virgin, Rhea. The plot is standard sword and sandal stuff with the exception of one unusual scene in which Romulus falls asleep in a temple and his future is debated by Mars the God of War and Venus the Goddess of Love. Genre regular Scilla Gabel appears in a supporting role as the woman who is loved and then spurned by Romulus in favor of Rhea. Roger Moore, as Romulus, looks so appropriate in period costuming that one wishes he had appeared in a worthier film. Comedy relief, of which there is an excess, is particularly annoying and dulls what little dramatic tension there is.

242 *Salome*

An Alla Nazimova Production (1922) 75 min.
Allied Distributors (1923)
    P–Alla Nazimova/D–Charles Bryant/W–Peter Winters/Based on the play by Oscar Wilde/C–Charles Van Enger/AD/CD–Natacha Rambova
    Cast–Nazimova (Salome), Nigel De Brulier (Jokaanan), Rose Dione (Herodias), Mitchell Lewis (Herod), Louis Dumar (Tigellinus), Frederick Peter (Naaman) with Earl Schenck, Arthur Jasmine

When Alla Nazimova ended her contract with MGM, she was determined to appear only in artistically significant films thereafter. She formed her own independent production company and her second film was an avant garde version of Oscar Wilde's controversial play. This daring movie retells the biblical tale of Salome, step-daughter of King Herod, and her infatuation with John the Baptist (herein called Jokaanan). Rejected by the holy man, Salome performs the Dance of the Seven Veils for her lecherous step-father and is given the severed head of Jokaanan as a reward. The stylized sets and costumes were designed by Nazimova's good friend Natacha Rambova who based them on the illustrations of Aubrey Beardsley. Rambova became the wife of Rudolph Valentino shortly after finishing her work on this film. *Salome* was directed by Nazimova's husband Charles Bryant and financed by Nazimova herself to the tune of $350,000. The picture was shelved for a year until a distributor could be found but then it was greeted by mixed reviews from the critics and indifference by the moviegoers. The movie lost most of its investment costs and became Nazimova's last film as an independent producer. Originally the running time was 75 minutes but it was later edited down to the 38 minute version which is available today.

243 *Salome*

Beckworth Productions
Columbia (1953) 103 min.
Technicolor
    P–Buddy Adler/D–William Dieterle/W–Harry Kleiner/M–George Duning, Daniele Amfitheatrof/C–Charles Lang/E–Viola Lawrence/AD–John Meehan/CD–Jean Louis, Emile Santiago
    Cast–Rita Hayworth (Salome), Stewart Granger (Claudius), Charles Laughton (Herod), Judith Anderson (Herodias), Sir Cedric Hardwicke (Tiberius), Arnold Moss (Micha), Basil Sydney (Pontius Pilate), Maurice Swartz (Ezra), Alan Badel (John the Baptist), Rex Reason (Marcellus)

Salome was Columbia Pictures' major entry in the biblical sweepstakes of the early fifties. The studio was know for its relatively low budget films and this was their costliest film since Frank Capra's *Lost Horizon* in 1937. To help recoup some of the costs, the lavish costumes and sets for *Salome* would be reused in such Columbia "B" pictures as *Serpent of the Nile* and *Slaves of Babylon*. At age thirty-five, Rita Hayworth was too old for the part of the teenage daughter of Herodias, but the film was produced by her own company, Beckworth, so who was going to argue the point? This is the least of its inaccuracies and *Salome* deserves its place in motion picture history as the film which most deviates from the biblical text. Adding insult to injury, a studio press release states that "there had to be the utmost in accuracy; there could be no slighting of the story, its theme and its several historic interpretations." Nevertheless, in an audacious departure from Scripture, Princess Salome becomes the unknowing victim of her scheming mother. Queen Herodias, played to the hilt by Judith Anderson, attempts to use her daughter's beauty to influence King Herod to behead John the Baptist. Eventually the misguided princess comes to her senses. To repent her evil ways she performs her infamous dance to save the life of John, rather than to have him killed. Of course, her honorable plan backfires and he is executed anyway. The film ends with Rita/Salome and Roman-tribune-turned-Christian Stewart Granger, lis-

Top: An example of Columbia's elaborate publicity campaign for *Salome* (1953). *Bottom:* Rita Hayworth as *Salome* (1953).

tening enraptured to the Sermon on the Mount. Add to this Charles Laughton's hammy performance as the lecherous King Herod and you have a truly over-the-top piece of entertainment. On the plus side, there are two things which almost make make the whole mess worthwhile—Charles Lang's breathtaking Technicolor photography and Rita's climactic Dance of the Seven Veils. The dance took two months of rehearsal and three days to film. It was created by Broadway choreographer Valerie Bettis.

Motion Picture: An elaborate spectacle, vaguely based on the Biblical story of Salome. The Dance of the Seven Veils is the climax of the sex-appeal angle of this extravaganza.

Life: Most authorities since St. Mark have regarded Salome as at least a willing accessory in the killing of John the Baptist. But the record is being set to rights by a new movie called *Salome*.

Photoplay: It's a lavish spectacle. The costumes alone are worth the price of admission.

244   *Samson*

(Sansone / Samson vs. Hercules)
Cineproduzioni Associate, Rome (1961) 95 min.
Totalscope / Eastman Color
U.S.–Medallion

   P–Mario Maggi / D–Gianfranco Parolini / W–Giovanni Simonelli, Gianfranco Parolini / M–Carlo Innocenzi / C–Francesco Izzarelli / E–Mario Sansoni / AD–Oscar D'Amico / CD–Vittorio Rossi

Brad Harris as *Samson* (1961) struggles against a typical peplum torture device.

Cast–Brad Harris (Samson), Alan Steel (Millstone), Serge Gainsbourg (Warkalla), Brigitte Corey (Jamine), Irena Prosen (Mila), Carlo Tamberlani (Botan) Mara Berni (Romilda) with Walter Reeves, Gianfranco Casparri, Manja Golec, Romano Ghini, Nick Stefanini

   The cast, crew, sets, and storyline of *Samson* were recycled for *The Fury of Hercules* with only the characters' names changed to protect the guilty. The major plot difference is that in this film Alan Steel plays Samson's likable, rough-housing buddy instead of a mute villain. In English language versions the Steel character is referred to as "Millstone," while in some foreign versions he is called "Hercules." Samson discovers that Mila, queen of the city of Sulim, has been deposed by her weak-willed half sister, Romilda. Romilda's evil advisor, Warkalla, has counseled her into unjustly persecuting her people. Samson joins the rebel forces, led by Millstone, in their attempts to restore Mila to the throne. This is a below average entry with poorly staged action sequences and very little originality. Brad Harris and Alan Steel work well together but this is the only interesting aspect of an otherwise unmemorable film.

245   *Samson and Delilah*

Paramount (1949) 131 min.
Technicolor

   P / D–Cecil B. DeMille / W–Jesse L. Laskey Jr., Fredric M. Frank / M–Victor Young / C–George Barnes / E–Anne Bauchens / AD–Hans Dreier, Walter Tyler / CD–Edith Head, Gile Steele, Dorothy Jeakins, Gwen Wakeling, Elois Jenssen

   Cast–Victor Mature (Samson), Hedy Lamarr (Delilah), George Sanders (Saran of Gaza), Angela Lansbury (Semadar), Henry Wilcoxon (Ahtur), Julia Faye (Hisham), William Farnum (Tubal), Olive Deering (Miriam), Rusty Tamblyn (Saul) with Fay Holden, Lane Chandler, Moroni Olson, William Davis, Laura Elliot, Jerry Austin, John Miljan, Frances J. McDonald, Arthur Q. Bryan, Fritz Leiber, Mike Mazurki, George Reeves

   In 1935 Cecil B. DeMille began plans to film the story of

Samson, possibly to star Henry Wilcoxon and Miriam Hopkins. Paramount studio head Adolph Zukor was skeptical about the potential popularity of a biblical subject with the moviegoing public and suggested that DeMille search elsewhere for material. In July 1946 DeMille revived the project and began to conduct story conferences on *Samson and Delilah*. Paramount executives were still leery of spending millions of dollars on a "Sunday School story" until DeMille confronted them with an artists' rendition of Samson and Delilah as he had conceived them for the motion picture. The sketch, which featured a muscular young man in a loincloth and a beautiful girl in an abbreviated costume, fully exploited the sexual aspects of the story that DeMille planned to emphasize. The executives were sold and gave DeMille a green light on the project. During the next two years further story conferences were held and the Minoan culture was thoroughly researched to provide a basis for the design of the Philistine sets and costumes. With the completion of *Unconquered* in 1947, DeMille turned his full attention to *Samson and Delilah*. An extensive search for a suitable actor and actress to fill the title roles was made. Steve Reeves was considered for the part of Samson but rejected as too inexperienced. Burt Lancaster was also up for the part but DeMille decided to pass on him as well. The vast number of actresses contemplated for Delilah included a highly unlikely Betty Hutton! DeMille finally settled on Victor Mature and Hedy Lamarr. In retrospect it is difficult to imagine anyone else in the title roles but, at the time of filming, DeMille had misgivings about his choice of stars. Mature aggravated DeMille with his continual refusal to perform any of the more dangerous stunt work expected of him. Russ Tamblyn remembers DeMille as a hard taskmaster who was not above humiliating a fourteen-year-old boy in front of hundreds of extras for forgetting his lines. Hedy Lamarr, on the other hand, spoke of DeMille fondly. During the filming she dispelled any misgivings he may have had in casting her and became one of his favorites. Lamarr, in her first color film, never looked lovelier or gave a better performance. She considered *Samson and Delilah* to be her finest film work. DeMille asked Lamarr to star

in his next picture, *The Greatest Show on Earth*, but the rigors of filming with the exacting director proved too much even for her and she declined. Victor Mature was undaunted by this early bout with antiquity and went on to become a regular player in epic films. Despite critical reaction that was even worse than usual for a DeMille film, *Samson and Delilah* made a fortune for Paramount in its original release and subsequent reissues. It also started the long cycle of epics which continued throughout the fifties and sixties. Few of these films could equal the spectacular destruction of the Temple of Dagon which occurs at the climax of *Samson and Delilah*. Accomplished at a cost of $140,000 by special effects expert Gordon Jennings, this sequence is one of the truly memorable moments in motion picture history.

AA Nominations: Best Color Cinematography, Special Effects, Musical Score, Color Art Direction*, Color Costume Design*

Motion Picture: Two years of writing and research has unearthed as much hate, passion, treachery, murder, violence and lust as you will find in any one movie (until the next DeMille production comes along).

Photoplay: When Cecil B. DeMille makes a picture, two things are certain; it will be a spectacle and it will be good entertainment. *Samson And Delilah* offered DeMille the opportunity to outdo himself.

Variety: It's a fantastic picture for this era in its size, in its lavishness, in the corniness of its storytelling and in its old-fashioned technique. But it adds up to first-class entertainment.

246   *Samson and Delilah*

Comworld
ABC TV Network (1984) 96 min.
Color by DeLuxe
   P–Gregory Harrison, Frank Levy/D–Lee Philips/W–John Gay/Based on *Husband of Delilah* by Eric Linkletter/M–Maurice Jarre/C–Gerry Fisher/E–George Jay Nicholson/PD–Ed Wittstein/CD–Madeline Ann Graneto
   Cast–Belinda Bauer (Delilah), Antony Hamilton (Samson), Max Von Sydow (Sidka), Stephen Macht (Maluck), Jose Ferrer (High Priest), Maria Schell (Deborah), Victor Mature (Manoah), Jennifer Holmes (Varinia), Daniel Stern (Micah), Clive Revill (Raul), David S. Eisner (Arin), David Byrd (Elon) with Angelica Aragon, Rene Ruiz, Brandon Scott

While Samson (Antony Hamilton) sleeps Delilah (Belinda Bauer) gives him a haircut: *Samson and Delilah* (1984).

This made-for-television version of *Samson and Delilah* is notable for its brevity, particularly when compared to some of the long winded television epics which were to follow. This film is heavily influenced by DeMille's version of the story with much of the plotting and many of the secondary characters patterned after that venerable spectacle. The chief departure is at the end. In this version, Delilah escapes from the destruction of the Philistine temple and takes the body of Samson back to his people. This makes for a surprisingly moving conclusion. Filmed inexpensively in Mexico, the sets and backgrounds often have a very "unbiblical" appearance. There are compensations to be found in the

Elizabeth Hurley, Eric Thal, and Dennis Hopper in the 1996 version of *Samson and Delilah*.

interesting cast, not the least of which is Antony Hamilton as Samson. Often looking more like Hercules in the beefcake epics of the sixties, Hamilton may not have been the best actor in the world but he was one of the most handsome. The director seems to have been determined to show him off to the best advantage by providing maximum exposure as much as possible. Hamilton had been a dancer with the Australian Ballet Company and a model before being chosen over actor Jon-Erik Hexum for the part of Samson. He later replaced Hexum in the TV series *Cover Up* after that actor's tragic accidental death on

the set. Hamilton was also considered to replace Roger Moore as James Bond but he was passed over by the producer because of his openly gay lifestyle. He died in 1995. *Samson and Delilah* also marks the final film appearance of Victor Mature, who was lured out of retirement to play Samson's father.

247   *Samson and Delilah*

(Sansone e Dalila)
A Turner/Lube/Lux Vide/Beta Film/Rai Uno Production
U.S.–TNT Network (1996) 182 min
Color

P–Gerald Rafshoon, Lorenzo Minoli/D–Nicholas Roeg/W–Allan Scott/M–Marco Frisina/C–Raffaele Mertes/E–Michael Ellis/PD–Paolo Biagetti/ CD–Enrico Sabbatini

Cast–Elizabeth Hurley (Delilah), Eric Thal (Samson), Dennis Hopper (Tariq), Michael Gambon (Rehamun), Diana Rigg (Mara), Ben Becker (Sidqa), Paul Freeman (Manoah), Jale Arikan (Naomi), Daniel Massey (Ira) with Karl Tessler, Luke Mullaney, Tim Gallagher, Sebastian Knapp, Pinkes Braun, Debora Caprioglio, Alessandro Gassman, Mark McGann

The fifth in the series of Turner Bible movies is an interesting but greatly flawed adaptation of the familiar story of strength and seduction. Eric Thal is a complex Samson whose most difficult battle is within himself. Elizabeth Hurley performs her seductive duties surprisingly well and, of course, looks gorgeous. But even the presence of these two attractive leads can't rescue this overlong adaptation from its dull execution. The famous biblical love story is overwhelmed by the serious tone and excessive piety which undermines much of this series. The most noteworthy thing about *Samson and Delilah* is Dennis Hopper in the role of a Philistine general. This is another one of those peculiar instances of miscasting which so often turn up in epic cinema. Hopper, looking extremely uncomfortable in his costume and wig, struggles in vain to overcome the "What am I doing here?" aura that surrounds him.

Variety: Rich and captivating in its visual dynamics, *Samson and Delilah* is, for all its tedious interludes, a sensitively wrought production marked with an obvious attention to detail.

248   *Samson and the Mighty Challenge*

(Ercole, Sansone, Maciste e Ursus: Gli Invincibili; Hercules, Samson, Maciste and Ursus: The Invincibles)
Senior Cinematografica, Rome–Les Filmes Regent, Paris–Productores
Exibidores Film S.A., Madrid (1964) 95 min.
Ultrapanoramic/Eastman Color
P–Giorgio Cristallini/D–Girogio Capitani/W–Alessandro Continenza, Roberto Gianviti/M–Piero Umiliani/C–Carlo Bellero/E–Roberto Cinquini/AD–Franco Ramacci/CD–Vittorio Rossi

Cast–Alan Steel (Hercules), Howard Ross (Maciste), Nadir Baltimore (Samson), Yann Lavor

(Ursus) with Livio Lorenzon, Valentino Macchi, Nino Marchetti, Helene Chanel, Nino del Fabbro, Arnaldo Fabrizio, Luciano Marin, Elisa Montes, Attilio Tosato, Moira Orfei, Maria Luisa Ponte, Conrado San Martin, Carlo Tamberlani, Lia Zoppelli

As the Universal horror film cycle of the thirties and forties came to an end and ideas began to run out, the producers decided to incorporate more and more of their monster characters into one film. First, Frankenstein met the Wolf Man and, soon after, Dracula as well. The final step was to burlesque all of the classic monsters in one film with Abbott and Costello as their foils. The European peplum films paralleled this idea as they began to feature several of their legendary heroes in a single film. In one early effort, Hercules meets Ulysses, while Hercules, Samson and Ulysses turned up together a few years later in another film. *Samson and the Mighty Challenge* incorporates four of the major characters of the peplum films in a dismal parody of the genre which is short on satire and long on slap-stick. Hercules (Alan Steel with peroxide blond hair) defies his father Zeus and embarks on a life based on the pursuit of pleasure. He arrives in Lydia where he falls head over heels in love with the queen's daughter, Omphale. Since Hercules is an empty-headed and arrogant braggart, Omphale refuses to marry him. Besides, she is already in love with the son of the barbarian chieftain, who is threatening to attack the kingdom of her mother. In an attempt to outwit Hercules, Omphale agrees to marry him if he can defeat Samson, reputedly the strongest man in the world. Three of the queen's ministers set out for Judea to find Samson. Along the way they encounter a brawling troublemaker. This is Ursus, a slave who has escaped from the arena in Rome. The three men finally arrive at the farm of Samson, who agrees to accompany them back to Lydia. Samson's wife Delilah, distraught over her husband's departure, cuts his hair and thereby robs him of his strength. The Lydians, refusing to believe that Samson is now weak, take him back to Greece. On the return trip they are joined by Ursus and Maciste (played by Howard Ross aka Red Ross aka Renato Rossini). After endless rough-housing by the four heroes, Omphale is finally allowed to wed the man of her choice and the four

It will take a miracle to get Gordon Scott out of this sticky situation in *Samson and the Seven Miracles of the World* (1962).

strongmen ride off into the sunset toward Judea. The screenplay's sole virtue lies in its attempt to provide an explanation of each of the heroes' backgrounds. The background score, which is dreadful, employs anachronistic modern music to emphasize the comic scenes.

249   *Samson and the Seven Miracles of the World*

(Maciste alla Corte del Gran Khan; Maciste at the Court of the Grand Khan)
Panda Film, Rome-Gallus Film, Paris (1962) 80 min.
Dyaliscope / Technicolor
U.S.–American-International
ColorScope
  P–Ermanno Donati, Luigi Carpentieri / D–Riccardo Freda / W–Oreste Biancoli, Duccio Tessari / M–Carlo Innocenzi / Les Baxter (U.S. version) / C– Riccardo Pallottini
  Cast–Gordon Scott (Samson), Yoko Tani (Princess Lei-Ling), Helene Chanel (Kiutai), Dante Di Paolo (Bayan), Gabriele Antonini (Cho) with Leonardo Severini, Valery Inkijinoff, Chut-La-Chit, Luong-Ham-Chau, Tonino Chou, Franco Ressel, Sergio Ukmar

  Thirteenth-century China is suffering under the rule of the cruel Tarter, Garak. Garak has murdered the emperor and now plans to assassinate the remaining members of the royal family, Prince Ti-Sung and Princess Lei-Ling. Into this unhappy situation strides the mighty Samson, incongruously clad in a brief loincloth, ready to right all wrongs until justice triumphs. Samson joins the guerrilla forces who oppose Garak and together they organize the people in revolt against the Tarter overlord. Gordon Scott (real name: Gordon Werschkul), who had previously appeared as Tarzan, stars in what was the first of many muscleman roles. He would go on to become one of the most prolific performers in peplum films.

250　*The Saracen Blade*

Columbia (1954) 76 min.
Technicolor
　P–Sam Katzman/D–William Castle/W–DeVallon Scott, George Worthington Yates/Based on the novel by Frank Yerby/M–Mischa Bakaleinikoff/C–Henry Freulich/E–Gene Havlick/AD–Paul Palmentola
　Cast–Ricardo Montalban (Pietro), Betta St. John (Iolanthe), Rick Jason (Enzio), Carolyn Jones (Elaine), Whitfield Connor (Frederick II), Michael Ansara (Siniscola), Nelson Leigh (Issac), Pamela Duncan (Zenobia), Edgar Barrier (Rogliano) with Frank Pulaski, Leonard Penn, Nyra Monssour, Edward Coch, Gene D'Arcy, Poppy Deluando

Another is the series of "poor man's" epics produced at Columbia in the early fifties. When his beloved Iolanthe is forced to marry for political reasons, Pietro Donati journeys to the Holy Land to join the Crusaders in their battle against the Saracens. This offering from the Sam Katzman–William Castle team is typically lacking in memorable material but, once again, Henry Freulich's Technicolor photography is dazzling. Pamela Duncan, who portrays the Saracen beauty Zenobia, later starred in two of Roger Corman's classic fifties horror films, *The Undead* and *Attack of the Crab Monsters* (both released in 1957).

Gianni Garko as the shepherd and Norman Wooland as the king in *Saul and David* (1965).

251　*Saul and David*

(Saul e David)
San Pablo, Madrid–San Paolo, Rome (1964) 120 min.
Panorama/Eastman Color
U.S.–World Entertainment Corp. (1965)
　P–Toni Di Carlo/D–Marcello Baldi/W–Ottavio Jemma, Flavio Nicholini, Marcello Baldi, Tonino Guerra/M–Teo Usuelli/C–Marcello Masciocchi/E–Guiliana Attenni/AD–Ottavio Scotti/CD–Giorgio Desideri
　Cast–Norman Wooland (Saul), Gianni Garko (David), Stefy Lang (Goliath), Luz Marquez (Abigail), Virgilio Teixeira (Abner), Elisa Cegani (Akhinoam), Antony Mayans (Jonathan), Pilar Clement (Michal), Carlos Casaravilla (Samuel) with Marco Paoletti, Giorgio Cerioni, Andrea Scire, Paolo Gozlino, Barta Berry, Dante Maggio

Another is the series of biblical films produced by the Paulus Brothers (see *The Great Leaders*). Though overlong and talky, *Saul and David* does have a pair of fine performances at its core. Norman Wooland is excellent as the tormented King of Israel who sees in the boy David all the qualities of greatness he has lost. Gianni Garko, as the adult David, presents a far more believable characterization than either Ivo Payer in *David and Goliath* or Richard Gere in *King David*. Although *Saul and David* has many of the same limitations as the other Paulus Brothers productions, it is by far the best film in the series from a dramatic point of view. The U.S. press material for the American release of *Saul and David* is memorable for its inaccuracies. In addition to stating that Norman Wooland portrays David, one press release declares that "Stefy Lang is an internationally famous actress who has appeared on stage and screen in all countries throughout the world." In actuality, Stefy Lang is the actor who plays Goliath.

252　*The Secret Seven*

(Gli Invincibili Sette; The Invincible Seven)
Columbus S.p.A., Rome–Atenea Film, Madrid (1964) 94 min.
Techniscope/Eastman Color
U.S.–Metro-Goldwyn-Mayer (1965)

Tony Russell comes to the aid of Helga Line in *The Secret Seven* (1965).

P–Joseph Fryd/D–Alberto De Martino/W–Alberto De Martino, Alessandro Continenza/M–Carlo Franci/C–Eloy Mella/E–Otello Colangeli/AD–Piero Poletto/CD–Mario Giorsi

Cast–Tony Russel (Leslio), Helga Line (Lydia), Massimo Serato (Axel), Gerard Tichy (Rabiro), Renato Baldini (Kadem), Livio Lorenzon (Rubio), Barta Barry (Baxo), Joseph Marco (Luzar) with Kriss Huerta, Gianni Solaro, Francesco Sormano, Emma Baron, Pedro Mari, Tomas Blanco, Renato Montalbano

Following the fall of Athens in the fourth century B.C., the tyranny of Sparta swept through the Middle East. In the city of Sidon two brothers, Axel and Leslio, join forces with five rebel slaves to oppose the unjust rule of the mercenary Spartan invaders. Leslio had once been in love with Lydia, who is now the mistress of the Spartan tyrant Rabirio. Lydia and Leslio renew their romance and she helps him in his fight against Rabirio and his Spar-

tans. *The Secret Seven* transfers the basic plot of *The Magnificent Seven* into a peplum film. The spirit is close to that of a western film with the action culminating in a stampede of wild horses. A followup, *The Spartan Gladiators*, appeared the following year.

253   *Serpent of the Nile*

Columbia (1953) 73 min.
Technicolor

P–Sam Katzman/D–William Castle/W–Robert E. Kent/M–Mischa Bakaleinikoff/C–Henry Freulich/E–Gene Havlick/AD–Paul Palmentola/CD–Jean Louis

Cast–Rhonda Fleming (Cleopatra), William Lundigan (Lucilius), Raymond Burr (Mark Antony), Jean Byron (Charmion), Michael Ansara (Florus), Michael Fox (Octavius), Conrad Wolfe (Assassin), John Crawford (Domitius), Jane Easton (Cytheris), Robert Griffin (Brutus), Frederic Best (Marculius), Julie Newmeyer (Golden Girl)

Fictitious love triangle: Lucilius (William Lundigan), Cleopatra (Rhonda Fleming), and Mark Antony (Raymond Burr) in *Serpent of the Nile* (1953).

Serpent of the Nile is the Sam Katzman–William Castle version of the Antony and Cleopatra story, filmed on a shoestring budget. Katzman was Columbia's resident producer of low budget, second feature pictures. Castle was, at this time, just another of Columbia's mediocre contract directors. The film is fairly standard stuff, although it is definitely a notch above *Slaves of Babylon*, which came from the same producer/director team. Rhonda Fleming is a beautiful Cleopatra and her costumes are imaginative, even if not authentic. The screenplay has Cleopatra married to Antony for purely political reasons. The real object of her desire is Lucilius, a Roman centurion who goes to Egypt to protect Antony from Cleopatra's treachery. Raymond Burr overplays his part so badly that it is easy to understand Cleopatra's longing to be rid of him. On the other hand, William Lundigan is so dull you wonder what she could possibly see in him. There is a barge scene obviously inspired by the DeMille version (which had been reissued the previous year), but not so elaborate or well staged. Julie Newmar (then Newmeyer) appears in this sequence as a gold-painted dancing girl. Henry Freulich's Technicolor photography is the film's greatest asset. *Serpent of the Nile* is best summed up by a line of dialogue from the script: "Dig beneath this veneer of gold and find emptiness."

254 *The Seven Magnificent Gladiators*

A Golan-Globus Production
Cannon Films (1983) 86 min.
Technicolor
U.S.–MGM/UA
    P–Alexander Hacohen/D–Bruno Mattei/W–

Lou Ferrigno is the leader of *The Seven Magnificent Gladiators* (1983).

Claude Fragassi/M–Dov Seltzer/C–Silvano Ippoliti/E–A. Swyftte/AD–Amedeo Mellone/CD–Belle Crandall

Cast–Lou Ferrigno (Han), Sybil Danning (Julia), Brad Harris (Scipio), Dan Vadis (Nicerote), Carla Ferrigno (Pandora), Yehuda Efroni (Emperor), Mandy Rice-Davies (Lucilla), Robert Mura (Vendrix), Barbara Pescate (Ankara), Ivan Beshears (Goliath)

This was the first in a series of attempts to revive the peplum movies in Italy during the eighties. *The Seven Magnificent Gladiators* actually comes close to recapturing the spirit of the original films but lacks their naive charm. Cinematographer Silvano Ippoliti, who had photographed many of the original peplum films, and the casting of Brad Harris and Dan Vadis, two of the principal stars from that era, provide further links with the past. The plot is another reworking of the western *The Magnificent Seven*, which itself was a remake of *The Seven Samurai*. In this version, Lou Ferrigno leads a band of renegade gladiators, including Sybil Danning and Brad Harris, in protecting a village which is being terrorized by Dan Vadis and his gang of murderous bandits. Ferrigno's real life wife, Carla, plays his onscreen sweetheart. Lou Ferrigno was born in Brooklyn and began weight training at the age of 14 to compensate for his deafness. Later, as a professional bodybuilder, he won the title of Mr. Universe two years in a row. He gained even wider public recognition in the television series *The Incredible Hulk*. During the making of *The Seven Magnificent Gladiators*, Brad Harris suggested to Ferrigno that he should star in a remake of *Hercules*, which he did immediately thereafter.

255   Seven Slaves Against the World

(Gli Schiavi Più Forti del Mondo)
Leone Films S.r.L. (1964) 96 min.
Techniscope/Technicolor
U.S.–Paramount (1965)

P–Elio Scardamanglia/D–Michele Lupo/W–Roberto Gianviti, Michele Lupo/M–Francesco De Masi/C–Guglielmo Mancori/E–Alberto Gallitti/AD–Pier Vittorio Marchi/CD–Walter Patriarca

Cast–Roger Browne (Marcus), Gordon Mitchell (Balisten), Scilla Gabel (Claudia), Giacomo Rossi Stuart (Gaius), Arnaldo Fabrizio (Goliath) with Germano Longo, Carlo Tamberlani, Alfredo Rizzo, Aldo Pini, Adriano Vitale, Luciana Vincenzi, Pietro Marescalchi, Aldo Pedinotti, Mario Novelli

One of three films directed by Michele Lupo in 1964 and starring Roger Browne. In *Seven Slaves Against the World*, Gaius, the deposed commander of a Roman slave camp, plots to undermine the authority of his replacement, Marcus, by inciting the slaves to revolt. The slaves escape and the Roman governor blames Marcus, who must flee for his life. Six of the runaway slaves aid Marcus and ask him to join them in their attempt to gain enough money to leave the country. They become gladiators and soon gain fame as the finest fighters in the arena. Marcus is able to use his position of anonymity to expose Gaius' plan to overthrow the governor. His valor enables him to obtain pardons for his companions and himself. The other two films in this trio are *Revenge of the Gladiators* and *Seven Rebel Gladiators* (aka Sette Contro Tutti; Seven Against All).

Gordon Mitchell (center) is taken captive in *Seven Slaves Against the World* (1965).

256 79 A.D.

(Anno 79–La Distruzione di Ercolano; The Destruction of Herculaneum)
Cineproduzioni Associate, Rome–C.F.P.C., Paris (1962) 113 min.
Totalscope / Eastman Color
U.S.–American-International
    P–Mario Maggi / D–Gianfranco Parolini / W–Giorgio Simonelli, Gianfranco Parolini / M–Carlo Franci / C–Francesco Izzarelli / E–Edmondo Lozzi / AD–Nico Matul
    Cast–Brad Harris (Marcus Tiberius), Susan Paget (Livia), Mara Lane (Diomira), Jacques Berthier (Tirteo), Jany Clair (Myrta), Carlo Tamberlani (Furio), Philippe Hersent (Titus), Ivy Stewart (Claudia), Isarco Ravaioli (Licinius) with George Menadovic, Vladimer Leib, Nick Stefanini, Pino Mattei, Ignazio Dolce, Roy Martino, Mila Kaciceva, Giuseppe Narotti

    There's treachery afoot in ancient Rome and Marcus Tiberius and his quartet of buffoonish companions are going to get to the bottom of it. They trace the trouble to Herculaneum (the other city that would be destroyed by the eruption of Mount Vesuvius). Once again an evil nobleman is committing crimes and trying to blame it on the local Christians. Marcus and company masquerade as gladiators to infiltrate enemy territory. They are discovered and sentenced to be crucified. The eruption of Vesuvius occurs in the nick of time and saves our heroes from execution. *79 A.D.* is overlong and has a muddled plot which consists of lots of action and little else. The same cast and director scored somewhat better the same year with *The Old Testament*. The volcanic eruption scenes are, for the most part, stock footage from the 1959 version of *The Last Days of Pompeii*.

257 The Shame of the Sabine Women

(El Rapto de las Sabinas; The Rape of the Sabine Women)

Lorenza Velazquez adores Lex Johnson in *The Shame of the Sabine Women* (1962).

Constelacion Films (1962) 80 min.
Mexicscope/Eastman Color
U.S.–United Producers Releasing Organization
    P/D/W–Albert Gout/M–Gustavo Cesar Carrion/C–Alex Phillips/E–Jorge Bustor
    Cast–Lex Johnson (Hostes), William Rubinskis (Romulus), Lorenza Velazquez (Hersilia), Teresa Velazquez (Rhea), Luis Induni (Titus Tacio), Leandro Vizcaino (Horacio), Juanita Crespi (Egea), Juan Monfort (Acron) with Victor Vayo, Antonio Palmer, Julio Albadalejo, Clotilde Gijon, Marin Rodriguez, Salvador Torrvella, Angel Lombarte

    The Shame of the Sabine Women is a Spanish-Mexican coproduction which covers much of the same territory as *Romulus and the Sabines*, an Italian-French production filmed the previous year. The production values are not on as grand a scale as its predecessor but, fortunately, the comedy relief in this version is a bit more restrained. The film begins with a brief sequence depicting the conflict between the brothers Romulus and Remus, resulting in the death of Remus. Following the death of this brother, Romulus establishes the new city of Rome on the spot where Remus was killed. Unfortunately, there are no women to help propagate the fledgling race of Romans and the men must look to the village of the Sabines for assistance. The Sabine women are repulsed by the barbaric Romans and refuse to cooperate. At this point the Romans decide to take things into their own hands, literally. The main action centers on Lex Johnson as Romulus' faithful aide, Hostes, and his attempts to tame a willful Sabine maiden. Writer-director Albert Gout, who filmed a version of *Adam and Eve* in 1956, is quite successful at duplicating the look and feel of the European peplum films. In the U.S. version of this film Teresa and Lorenza Valezquez are billed as Tresa and Lorena Doude.

258   *Siege of Syracuse*

(L'Assedio di Siracusa)
A Galatea-Glomer-Lyre Production (1962) 96 min.
Dyaliscope/Eastman Color
U.S.–Paramount

P–Enzo Morelle/D–Pietro Francisci/W–Ennio De Concini, Pietro Francisci/M–Angelo Francesco Lavagnino/C–Carlo Carlini/E–Nino Baragli/AD–Ottavio Scotti/CD–Gaia Romanini

Cast–Rossano Brazzi (Archimedes), Tina Louise (Diana), Sylva Koscina (Clio), Alberto Farnese (Marcello) with Enrico Maria Salerno, Gino Cervi, Luciano Marin, Alfredo Varelli

When Syracuse is threatened by both the Romans and the Carthaginians, the defense of the city is entrusted to the brilliant physicist Archimedes. However, very little screen time is spent on his scientific achievements. The main focus of the screenplay is Archimedes' love for the beautiful dancing girl, Diana. Their relationship is not an easy one as Archimedes is already promised to another woman. When Diana reveals that she is pregnant with the child of Archimedes, her stepbrother puts her on a ship sailing for Rome. During an escape attempt Diana is injured and stricken with amnesia. Diana marries the Roman consul Marcello and Archimedes marries his betrothed, Clio. Years later, Archimedes is in Rome to negotiate an alliance and he discovers that Diana is now married to the consul. The shock of seeing him again restores her memory but Diana cannot abandon her husband and children. Shortly after his return to Syracuse, Clio is killed in a chariot accident. Rome invades Syracuse and Marcello is a casualty in the battle. At long last, the lovers are (rather conveniently) reunited. Pietro Francisci directs with his usual flair for action and romance. Francisci began directing in 1934 and for many years specialized in travelogues and documentaries. In the early fifties he switched to action-oriented costume dramas. Following the success of *Hercules* (1958), Francisci devoted the majority of his later career to the epic genre. His final film was *Sinbad i il Califfo di Bagdad*, made in 1973.

259　*Siege of the Saxons*

A Charles H. Schneer Production/An Ameran Film Columbia (1963) 85 min.
Eastman Color

Produced by Jud Kinberg/D–Nathan Juran/W–John Kohn, Jud Kinberg/M–Laurie Johnson/C–Wilkie Cooper, Jack Mills/E–Maurice Rootes/AD–Bill Constable

Cast–Janette Scott (Katherine), Ronald Lewis (Robert), Ronald Howard (Edmund), John Laurie (Merlin), Mark Dignam (King Arthur) with Jerome Willis, Francis De Wolff, Charles Lloyd Pack, Peter Mason

During the twentieth year of his reign, King Arthur's position is threatened by the usurper Edmund of Cornwall. To protect his daughter, Princess Katherine, he sends her into hiding. Arthur is killed when Edmund and his Saxons attack Camelot. Edmund attempts to find Katherine so that he can marry her and legitimize his claim to the throne. As Edmund is about to be crowned king, Merlin appears at the ceremony and challenges him to draw the sword Excalibur from its scabbard. Only the rightful monarch is able to do this and when Edmund fails he forfeits his claim to rule. Katherine easily withdraws the sword and her army defeats the Saxon invaders. *Siege of the Saxons* is an entertaining programmer—inexpensive, but well made nevertheless. As with many of the low budget British productions made at this time, an excellent cast of performers helps to elevate the material. Ronald Howard, who plays the villainous Edmund of Cornwall, is the son of actor Leslie Howard.

260　*The Sign of the Cross*

Paramount (1932) 124 min.

P/D–Cecil B. DeMille/W–Waldemar Young, Sidney Buchman/Based on the play by Wilson Barrett/M–Rudolph Kopp/C–Karl Struss/E–Anne Bauchens/AD/CD–Mitchell Leisen

Cast–Fredric March (Marcus Superbus), Elissa Landi (Mercia), Claudette Colbert (Poppaea), Charles Laughton (Nero), Ian Keith (Tigellinus), Harry Beresford (Flavius), Vivian Tobin (Dacia), Arthur Hohl (Titus), Tommy Colon (Stephanus), Clarence Burton (Servilius), Harold Healy (Tibul), Robert Manning (Philodemus), Ferdinand Gottschalk (Glabrio), Joyzella Joyner (Ancaria) with Nat Pendleton, William V. Mong, Richard Alexander, Joe Bonomo

One day in 1932 on the Paramount studio lot, Cecil B. DeMille walked up to Claudette Colbert and asked her, "How would you like to play the wickedest woman in the world?" Up until then Colbert was known primarily for her work in light comedy roles but DeMille had sensed in her an ability for drama. His intuition paid off and her performance as Poppaea, the evil Empress of Rome, is the

Nero (Charles Laughton, center) sings as Rome burns: *The Sign of the Cross* (1932).

highlight of *The Sign of the Cross*. Whether dressed in Mitchell Leisen's exotic costumes or reposing nude in a milk bath, she is never anything less than splendid. The film is based on a play by Wilson Barrett which had already spawned a 1914 movie version. The plot is very similar to that of *Quo Vadis*, with a handsome Roman tribune falling in love with a beautiful Christian girl during the reign of the emperor Nero. To further complicate their romance, the tribune is also desired by Nero's wife, Poppaea. One major difference is that in *The Sign of the Cross*, the hero and heroine both die in the arena at the end. This film marked DeMille's return to Paramount following several years absence as an independent producer. The subsequent success of this film was so great that studio executive Adolph Zukor offered DeMille a permanent place at Paramount. In 1944 DeMille released his "modernized" version of *The Sign of the Cross* which included an eleven minute prologue showing American bombers flying over a war-torn Rome. He reasoned that this would give the film more immediacy for World War II–conscious audiences. Several scenes were

trimmed for the reissue due to strict censorship codes which did not exist in 1932. Some of the gamier sequences included a shot of a naked girl tied to a stake about to be ravaged by a gorilla and an attempt by dancer Joyzella Joyner to seduce Elissa Landi. Thankfully Colbert's milk bath and the Amazon women fighting pygmies in the arena were retained.

AA Nomination: Best Cinematography

Films and Filming: *The Sign of the Cross* typifies the best and the worst of [DeMille's] excesses. Characterisation and plot are sparse, yet most of the performances are adequate, whilst the direction is cleverly controlled in its contrivance.

Movie: By no means one of his best, it still contains all the ingredients of a great epic film.

261   *Sign of the Gladiator*

(Nel Signo de Roma; The Sign of Rome)
A Glomer Production (1959) 98 min.
Dyaliscope / Eastman Color
U.S.–American-International 80 min.
ColorScope
P–Vittorio Musy-Glory / D–Guido Brignone /

Georges Marchal must decide between his love for Anita Ekberg and his duty to Rome in *Sign of the Gladiator* **(1959).**

W–Sergio Leone, Guido Brignone, Giuseppe Mangione, Francesco Thellung, Francesco De Feo/M–Angelo Francesco Lavagnino/C–Luciano Trasatti/E–Nino Baragli/AD–Ottavio Scotti/CD–Vittorio Nino Novarese

Cast–Georges Marchal (Marcus Valerius), Anita Ekberg (Zenobia), Lorella De Luca (Bathsheba), Jacques Sernas (Julian), Folco Lulli (Semanzio), Chelo Alonso (Erika), Alberto Farnese (Marcel), Mimmo Palmara (Lator), Alfredo Varelli (Ito), Sergio Sauro (Tullius), Gino Cervi (Aurelian) with Paul Muller, Arturo Dominici

American-International Pictures temporarily abandoned teenage exploitation films and attempted to move into the realm of the blockbuster with this lavish historical import. Re-edited and retitled, *Sign of the Gladiator* was given AIP's usual saturation release accompanied by reams of publicity. The film did well enough for the company to pick up scores of other European mini-epics for distribution in the United States. *Sign of the Gladiator* is fairly unremarkable, as peplum films

go, but it does boast a better than average cast. The story is set during the reign of the Roman emperor Aurelian. General Marcus Valerius goes to the kindom of Palmyra posing as an expatriate to win the trust of Queen Zenobia. Valerius and Zenobia fall in love but he cannot forget his allegiance to Rome. Finally, Valerius causes the fall of Zenobia's empire and she is sent to Rome to be prosecuted for her rebellion. Cuban dancer Chelo Alonso, fresh from the *Folies Bergères*, appears in her first epic role. Battle sequences were directed by Riccardo Freda.

Variety: Sign of the Gladiator is a crudely made spectacle. The deepest thing about it is Anita Ekberg's cleavage.

262   *Sign of the Pagan*

Universal-International (1954) 92 min.
CinemaScope/Technicolor

P–Albert J. Cohen/D–Douglas Sirk/W–Oscar Brodney, Barre Lyndon/M–Frank Skinner, Hans J.

Jack Palance, Jeff Chandler and Ludmilla Tcherina in a publicity pose for *Sign of the Pagan* (1954).

Salter/C–Russell Metty/E–Milton Carruth, Al Clark/AD–Alexander Golitzen, Emrich Nicholson/CD–Bill Thomas

 Cast–Jeff Chandler (Marcian), Jack Palance (Attila), Ludmilla Tcherina (Pulcheria), Rita Gam (Kubra), Jeff Morrow (Paulinus), George Dolenz (Theodosius), Allison Hayes (Ildico) with Alexander Scourby, Sara Shane, Eduard Franz, Moroni Olson, Leo Gordon, Pat Hogan, Howard Petrie, Michael Ansara, Rusty Wescoatt, Charles Horvath

On his way from Rome to Constantinople, the Roman centurion Marcian is wounded and taken as a prisoner to the camp of Attila the Hun. Attila admires the Roman's courage and spares his life. When Marcian learns of Attila's plan to march on the Roman empire, he escapes to warn the emperor Theodosius. The emperor ignores the warning and attempts to make the barbarians his allies. His sister Pulcheria realizes the futility of this and, with the help of Marcian, stages a revolt which gains her control of the kingdom from her brother. Under her leadership, the Romans march against Attila and his men. *Sign of the Pagan* was one of Universal's early forays into the realm of large-scale film making. Actually, a number of skillful matte paintings make the film look more expensive than it was. Jeff Chandler, then the studio's top leading man, took time off from his usual frontier characters to play a Roman centurion. Originally he had been offered the part of Attila but refused it because he did not feel it was in keeping with his "good guy" image. Jack Palance, in his first of many epic film roles, plays Attila to good effect and easily steals the picture away from Chandler. Ballerina Ludmilla Tcherina is very wooden as the object of Jeff Chandler's affections. Reportedly, she was so difficult during the filming of *Sign of the Pagan* that Universal abandoned plans to star her in any future films. Allison Hayes, who later gained fame as a horror movie queen, can be seen in one of her earliest screen roles as Ildico, the wife of Attila. She very effectively plays her pivotal part without even speaking a line of dialogue. Douglas Sirk would soon find his niche as the director of a series of glossy soap operas for Universal, including *Written on the Wind* (1956) and *Imitation of Life* (1959). *Sign of the Pagan* was Universal's second movie to utilize the new CinemaScope widescreen process. To ensure maximum bookings, a standard screen version was filmed simultaneously.

Photoplay: The sweep of savage armies and the clash of ancient battles build up plenty of visual excitement. Plots and counterplots are sometimes a bit confusing, but events move fast.

Screen Stories: Christians and pagans battle it out on the CinemaScope screen. With such stalwart sons as Jeff [Chandler] to protect her, it is a wonder that Rome ever declined and fell.

263   The Silver Chalice

Warner Bros. (1955) 144 min.
CinemaScope/WarnerColor

P/D–Victor Saville/W–Lesser Samuels/Based on the novel by Thomas B. Costain/M–Franz Waxman/C–William V. Skall/E–George White/PD–Rolf Gerard/AD–Boris Leven/CD–Marjorie Best

Cast–Virginia Mayo (Helena), Pier Angeli (Deborra), Jack Palance (Simon), Paul Newman (Basil), Walter Hampden (Joseph), Joseph Wiseman (Mijamin), Alexander Scourby (Luke), Lorne Greene (Peter), David J. Stewart (Adam), Herbert Rudley (Linus), Jacques Aubuchon (Nero) E.G. Marshall (Ignatius), Michael Pate (Aaron), Shawn Smith (Poppaea) with Peter Reynolds, Natalie Wood, Mort Marshall, Booth Coleman, Terence de Marney, Robert Middleton, Albert Dekker

Hoping to duplicate the box office success of Fox's *The Robe*, Warner Bros. produced *The Silver Chalice*, based on another best-selling religious novel about a holy relic belonging to Jesus. The complicated plot involves Basil, a talented artist who is sold into slavery. He is bought and freed by the Apostle Luke who takes him to the home of Joseph of Arimathea. Joseph is in possession of the cup from which Jesus drank at the Last Supper and he requests that Basil fashion a silver chalice to enshrine it. A band of zealots is searching for the cup in order to defame the followers of Jesus. They enlist the help of Simon the Magician, whose mistress, Helena, is having an affair with Basil. To add further entanglements to the plot, Joseph's granddaughter, Debbora, is also in love with the artist. The story culminates in Rome at the court of Nero. The movie's main attributes are a strong cast and the wonderfully stylized sets. These sets were designed by Boris Leven who worked closely with Rolf Gerard, production designer for the Metropolitan Opera Company. Particular attention was paid to the use of color throughout. Leven, Gerard and director Victor Saville wanted to ensure that audiences would not be distracted away from the principal characters in a scene by the indiscriminate use of color. The sets and costumes were carefully designed to enhance the

Jack Palance, Robert Middleton and Virginia Mayo on one of the stylized sets for *The Silver Chalice* (1955).

drama rather than detract from it. Unfortunately, all of this creative effort was lost on contemporary critics and audiences who found the meticulous design of the film to be anachronistic. The large cast is dominated by Jack Palance's delightfully villainous performance as Simon the Magician. Pier Angeli is gentle and sincere as Deborra. As the temptress Helena, Virginia Mayo sports the most bizarre pair of eyebrows in antiquity. This, combined with her pale skin and exotic costuming, helps to create the perfect image of wanton decadence. Paul Newman, in his film debut, is handsome, though a bit wooden, as Basil. Years later, when the film had its television premiere in Los Angeles, Newman took out an advertisement in the newspaper decrying his performance with the hope of discouraging viewers from watching. The result

was one of the highest rated movies shown on a local television station up to that time.

AA Nomination: Best Color Cinematography, Musical Score

Screen Stories: Pageant of the Roman Empire, with handsome sets.

264   *The Sin of Adam and Eve*

(El Pecado de Adan y Eva)
Dimension Pictures (1972) 72 min.
MetroColor

P/D/W–Michael Zachary (Miguel Zacarias)/ M–Edward Norton/C–Robert Solano/E–Gloria Shoemann/Montage sequences created by Johann Verros

Cast–George Rivers/Jorge Rivero (Adam), Candy Wilson/Candy Cave (Eve) and Charles L. Campbell as The Voice

Jorge Rivero is the hunkiest Adam on film in
***The Sin of Adam and Eve* (1972).**

The Sin of Adam and Eve is a Mexican film produced in 1967. Dimension Pictures, an independent releasing company, picked up the picture for distribution in the United States in 1972. The movie was recut and the names of the actors and director were anglicized. Jorge Rivero, the popular beefcake star of innumerable Mexican films, became the "famous European star" George Rivers. He actually comes across more as Tarzan than Adam since the silly scenario has him fighting sundry jungle beasts while dressed in a loin cloth. In reality, the film is pure exploitation masquerading under the guise of an "artistic" biblical drama. The execution is naive and the acting is amateurish. The brief dialogue sequences are made all the more ridiculous by the dreadful dubbing. Jorge Rivero and Candy Cave do manage to appear totally unselfconscious about their nudity.

265   *Sins of Jezebel*

A Robert L. Lippert, Jr., Production
Lippert Pictures (1953) 74 min.
Ansco Color

P–Sigmund Neufeld / D–Reginald Le Borg / W–Richard Landau / M–Bert Shefter / C–Gilbert Warrenton / E–Carl Pierson / AD–Frank Sylos / CD–Riley Thorn

Cast–Paulette Goddard (Jezebel), George Nader (Jehu), Eduard Franz (Ahab), John Hoyt (Elijah), John Shelton (Loram), Margia Dean (Deborah), Ludwig Donath (Naboth) with Joe Besser, Carmen d'Antonio

During the biblical movie boom of the early fifties three studios announced forthcoming motion pictures to be based on the story of Jezebel. The most promising of these seemed to be the 20th Century–Fox production *The Story of Jezebel* which would be filmed in the new CinemaScope widescreen process. The other two films were from the "poverty row" companies Allied Artists (*The Siren Jezebel*) and Lippert Pictures (*Sins of Jezebel*). Only the latter film was actually made and it is so inferior that one wishes that either of the others had been completed instead. Robert L. Lippert later said that *Sins of Jezebel* was one of the only films his company had produced that he was proud of. This should indicate the general quality of their output. Filmed in "glorious" Ansco Color, *Sins of Jezebel* has the dubious distinction of being one of the "cheesiest" looking epics ever made. Paulette Goddard, at a low point in her career, is definitely over the hill as the temptress Jezebel, especially when compared to her handsome leading man (a young George Nader in his pre–Universal days). She does try and bring some humanity to the primarily unsympathetic role of the pagan princess who marries the King of Israel and attempts to introduce her false gods into his country. John Hoyt does double duty as Elijah the Prophet and the modern on-screen narrator. The money, what there was of it, seems to have suddenly run out before the end because the narrator appears and fills the audience in on events that would normally have been the climax. The story of Jezebel is filled with all the elements that made these films so popular—i.e., sex, violence, and a bit of religion. It is a great pity that a better film couldn't have been produced from the material.

Motion Picture Herald: Discloses itself to be primarily a dramatic film which stresses the

George Nader kneels before his evil queen (Paulette Goddard) in *Sins of Jezebel* (1953).

sexiness and sinfulness of one of the most wicked women who ever lived. Picture should therefore attract the large segment of the picturegoers who like "sex and sin" in their film fare.

266 *The Sins of Pompeii*

(Gli Ultimi Giorni di Pompei/The Last Days of Pompeii)
Universalia, Rome–Franco London Films, Paris (1949) 110 min.
U.S.–Visual Drama Inc.
  P–Salvo d'Angelo/D–Marcel L'Herbier, Paolo Moffa/W–Marcel L'Herbier, Jean Laviron, Pierre Brive/Based on the novel *The Last Days of Pompeii* by Edward Bulwer-Lytton/M–Roman Vlad/C–Roger Herbert/CD–Veniero Colasanti
  Cast–Micheline Presle (Helene), Georges Marchal (Lysias), Marcel Herrand (Arbax), Jacques Catelain (Clodius), Adriana Benetti (Nydia), Laure Alex (Julia), Peter Trent (Salluste), Marcelle Rovena (Magician), Alain Quercy (Lepidus), Antonio Pierfederici (Olinthus)

  This version of *The Last Days of Pompeii* was one of the first European epics to follow in the

footsteps of *Fabiola*. It was filmed at Cinecitta Studios in Rome and on location at the arena of Verona. It has received very limited exposure in the United States and lacks an easily recognizable cast, with the exception of a very young Georges Marchal, who was to become a staple of such films. One reason for its poor distribution in the U.S. may have been that R.K.O. decided to reissue their 1935 version of the same story in 1949. A title change to *The Sins of Pompeii* did little to increase its chances of success. Although the 1949 version is marginally better than the R.K.O. film, it still lacks the sheer bravado of the 1959 remake starring Steve Reeves. Paolo Moffa, who co-directed *The Sins of Pompeii*, was the producer of the 1959 version.

267 *Sins of Rome*

(Spartaco; Spartacus)
Spartacus Consortium Production (1953) 120 min.
U.S.–R.K.O. (1954) 71 min.
  P–Roberto Fabbri/D–Riccardo Freda/W–Jean Ferry, Maria Bori, Gino Visentini, Riccardo Freda/

Spartacus (Massimo Girotti) is temporarily bewitched by a treacherous Roman beauty (Gianna Maria Canale) in *Sins of Rome* (1954).

M–Renzo Rosselini/C–Gabor Pogany/E–Mario Serandrei/AD–Franco Lolli/CD–Dina Di Bari

    Cast–Massimo Girotti (Spartacus), Ludmilla Tcherina (Amitys), Yves Vincent (Octavius), Gianna Maria Canale (Sabina), Carlo Ninchi (Crassus), Vittorio Sanipoli (Rufus) with Nerio Bernardi, Carlo Giustini, Cesare Beccarini, Umberto Silvestri, Mimmo Palmara

In 75 B.C. the Thracian slave, Spartacus, is loved by Sabina, the wanton daughter of the Roman general Crassus, but he is in love with her handmaiden Amytis. When he rejects Sabina's advances, she has him sent to the arena to be trained as a gladiator. Spartacus escapes and leads the other slaves in a revolt against the Roman oppression. When his troops are eventually defeated, he dies on the battlefield in the arms of Amytis. Very little of the historical facts about Spartacus are evident in this film and when compared to the1961 version, *Sins of Rome* definitely comes up short. This does not mean that it isn't successful as entertainment. The film actually has much to recommend it. The stunning black and white cinematography of Gabor Pogany is a major attribute. Massimo Girotti gives a superior performance as Spartacus and Gianna Maria Canale has never been more beautiful than she is as the iniquitous Sabina. Ludmilla Tcherina is less successful as Amytis,

although she does get an opportunity to display the talents as a ballerina that brought her fame in films like *Tales of Hoffman* (1951). It is difficult to judge the story fairly in the extremely truncated English language version since it was cut to almost half its original length. Mimmo Palmara, in one of his first film roles, can be spotted briefly as a member of Spartacus' slave army.

268   *The Slave*

(Il Figlio di Spartacus; The Son of Spartacus)
A Titanus-Arta Cinematografica S.p.A. Production (1962) 100 min.
CinemaScope/Eastman Color
U.S.–Metro-Goldwyn-Mayer (1963)
    P–Franco Palaggi/D–Sergio Corbucci/W–Andriano Bolzoni, Bruno Corbucci, Giovanni Grimaldi/M–Piero Piccioni/C–Enzo Barboni/E–Ruggero Mastroianni/AD–Ottavio Scotti, Riccardo Domenici/CD–Mario Giorsi

    Cast–Steve Reeves (Randus), Jacques Sernas (Vezio), Gianna Maria Canale (Clodia), Claudio Gora (Crassus), Ivo Garrani (Julius Caesar), Enzo Fiermonte (Gular) with Ombretta Colli, Roland Bartrop, Franco Balducci, Renato Baldini, Benito Steffanelli, Gloria Parri

In 48 B.C. Rome is ruled by the triumvirate of Julius Caesar, Crassus and Pompey. Fearing treachery, Caesar sends his loyal officer Randus from Alexandria to the Roman province of Lydia to spy on Crassus. While on his journey, Randus is captured by Lydian slave traders who refuse to believe his claim of being a Roman officer. One of the other captives is a former gladiator who had fought beside the great Spartacus. He recognizes the amulet worn by Randus and knows that he must be the son of Spartacus. Randus organizes an uprising against the slave traders and escapes his captors. At the court of Crassus he is excepted as an ally. When Randus witnesses the cruelties inflicted on the slaves by Crassus he goes to the slave stronghold at the City of the Sun and claims his father's sword and armor, vowing to fight against the Roman oppressors. This is a credible, action oriented se-

Steve Reeves is the son of Spartacus in *The Slave* (1963).

quel to Spartacus, featuring one of Steve Reeves' best performances and a strong supporting cast of familiar faces. The production values are well above average, heightened by some excellent location photography in Egypt.

ABC Film Review: Among scenes of barbaric splendor this exciting drama is packed with battles, intrigue and murder, with brief intervals for romance.

269   Slave of Dreams

De Laurentiis Entertainment
U.S.–Showtime TV Network (1995) 96 min.
Color

P–Dino and Martha De Laurentiis/D–Robert M. Young/W–Ron Hutchinson/M–Christopher Tyng/C–Giuseppe Maccari/E–Norman Buckley/PD–Pier Luigi Basile/AD–Marco Trentini/CD–Sergio Ballo, Gabriella Pescucci

Cast–Adrian Pasdar (Joseph), Edward James Olmos (Potiphar), Sherilyn Fenn (Zulaikha) with Philip Newman, Nabil Shaban, Orso Maria Guerrini, Nadim Sawalha, Kevork Malikyan, Anthony Samuel Selby

An obvious attempt to cash in on the TNT version of the same biblical story but with none of the class or sincerity of that production. The plot concentrates on the Potiphar portion of Joseph's story with Sherilyn Fenn a vast improvement over Leslie Anne Warren as Potiphar's wife. For once, the part is somewhat sympathetically written and not played as a frustrated nymphomaniac. Adrian Pasdar is a very sexy Joseph and full advantage is taken to show him off in a loincloth as much as possible.

270   The Slave of Rome

(La Schiava di Roma/Blood of the Warriors)
Atlantica Cinematografica (1961) 91 min.
Totalscope/Eastman Color
U.S.–Medallion (1964)

P–Marco Vicario/D–Sergio Grieco/W–Franco

Rossana Podesta confronts Mario Petri in *The Slave of Rome* (1964).

Prosperi, Silvano Reina, Marco Vicario/M–Armando Trovajoli/C–Vincenzo Seratrice/E–Enzo Alfonsi/AD–Franco Lolli/CD–Mario Giorsi

Cast–Guy Madison (Marcus Valerius), Rossana Podesta (Anthea), Giacomo Rossi Stuart (Claudius), Mario Petri (Lyciros) with Ignazio Leone, Raffaele Baldassarre, Nando Poggi, Goffredo Unger, Nazzaro Zemperla, Antonio Basile, Angelo Bastianoni, Stefano Delic, Mirko Boman

Once again it's Rome vs. the barbarian hordes. A small band of Romans, led by Marcus Valerius, is sent out to fight the much larger army of the Gauls. The Romans are presented as a very sympathetic lot while the barbarians live up to their name. Their idea of entertainment at dinner is burning someone's eyes out with a torch. The Gallic leader hopes to make peace with the Romans but he is opposed by the headstrong and treacherous warrior Lyciros. Anthea, the daughter of the chieftain, dons her armor and leads the first assault on the Romans. She is taken captive but treated kindly by Marcus, who saves her from rape by one of the mercenaries employed in his troop. Her father negotiates for her release but Lyciros turns the peaceful plan into a trap in which her father is killed. Anthea, who has fallen in love with Marcus, now willingly joins the Romans. In a climactic confrontation, the Romans and Gauls kill each other off, leaving only Marcus and Anthea alive on the blood soaked battlefield. Mario Ciano was an assistant director on this film, much of which was made on location in Yugoslavia.

271   Slave Queen of Babylon

(Io, Semiramide; I Am Semiramis)
APO Film–Globe Films International (1962) 101 min.
CinemaScope/Eastman Color
U.S.–American-International

P–Aldo Pomilia/D–Primo Zeglio/W–Fede Arnaud, Alberto Liberati, Primo Zeglio/M–Carlo Savina/C–Alvaro Mancori/E–Alberto Gallitti/AD–Franco Lolli/CD–Maria Baroni

Cast–Yvonne Furneaux (Semiramis), John Ericson (Kir), Renzo Ricci (Minurte), Gianni Rizzo (Ghelas), Lucio De Santis (Marduk), Germano Longo (Onnos) with Antonio Corevi, Ugo Sasso, Umberto Silvestri, Jose Torres, Calisto Calisti, Nino Di Napoli, Massimo Giuliani, Mario Laurentino, Piero Pastore, Mario Pissante, Valerie Camille

Semiramis is the beautiful but scheming consort of Minurte, the king of Nineveh. The mighty general Onnos returns from battle with the intention of usurping the throne. Semiramis pretends to love him and convinces him to abandon his plan. Among the prisoners of war taken by Onnos is Kir, the king of Dardania. Semiramis is instantly attracted to the handsome captive and the jealous Onnos attempts to have him killed. Semiramis intervenes and Kir is pardoned by King Minurte who invites him to instruct the young heir to the throne in the arts of battle. Semiramis and Kir begin a torrid love affair but when the opportunity for her to marry Minurte and become queen arises, she allows ambition of overrule her heart. Onnos uses this as an excuse to arrest Kir and have him executed. Kir escapes but Semiramis believes that he has been killed and that Minurte ordered the execution. She devises a plan to assassinate the king and assumes his throne as ruler. One of Semiramis' first edicts is an order for the Dardanian slaves to build her new city of Babylon. Later, she visits the building site not knowing that Kir has rejoined his people as a slave to give them hope. When Onnos and his soldiers attack the camp, Kir and his men join Semiramis' guards to quell the onslaught. The grateful queen, relieved to discover that the man she loves is still alive, restores Kir to his rightful place of eminence. Kir, however, has never forgiven her for abandoning him to marry Minurte. When Semiramis discovers that Kir plans to take over Nineveh for his Dardinians, she poisons him to protect her throne. As she speaks over his funeral pyre, one of Kir's men shoots an arrow into Semiramis' heart. Unable to overcome their differences in life, the two lovers are now united on the pyre in death. This

interesting and elaborate Italian production has two extremely attractive lead performers. John Ericson looks so natural in the period costuming that it is surprising that this was his only Euro epic. Yvonne Furneaux is as gorgeous as ever but the lack of passion in her performance sometimes causes the film to be less affecting than it could have been.

272 *Slaves of Babylon*

Columbia (1953) 82 min.
Technicolor
  P–Sam Katzman / D–William Castle / W–DeVallon Scott / M–Mischa Bakaleinikoff / C–Henry Freulich / E–William A. Lyon / AD–Paul Palmentola
  Cast–Richard Conte (Nahum), Linda Christian (Panthea), Maurice Swartz (Daniel), Terrance Kilburn (Cyrus), Michael Ansara (Belshazzar), Ruth Storey (Rachel), Leslie Bradley (Nebuchadnezzar), John Crawford (Avil), Ric Rowen (Arrioch), Robert Griffin (Astyages) with Beatrice Maude, Wheaton Chambers, Paul Purcell, Julie Newmeyer, Ernestine Barrier

In 1953 Warner Bros. announced their plans to film a big budget spectacular entitled *Daniel and the Woman of Babylon*, to be adapted from the Book of Daniel in the Old Testament. Columbia's resident producer Sam Katzman, sometimes known as the "King of the Quickies," rushed a film based on the same source

A Jewish slave (Richard Conte) loves a Babylonian princess (Linda Christian) in *Slaves of Babylon* (1953).

into production. Consequently, the Warner Bros. project never materialized. The plot of *Slaves of Babylon* deals with the fall of Babylon to Cyrus the Persian, with the emphasis on a love affair between a Hebrew slave and a scheming princess. The pivotal character of Daniel is forced to take a back seat to these proceedings. The haste in filming Columbia's *Slaves of Babylon* is apparent in the cheap quality of the overall production. The sets and costumes are, for the most part, leftovers from *Salome*, filmed earlier the same year. In addition to the poor production values, the film also suffers from a dull script, routine performances, and the uninspired direction of William Castle. Castle would later gain considerable fame as a director of horror films, including *House on Haunted Hill*, *The Tingler*, and *Strait-Jacket*. Richard Conte's performance and appearance as the Hebrew slave Nahum seems far better suited to a gangster film than a historical spectacle. Linda Christian, though extremely beauiful as Princess Panthea, is decorative and little more.

273   *Sodom and Gomorrah*

(Sodoma e Gomorra / The Last Days of Sodom and Gomorrah)
A Titanus Production (1962) 154 min.
Eastman Color
U.S.–A Goffredo Lombardo and Joseph E. Levine Presentation
20th Century–Fox (1963)
Color by DeLuxe
    P–Goffredo Lombardo / D–Robert Aldrich / W–Hugo Butler, Giorgio Prosperi / M–Miklos Rozsa / C–Silvano Ippoliti, Mario Montuori, Cyril Knowles / E–Peter Tanner / AD–Ken Adam / CD–Giancarlo Bartolini Salimbeni / Prologue and Main Title designed by Maurice Bender
    Cast–Stewart Granger (Lot), Pier Angeli (Ildith), Stanley Baker (Astaroth), Rossana Podesta (Shuah), Anouk Aimee (Queen Bera), Claudia Mori (Maleb), Scilla Gabel (Tamar), Rik Battaglia (Melchir), Giacomo Rossi Stuart (Ishmael), Mimmo Palmara (Arno) with Feodor Chaliapin, Aldo Silvani, Enzo Fiermonte, Antonio De Teffe, Gabriele Tinti, Daniele Vargas, Alice and Ellen Kessler, Mitzuko Takara, Giovanna Galletti, Massimo Pietrobon, Andrea Tagliabue

Sodom and Gomorrah can truly be called a multi-national production. The exteriors were filmed in Ouarzazate, Morocco, and the interiors at the Titanus studios in Rome. The principal cast members are British, Italian and French. The director was an American. The project had been on Titanus' production schedule for over eight years but actual filming was delayed while a vast amount of research could be conducted and the necessary financing could be arranged. Various locations were considered but Robert Aldrich finally decided on Ouarzazate. The location, though scenically ideal, created a number of hardships for the cast and crew. Daytime temperatures often rose to over 110 degrees and at night dropped to freezing. The exterior location shooting lasted 100 days. What Goffredo Lombardo had conceived as a $5 million dollar production had risen in cost considerably. Titanus was forced to seek additional financing elsewhere and found it with American movie entrepreneur Joseph E. Levine. The eventual cost of the film was $8 million. The extensive use of location photography gives *Sodom and Gomorrah* a realistic quality that many other epics lack. All of the effort was lost on American critics and audiences, who dismissed it as just another dubbed European costume picture and ignored it almost totally. In Europe, however, the film was a box office success. In the United Kingdom alone it became one of the biggest moneymakers ever released by the Rank Organisation. London critics were also quick to praise the technical aspects and the action sequences. Robert Aldrich's direction keeps the story moving at a rapid pace. Italian director Sergio Leone had been hired as a second unit director. His degree of contribution varies greatly depending on the source of information. Leone enthusiasts claim that his input was extensive and that the results are obvious. Indeed, many European posters for the film list him as co-director. Books about Robert Aldrich say that he only worked on the film a few weeks before he was fired by the director. At any rate, Leone's name does not appear in the on-screen credits at all. Dimitri Tiomkin was originally contracted to compose the background score but he was forced to decline due to health problems. Miklos Rozsa replaced him and the fortunate result is one of his most dynamic scores. Rozsa, however, hated the movie and in his autobiography said that it "was like a parody of the genre." Special men-

Robert Aldrich directs Rossana Podesta, Pier Angeli, Stewart Granger and Anouk Aimee in *Sodom and Gomorrah* (1963).

tion should also be made of Maurice Bender's impressive opening credits. They instantly establish the tone of the film to follow with a succession of exotic and beautifully photographed images. The cast is generally quite good. Rossana Podesta turns in one of the best performances as Lot's wayward daughter and Anouk Aimee is a perfectly malevolent Queen of Sodom. At the same time as this version of the story was starting production, producer Fred Gebhardt announced an American-Swedish co-production based on M. Agrest's theory that space travelers landed on Earth centuries ago and caused the destruction of the twin cities. This film was never made.

Time: As for the treatment of Sodom's sins, customers could probably see more sex in the back row balcony than is shown on the screen.

Cinema: Aldrich's inventive use of special effects, new viewpoint on the erotic costume, and uncanny understanding of occult sadism

point a direction that he might have gone. As the film is, it fails brutally.

Modern Screen: The oft-told story of Lot is brought to the screen in this rousing spectacle which, in spite of the cast of thousands, exciting special effects and all the other embellishments of gore and orgy, still doesn't lose sight of the basic human elements involved.

274   *Solomon*

(Salomone)
A Five Mile River Films Ltd/Lube/Lux Vide Production (1997) 172 min
Color
U.S.–Cable television release

P–Lorenzo Minoli, Gerald Rafshoon/D–Roger Young/W–Bradley T. Winter/M–Patrick Williams/C–Raffaele Mertes/E–Benjamin Weissman/PD–Paolo Biagetti/CD–Simonetta Leoncini, Giovanni Viti

Cast–Ben Cross (Solomon), Vivica A. Fox (Sheba), Max Von Sydow (David), Anouk Aimee (Bathsheba), G.W. Bailey (Azarel), Maria Grazia

Cucinotta (Abishag), David Suchet (Joab), Richard Dillane (Jeroboam), Ivan Kaye (Adonijah), Dexter Fletcher (Rehoboam), Umberto Orsini (Nathan), Roger Hammond (Zadok) with Stefania Rocca, Thom Hoffman, Vadim Glowna, Michael Culkin, Pete Lee-Wilson, Marta Zoffoli, Stefan Gubser

The long and troubled reign of King Solomon is the focus of this installment in the Lube/Lux Vide series "La Bibbia." It was the first to be released to American television without the participation of Turner Broadcasting. It is also one of the finest entries in the series. The detailed and episodic narrative begins with the struggle between Solomon and his brother Adonijah for the throne of their dying father David. With the aid of his cunning mother Bathsheba, Solomon becomes King of Israel and Adonijah is killed. The next part of the story focuses on Solomon's wise and productive rule, culminating in the building of a magnificent temple to God. Although Solomon takes many wives it isn't until the beautiful Queen of Sheba visits Jerusalem that he discovers true love. Sheba remains in Israel and bears Solomon a son. When Solomon attempts to make the child his heir, the priests and his people oppose his decision and Sheba must return to her own kingdom. Distraught over the absence of his beloved, Solomon's wisdom fails and he turns to the worship of false gods. The golden age of Solomon ends with his death. The Twelve Tribes of Israel become divided when his imprudent son Rehoboam ascends to the throne. Ben Cross is splendid as Solomon and successfully portrays the diversity of this multifaceted king. The supporting cast is excellent with Anouk Aimee a standout as the crafty Bathsheba. Special mention should also be made of the beautiful symphonic background score by Patrick Williams. It is the best score in this series of TV biblical films and often recalls the music of the great Hollywood epics. It helps to give *Solomon* a sense of grandeur that other entries in this series sometimes lack.

275 *Solomon and Sheba*

A King Vidor Production/An Edward Small Presentation
United Artists (1959) 139 min.
Super Technirama 70/Technicolor

P–Ted Richmond/D–King Vidor/W–Anthony Veiller, Paul Dudley, George Bruce/From a story by Crane Wilbur/M–Mario Nascimbene/C–Freddie Young/E–John Ludwig/AD–Richard Day, Alfred Sweeney/CD–Ralph Jester
Cast–Yul Brynner (Solomon), Gina Lollobrigida (Sheba), George Sanders (Adonijah), Marisa Pavan (Abishag), David Farrar (Pharaoh), John Crawford (Joab), Finley Currie (David), Laurence Naismith (Hezrai), Jose Nieto (Ahob), Harry Andrews (Baltor), Julio Bena (Zadok), Alejandro Rey (Sittar), Jack Gwilliam (Josiah) with Maruchi Fresno, William Devlin, Jean Anderson, Felix de Pomes

Solomon and Sheba had been filming in Spain for two months when, on November 15, 1958, while filming a strenuous sword fight with George Sanders, Tyrone Power was stricken with a fatal heart attack. He was only 44 years old. Four million dollars had already been spent and the film was 75 percent completed when this tragedy occurred. Unfortunately the director, King Vidor, had reversed the usual practice of shooting crowd scenes and long shots last. Without the necessary close-ups, the footage of Power was unusable. Rather than discontinue the project and collect the insurance, United Artists' executives decided to begin again with Yul Brynner in the Solomon role. Brynner viewed the three hours of existing footage and decided to abandon Power's cerebral concept of a man torn between desire and duty. He then demanded a rewrite more in keeping with his virile screen personality. In retrospect, it is difficult to imagine Power as the young Solomon. Photos taken at the time show him looking rather old and tired. There were two other changes of cast when the filming was resumed. Finlay Currie replaced Noel Purcell in the part of King David and Jack Gwillim replaced Maurice Marsac as Josiah. Gina Lollobrigida, as the seductive Queen of Sheba, wore some of the most daring costumes seen in films, up to that time. One, in fact, proved too daring. During the orgy sequence, Lollobrigida wore a two-piece outfit consisting mostly of a short diaphanous veil on top and a long skirt on the bottom. When she undulated to the music the veil would not stay in place. Rather than risk the ire of the censors, a "pagan brassiere" was designed to replace the offending piece of apparel. The film is close to the spirit of DeMille, with lots of sex

Noel Purcell (as King David) crowns Tyrone Power (as Solomon) in the scuttled version of *Solomon and Sheba* (1959).

and spectacle followed by a reel of redemption. When King David dies, he leaves the rule of Israel in the hands of his youngest son, Solomon. The Pharaoh of Egypt, thinking that the inexperienced youth will be an easy target, joins forces with the Queen of Sheba to plot his downfall. Sheba journeys to Israel under the guise of friendship and promptly falls in love with Solomon, thereby forsaking her pact with the pharaoh. Solomon incurs

Yul Brynner and Gina Lollobrigida as *Solomon and Sheba* (1959).

the wrath of God by responding in kind to the pagan queen. When all seems lost, divine intervention saves the day but, in repentance for their sins, the two lovers must part. This was the final film in King Vidor's long and distinguished career.

Time: Two hours of full-color, wide-screen lust, in which all of Solomon's love affairs are lumped into one. In the case of Solomon this makes quite a lump, but Lollobridiga does her breasty best to fill the part.

Motion Picture: When you see that title, you

take it for granted that the big screen's going to be jammed with color and action, romance and religious sentiment. And you're not disappointed.

276   *Solomon and Sheba*

De Laurentiis Entertainment
U.S.–Showtime TV Network (1995) 120 min.
Color
    P–Dino and Martha De Laurentiis/D–Robert M. Young/W–Ronni Kern/M–David Kitay/C–Giuseppe Maccari/E–Arthur Coburn/PD–Pier Luigi Basile/ AD–Marco Trentini/CD–Gabriella Pesucci
    Cast–Halle Berry (Nikaule), Jimmy Smits (Solomon), Nicholas Grace (Jeroboam) with Kenneth Colley, Ruben Santiago Hudson, David John Pope, Chapman Roberts, Hugh Quarshie, Nadim Sawalha, Miguel Brown, Laura Fuino, Norman Buckley, Paul Costello, Christian Anderson, Sergio Smacchi

    While crossing the desert on her way to Jerusalem, the Queen of Sheba discovers the gold mines of Ophir. She attempts to use this information in her plan to make an ally of King Solomon. Solomon's evil advisor Jeroboam has plans of his own to take the throne from his king. The famous biblical romance is reduced to a search for gold in this unforgivably dull TV movie. The only asset is the beauty of Halle Berry as the Queen of Sheba. After two feeble attempts, the De Laurentiis Entertainment series of biblical films for Showtime thankfully ended.
    Variety: King Vidor's $6 million–plus spectacle concerning the same story and starring Yul Brynner and Gina Lollobrigida wasn't any more biblical, but it sure was entertaining.

277   *Son of Cleopatra*

(Il Figlio de Cleopatra)
A Seven Film–Tiki Production, Rome (1965) 103 min.
Techniscope/Technicolor
U.S.–Metro-Goldwyn-Mayer
    P–Cleto Fontini, Francesco Thellung/D–Ferdinando Baldi/W–Ferdinando Baldi, Franco Airoldi, Cleto Fontini/M–Carlo Rustichelli/C–Adalberto Albertini/E–Otello Colangeli/CD–Ditta Peruzzi
    Cast–Mark Damon (El Kabir/Caesarion), Scilla Gabel (Livia), Arnoldo Foa (Caesar Octavian), Livio Lorenzon (Petronius) with Alberto Lupo, Paolo Gozlino, Samira Ahmed, Shoukri Sarhan, Layla Fawzi, Yehia Shaheen, Franco Fantasia, Abdel Khalek Saleh, Mahmoud Farag, Alberto Cevenini, Ivan Basta, Hassen Yousef, Corrado Annicelli

    Son of Cleopatra is yet another attempt to cash in on all of the publicity given to the Taylor/Burton *Cleopatra*. This time, however, a definite attempt is made to link the two films. It seems that Caesarion, the son of Julius Caesar and Cleopatra, did not die at the hands of Octavian's soldiers. He was taken to the desert tribes where he has grown to manhood, ignorant of his royal origins. As "El Kabir," a kind of Egyptian Robin Hood, he leads his people in revolt against the cruel Romans who oppress them. When he takes captive the beautiful daughter of the governor of Alexandria, the Romans escalate their attempts to capture him. Extensive location filming in Egypt sets this a notch above the others of its type and Mark Damon and Scilla Gabel are very appealing in the lead roles.

278   *Son of Hercules in the Land of Darkness*

(Ercole l'Invincible; Hercules the Invincible)
A Metheus Production (1963) 81 min.
Techniscope/Technicolor
U.S.–Embassy (1964)
    P–Lewis Mann/D–Al World (Alvaro Mancori)/W–Kirk Mayer, Pat Kein, Al World/M–Frank Mason (Francesco De Masi)/C–Claude Haroy/E–Frank Robertson/CD–Anna Maria Chretien
    Cast–Dan Vadis (Argolis), Ken Clark (Kaboal) with Carla Calo, Spela Rozin, John Simons, Janette Barton, Hugo Arden/Ugo Sasso, Red Ross/Renato Rossini, Kirk Bert, Sara Laurier, Rosemary Lindt, Michaela Ariston

    Typical peplum foolishness worth mentioning mainly because it was altered with the hope of creating a television series called *The Sons of Hercules*. The feature length film, which had shown as part of the Embassy "Sons of Hercules" movie package, was edited down to two black and white episodes, each running approximately thirty minutes. Narration was used to fill in the gaps left by the editing. After a brief prologue, consisting of clips from several of the other Hercules films, *The Land of Darkness* Part One begins with Argolis, one of the many sons of Hercules, rescuing the beautiful Princess Telka from a lion. As a reward, her father promises

More chains and muscles: Dan Vadis as the *Son of Hercules in the Land of Darkness* (1964).

Argolis her hand in marriage if he will first slay the resident dragon. He accomplishes this with the aid of the dragon sequence lifted intact from *Hercules* (1959). The sudden appearance of a band of marauding barbarians called the Demios, further complicates matters. At this point the first episode abruptly ends. Up to now the film seems to be a precursor to the "Conan" style sword and sorcery films of the eighties, with its fictitious Dark Ages setting and barbaric warriors. Part Two begins with a lengthy recap of the first half and soon degenerates into a typical underground-kingdom-ruled-by-a-beautiful-but-evil-queen plot. Although Argolis gains the trust of the queen when he saves her life from a rampaging elephant, she is assassinated and Telka becomes the prime suspect. The evil warrior Kaboal (Ken Clark in Fu-Manchu makeup) has masterminded this plot to put his girlfriend on the throne. Argolis rescues Telka and releases

a lava flow which destroys the kingdom of the Demios. Although Dan Vadis (real name: Constantine Daniel Vafiadis) is an able hero, there is little else to recommend *The Land of Darkness*. Why the powers that be chose this unremarkable film as the pilot to launch a new series is beyond comprehension.

279   Son of Hercules in the Land of Fire

(Ursus nella Terra di Fuoco / Ursus in the Land of Fire)
Cine Italia Films (1963) 87 min.
Dyaliscope / Eastman Color
U.S.–Embassy (1964)
   D–Giorgio Simonelli / W–Marcello Cirociolini, Luciano Martino / M–Carlo Savina / C–Luciano Trasatti / AD–Romano Paxuell Berti
   Cast–Ed Fury (Ursus), Claudia Mori (Mila), Luciana Gilli (Diana) with Adriano Micantoni, Pietro Ceccarelli, Giuseppe Addobbati, Mireille Granelli, Nando Tamberlani

Ed Fury defends himself in *Son of Hercules in the Land of Fire* (1964).

The handsome and amiable Ed Fury (real name: Edmund Holovchik) returns as Ursus. This time around he is falsely accused of kidnapping the local princess. It's all part of an attempt by the evil Hamilan to discredit the muscular do-gooder. Ursus evades capture but is buried in a landslide during a volcanic eruption. Taking advantage of Ursus' absence, Hamilan kills the king and assumes his position as ruler. Ursus, who was not killed after all, comes to the city in disguise to battle Hamilan's five giant warriors in a tournament. Ursus defeats them but he is immediately taken prisoner and tortured. The populace, fed up with Hamilan, rescues Ursus and together they defeat the tyrant.

280   *Son of Samson*

(Maciste nella Valle dei Re; Maciste in the Valley of the Kings)
Jolly Films, Rome–Borderie-Gallus Films, Paris (1960) 90 min.

Totalscope/Technicolor
U.S.–A Samuel Schneider Presentation
Medallion (1962)
      P–Ermanno Donati, Luigi Carpentieri/D–Carlo Campogalliani/W–Oreste Biancoli, Ennio De Concini/M–Carlo Innocenzi/C-Riccardo Pallotini/E–Roberto Cinquini/AD–Oscar D'Amico/CD–Maria De Matteis
      Cast–Mark Forest (Maciste), Chelo Alonso (Queen Smedes), Angelo Zanolli (Kenamun), Vira Silenti (Tekaet), Federica Ranchi (Nofret), Carlo Tamberlani (Armitee) with Peter Dorric, Nino Musco, Ignazio Dolce, Andrea Fantasia

Maciste (Mark Forest at his bulkiest) turns up in ancient Egypt where the evil ruler of Tanis, Queen Smedes, is making it tough for the local slave population. Kenamun is the son of the true king, who was assassinated by Smedes and her Persian allies. Maciste vows to restore the prince to his rightful place of eminence. Smedes, however, drugs Kenamun and plans to marry him to solidify her claim to the throne. When Maciste comes to the

Maciste (Mark Forest, right) befriends the pharaoh (Angelo Zanolli, center, in helmet) in *Son of Samson* (1962).

palace, Smedes is fascinated by his power and attempts to seduce him. He pretends to have fallen under her spell in order to rescue Kenamun. Following the usual feats of strength, Maciste is finally able to liberate the people from their oppressors and revive Kenamun from his trance. The Egyptian sets in *Son of Samson* are patterned after those in DeMille's *The Ten Commandments*, but on a decidedly smaller scale. The North African location photography is an attribute and the action moves along at a nice pace.

281 *Spartacus*

Bryna Productions
Universal-International (1960) 197 min.
Super Technirama 70/ Technicolor
  P–Edward Lewis/D–Stanley Kubrick/W–Dalton Trumbo/Based on the novel by Howard Fast/M–Alex North/C–Russell Metty/E–Robert Lawrence/PD–Alexander   Golitzen/AD–Eric

Orbom/CD–Bill Thomas, Valles/Main Titles and Design Consultant–Saul Bass/Historial and Technical Advisor–Vittorio Nino Novarese
  Cast–Kirk Douglas (Spartacus), Laurence Olivier (Crassus), Jean Simmons (Varinia), Charles Laughton (Gracchus), Peter Ustinov (Batiatus), John Gavin (Julius Caesar), Tony Curtis (Antoninus), Nina Foch (Helena), Herbert Lom (Tigranes), John Dall (Glabrus), John Ireland (Crixus), Joanna Barnes (Claudia) with Charles McGraw, Harold J. Stone, Woody Strode, Peter Brocco, Paul Lambert, Robert J. Wilke, Nicholas Dennis, John Hoyt, Frederic Worlock, Dayton Lummis

  In 1957, Howard Fast's novel *Spartacus* was brought to the attention of Kirk Douglas by an associate as a possible follow-up film to the recently completed *The Vikings*. Douglas decided to produce the film through his company Bryna, as he had *The Vikings*, for release by United Artists. To his dismay he learned that United Artists had already committed to a project dealing with the same subject called

Reynold Brown artwork of Kirk Douglas as *Spartacus* (1960).

The Gladiators, directed by Martin Ritt and starring Yul Brynner and Anthony Quinn. Undaunted, Douglas took his project to Universal, who agreed to distribute the film. A first screenplay by author Fast was rejected and Dalton Trumbo was hired to fashion a new one. Douglas took a chance in hiring Trumbo who had been blacklisted during the McCarthy era. When Douglas insisted that Trumbo's name be on the film, the blacklist was broken. David Lean was approached as a possible director but he declined. Laurence Olivier, Charles Laughton and Peter Ustinov were cast and the role of Antoninus was created as a favor to Tony Curtis who wanted to appear in the film to fulfill a final contract commitment to Universal. At this point, United Artists abandoned their plans for the picture with Brynner. For his leading lady Douglas considered Elsa Martinelli, Ingrid Bergman and Jeanne Moreau, but all were un-

available. He finally chose an unknown German actress named Sabina Bethmann to play his on screen love, Varinia. Universal insisted on Anthony Mann for director and shooting finally began in January 1959. A month later is became clear that both Mann and Bethmann were not working out. Anthony Mann was replaced by Stanley Kubrick, although much of the footage Mann shot of the gladiator school remains in the film. Jean Simmons, already a veteran of many epics, took over the part of Varinia. The resulting film has often been termed "the thinking man's spectacle" and *Spartacus* is indeed both literate and spectacular. Dalton Trumbo's screenplay gives the script a sense of immediacy that stories set is so distant a period of time often lack. The cast is, for the most part, praiseworthy. Tony Curtis is the major liability. He is ten years too old for the part of the youthful Antoninus and, as usual, his delivery is inappropriate for

Costume test for *Spartacus* (1960) with John Gavin wearing Jeff Chandler's armor from *Sign of the Pagan*.

a historical film. Although *Spartacus* was heralded at the time as the most expensive movie ever to be made completely in Hollywood, some of the battle scenes were filmed in Spain and employed some 8,000 members of the Spanish army as extras. When the film opened in New York and Los Angeles in October 1960, it had already been cut from 197 minutes to 182 minutes by the studio. A 1967 re-release was edited down to 161 minutes. In 1991 a major restoration of *Spartacus* restored the film to its original 197 minute running time.

AA Nominations: Best Supporting Actor (Peter Ustinov)*, Editing,

Musical Score, Color Cinematography*, Color Art Direction*, Color

Costume Design*

Show Business Illustrated: The revolt of gladiators in ancient Rome splashes colorfully, if cruelly, across the wide-wide screen.

Films and Filming: The film goes back to the rip-roaring days of the big spectaculars and includes battles, suicide, crucifixions, murder, fights to the death, illicit love: in fact, it has got everything!

282   *Spartacus and the Ten Gladiators*

(Spartaco e i Dieci Gladiatori/Day of Vengeance)
Cineproduzioni Associate, Rome–Producciones Cinematograficas
Balcazar, Barcelona–Les Films Copernic, Paris (1964) 99 min.
Techniscope/Technicolor
U.S.–Four Star

P–Armando Morandi/D–Nick Nostro/W–Nick Nostro, Simon Sterling (Sergio Sollima)/M–Carlo Savina/C–Tino Santoni/E–Bruno Mattei/AD–Giorgio Postiglione/CD–Massimo Bolognaro

Cast–Dan Vadis (Rocca), Helga Line, John Heston, John Warrell, Ursula Davis, Julian Dower, William Bird, Gianni Rizzo, Milton Reid, Alan Lancaster, Frank Oliveras, Marco Vassilli, Gordon Steve/Ugo Sasso, Jeff Cameron, Sal Borghese, Fred Hudson, Don Messina

This prequel to *The Ten Gladiators* is set in 73 B.C., which places it over 100 years before the previous film. Miraculously the ten gladiators look the same age as they do a century later, but then logic was never a strong point of the peplum films. Once again, Don Vadis stars as Rocca, the leader of a gang of outcast gladiators who are banished from the arenas of Rome for daring to interfere when a father and son are ordered to fight each other to the death. While wandering about the countryside they rescue the daughter of a nobleman from a band of brigands who have attempted to raid her caravan. They accompany her to the home of her father who tells them that the land is being terrorized by the slave army of the renegade Spartacus. He hires the glad-

iators to find Spartacus and capture him. It isn't long before the ten lovable lunkheads realize they are fighting on the wrong side. Rocca and his men eventually join the army of Spartacus and fight with him against the forces of Rome. *Spartacus and the Ten Gladiators* is marginally better than its predecessor. It is memorable because of its relatively light-hearted approach to the material and the affability of its leading man, Dan Vadis. The final film in the ten gladiator trilogy is *The Triumph of the Ten Gladiators.*

283   *The Spartan Gladiators*

(La Rivolta dei Sette; The Revolt of the Seven)
Sanson Films S.r.L. Production (1964) 87 min.
CinemaScope/Eastman Color
U.S.–Metro-Goldwyn-Mayer (1966)

P–Joseph Fryd/D–Alberto De Martino/W–Alessandro Continenza, Alberto De Martino, Chen Morrison/M–Francesco Mannino/C–Pier Ludovico Pavoni/E–Otello Colangeli/AD–Piero Poletto/CD–Mario Giorsi

Cast–Tony Russel (Karos), Massimo Serato, Nando Gazzolo, Livio Lorenzon, Piero Lulli, Helga Line, Paula Pitti, Renato Rossini/Red Ross, Pietro Capanna, Walter Maestosi, Gaetano Quartararo, Nando Angelini

Karos, a young Spartan man attempting to aid his mortally wounded brother, is suspected of being a rebel and is sentenced to a gladiatorial school. He escapes and hides with a caravan of traveling actors. Soon he joins forces with the rebels in their search for a golden statue which holds information necessary to overthrow a would-be tyrant. This is a fairly undistinguished follow up to *The Secret Seven*, with Tony Russel and his freedom fighters opposing yet another evil despot. Many of the names behind and in front of the camera are the same as before and the story covers much of the same ground as its predecessor. As with many of Alberto De Martino's movies the spirit of the Western is translated into peplum terms. As in the previous film there is a stampede; this time it's cattle rather than horses.

Films and Filming: The Spartan Gladiators is a clearcut and efficient piece of work with about two attempts at something a little stylish. A success in its modest way.

Basil Sydney as King Saul and Jeff Chandler as David in *A Story of David* (1961).

284   *A Story of David*

(David the Outlaw)
A Scoton Ltd. Production (1960) 104 min.
Eastman Color
U.S.–ABC TV Network (1961) 99 min.
   P–George Pitcher, William Goetz/D–Robert McNaught/W–Gerry Day, Terence Maple
   Cast–Jeff Chandler (David), Basil Sydney (Saul), Barbara Shelley (Abigail), Peter Arne (Doeg), David Knight (Jonathan), Donald Pleasence (Nabal), Robert Brown (Jashobeam), Richard O'Sullivan (Abiathar), Angela Brown (Michal) with David Davies, John Van Eyssen, Charles Carson, Zena Marshall, Martin Wyldeck, Lynn Gray

   This biblical drama, British produced and filmed in Israel, was one of the first motion pictures to have its world premiere on American television. It was released theatrically throughout the rest of the world a year after Jeff Chandler's untimely death in 1961. As the title suggests, the plot of the film recounts only a portion of David's story. King Saul drives David into exile when he suspects that the former shepherd is trying to take the throne of Israel for himself. Jeff Chandler, although too old to play the youthful David, nevertheless turns in one of the best performances of his career. Sadly, the film has vanished into limbo and has not been shown for several years.

285   *The Story of David*

A Milberg Theatrical Production
Columbia Pictures Television (1976) 191 min.
Color
   Produced by Mildred Freed Alberg/W–Ernest Kinoy/M–Laurence Rosenthal/C–John Coquillon/E–Sidney Katz
   Part One: "David and King Saul"/D–Alex Segal, David Lowell Rich/AD–Kuli Sander/CD–Judy Moorcroft, Rochelle Zaltzman
   Cast–Timothy   Bottoms   (David),   Anthony

Quayle (Saul), Oded Teumi (Jonathan), Mark Dignam (Samuel), Norman Rodway (Joab), Yehuda Efroni (Abner), Tony Tarruella (Goliath), Irit Ben Zur (Michal)

Part Two: "David the King"/D–David Lowell Rich/AD–Kuli Sander, Fernando Gonzalez/CD–Judy Moorcroft, Tony Pueo

Cast–Keith Michell (David), Jane Seymour (Bathsheba), Barry Morse (Jehosephat), Susan Hampshire (Michal), Brian Blessed (Abner), Norman Rodway (Joab), Nelson Modlin (Absalom), David Collings (Nathan)

Of all the Old Testament personages, David has had the most filmic incarnations. This made-for-television movie is one of the more impressive depictions of the story of the shepherd boy who became the King of Israel. The movie is divided into two parts. Part One shows how the young David came into the house of Saul, the aging and troubled leader of Israel. David is able to soothe Saul's increasingly violent fits of madness by singing to him. The Philistines dare the Israelites to find a soldier brave enough to face the giant warrior Goliath in single combat and David accepts the challenge. David defeats Goliath and goes on to become Israel's greatest fighter. The adulation of the people incurs the jealousy and wrath of Saul when they proclaim "Saul has slain his thousands and David his ten thousands." David must flee for his life and does not return until he learns that Saul and his son Jonathan have been slain in a battle with the Philistines. David is proclaimed King of Israel.

Part Two focuses on the rule of King David; a reign fraught with poor judgments and conflict. Hoping to reunite the tribes of Israel, David strives to make his ascension to the throne acceptable to the people. To do this he forces Saul's daughter Michal to leave her husband and take her place as his wife. Many wives later, David sees the beautiful Bathsheba and wants her for his own, although she is already married to Uriah the Hittite. David causes Uriah to be slain in battle and then marries Bathsheba. When David is older, his many wives connive for their sons to be named heir to the throne. There is little peace for David in his old age.

The Story of David is treated like two separate films with a different cast for each. Only Norman Rodway appears in both as David's troublesome nephew Joab. This is a bare bones production filmed in Israel. There are no "casts of thousands" and the sets are all existing locations. Fortunately the quality of the acting and writing are such that one can overlook the deficiencies in the physical production and concentrate on the cerebral aspects. Both Timothy Bottoms and Keith Michell turn in good performances as the younger and older David respectively. Susan Hampshire is wasted in her brief appearance as the older Michal but Jane Seymour, at the height of her beauty, brings a sly edge to her performance as Bathsheba.

286   *The Story of Jacob and Joseph*

A Milberg Theatrical-Screen Gems Production
ABC TV Network (1975) 96 min.
Color

P–Mildred Freed Alberg/D–Michael Cacoyannis/W–Ernest Kinoy/M–Mikis Theodorakis/C–Ted Moore (Jacob), Austin Dempster (Joseph)/E–Kevin Connor/AD–Kuli Sander/CD–Judy Moorcroft

Cast–Keith Michell (Jacob), Tony Lo Bianco (Joseph), Colleen Dewhurst (Rebecca), Herschel Bernardi (Laban), Harry Andrews (Issac), Julian Glover (Esau), Yossef Shiloah (Pharaoh), Rachel Stone (Potipher's Wife), Yona Elian (Rachel) with Yehuda Efroni, Yossi Grabber, Bennes Maarden, Zila Karney

Alan Bates narrates two Bible stories which could be seen as cautionary tales illustrating the pitfalls of parental favoritism. Issac's wife Rebecca gives birth to twins. The firstborn, Esau, is the favorite of his father but Rebecca favors her other son Jacob. Rebecca conceives of a plan to gain Jacob his father's blessing and the birthright of the firstborn. Jacob, apparently history's first "mama's boy," reluctantly impersonates Esau and does indeed obtain the blessing and birthright. He also incurs the hatred of his brother and must flee for his life. Jacob gets a taste of his own medicine when his uncle substitutes one daughter for another in Jacob's marriage bed. Jacob eventually ends up with two wives and twelve sons, greatly favoring number eleven who is called Joseph. His ten jealous elder brothers sell Joseph into slavery and tell their father that he has been killed. Joseph ends up in

Keith Michell (center) as Jacob: *The Story of Jacob and Joseph* (1975).

Egypt and becomes the trusted advisor of Pharaoh. In due time, Joseph is reunited with his family and forgives his brothers. This filmed in Israel TV movie set the precedent for many of the biblical television dramas that would follow. The spare production and realistic tone are the antithesis of what had defined the typical Hollywood Bible epic. During the "Joseph" sequence, a brief location shot from Columbia's jettisoned *Joseph and His Brethern* is used.

287   The Story of Mankind

A Cambridge Production
Warner Bros. (1957) 100 min.
Technicolor
    P/D–Irwin Allen/W–Irwin Allen, Charles Bennett/Based on the book by Hendrik van Loon/M–Paul Sawtell/C–Nick Musuraca/E–Roland Gross, Gene Palmer/AD–Art Loel/CD–Marjorie Best
    Cast–Ronald Colman (Spirit of Man), Vincent Price (Mr. Scratch), Sir Cedric Hardwicke (High Judge), Hedy Lamarr (Joan of Arc), Virginia Mayo (Cleopatra), Peter Lorre (Nero), Agnes Moorhead (Queen Elizabeth I), Charles Coburn (Hippo-

crates), Francis X. Bushman (Moses), Marie Wilson (Marie Antoinette), Dennis Hopper (Napoleon), Marie Windsor (Josephine) with John Carradine, Reginald Gardiner, Cathy O'Donnell, Helmut Dantine, Edward Everett Horton and the Marx Brothers

Irwin Allen's first "disaster film" was this serio-comic adaptation of Hendrik van Loon's widely read book. Producer Bernard Foyer had originally acquired the rights to the book in 1953 and planned on using it as the basis for a series of films. Somehow it ended up with Irwin Allen, who had been responsible for the Academy Award–winning documentary *The Sea Around Us* in 1953. Following the invention of the Super H-Bomb, the Devil and the Spirit of Man meet before the High Tribunal in Outer Space to debate the future of man on Earth. This potted history of mankind is presented in a series of vignettes which utilize a plethora of mismatched stock footage from past motion pictures. Also on hand is a vast array of stars who are mostly miscast as various historical personages. These brief peeks at the different ages of man are un-

Helmut Dantine as Mark Antony and Virginia Mayo as Cleopatra in *The Story of Mankind* (1957).

funny misfires; badly written, badly directed and badly performed. Particularly dire are Virginia Mayo as a campy Cleopatra, Peter Lorre as Nero and Agnes Moorhead as Queen Elizabeth I. Only Ronald Colman and Vincent Price manage to come out of this mess fairly unscathed.

Los Angeles Mirror News: Hendrik van Loon's monumental work has now been made into a Technicolor movie and it is anything but monumental.

288   *The Story of Ruth*

20th Century–Fox (1960) 132 min.
CinemaScope / Color by DeLuxe
   P–Samuel E. Engel / D–Henry Koster / W–Norman Corwin / M–Franz Waxman / C–Arthur E. Arling / E–Jack W. Holmes / AD–Lyle Wheeler, Stuart Ross / CD–Vittorio Nino Novarese
   Cast–Elana Eden (Ruth), Stuart Whitman (Boaz), Tom Tryon (Mahlon), Peggy Wood (Naomi), Viveca Lindfors (Eleilat), Jeff Morrow (Tob), Thayer David (Hedak), Les Tremayne (Elimelech), Eduard Franz (Jehoam), Leo Fuchs (Sochin), Ziva Rodann (Orpah), Lily Valenty (Kera), John Gabriel (Chilion) with Basil Ruysdael, John Banner,

Adelina Pedroza, Sara Taft, Daphna Einhorn, Berry Kroeger, Peter Coe

   From the director of *The Robe* comes this beautiful and tasteful depiction of one of the best-loved Bible narratives. *The Story of Ruth* is told with reverence and considerable restraint. It is probably the most understated biblical film ever to come out of Hollywood, never resorting to the sensationalism apparent in similar productions. The story is divided into two distinct parts. The first half contains most of the grandeur and action as it shows Ruth's early life as a priestess of the pagan god Chemosh in the land of Moab. Through the love and understanding of the gentle Mahlon, a young Hebrew artisan, she comes to know and believe in Jehovah. When Ruth interferes with a human sacrifice to Chemosh, Mahlon is imprisoned for his subversive influence. Ruth engineers his escape but Mahlon is mortally wounded in the attempt. As Mahlon lies dying, he and Ruth exchange wedding vows. The latter part of the film concentrates on Ruth's relationships with her mother-in-law Naomi and their kinsmen, Tob and Boaz. Ruth goes with Naomi to her home in Bethlehem but the people are reluctant to take a Moabitess into their fold. Ruth is unjustly accused of idolatry but she is able to prove her innocence. She falls in love with Boaz but the arrogant Tob claims his right as next of kin to take her as his wife. At their wedding celebration, Ruth publicly declares her love for Boaz and the humiliated Tob renounces his claim on her. Boaz marries Ruth, thereby founding the dynasty that would eventually produce David, King of Israel. Most of the publicity that surrounded the filming of *The Story of Ruth* dealt with the search for an actress to play the title role. Seven months and over $200,000 were spent trying to find an actress with the qualities necessary to portray Ruth. More than 300 women were interviewed and tested. One early contender was Ursula Andress (who gained fame two years later in *Dr. No*) but her command of the English language was not good enough at the time to assay the demanding role. A twenty-year-old actress named Elana Eden was flown to London from Israel to test for Anne in *The Diary of Anne Frank* but got the part of Ruth

Ruth (Elana Eden) pauses before a statue of the god Chemosh in *The Story of Ruth* (1960).

instead. Her gentle, low-key performance is in perfect harmony with the overall tone of the film. Unfortunately, *The Story of Ruth* was not a resounding box office success and no further parts for Eden were forthcoming. Franz

Waxman contributes one of his loveliest and most inventive scores for this greatly underrated movie.

Screenland: Undoubtedly one of the best of the recent biblical stories. This one combines spectacle in plenty with great warmth and intimacy.

Modern Screen: Those familiar with the biblical story will find emphasis laid on certain points in the film which were rather insignificant in the original written words. Nevertheless, this is a beautiful production and one that should be seen by everyone.

Photoplay: The opening scenes are loaded with the pageantry you expect in biblical epics. But the rest of the picture stays on the personal level.

289 *Sudan*

Universal (1945) 76 min.
Technicolor
P–Paul Malvern / D–John Rawlins / W–Edmund L. Hartmann / M–Milton Rosen / C–George Robinson / E–Milton Carruth / AD–John B. Goodman, Richard Riedel / CD–Vera West
Cast–Maria Montez (Naila), Jon Hall (Merab), Turhan Bey (Herua), Andy Devine (Nebka), George Zucco (Horadef) with Robert Warwick, Phil Van Zandt, Harry Cording, George Lynn, Charles Arnt

During the 1940s, Universal studios produced a series of exotic Technicolor extravaganzas starring Maria Montez and Jon Hall. The last of these was made in 1944 under the title *Queen of the Nile* and released the following year as *Sudan*. As with the other films in this series (*Arabian Nights*, *Cobra Woman*, *White Savage*, etc.) the emphasis was on colorful escapism, not history. The King of Khemmis is murdered and his daughter Princess Naila vows vengeance on the rebel leader Herua, whom she believes killed her father. In truth, it is her father's evil advisor, Horadef, who committed the crime. Naila goes into the desert in search of Herua but Horadef has her captured and sold into slavery. With the help of two rogues, Merab and Nebka, Naila escapes the slave traders. When Horadef attempts to recapture her, Naila is

Maria Montez and Jon Hall star in their last film together, *Sudan* (1945).

rescued by a handsome stranger and taken to his desert stronghold. The two are beginning to fall in love when he confesses to her that he is the rebel Herua. Still believing that he is responsible for her father's death, Naila lures Herua to Khemmis where he is taken prisoner and sentenced to be executed. Knowing that Naila really loves Herua, Merab devises a plan which allows him to escape. Merab is arrested and tortured until Naila agrees to lead Horadef and his soldiers to Herua's hidden encampment in the mountains. By now Naila knows that Horadef is her father's murderer. As she leads Horadef and his troops through the mountain pass, Herua's followers cause an avalanche which destroys the villain and his men. Naila and Herua are reunited and ride off into the sunset. No matter what the setting, the plot and characters of these films were interchangeable, but *Sudan* differs from the previous entries in the series in that Tur-

han Bey is the hero and Jon Hall is the sidekick. Prior to this, Hall always ended up with Montez at the fadeout. *Sudan* has breathtaking Technicolor photography and beautiful matte paintings, which give the film a sense of grandeur which belies the relatively meager budget.

290   *The Sword and the Cross*

(Le Schiave de Cartagine; The Slaves of Carthage)
A Cines-Yago Production (1957) 87 min.
Cinetotalscope / Ferraniacolor
U.S.–Valiant Films (1960)

P–Italo Zingarelli / D–Guido Brignone / W–Francesco De Feo, Mario Guerra, Nicola Manzari, Francesco Thellung, Guido Brignone / M–Enzo Masetti / C–Adalberto Albertini / E–Jolanda Benvenuti / AD–Franco Lolli / CD–Enzo Bulgarelli

Cast–Gianna Maria Canale (Julia Martia), Jorge Mistral (Marcus Valerius), Marisa Allasio (Lea), Ana Luisa Peluffo (Esther), Ruben Rojo (Flavius Metellus), Luigi Pavese (Publius Cornelius) with Albert

Gianna Maria Canale wicked again in *The Sword and the Cross* (1960).

6575-29

This time around it is Jean Wallace and Cornel Wilde as Guinevere and Lancelot in *Sword of Lancelot* (1963).

Hehn, Marcello Giorda, Nietta Zocchi, Ugo Sasso, Herman Cobos

The Sword and the Cross relates the plight of two sisters from Carthage who are sold to the cruel daughter of the proconsul of the Roman province of Cilica. The sisters, Esther and Lea, are imprisoned when their mistress, Julia Martia, discovers that they are Christians. Marcus Valerius, a Roman officer, has fallen in love with Lea. When Marcus speaks out in the Senate in defense of the Christians he is branded a traitor and barely escapes capture. Julia, who also loves Marcus, flies into a jealous rage and tortures Lea until she is blinded. A mass execution of the Christians in ordered but Marcus and his loyal soldiers descend on the site of the would-be massacre. In the ensuing battle, Julia is killed and the Christians are freed. Marcus marries Lea and is elected as the new proconsul. Gianna Maria Canale, already a veteran of the epic genre (*Sins of*

Rome and *Theodora, Slave Empress*) went on to portray the icy temptresses of many peplum films. Marisa Allasio had her big break at international stardom in 1958, co-starring with Mario Lanza in *Seven Hills of Rome*. Shortly thereafter she married a count and retired from the film industry.

291   *Sword of Lancelot*

(Lancelot and Guinevere)
An Emblem Production
Universal (1963) 116 min.
Panavision/Technicolor

P–Cornel Wilde, Bernard Luber/D–Cornel Wilde/W–Richard Schayer, Jefferson Pascal/M–Ron Goodwin/C–Harry Waxman/E–Frederick Wilson/AD–Maurice Carter/CD–Terence Morgan

Cast–Cornel Wilde (Lancelot), Jean Wallace (Guinevere), Brian Aherne (Arthur), Adrienne Corri (Vivian), George Baker (Sir Gawain), Mark Dignam (Merlin) with Archie Duncan, Michael

Guy Madison and Eleonora Rossi Drago are relieved at the death of Jack Palance (on the floor) in *Sword of the Conqueror* (1962).

Meacham, Iain Gregory, Reginald Beckwith, John Barrie, Graham Stark

Cornel Wilde's version of the King Arthur-Lancelot-Guinevere love triangle has been strangely neglected, although it is one of the finer interpretations of the story that has been filmed. It certainly has more depth of emotion than the better known but essentially shallow MGM version *Knights of the Round Table* (1954). Wilde's direction of the more intimate scenes gives them a sense of romance and tragedy which is enhanced by Ron Goodwin's moving background score. The performances are good; however, Cornel Wilde's French accent, seemingly a leftover from his role in DeMille's *The Greatest Show on Earth* (1952), is often annoying. Brian Aherne reprises the role of King Arthur he had previously played in *Prince Valiant* (1954).

292   *Sword of the Conqueror*

(Rosmunda e Alboino)
A Titanus Production (1962) 95 min.
CinemaScope/Eastman Color
U.S.–United Artists
    P–Gilberto Carbone/D–Carlo Campogalliani/ W–Roberto Gianviti, Alessandro Ferrau, Paolo Barbara, Primo Zeglio/M–Carlo Rustichelli/C– Raffaele Masciocchi/E–Mario Serandrei/AD–Massimo Tavazzi/CD–Giuliana Ghidini
    Cast–Jack Palance (Alboin), Eleonora Rossi Drago (Rosmund), Guy Madison (Amalchi), Edy Vessel (Matilda), Ivan Palance (Ulderic), Vittorio Sanipoli (Wolfgang) with Carlo D'Angelo, Andrea Bosic, Raffaele Baldassarre, Calisto Calisti, Guido Celano, Walter Grant, Aldo Pini

After the fall of the Goth empire, the Lombards are in constant conflict with the Gepidae. Alboin, the Lombard king, offers peace terms to the Gepidae if their princess, Rosmund, is given to him in marriage. Rosmund, who is in love with the warrior Amalchi, refuses and , in retaliation, her father is beheaded by Alboin. Alboin forces Rosmund into marriage and Amalchi is imprisoned when he attempts to rescue her. Amalchi escapes and challenges Alboin to a duel in the bridal chamber. As Alboin is about to kill Amalchi, Rosmund stabs him to death with her dagger. The battle sequences are impressive, albeit more gory than usual. By now Jack Palance had become an old hand at playing barbarian chieftains.

293   *Sword of the Valiant*

A Golan-Globus Production
Cannon Films (1982) 101 min.
Color

P–Menahem Golan, Yoram Globus/D–Stephen Weeks/W–Philip Breen, Howard Penn, Stephen Weeks/M–Ron Geesin/C–Freddie Young/E–Richard Marder/PD–Maurice Fowler/CD–Shuna Harwood

Cast–Miles O'Keefe (Sir Gawain), Sean Connery (The Green Knight), Trevor Howard (King Arthur), Leigh Lawson (Humphrey), Emma Sutton (Morgan Le Fay), Peter Cushing (Seneschal), Douglas Wilmer (The Black Knight) with Thomas Heathcote, Lila Kedrova, John Rhys-Davies, Ronald Lacey, David Rappaport, Cyrielle Claire

Gawain, a young squire at the court of Camelot, is the only person to stand up to the treacherous Green Knight when he threatens the honor of King Arthur. For his bravery, Gawain is knighted and must now face the Green Knight in battle. Based on the epic poem written in the late fourteenth century by an anonymous author, this is British director Stephen Weeks' second film version of the story. He had first filmed it as *Gawain and the Green Knight* in 1973 starring Murray Head as Sir Gawain

and Nigel Green as the Green Knight. Although the latter version has a bigger budget, it is no real improvement over the original. Ex-Tarzan Miles O'Keefe is horribly wooden as Sir Gawain and, to make matters worse, he is saddled with one of the worst wigs in film history. The sole reasons for watching are Sean Connery, who makes memorable appearances at the beginning and end of the film as the Green Knight, and Peter Cushing as the villainous Seneschal.

294   *The Tarters*

(I Tartari)
Lux Film (1961) 83 min.
Totalscope/Technicolor
U.S.–Metro-Goldwyn-Mayer

P–Alessandro Tasca/D–Richard Thorpe/W–

Victor Mature and Liana Orfei in a publicity pose for *The Tarters* (1961).

Sabatino Ciuffini, Ambrogio Molteni, Mario Fratini, Oreste Palella, Emimmo Salvi, Domenico Salvi, Julian De Kassel/M–Renzo Rossellini/C–Americo Gengarelli/E–Maurizio Lucidi/AD–Oscar D'Amico/CD–Giovanna Natili

Cast–Victor Mature (Oleg), Orson Welles (Burandai), Liana Orfei (Helga), Bella Cortez (Samia), Folco Lulli (Togrul), Luciano Marin (Eric), Furio Meniconi (Sigrun), Arnoldo Foa (Chu Lung) with Pietro Ceccarelli, Renato Terra

Vikings battle Tarters on the Russian Steppes in this action adventure. Oleg, a Viking chieftain, and his people try to peacefully coexist with the Tarters but they are opposed by the Tarter Khan, Burundai. When Burundai's brother is killed by Oleg, war is declared. The Vikings capture Samia, the niece of Burandai and, in turn, the Tarters abduct Helga, the wife of Oleg. Samia is well treated and falls in love with Eric, the younger brother of Oleg. On the other hand, Helga is raped by Burundai and then given over to his men for their pleasure. When Helga dies of the assault, the Vikings and Tarters engage in a bloody battle to the death. Orson Welles is the standout in the cast by virtue of sheer girth alone. He also squints a great deal of the time in an effort to appear insidious. Victor Mature, in the last of his epic roles, suffers from the fact that much of his dialogue has been dubbed by another actor. Often a single line of dialogue is partially delivered by Mature and then his dubber. For anyone familiar with Mature's voice, this is very disconcerting. An interminable climactic scene reveals the all too obvious substitution of stunt doubles for Welles and Mature. Despite these negative factors, *The Tarters* does have energy and a certain amount of style. The major set in the film is the Khan's palace and it is both colorful and spectacular. Luciano Marin and Bella Cortez are an attractive pair of young lovers and Liana Orfei gives a noteworthy performance as the ill-fated Helga.

295   *The Ten Commandments*

Paramount (1923) 146 min.

P/D–Cecil B. DeMille/W–Jeanie Macpherson/C–Bert Glennon, Ray Rennahan (Color photography)/E–Anne Bauchens/AD–Paul Iribe

Cast–Prologue–Theodore Roberts (Moses), Charles de Roche (Rameses), Estelle Taylor (Miriam), James Neill (Aaron), Lawson Butt (Dathan) with Julia Faye, Terrence Moore, Nobel Johnson, Clarence Burton, Gino Corrado, Pat Moore

Modern Story–Richard Dix (John McTavish), Rod La Rocque (Dan McTavish), Edythe Chapman (Mrs. McTavish), Leatrice Joy (Mary), Nita Naldi (Sally), Robert Edeson (Redding) with Charles Ogle, Agnes Ayres

The biblical section of DeMille's first version of *The Ten Commandments* serves as a prologue to a modern morality story and runs approximately fifty minutes. It begins with scenes showing the hard labor forced on the Israelites by the Egyptians. Their prayers for a deliverer are answered when Moses comes to Egypt to free them from bondage and lead them to the promised land. In style and execution the scenes showing the Exodus from Egypt and the parting of the Red Sea differ very little from those in the 1956 remake, proving the point of DeMille detractors that he never advanced as a filmmaker beyond the silent era. Even the exterior Egyptian sets were copied for the remake with few changes evident. Julia Faye, who was reportedly DeMille's mistress for many years, plays Pharaoh's wife. She was a regular performer in DeMille films throughout the decades and eventually appeared in a supporting role in the 1956 version of *The Ten Commandments*. DeMille had previously employed the idea of using sequences set in ancient times as moral lessons for his modern characters in such films as *Male and Female* (1919) and *Manslaughter* (1922). *The Ten Commandments* took this concept to new heights with the flashback becoming the most elaborate and memorable part of the film. Early two-strip Technicolor was utilized on these scenes while the modern story is in black and white. After the spectacle and power of the Moses story, the remainder of the film is an anticlimax. The modern story is concerned with two very dissimilar brothers who are both in love with the same girl. The younger brother, Dan, embarks on a life of sin, vowing to break all of the Ten Commandments in defiance of God. The other brother, John, is a God-fearing man who stands steadfastly on the side of good. Dan wins the girl and grows wealthy due to some shady business dealings. John remains

A young Moses (Charlton Heston) kneels before the pharaoh (Sir Cedric Hardwicke) as Rameses (Yul Brynner) and Nefretiri (Anne Baxter) look on in *The Ten Commandments* (1956).

poor but honest. Dan eventually gets his just desserts when he contracts leprosy from an avaricious wanton, played in best vamp style by Nita Naldi. Heavy handed and melodramatic, the modern section of *The Ten Commandments* is a poor follow-up to the biblical prologue.

Photoplay: The greatest theatrical spectacle in history. It will last as long as the film on which it is recorded.

296   *The Ten Commandments*

A Motion Picture Associates, Inc. Production
Paramount (1956) 221 min.
VistaVision/Technicolor

P/D–Cecil B. DeMille/W–Aeneas MacKenzie, Jessie L. Lasky, Jr., Jack Garris, Fredric M. Frank/M–Elmer Bernstein/C–Loyal Griggs/E–Anne Bauchens/AD–Hal Pereira, Walter Tyler, Albert Nozaki/CD–Edith Head, Ralph Jester, John Jenson, Dorothy Jeakins, Arnold Friberg

Cast–Charlton Heston (Moses), Yul Brynner (Ramses), Anne Baxter (Nefretiri), Yvonne De Carlo (Sephora), Edward G. Robinson (Dathan), Debra Paget (Lilia), John Derek (Joshua), Sir Cedric Hardwicke (Sethi), Martha Scott (Yochabel), Nina Foch (Bithiah), Judith Anderson (Memnet), Vincent Price (Baka), John Carradine (Aaron), Eduard Franz (Jethro), Olive Deering (Miriam), Donald Curtis (Mered), Douglas Dumbrille (Jannes), Ian Keith (Rameses I), Henry Wilcoxon (Pentaur), Julia Faye (Elisheba) with Lawrence Dobkin, H.B. Warner, Frank DeKova, Woody Strode, Esther Brown, Fraser Heston, Joan Woodbury, Touch Connors, Michael Ansara

Following the release of his non-genre *The Greatest Show on Earth* in 1952, Cecil B. DeMille began to review properties for his next motion picture. He briefly considered doing films about Queen Esther or Helen of Troy but finally decided on a remake of his 1923 silent success *The Ten Commandments*. While the original version had cost $1.4 million, the new version was budgeted at $8 million. The

115/5-F-29-B

cost of the film eventually rose to $13.5 million, making it the most costly movie made up to that time. Expanding the biblical prologue of the first film into nearly fours hours of screen time also made it the longest. Although the life of Moses is one of the most extensive narratives in the Old Testament, details of his early life in the court of Egypt are omitted. To fill in the gaps DeMille turned to a variety of sources, including the novel *Prince of Egypt* by Dorothy Clark Wilson. The result was a theoretical, but highly plausible love triangle between Moses, Rameses and the Throne Princess, Nefretiri. The cast and crew consisted of many people who had worked with DeMille in the past. The first actor signed was Yul Brynner. DeMille attended a Broadway performance of *The King and I* and offered the part of Rameses to Brynner during the intermission. Cornel Wilde was originally cast as Joshua but he was replaced by John Derek before filming began. DeMille had wanted to have Claudette Colbert play the part of Bithiah but this never panned out. Paramount had hoped that DeMille would utilize some of their contract players like William Holden and Audrey Hepburn but the director was adamant about selecting his own cast. Unlike many "all-star" spectaculars, DeMille makes good use of his cast by giving them "real" parts to play and not mere "cameos" inserted for the sake of marquee value. Charlton Heston and Yul Brynner are effective in the lead roles of Moses and Rameses although, as presented by the script writers, these characters are somewhat one-dimensional. In this instance DeMille falls into that old trap of showing historical personages as figureheads rather than human beings. Moses is completely good throughout the film while Rameses is totally villainous. Nefretiri is one of the few principal characters in the drama whose personality shows any development during the course of the action. This is typical of many DeMille films. He preferred to use a female character as the catalyst who sparks off the dramatic chain of events. Consequently, the leading lady roles in DeMille films are usually far better defined than those of the leading men. The filming of *The Ten Commandments* was a colossal undertaking, particularly since DeMille was seventy-five years old at the time. He came close to not finishing it when, while on location in Egypt, he suffered a heart attack. The doctors prescribed total bed rest in an oxygen tent. DeMille stated, "I would rather be a dead director on the set than a live director in an oxygen tent," and carried on as usual until the picture was completed. Victor Young, who had composed the music for all of DeMille's films since 1940, was set to score *The Ten Commandments*. At the last minute he was forced to bow out due to illness and died later that same year. It was the last film to be directed by DeMille but it proved to be his most popular. Audiences were dazzled by the constant procession of Technicolored pomp and pageantry, but they were moved by the religious aspects as well. Despite its box office success, *The Ten Commandments* suffered many of the critical lambastes that had plagued DeMille throughout his career. Some critics found it "artificial" and "too flashy" but few could deny it had enormous scope and crowd-pleasing potential. It sums up the best, and worst, aspects of the epic genre and is probably the ultimate example of the "Hollywood Spectacle."

AA Nominations: Best Picture, Color Cinematography, Color Art Direction, Color Costume Design, Sound, Editing, Special Effects*

Motion Picture: Cecil B. DeMille's latest movie leaves one stunned by sheer size. Unfortunately, in recent years, other movies about similar subjects have made many aspects of this period of history seem like movie clichés, which removes some of the impact of Mr. DeMille's work.

Modern Screen: To say this picture is monumental may not be going far enough. Obviously, no expense was spared in filming this production. The miracles are events not left to the imagination. They are all here, by God. Or, at least, by Cecil B. DeMille.

Life: Soon the longest, most costly, most monumental movie in all the history of moviemaking will begin unfolding its three hours and 41 minutes of biblical pageantry. The result is a film of reverent and massive magnificence.

Opposite: Moses leads the Exodus from Egypt: *The Ten Commandments* (1956).

Dan Vadis is one of *The Ten Gladiators* (1963).

297   *The Ten Gladiators*

(I Dieci Gladiatori / Ten Desperate Men / Revolt of
  the Gladiators)
Cineproduzioni Associate, Rome (1962) 104 min.
Supertotalscope / Eastman Color
U.S.–American-International (1963)

   P–Piero Lazzari / D–Gianfranco Parolini / W–Gianfranco Parolini, Giovanni Simonelli, Sergio Sollima / M–Angelo Francesco Lavagnino / C–Francesco Izzarelli

   Cast–Roger Browne (Glaucus), Susan Paget
(Livia), Dan Vadis (Rocca), Gianni Rizzo (Nero),
Mimmo Palmara (Tigellinus), Margaret Taylor
(Poppaea) with Mirko Ellis, Ugo Sasso, John Lit-
tlewords, Marco Vassilli

   The Ten Gladiators is the first in a series of
films starring Dan Vadis as the rebel gladiator
Rocca. However, it is actually the final installment in the trilogy as the Vadis character
dies at the end. The other two films must be
considered prequels as they are set in time periods prior to the reign of Nero. In this film,
Rocca and his gladiator friends are mistaken
for a band of hooded zealots who oppose the
rule of Nero and his wife Poppaea. They are
taken prisoner by the troops of Nero's henchman Tigellinus and forced to fight in the
arena. The gladiators escape to join the zealots in their battle against tyranny and help to
aid the persecuted Christians. The plot alter-
nates between the light-hearted, back-slap-
ping camaraderie of the gladiators and the
more serious aspects of this particular era in
history. The combination is not always a ho-
mogeneous one this time around.

298   *The Terror of Rome Against the Son of Hercules*

(Maciste, Gladiatore di Sparta; Maciste, Gladiator
  of Sparta / Maciste and the 100 Gladiators)

Mark Forest fights an unconvincing anthropoid in *The Terror of Rome Against the Son of Hercules* (1964).

Prometeo S.r.L. and Sancro Film, Rome–Les Filmes Jacques Leittienne and Unicite, Paris (1964) 100 min.
Techniscope / Technicolor
U.S.–Embassy
   D–Mario Caiano / W–Mario Amendola, Alfonso Brescia, Albert Valentin / M–Carlo Franci / C–Pier Ludovico Pavoni / E–Nella Nannuzzi / AD–Pier Vittorio Marchi / CD–Mario Giorsi
   Cast–Mark Forest (Maciste), Marilu Tolo (Olympia), Elisabeth Fanty (Silvia) with Robert Hundar, Peter White, Lea Monaco, Ugo Attanasio, Ferruccio Amendola, Renato Navarrini, Jacques Stany, Enrico Salvatore, Bruno Ukmar, Giuliano Giuliani

   Mark Forest flexes his muscles once again as Maciste, the champion gladiator of the Roman arena. This time he saves a group of Christians from the lions during the reign of the emperor Vitellius. Although he is desired by the beautiful Roman patrician Olympia, his heart belongs to the innocent Christian girl Silvia. To save Silvia from persecution he must fight against the "Terror of Rome"—a man in a very unconvincing ape costume. Better than average production values and Mark Forest's presence place this a notch above others of its type. In some versions of this film, the Mark Forest character is referred to as Poseidon rather than Maciste.

299   *Tharus, Son of Attila*

(Tharus, Figlio di Attila)
P.T. Cinematografica (1962) 89 min.
Widescreen Telecolor
U.S.–Medallion
   P–Michaelangelo Ciafre / D–Roberto Montero / W–Leo Bomba, Roberto Montero / M–Alexandre Derevitsky, Mario Migliari / C–Giuseppe La Torre / E–Enzo Alfonsi / AD–Giuseppe Ranieri, Oscar D'Amico / CD–Giorgio Desideri
   Cast–Jerome Courtland (Tharus), Lisa Gastoni

Mimmo Palmara is the enemy of Rik Von Nutter and Jerome Courtland, who plays *Tharus, Son of Attila* (1962).

(Tamal), Mimmo Palmara (Cudrun), Livio Lorenzon (Hatun), Rik Von Nutter (Otto), John McDouglas (Bholem) with Liana Dori, Daniele Igor, Cristina Martel, Lorenzo Artole, Renato Montalbano

This is a little-known film which received poor distribution in the United States prior to its video release. Although you might suspect that this is a sequel to *Attila the Hun* starring Anthony Quinn, the plot has little to do with Attila aside from a brief mention at the beginning. The story occurs several years after Attila's death. Attila's son, Tharus, now grown to manhood, is sent by his uncle, King Bholem, to infiltrate the encampment of his enemy Hatun. He succeeds in his task but falls in love with Tamal, the daughter of the rival chieftain. Tamal is also attracted to Tharus but, unfortunately, she has already been promised in marriage to the evil warrior Cudrun. Tharus and Tamal attempt to run away

together but they are captured and Tharus is whipped. Cudrun murders Hatun and then allows Tharus to escape. Cudrun tells Tamal that Tharus is responsible for her father's death and she reluctantly agrees to honor their marriage pact. During the marriage festivities, King Bholem and his warriors attack the camp. Tharus kills Cudrun and convinces Tamal of his innocence. The film is worth noting primarily because it presents Mimmo Palmara (clad in a variety of chest accentuating costumes) with one of his largest roles, albeit a villainous one. He gives such a convincing performance that it is difficult to understand why he was not able to make the transition to leading man in future peplum films. Nevertheless, he does have the distinction of being one of the genre's most frequent and versatile performers. American actor Jerome Courtland is far less impressive in the title role. He later became a director of such primetime TV soaps as *Dynasty*, *Falcon Crest* and *Knot's Landing*.

300   *Theodora, Slave Empress*

(Teodora, Imperatrice di Bisanzio; Theodora, Empress of Byzantium)
Lux Film, Rome–Lux Compagnie Cinematographique, Paris (1954) 124 min.
Pathécolor
U.S.–I.F.E. Releasing Corp. 88 min.
   D–Riccardo Freda/W–Rene Wheeler, Raniere Cochetti, Claude Accursi, Riccardo Freda/M–Renzo Rossellini/C–Rodolfo Lombardi/E–Mario Serandrei AD–Antonio Valente, Filiberto Sbardella/CD–Veniero Colasanti
   Cast–Gianna Maria Canale (Theodora), Georges Marchal (Justinian), Renato Baldini (Arcal), Henri Guisol (Cappadocia), Irene Papas (Faidia), Carletto Sposito (Scarpios), Nerio Bernardi (Belisario), Olga Solbelli (Egina), Alessandro Fersen (Metropolita), Lois Gizza (Smirnos) with Umberto Silvestri, Mario Siletti, Oscar Andriani, Giovanni Fagioli

Justinian, Emperor of Byzantium, goes out among his people dressed as a commoner and meets Theodora, the daughter of a stable-keeper. Fascinated by her beauty, he attempts to make love to her but she rejects his advances. Later, during the annual chariot race, Theodora represents the common people and drives a chariot against Justinian. She wins the race and Justinian invites her to the palace where he asks her to be his mistress. When Theodora refuses, Justinian proposes marriage. As empress, Theodora champions the causes of her people, to the displeasure of the prime minister, Cappodocia. In order to be rid of her, Cappodocia convinces Justinian that his new wife is unfaithful. Theodora is forced to flee for her life. She joins the rebel forces who are planning a revolt against the cruel edicts of Cappodocia but the plan fails and she is captured. Justinian learns the truth as Theodora is about to be executed and saves her. Gianna Maria Canale had been brought to America in 1950 to star with Van Johnson in *Go for Broke*. She declined to stay in Hollywood and returned to Europe where she be-

Georges Marchal loves Gianna Maria Canale as *Theodora, Slave Empress* **(1954).**

came one of the most recognizable faces in peplum films. In *Theodora, Slave Empress* she is the heroine and not the cold-blooded villainess which would become her standard screen persona. In 1957 she again starred for director Riccardo Freda in the Euro horror film *I Vampiri*.

301   *The 13th Warrior*

A Crichton/McTiernan Production
Touchstone Pictures (1999) 103 min.
A Buena Vista Release
Panavision/Technicolor

P–John McTiernan, Michael Crichton, Ned Dowd/D–John McTiernan/W–William Wisher, Warren Lewis/Based on the novel *Eaters of the Dead* by Michael Crichton/M–Jerry Goldsmith/C–Peter Menzies Jr./E–John Wright/PD–Wolf Kroeger/CD–Kate Harrington

Cast–Antonio Banderas (Ahmed), Omar Sharif (Melchisidek), Vladimir Kulich (Buliwyf), Dennis Storhoi (Heger), Daniel Southern (Edgtho), Neil Maffin (Roneth), John DeSantis (Ragner) with Clive Russell, Mischa Hausserman, Diane Venora, Oliver Sveinall, Tony Curran

A young Arab poet is exiled from Baghdad because he has fallen in love with a married woman. Heading north with a caravan, he encounters a shipload of Vikings who recruit him as the 13th warrior in their crusade against an ages old evil which is menacing their people. Returning with the Vikings to their homeland, Ahmed discovers that the enemy is a demonic tribe of creatures who steal the heads of their victims and gnaw on the corpses. In actuality these cannibalistic monsters are fierce warriors who dress in animal skins to frighten their adversaries. Most of the emotional conflict in this film arises from the differences between the refined Arab and the brutal but noble Vikings. At first they are at odds but eventually they learn to respect each other despite their variant beliefs. There isn't much plot here; just a series of violent and bloody battle sequences, but the action moves along at a vigorous pace. From a technical standpoint *The 13th Warrior* is outstanding, with breathtaking cinematography and an evocative background score.

302   *Thor and the Amazon Women*

(Le Gladiatrici/The Amazon Women)
Italia–Cornet Films (1963) 85 min.
Totalscope/Eastman Color
U.S.–Wilcox

P–Alfredo Guarini/D–Antonio Leonviola/W–Antonio Leonviola, Maria Sofia Scandurra/M–Roberto Nicolosi/C–Memmo Mancori/E–Roberto Cinquini/AD–Oscar D'Amico/CD–Serenilla Staccioli

Cast–Joe Robinson (Thor), Susy Andersen (Tamar), Maria Fiore (Amazon Captain), Harry Baird (Ubaratutu), Alberto Cevenini (Hamok) with Carla Foscari, Janine Hendy, Tony Ante, Robert Baca, Anna Majurec

Thor and the Amazon Women is a semi-sequel to *Taur the Mighty* (1963) which was originally entitled *Tarzan, King of Brutal Force*. The Edgar Rice Burroughs' estate prevented the film from being released with the Tarzan title so the name of the main character was changed to Taur. By the time the sequel was released the name had been further changed to Thor. No matter what name it goes by *Thor and the Amazon Women* is about as bad as they come. Thor battles the Njala civilization, which is a society dominated by women and ruled over by the cruel Queen Nera. Nera captures Tamar, heir to the throne of Balylon, and forces her to become a "gladiatrix." Thor and his faithful companion Ubaratutu set out to rescue her. The resulting high camp adventure often has to be seen to be believed. The action sequences are punctuated with silly sound effects and even sillier dialogue. The character of Thor (played by British bodybuilder Joe Robinson) actually has very little screen time. The majority of the film is devoted to the clumsily staged gladiatorial combats between the buxom Amazons. Ubaratutu is depicted as a sort of muscular Stepin Fetchit. The scene where Queen Nera puts him on a revolving platform and makes him flex his muscles for her amusement is ludicrous in the extreme. Even worse are some of Susy Andersen's speeches about the inferiority of women, guaranteed to make any feminist cringe.

Hero Alan Steel (left) confronts bad guy Mimmo Palmara (right) in *The Three Avengers* (1964).

303   *The Three Avengers*

(Gli Invincibili Three; The Invincible Three / Ursus
the Invincible)
A Cine Italia Production (1964) 98 min.
Totalscope / Eastman Color
U.S.–ABC Films
   P–Giuseppe Fatigati / D–Gianfranco Parolini /
W–Lionello De Felice, Arnaldo Marrosu, Gian-
franco Parolini / M–Angelo Francesco Lavagnino /
C–Francesco Izzarelli / E–Edmondo Lozzi / AD–Ro-
mano Paxuell Berti / CD–Mario Giorsi
   Cast–Alan Steel (Ursus), Rosalba Neri (Demora),
Lisa Gastoni, Mimmo Palmara, Carlo Tamberlani,
Orchidea De Santis, Vassili Karamesinis, Nello
Pazzafini, Alberto Dell'Acqua, Tony Maggio, Pino
Mattei, Gianni Rizzo

   The city of Attra is tyrannized by an evil
man who claims that he is Ursus. He has completely dominated the king and is now trying
to dispense with Dario, the crown prince. Into
the city comes the real Ursus and his two daffy
companions. Prince Dario enlists their aid in
trying to make peace with the Tanusi, a no-
madic people who have long been the enemies of Attra. Dario arranges a contest between the false Ursus representing Attra and
the real Ursus representing the Tanusi, with
the winner deciding the peace terms. The impostor wins through treachery, and Ursus is
temporarily blinded. False Ursus has the king
murdered and then puts the blame on Dario.
Fortunately, Ursus regains his sight and, with
the help of his companions, makes sure that
right triumphs over evil. *The Three Avengers*
might better have been called "Ursus and the
Two Stooges." There is an excess of lame
comic highjinks thanks to Ursus' two goofy
friends, who are far more annoying than
funny. The best things about this film are
Mimmo Palmara, shown to good advantage as
the evil Ursus, and Rosalba Neri in a rare sympathetic role.

304   *The Three Hundred Spartans*

(Lion of Sparta)
20th Century–Fox (1962) 114 min.
CinemaScope/Color by DeLuxe

P–Rudolph Mate, George St. George/D–Rudolph Mate/W–George St. George, Ugo Liberatori, Remigio Del Grosso, Giovanni D'Eramo, Gian Paolo Callegari/M–Manos Hadjidakis/C–Geoffrey Unsworth/E–Jerome Webb/AD–Arrigo Equini

Cast–Richard Egan (Leonidas), Ralph Richardson (Themistocles), Diane Baker (Ellas), Barry Coe (Phylon), David Farrar (Xerxes), Donald Houston (Hydarnes), Anna Synodinou (Gorgo), Kieron Moore (Ephialtes) with John Crawford, Robert Brown, Laurence Naismith, Anne Wakefield, Ivan Triesault, Charles Fawcett, Michael Nikoliankos, Sandro Giglio, Anna Raftopoulou, Dimos Starenios

Xerxes, the King of Persia, assembles an enormous army and marches on Greece. King Leonidas of Sparta offers to lead the Greek states into battle but his strategies are continually rejected by the Greek Council. He decides to take his personal bodyguard of 300

Richard Egan is the courageous Spartan king Leonidas in *The Three Hundred Spartans* (1962).

men to Thermopylae in a desperate attempt to hold off the Persians. Using brilliant military tactics, the Spartans hold off the Persian army with few casualties. Just when victory seems possible, the Greeks are ambushed from behind and the 300 valiant warriors are massacred by the Persian forces. The action sequences in *The Three Hundred Spartans* are very well staged but the film's weak point is the tepid, and totally superfluous, romantic element between Barry Coe and Diane Baker. Ironically, two years before, Richard Egan had portrayed Xerxes (also known as Ahasuerus) in *Esther and the King*.

305   *The Three Stooges Meet Hercules*

A Normandy Production
Columbia (1961) 89 min.

P–Norman Maurer/D–Edward Bernds/W–Elwood Ullman/M–Paul Dunlap/C–Charles Welborn/E–Edwin Bryant/AD–Don Ament

Cast–The Three Stooges (Larry, Moe and Curly Joe), Samson Burke (Hercules), Quinn Redeker (Schyler Davis), Vicki Trickett (Diane), George N. Neise (Mr. Dimsal/King Odius) with Emil Sitka, Hal Smith, John Cliff, Lewis Charles, Barbara Hines, Terry Huntingdon, Diana Piper, Gregg Martell, the McKeever Twins

It seems that even the mighty Hercules was not to be spared the inanity of the Three Stooges. In this mildly humorous comedy send up of peplum films, the Stooges and their scientist friend, Schyler, build a time machine which transports them to ancient Greece. In no time at all, they succeed in antagonizing the King of Ithaca, who sentences them to be galley slaves. The strenuous rowing transforms Schyler into a muscleman. After they all escape from the ship, the Stooges pass him off as Hercules in order to make money. When the real Hercules gets wind of this he challenges Schyler to a test of strength in the arena. Hercules is defeated and Schyler and the Stooges return to their own time via some stock footage scenes from other Columbia movies. By 1961 the Three Stooges had become a bit long of tooth for their childish antics, so much of the slapstick seems even more forced and foolish than usual.

Hercules (Samson Burke, in chariot) salutes his emperor in *The Three Stooges Meet Hercules* (1961).

306   *Titus*

Clear Blue Sky/Overseas Filmgroup/Urania Pictures/NDF Productions
U.S.–Fox Searchlight (1999) 162 min.
Widescreen/DeLuxe Color
P–Jody Patton, Conchita Airoldi, Julie Taymor/ D/W–Julie Taymor/Based on the play *Titus Andronicus* by William Shakespeare/M–Elliot Goldenthal/C–Luciano Tovoli/E–Francoise Bonnot/ PD–Dante Ferretti/CD–Milena Canonero

Cast–Anthony Hopkins (Titus Andronicus), Jessica Lange (Tamora), Alan Cumming (Saturninus), Colm Feore (Marcus), James Frain (Bassianus), Laura Fraser (Lavinia), Harry Lennix (Aaron), Angus Macfayden (Lucius), Matthew Rhys (Demetrius), Jonathan Rhys-Meyers (Chiron) with Kenny Doughty, Osheen Jones, Blake Ritson, Colin Wells, Geraldine McEwan

In A.D. 400 the great general Titus Andronicus returns to Rome in triumph. He has conquered the Goths and brought back their queen, Tamora, and her three sons as captives. The emperor has died and Titus is offered his throne. He declines and passes the crown to the emperor's eldest son Saturninus. Titus offers Tamora's firstborn as a sacrifice to the gods, thereby earning her undying hatred. Through an unfortunate turn of events, Titus incurs the displeasure of Saturninus who has taken Tamora as his empress. Thus begins a cycle of revenge and murder that culminates in a bloodbath of major proportions. Julie Taymor, fresh from her triumph as director of *The Lion King* on Broadway, makes her cinematic directorial debut with this unique adaptation of Shakespeare's *Titus Andronicus*. It is an audacious and imaginative movie which mixes contemporary styles with those of ancient Rome and Thirties fascism to stunning effect. The performances are first rate and, despite a lengthy running time, the action never flags. It is also an extremely gruesome affair, featuring what may well be the most heinous act of revenge ever conceived.

New York Times: Ms. Taymor has respected

both an ancient work of art and a modern company of screen actors. Her reward is to have created something very special.

Variety: Theatrical wizard Julie Taymor strides boldly into the feature film arena with "TITUS" and emerges with a conditional victory.

Time: Julie Taymor takes Shakespeare's goriest play and makes it vivid, relevant and of elevating scariness. Taymor keeps the eye as busy as the ear; she embellishes the story without disfiguring it.

307 *The Triumph of Hercules*

(Il Trionfo di Ercole / Hercules vs. the Giant Warriors / Hercules and the Ten Avengers)
P.C. Produzione Cinematografica, Rome—Les Filmes Jacques Leitienne and Unicite, Paris (1964) 90 min.
Cromoscope / Eastman Color
U.S.—John Alexander Films (1965)
P–Alberto Chimenz, Vilo Pavoni / D–Alberto De Martino / W–Roberto Gianviti, Alessandro Ferrau / M–Francesco De Masi / C–Pier Ludovico Pavoni / E–Otello Colangeli / PD–Carlo Gentili / AD–Pier Vittorio Marchi / CD–Nadia Vitale
Cast–Dan Vadis (Hercules), Pierre Cressoy (Milo), Moira Orfei (Pasiphae), Marilu Tolo (Ati), Piero Lulli (Herus), Enzo Fiermonte (Eurystheus), Renato Rossini (Gordius) with Aldo Cecconi, Pietro Capanna, Nino Marchetti, Anna Maria Mostari, Gaetano Quartararo, Jacques Stany, Nazzareno Zamperla

Prince Milo causes the murder of his uncle the King of Mycenae and then sets his sights on stealing the throne from his cousin, Princess Ati. Milo's mother is the powerful sorceress Pasiphae. To aid her ambitious son she gives him a dagger which conjures up seven indestructible golden warriors when it is removed from its scabbard. Hearing of the king's death, Hercules comes to Mycenae and participates in a contest to win the hand of Ati. Milo has Ati kidnapped and then convinces Hercules that it was done by the local villagers. Hercules goes berserk and when he kills an innocent man Zeus takes away his son's strength as punishment. Deprived of his great strength, Hercules is taken prisoner by Milo's soldiers. Only when the life of Ati is in gravest danger does Zeus restore Hercules' powers. Hercules defeats the seven golden warriors

and Milo is killed while trying to escape. To avenge the death of her son, Pasiphae takes on the form of the princess and Hercules must decide which of the two is the real Ati in order to save her life. The production values of *The Triumph of Hercules* are average for a film of its type and the plot, though fairly standard, is fast moving. The seven golden warriors are a nice touch, although they are dispatched rather easily by a Hercules-induced cave-in.

308 *Triumph of the Son of Hercules*

(Il Trionfo di Maciste; The Triumph of Maciste)
York Film, Rome (1961) 87 min.
Totalscope / Eastman Color
U.S.—Embassy (1963)
P–Roberto Capitani, Luigi Mondello / D–Amerigo Anton (Tanio Boccia) / W–Arpad De Riso, Nino Scolaro / M–Carlo Innocenzi / C–Oberdan Troiani / E–Gino Talamo / AD–Amedeo Mellone / CD–Walter Petrarca
Cast–Kirk Morris (Maciste), Cathia Caro (Antea), Ljuba Bodin (Tenefis), Cesare Fantoni (Agadon), Giulio Donnini (Omnes), Attilio Dottesio (Arsino), Bruno Tocci (Tabos), Aldo Bufi Landi (Themail), Carla Calo (Yalis) with Salvatore Lago, Piero Leri, Lucia Randi, Alfredo Salvadori, Calisto Calisti

Adriano Bellini was one of the few homegrown Italian muscleman to make it big in peplum films. As Kirk Morris, the former gondolier starred in several films as Maciste, a part he repeats in *Triumph of the Son of Hercules.* Set in ancient Egypt, for no good reason other than to reuse sets and costumes from *Queen of the Nile*, this is one of the poorer entries in the series. The evil queen Tenefis sits of the throne of Memphis. Her people live in fear because she is in league with the Yuri Men, monsters who sacrifice maidens to their insatiable fire god. Enter Maciste, to right all wrongs and restore the throne to the rightful heir. Maciste is captured and taken to Tenefis who immediately falls for the handsome hunk. Fortunately for her, she possesses a magic scepter, the touch of which makes Maciste forget everything and become her devoted slave. Eventually Maciste regains his senses and is able to destroy the Yuri Men, their fire god and the iniquitous queen. To pad the running time, the producers cut in a

And even more muscles and chains: Kirk Morris in *Triumph of the Son of Hercules* (1963).

big chunk of action footage from *Maciste al-l'Inferno* (aka *The Witch's Curse*). Although Kirk Morris also starred in this film, his hairstyle and costume are quite different causing a very noticeable lack of continuity.

309   *The Triumph of the Ten Gladiators*

(Il Trionfo dei Dieci Gladiatori)
Cineproduzioni Associate, Rome (1964) 100 min.
Techniscope / Technicolor
U.S.–Four Star (1965) 94 min.

D–Nick Nostro / W–Nick Nostro, Simon Sterling (Sergio Sollima) / M–Carlo Savina / C–Tino Santoni / E–Enzo Alfonsi

Cast–Dan Vadis (Rocca), Helga Line, Stanley Kent, Leontine May, Alina Zalewska, William Bird, Carlo Tamberlani, Don Messina, Gordon Steve / Ugo Sasso, Sal Borgese, Gianni Rizzo, John Heston, Enzo Fiermonte

Those ten good-natured musclebound hunks are back and the wide screen can barely contain this sea of skin. The proconsul of Rome dispatches the ten gladiators to a province in Asia Minor to kidnap the local queen. Actually the proconsul is in league with the queen's ruthless prime minister who wants her out of the way. The gladiators learn that a masked raider has been committing rebellious acts in response to the unfair edicts of the government. Eventually the gladiators discover that the masked raider is none other than the queen herself, who is attempting to protect her subjects. They realize that they have been duped into serving on the wrong side and join forces with the queen to oust the prime minister and restore order to her kingdom. Once again Rocca and his pals laugh in the face of danger. This time around there are even more comic situations than in *The Ten*

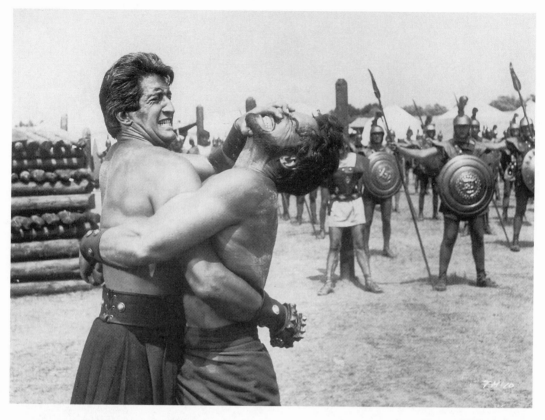

Ajax (Mimmo Palmara) and Aeneas (Steve Reeves) attempt to settle the Trojan War man to man in *The Trojan Horse* (1962).

Gladiators. There is even one sequence where they all dress up in drag and apparently enjoy it!

310 *The Trojan Horse*

(La Guerra di Troia; The War of Troy / The Wooden Horse of Troy)
Europea Cinematografica, Rome–Les Filmes Modernes, Paris
(1961) 105 min.
Euroscope / Eastman Color
U.S.–Colorama Features (1962)

P–Campo Bigazzi / D–Giorgio Ferroni / W–Ugo Liberatore, Federico Zardi, Giorgio Stegani, Giorgio Ferroni / M–Giovanni Fusco / C–Rino Filipponi / E–Antonietta Zita / AD–Pier Vittorio Marchi

Cast–Steve Reeves (Aeneas), John Drew Barrymore (Ulysses), Juliette Mayniel (Creusa), Edy Vessel (Helen), Lydia Alfonsi (Cassandra), Warner Bentivegna (Paris), Luciana Angelillo (Andromache), Arturo Dominici (Achilles), Mimmo Palmara (Ajax), Nerio Bernardi (Agamemnon), Nando Tamberlani (Menelaus), Carlo Tamberlani (Priam)

In the last year of the Trojan War, Ulysses devises his famous plan to breech the city walls. The Greeks build a colossal wooden horse which the Trojans take into their city, believing it to be a gift from the gods. Hidden inside are Greek warriors who open the city gates and thus bring about the fall of Troy. The screenplay offers very little in the way of innovation other than making Aeneas the focus of the conflicts. This is predictable considering Steve Reeves is the star. The accent is on action with Reeves performing the requisite feats of strength. Helen and Paris are a distinctly unsympathetic pair and Menelaus takes his revenge on them both in the final reel. Aeneas escapes the destruction of Troy with several companions to found the city of Rome and star in the sequel *The Avenger*.

311   *The Trojan Women*

Cinerama Releasing (1971) 105 min.
Color
  P–Anis Nohra/D/W/E–Michael Cacoyannis/
Based on the play by Euripides/M–Mikis Theodor-
akis/C–Alfio Contini/AD–Nicholas Georgiadis/
CD–Annalisa Nasalli-Rocca
  Cast–Katharine Hepburn (Hecuba), Irene Papas
(Helen), Vanessa Redgrave (Andromache), Gene-
vieve Bujold (Cassandra), Patrick Magee (Mene-
laus), Brian Blessed (Talthybius), Alberto Sanz
(Astyanax) with Pauline Letts, Anna Maria Espojo,
Pat Beckett, Elena Castillo

After the fall of Troy, the Trojan women
are held captive by the conquering Greeks.
The main characters are Hecuba, queen of
the fallen city, her mad daughter Cassandra,
Hecuba's daughter-in-law Andromache, and
the woman who caused the ten year war,
Helen. A Greek messenger arrives at the camp
to inform them of their fates. With four actresses of such high caliber in the lead roles,
you could easily suppose that the film would
be something special. Sadly, this is not the
case. Under Michael Cacoyannis direction this
version of Euripides tragedy is a static affair
filled with overwrought acting. The exception
is Brian Blessed who, as the Greek messenger,
gives an outstanding performance.
  British Photoplay: Michael Cacoyannis has
made his film in stark locations, glorious
monolithic rock which is utterly timeless …
but spoils it by allowing his leading ladies to
let mild hysteria cloy the issues.

312   *Troy*

Warner Bros/Village Roadshow
  Pictures (2004)
  P–Wolfgang Petersen, Diane
Rathburn, Colin Wilson, Gail Katz/
D–Wolfgang Petersen/W–David
Benioff/M—Gabriel Yared; C–Roger
Pratt/PD–Nigel Phelps
  Cast–Brad Pitt (Achilles), Eric
Bana (Hector), Orlando Bloom
(Paris), Diane Kruger (Helen), Brian
Cox (Agamemnon), Sean Bean
(Odysseus), Peter O'Toole (Priam),
Julie Christie (Thetis), Garrett Hed-
lund (Patroclus), Saffron Burrows
(Andromache), Rose Byrne (Bri-
seis), Brendon Gleeson (Menelaus),
James Cosmo (Glacus)

This $180 million plus epic began produc-
tion in April 2003 and is set to be released to
theatres in May 2004. Filming locations include England, Malta, and Mexico.

313   *Two Gladiators*

(I Due Gladiatori/La Fureur des Gladiateurs; The
  Fury of the Gladiators/Fight or Die)
Produzione Prometeo Film (1964) 97 min.
Techniscope/Eastman Color
U.S.–ABC Films
  P–Carlo Vassalle/D–Mario Caiano/W–Mario
Amendola, Alfonso Brescia/M–Carlo Franci/C–
Fausto Rossi/E–Nella Nannuzzi/AD–Pier Vittorio
Marchi/CD–Mario Giorsi
  Cast–Richard Harrison (Lucius), Moira Orfei
(Marcia), Mimmo Palmara (Commodus), Giuliano
Gemma (Orazius), Alberto Farnese (Leto), Piero
Lulli (Cleander) with Ivy Holzer, Mirko Ellis, Enzo
Fiermonte, Gianni Solaro, Renato Montalbano,
Nello Pazzafini

Following the death of the wise emperor
Marcus Aurelius his mad son Commodus becomes ruler of the Roman Empire. Lucius, a
Tribune, goes in search of Commodus' twin
brother, who was sent away at birth. He hopes
to convince the brother to replace his crazed
sibling as emperor and thereby save Rome
from his evil excesses. Richard Harrison once
again takes up the sword to defend the Empire
in this interesting variation on the reign of
Commodus, who is played with gusto by the
ever reliable Mimmo Palmara.

Richard Harrison is one of *Two Gladiators* (1964).

314 Two Nights with Cleopatra

(Due Notti con Cleopatra)
Excelsa-Rosa Film (1954) 80 min.
Ferraniacolor
U.S.–Ultra Pictures (1963)

P–Giuseppe Colizzi/D–Mario Mattoli/W–Ruggero Maccari, Ettore Scola/M–Armando Trovajoli/C–Karl Struss, Riccardo Pallottini/E–Roberto Cinquini/CD–Giuseppe Peruzzi

Cast–Sophia Loren (Cleopatra/Nisca), Alberto Sordi (Cesarino), Ettore Manni (Mark Antony), Paul Muller (Tortul), Rolf Tasna (Meros), Carlo Dale (Cocis), Alberto Talegalli (Enobarbus), Riccardo Garrone (Venus) with Nando Bruno, Gianni Cavalieri, Ugo D'Alessio, Ughetto, Cristina Fantoni

This Italian farce was Sophia Loren's second excursion into ancient Egypt. The previous year she had starred in *Aida*. Loren plays a duel role as the brunette Egyptian queen and a look-alike blonde prostitute named Nisca. She is so convincing and lovely in the part of Cleopatra that it is a pity she was never given the opportunity to play the role in a straight dramatic film. The scenes between Cleopatra and Mark Antony (portrayed by a young Ettore Manni) are played without comedy and hint at how effective Loren and Manni might have been given better material. Unfortunately, a majority of the footage in *Two Nights with Cleopatra* is devoted to the Italian comedian Alberto Sordi as an inept and irritating palace guard who substitutes the prostitute for the queen. Much ado is made about Cleopatra's supposed promiscuity and foolish jokes abound. First and foremost, the film is a vehicle for Sordi. Sophia Loren's nude bathing scene in this film garnered considerable publicity after she became a major star but, in actuality, it is less revealing than photos would suggest. *Two Nights with Cleopatra* remained unreleased in the United States until is was distributed by Ultra Pictures in 1963 to cash in on the Cleopatra craze of the early sixties. Also in 1963 that other popular Italian comedian Toto, starred in *Toto e Cleopatra* with Magali Noel as the Egyptian Queen. Directed by Fernando Cerchio, it was never released in the U.S.

315 Tyrant of Lydia Against the Son of Hercules

(Goliath e la Schiava Ribelle; Goliath and the Rebel Slave/Arrow of the Avenger)
F.I.A. Films, Rome–Georges De Beauregard-Gladiator Film, Paris
(1963) 86 min.
Euroscope/Eastman Color
U.S.–Embassy (1964)

P–Giorgio Agliani, Rudolph Solmsen/D–Mario Caiano/W–Gian Paolo Callegari, Albert Valentin/M–Carlo Franci/C–Pier Ludovico Pavoni/E–Nella Nannuzzi/CD–Mario Giorsi

Cast–Gordon Scott (Gordian/Goliath), Massimo Serato (Mazio), Mimmo Palmara (Artabazo), Serge Nubret (Milone), Gloria Milland (Zoe) with Ombretta Colli, Gabriele Antonini, Lea Kruger, Mirko Ellis, Paolo Petrini, Aldo Pini, Amedeo Trilli

As the army of Alexander the Great approaches Sardi, the capital of Lydia, Gordian, the captain of the palace guards, tries to persuade the ruler of the city to join forces with the young conqueror. The high priest believes that the city should join forces with Alexander's enemy the King of Persia. Herein lies the conflict of this routine peplum film which features a cast filled with genre regulars. There is little to distinguish this from the many other movies Gordon Scott starred in at this time. Scott was a lifeguard in Las Vegas when he was discovered by producer Sol Lesser, who subsequently starred him as Tarzan in five films. Onetime husband to actress Vera Miles, after their divorce Scott moved to Rome and became one of the most popular players in Italian genre cinema, switching from peplum films to Spaghetti Westerns when trends changed.

316 Ulysses

(Ulisse)
A Lux Film Production (1954) 104 min.
Technicolor
U.S.–Paramount (1955)

P–Dino De Laurentiis, Carlo Ponti/D–Mario Camerini/W–Franco Brusati, Mario Camerini, Ennio De Concini, Hugh Gray, Ben Hecht, Ivo Perilli, Irwin Shaw/Based on *The Odyssey* by Homer/M–Alessandro Cicognini/C–Harold Rosson/E–Leo Cattozzi/AD–Flavio Mogherini/CD–Giulio Coltellacci, Madame Gres

Cast–Kirk Douglas (Ulysses), Silvana Mangano (Penelope/Circe), Anthony Quinn (Antinous),

Ulysses (Kirk Douglas) and the sorceress Circe (Silvana Mangano): *Ulysses* (1955).

Rossana Podesta (Nausicaa), Franco Interlenghi (Telemachus), Daniel Ivernel (Eurilocus), Jacques Dumesnil (Alcinous), Elena Zareschi (Cassandra) with Sylvie, Evi Maltagliati, Ludmilla Dudarova, Tania Weber, Piero Lulli, Umberto Silvestri, Oscar Andriani, Alessandro Fersen, Ferruccio Stagni, Walter Brandi

Ulysses is an entertaining version of *The Odyssey* which benefits from an interesting cast and an elaborate production. For this co-production, Dino De Laurentiis and Carlo Ponti wisely cast well-known Hollywood star Kirk Douglas in the lead to ensure international exposure. Two of Italy's reigning glamour queens were featured as his costars. In a clever touch, Silvana Mangano plays both Ulysses' faithful wife Penelope and the sorceress Circe. Rossana Podesta, in her first epic role, is Nausicaa, the princess who rescues the shipwrecked Ulysses. To her, he recounts the story of his fateful ten-year voyage. With the city of Troy defeated, Ulysses and his men set sail home to Ithaca but the sea god Poseidon, who favored Troy, sends a storm to blow the ship off course. In the years that follow Ulysses and company undergo a series of adventures. These include encounters with the Cyclops Polyphemus (a highlight of the film with special effects by Eugen Shuftan) and the beautiful witch Circe, who turns men into pigs—literally! The screenplay, though faithful to the source, is mediocre, at best. Why it took seven writers, including the illustrious screenwriter Ben Hecht and author Irwin

Shaw, to pen the scenario, is a great mystery.

Photoplay: What we have here is a random selection of incidents—some well done, others silly—but nothing of the poetry, the vividness, the vitality of Homer. It could have been a great movie; it wasn't even good.

Movie Story: A spectacular costume drama of ancient Greece which will be one of the most talked-about pictures of the year. This is real greatness in movie-making adventure. Don't fail to see it.

317   Ulysses Against the Son of Hercules

(Ulisse Contro Ercole; Ulysses Against Hercules)
Compagnia Cinematografica Mondiale, Rome–Fides, Paris (1961) 99 min.
Totalscope/Eastman Color
U.S.–Embassy (1963)
P–Luigi Mannerini/D/W–Mario Caiano/M–

Ulysses (Georges Marchal) and Hercules (Michael Lane) are captives of the queen of the Bird People (Dominique Boschero) in *Ulysses Against the Son of Hercules* (1963).

Angelo Francesco Lavagnino/C–Alvaro Mancori/ E–Renato Cinquini/AD–Piero Filippone/CD– Mario Giorsi

Cast–Georges Marchal (Ulysses), Michael Lane (Hercules/Heracles), Alessandra Panaro (Helen), Gianni Santuccio (Lago) with Yvette Lebon, Eleonora Bianchi, Dominique Boschero, Nando Angelini, Tino Bianchi, Raffaele Baldassarre, Raffaella Cara, Gabriele Tinti, Raffaele Pisu

Hercules' beloved Helen is forced into marriage with another man. Before he has time to react, Jupiter sends him on a mission to capture Ulysses. Jupiter has decided that Ulysses has not been punished enough for blinding Polyphemus the Cyclops. Hercules will capture Ulysses who will then become Polyphemus' slave. Hercules hires a Phoenician pirate ship to ram Ulysses' vessel. Ulysses is taken captive but manages to set the ship on fire. Only he and Hercules get out alive. They swim ashore and are immediately captured by birdmen who take them to their queen. The queen tells the prisoners that they are to be sacrificed to a gigantic vulture god. They escape and Ulysses eludes recapture by Hercules. It's out of the frying pan and into the fire as Ulysses is taken prisoner by the Cave-dwellers of King Largo. The mad king is planning an attack on the kingdom ruled by Helen's father. Through the efforts of Ulysses, Largo is killed, Helen's people are saved and she and Hercules are reunited. When Hercules attempts to once again take Ulysses prisoner, Helen intervenes. Hercules begs for mercy from Jupiter and his plea is granted. Ulysses is free to return home. In the U.S. prints the name of the Hercules character is changed to Heracles, one of the sons of Hercules. He is played by Michael Lane who had previously appeared as the monster in *Frankenstein 1970* (1958).

318   *Up Pompeii*

Associated London Films/Anglo-EMI (1971) 90 min.
Technicolor
U.S.–No theatrical release
P–Ned Sherrin/D–Bob Kellett/W–Sid Colin/ Based on an idea by Talbot Rothwell/M–Carl Davis/C–Ian Wilson/E–Al Gill/PD–Seamus Flannery/CD–Jenny Lowe

Cast–Frankie Howerd (Lurcio), Michael Hordern (Ludicrus Sextus), Barbara Murray (Ammonia), Patrick Cargill (Nero) Julie Ege (Voluptua), Bernard Bresslaw (Gorgo), Madeline Smith (Erotica), Lance Percival (Bilius) with Bill Fraser, Roy Hudd, Rita Webb, Aubrey Woods

British comedian Frankie Howerd is a sort of one man "Carry On" gang. This feature version of his 1970 television series is a send up of Roman epics and is often reminiscent of *A Funny Thing Happened on the Way to the Forum* and *Carry On Cleo*. Howerd, as the slave Lurcio, talks to the camera quite a bit and the movie is basically little more than a series of lame double entendres executed in the most puerile style imaginable. There is one inspired scene where Michael Hordern, suffering a hangover from the previous night's orgy, hears every sound magnified beyond endurance. Also on the plus side are Julie Ege and Madeline Smith, two gorgeous "Glamour Girls" from the Hammer horror stable. The plot, such as it is, has Lurcio inadvertently becoming involved in a plot to assassinate the emperor Nero. Lurcio is "rescued" by the eruption of Mount Vesuvius in a charmingly cheesy special effects finale.

319   *Ursus in the Valley of the Lions*

(Ursus nella Valle dei Leoni)
A Cine Italia–Interfilm Production (1961) 82 min.
Totalscope/Eastman Color
U.S.–A Palisade International Presentation
Medallion (1962)
P–Fernando Cinquini/D–Carlo Ludovico Braglia/W–Giuseppe Mangione, Alessandro Continenza/M–Riz Ortolani/C–Giovanni Bergamini/ E–Renato Cinquini/AD–Romano Paxuell Berti

Cast–Ed Fury (Ursus), Alberto Lupo (Ayak), Gerard Herter (Lothar), Miora Orfei (Diana), Mary Marlon (Annia) with Michelle Malaspina, Giacomo Furia, Mariangela Giordano, Andrea Scotti, Elena Forte

Ursus, the infant son of a deposed monarch, is abandoned in the wilderness. He is rescued by lions and brought up as part of their family. When he grows to manhood he encounters a slave caravan and determines to free the captives. After rescuing them from their captors, Ursus returns with the liberated slaves to their city. This is the very city that was once ruled over by his father. With the aid of his lions, Ursus is able to overthrow the

Oh no! More chains! Ed Fury in *Ursus in the Valley of the Lions* (1962).

cruel ruler and regain his rightful place on the throne. *Ursus in the Valley of the Lions* is a mostly unsuccessful attempt at presenting a Tarzan-type story in peplum terms.

320 *The Vengeance of Ursus*

(La Vendetta di Ursus/ Ursus, the Mighty Warrior)
Spendor Film, Rome (1962) 99 min.
Techniscope/Eastman Color
U.S.–Medallion
P–Ferdinando Feliconi/D–Luigi Capuano/ W–Roberto Gianviti, Nino Scolaro, Marcello Cirociolini/M–Carlo Innocenzi/C–Oberdan Trojani/AD–Alfredo Montori
Cast–Samson Burke (Ursus), Wandisa Guida (Sira), Livio Lorenzon (Zagro), Nadine Sanders (Sabra), Nerio Bernardi (Alteo), Roberto Chevalier (Dario) with Gina Rovere, Gianni Rizzo, Franco Fantasia, Ugo Sasso, Ignazio Balsamo

Following his stint as Hercules in *The Three Stooges Meet Hercules*, Canadian body builder Samson Burke (real name: Sam Berg) went to

Italy to star in this, his only legitimate peplum film. The plot is fairly typical stuff. Sira, the princess of Lycea, is being forced into marriage with Zagro, the tyrant of Cadia, so that

Samson Burke protects Wandisa Guida in *The Vengeance of Ursus* (1962).

he can take over the kingdom of her father. Of course, Ursus intervenes and uses his tremendous strength to save the princess and her loyal followers. Livio Lorenzon is his usual dastardly self as the evil Zagro and, as always, makes the most of the part. Immediately after making *The Vengeance of Ursus*, Samson Burke appeared as Maciste in the Italian peplum parody *Toto Contro Maciste* (Fernando Cerchio; 1962). In this film Maciste threatens the city of Thebes and the pharaoh enlists the aid of "Totokamen" to help defeat him. In 1968, Samson Burke returned to the epic genre in *L'Odissea* (aka *The Adventures of Ulysses*), an eight hour mini-series made for Italian television. He appeared in heavy makeup as the Cyclops Polyphemus in an episode directed by the great Mario Bava.

321 *Venus Meets the Son of Hercules*

(Marte, Dio della Guerra; Mars, God of War)
S.p.A. Cinematografica–Incei Films (1962) 93 min.
Totalscope/Eastman Color
U.S.–Embassy (1963)
    D–Marcello Baldi/W–Alessandro Continenza, Marcello Baldi/M–Gino Marinuzzi/C–Marcello Masciocchi/E–Maurizio Lucidi/AD–Piero Poletto/CD–Mario Giorsi
    Cast–Roger Browne (Mars), Jackie Lane (Daphne/Venus), Massimo Serato (Antarus) with Dante Di Paolo, Linda Sini, John Kitzmiller, Renato Speziali, Michele Bally, John McDouglas, Renato Navarrini

Mars, God of War is one of the many films which were picked up and retitled by Embassy Pictures to be released as part of their "Sons of Hercules" TV package. The god Mars comes to Earth to save a city which is under siege by a tribe of African warriors (actually lots of Italian extras in black face). Due to the intervention of Mars, the city is saved. Before he returns to the heavens he falls in love with Daphne, a mortal, and begs his father Jupiter to allow him to live with her as an ordinary man. Jupiter agrees and provides his son with three thunderbolts to aid him in times of trouble. When Daphne is unwillingly consecrated as a Vestal in the temple of Venus, Mars attempts to liberate her. The goddess Venus takes on the form of Daphne and seduces him. While Mars dallies with Venus, the real Daphne is unjustly accused of murder and sentenced to death. Mars comes to his senses as Daphne is about to be fed to a giant man-eating plant. In the ensuing fracas, Daphne is mortally wounded. Jupiter takes pity on his grieving son and the lovers are reunited in heaven. Despite its convoluted plot, the film is of interest because it eschews the usual beefcake for a more fairy-tale approach. Roger Browne is a far more benevolent Mars than he was in *Vulcan, God of Fire* in which he plays the same god as a villain.

322 *The Viking Queen*

A Hammer–Seven Arts Production (1967) 91 min.
Technicolor
U.S.–Twentieth Century–Fox
Color by DeLuxe
    P–John Temple-Smith/D–Don Chaffey/W–Clarke Reynolds/M–Gary Hughes/C–Stephen Dade/E–James Needs, Peter Boita/PD–George Provis/CD–John Furniss
    Cast–Don Murray (Justinian), Carita (Salina), Donald Houston (Maelgan), Andrew Keir (Octavian), Niall MacGinnis (Tiberion), Adrienne Corri (Beatrice), Wilfred Lawson (The King), Nicola Pagett (Talia), Percy Herbert (Catus), Patrick Troughton (Tristram), Sean Caffrey (Fergus) with Denis Shaw, Philip O'Flynn, Brendan Mathews, Gerry Alexander, Patrick Gardiner, Paul Murphy, Arthur O'Sullivan

The Viking Queen was a change of pace for the famous British House of Horror, Hammer Films. This was another in the series of mini-spectaculars or "glamadventures," as Hammer called them, that followed in the wake of the highly successful *She* in 1965 and *One Million Years B.C.* in 1966. *The Viking Queen* lacks the fantasy elements prevalent in its predecessors and is primarily an adventure/romance. Director Don Chaffey takes full advantage of some wonderful location filming in the Wicklow Mountains of Ireland and employs a vast contingent of the Irish army in some of the large scale action sequences. The story has nothing to do with Vikings, other than a brief reference made in a single line of dialogue. Instead, the plot concentrates on the Roman occupation of Britain and the subsequent revolt led by a Boadicea-like queen named Salina against the oppressors. To complicate matters, Salina falls in love with Justinian, the Roman

Brad Jackson has the upper hand in his battle with the evil Richard Devon in Roger Corman's charmingly cheesy *Viking Women and the Sea Serpent* (1958).

commander, who is leading his troops against her people. Salina is played by Carita, a Finnish fashion model in her film debut. The strong supporting cast includes outstanding performances by Andrew Keir as a villainous Roman officer and Adrienne Corri as Salina's evil sister. Mysterious Druid rites and human sacrifices add typically horrific Hammer touches.

323   *The Viking Sagas*

A New Line–Gurian Production
New Line Cinema (1996) 83 min.
Technicolor
  P–Paul R. Gurian / D–Michael Chapman / W–
Dale Heard, Paul R. Gurian, Michael Chapman /
M–George S. Clinton / C–Dean Lent / E–Laurence
Jordan / PD–Bryce Perrin / CD–Pamela Tait
  Cast–Ralf Moeller (Kjartan), Ingibjorg Stefans-
dottir (Gudrun), Sven-Ole Thorsen (Gunnar) with
Henrik Olafson, Thorir Waagfjord, Raimund
Harmstorf, Magnus Jonsson, David Kristiansson,
Magnus Olafson

  German bodybuilder Ralf Moeller is Kjartan, a Viking prince in Iceland. When his fa-

ther the king is slain by a band of villainous warriors, Kjartan escapes with the Ghost Sword, a symbol of good which will help him to free his people from tyranny. He is taught to fight by the famous warrior Gunnar and falls in love with the beautiful Gudrun. That's about it for story and what remains is a series of sword fights. Shot in Iceland , the film was directed by Michael Chapman who was cinematographer on Martin Scorsese's *Raging Bull*. *The Viking Sagas* is a confused, gory affair (at one point a character slowly pulls out his own intestines). Despite extensive narration, there isn't much of a coherent plot line and what little story there is moves along at a crawl.

324   *Viking Women and the Sea Serpent*

A Malibu Production
American-International (1958) 70 min.
  P / D–Roger Corman / W–Lawrence Louis Gold-
man, Irving Block / M–Albert Glasser / C–Monroe

P. Askins/E–Ronald Sinclair/AD–Bob Kinoshita/ SVE–Jack Rabin, Louis De Witt, Irving Block

Cast–Abby Dalton (Desir), Susan Cabot (Enger), Brad Jackson (Vedric), June Kenney (Asmild), Richard Devon (Stark), Jay Sayer (Senja), Betsy Jones-Moreland (Thyra), Jonathan Haze (Ottar), Gary Conway (Jarl) with Lynn Bernay, Sally Todd, Mike Forrest (aka Michael Forest), Wilda Taylor

Roger Corman's first attempt at the epic film genre surpasses even his *Atlas* (1961) for sheer cheapness. The actual title of the film is *The Saga of the Viking Women and Their Voyage to the Waters of the Great Sea Serpent*. Obviously this had limited marquee potential so it was shortened in the advertising campaign. The title tells it all: A tribe of ninth-century Viking women go to sea in search of their missing menfolk, where they encounter a variety of dangers including a sea serpent. Despite some exciting poster art, the movie is merely another in the long line of exploitation films produced by American International Pictures and geared to make a quick buck in the teenage market. Roger Corman and AIP had been duped by Jack Rabin and Irving Block into believing that they could deliver a spectacular motion picture, spending a minimum amount of money, by utilizing their special effects expertise. By the time Corman realized the gravity of his mistake, the picture was already well into the ten-day shooting schedule. Actually, the special effects are rather good and include some nicely realized matte paintings in addition to the sea serpent of the title. The cast is made up of members of Corman's stock company and, to their credit, they try hard to make something out of the material at hand. This couldn't have been easy with a script peppered with lines like "She gives me the creeps" and "You big slob." Authentic Viking lingo no doubt.

325   *The Vikings*

A Kirk Douglas–Bryna Production
United Artists (1958) 114 min.
Technirama/Technicolor
P–Jerry Bresler/D–Richard Fleischer/W–Calder Willingham/Based on the novel *The Viking* by Edison Marshall/M–Mario Nascimbene/C–Jack Cardiff/E–Elmo Williams/PD–Harper Goff

Cast–Kirk Douglas (Einar), Tony Curtis (Eric), Ernest Borgnine (Ragnar), Janet Leigh (Morgana), James Donald (Egbert), Alexander Knox (Father Godwin), Frank Thring (Aella), Maxine Audley (Enid) with Eileen Way, Eric Conner, Dandy Nichols, Per Buckhoj, Almet Berg

Kirk Douglas' four million dollar production is the granddaddy of all the Viking films that were to follow but, like his later production of *Spartacus*, it suffers from the miscasting of Tony Curtis in a major role. One need only view *The Blackshield of Falworth* (Rudolph Mate; 1954) to realize how inappropriate Curtis is for this type of picture. He may cut a dashing figure visually but his delivery is pure Bronx. This gripe aside, *The Vikings* is an exciting and elaborate movie. A thirty-acre Viking village was built in Norway and three full-size replicas of authentic Viking ships were constructed for use in the film. These were completely operable by sail or oars. Filmed on location in the Norwegian fjords, *The Vikings* tells of the rape of the British queen Enid by Ragnar the Viking and the subsequent birth of their son Eric. Eric becomes a slave to the Vikings, who do not know that he is the son of their leader. Ragnar's other son

Tony Curtis and Janet Leigh dread the arrival of Kirk Douglas in *The Vikings* (1958).

Einar and Eric become bitter enemies and rivals for the hand of the Welsh princess Morgana. They must set aside their differences when the English king Aella murders Ragnar and takes Morgana captive. Einer and Eric lead the Viking forces in a siege on Aella's castle. With Aella defeated, the brothers engage in a duel to the death for possession of Morgana. Kirk Douglas gives a bravura performance as the villainous Einar and seems to be enjoying himself immensely. The animated prologue was designed by UPA studios and features narration by Orson Welles.

326   *Vulcan, God of Fire*

(Vulcano, Figlio di Giove; Vulcan, Son of Jove)
Juno-Rome Productions (1962) 76 min.
Supercinescope / Eastman Color
U.S.–No theatrical release
   P–Decio Salvi / D–Emimmo Salvi / W–Ambrogio Molteni, Gino Stafford, Benito Ilforte, Emimmo Salvi / M–Marcello Giombini / C–Mario Parapetti / E–Otello Colangeli / AD–Ambrogio Molteni / CD–Augusta Morelli
   Cast–Rod Flash Ilush (Vulcan), Bella Cortez (Aetna), Roger Browne (Mars), Gordon Mitchell (Pluto), Liliana Zagra (Venus) with Furio Meniconi, Omero Gargano, Yonne Scire, Salvatore Furnair, Ugo Sabetta, Paolo Pieri, Anna Gorassini

This curiosity is surely one of the oddest films in the peplum cycle. The main characters are gods from Mount Olympus, which apparently doesn't prevent them from suffering from the same pettiness and deceit as mortals. None of the ethereal stateliness of the Olympus of *Jason and the Argonauts* is in evidence here. The beautiful Venus (complete with a sixties' bouffant hairdo) dallies with Adonis and a jealous Hera, Queen of the Gods, demands that Zeus punish her. What worse punishment, reasons Zeus, than marriage? Venus must choose between Vulcan, God of Fire and Mars, God of War. Before she can make her decision, Pluto, God of the Underworld, convinces Mars that he must kidnap Venus and take her to Earth. Vulcan follows Mars in hot pursuit. Shortly after his arrival on Earth, Vulcan rescues Aetna, daughter of Neptune, from a tribe of lizard men. Vulcan and Aetna soon fall in love but before they can ride off into the sunset, Vulcan discovers that Mars and Venus have joined the

Thracian army in a plan to invade Mount Olympus (a poor matte painting hovering in the background). A potentially interesting concept is botched by poor production values and some terrible performances. "Guest Star" Gordon Mitchell is especially dreadful as Pluto. Rod Flash Ilush appeared in later films using the name Richard Lloyd.

327   *War Gods of Babylon*

(Le Sette Folgori di Assur; The Seven Thunderbolts
   of Assur / The Seventh Thunderbolt)
(1962) 82 min.
CinemaScope / Technicolor
U.S.–American-International
   D–Silvio Amadio / W–Sergio Spina, Gino De Santis, L. De Simone / M–Angelo Francesco Lavagnino / C–Tino Santoni / CD–Maria Baroni
   Cast–Howard Duff (Sardanapale), Jackie Lane (Myrrha), Luciano Marin (Shamash) with Giancarlo Sbraglia, Arnoldo Foa, Luigi Borghese, Calisto Calisti, Stelio Candelli, Jose Greci, Nico Pepe, Omar Zolficar

Sardanapale, King of Nineveh, conquers Babylon and places his younger brother, Shamash, on the throne. The Babylonian people are resentful and oppose his rule. Sardanapale and Shamash both fall in love with the beautiful hostage Myrrha causing a rift in their relationship which weakens their hold on Babylon. The Babylonians are about to stage an uprising when Zoroastre, a messenger of the gods, appears and foretells the downfall of Nineveh. A tremendous cloudburst causes the Tigris River to overflow and floods the city of Nineveh, destroying the tyrannical rule of Sardanapale.

328   *The War Lord*

A Court Production
Universal (1965) 123 min.
Panavision / Technicolor
   P–Walter Seltzer / D–Franklin Schaffner / W–John Collier, Millard Kaufman / Based on the play *The Lovers* by Leslie Stevens / M–Jerome Moross / C–Russell Metty / E–Folmar Blangsted / AD–Alexander Golitzen, Henry Bumpstead / CD–Vittorio Nino Novarese
   Cast–Charlton Heston (Chrysagon), Rosemary Forsyth (Bronwyn) Richard Boone (Bors), Guy Stockwell (Draco), James Farentino (Marc), Niall MacGinnis (Odins) with Maurice Evans, Henry Wilcoxon, Michael Conrad, Sammy Ross, Woodrow Parerey, John Anderson, Alan Jaffe, Dal Jenkins

Poster art of Charlton Heston as *The War Lord* (1965).

In eleventh-century Normandy, the Norman knight Chrysagon is sent to be overlord of a Druid village. When he exercises the "Right of the First Night" with a local virgin bride, the serfs turn against him. The girl, Bronwyn, falls in love with Chrysagon and chooses to remain by his side, setting off a tragic chain of events. Based on the play *The Lovers* by Leslie Stevens, Charlton Heston had originally been approached to star in the Broadway stage production. He declined, but remained intrigued by the story. In 1962 Hes-

Susy Anderson and Ettore Manni drink a toast in *War of the Zombies* (1965).

ton and producer Walter Seltzer decided to buy the screen rights. When production began two years later, Diane Baker was originally mentioned for the role of Bronwyn and Gary Raymond for Draco. These parts were finally played by Rosemary Forsyth and Guy Stockwell, who both give memorable performances. Universal executives were unwilling to finance any location filming in England so the "English" marshes were actually located at a waterfowl reserve in Colusa, California. The finished movie clocked in at two hours and fifty-four minutes. Universal responded by cutting the film to just over two hours length. Charlton Heston has said that this is one of his own personal favorites among his films and hopes that one day a restored version will be made available.

329   *War of the Zombies*

(Roma Contro Roma; Rome Against Rome / Night Star, Goddess of Electra)

A Galatea Production (1964) 110 min.
Widescreen / Eastman Color
U.S.–American-International (1965) 85 min.
ColorScope
P–Ferruccio de Martino, Massimo de Rita / D–Giuseppe Vari / W–Piero Pierotti, Marcello Sartarelli / M–Roberto Nicolosi / C–Gabor Pogany / AD–Giorgio Giovannini / CD–Trini Grani
Cast–John Drew Barrymore (Aderbal), Susy Andersen (Tullia), Ettore Manni (Gaius), Ida Galli (Rhama) with Mino Doro, Phillippe Hersent, Matilde Calnan, Giulio Maculani, Ivo Staccioli, Livia Contardi, Antonio Corevi

A large shipment of gold disappears on its way to Rome and the centurion Gaius is sent to Armenia to investigate. Aderbal, high priest of the goddess Electra, has stolen the treasure in an attempt to organize a revolt. Aderbal is assisted in his plan by Tullia, the wife of the Roman emissary, Lutezius. When Lutezius is murdered, Gaius is accused of the crime and must fight to prove his innocence. Using the magic powers of Electra, Aderbal resurrects an army of dead Roman soldiers to use them in his plans to conquer Rome. The zombie soldiers are gaining the upper hand in a battle with the Roman troops but when Gaius kills Aderbal, the spell is broken. Always searching for the most exploitable angle, American-International Pictures bought the rights to this sword and sandal movie and attempted to pass it off as one of their horror entries. The result is a film which never succeeds on either level due, in part, to the second rate direction of Giuseppe Vari. *War of the Zombies* does have some imaginative sets, in particular, the caverns of Aderbal, dominated by the gigantic stone head of the one-eyed goddess. The most effective sequence, showing the resuscitated soldiers riding off to battle in slow motion, has a haunting quality that the remainder of the film lacks.

330 *The Warrior and the Slave Girl*

(La Rivolta dei Gladiatori; The Revolt of the Gladiators)
Alexandra P.C., Rome–Atenea, Madrid (1958) 89 min.
Supercinescope/Eastman Color
U.S.–Columbia (1959)

P–Virgilio de Blasi/D–Vittorio Cottafavi/W–Ennio De Concini, Francesco De Feo, Gian Paolo Callegari, Duccio Tessari/M–Roberto Nicolosi/C–Mario Pacheco/E–Julio Pena/AD–Antonio Simont, Vittorio Rossi/CD–Enzo Bulgarelli

Cast–Gianna Maria Canale (Amira), Georges Marchal (Asclepius), Ettore Manni (Marcus Numidius), Rafael Calvo (Lucanus), Mara Cruz (Zahar), Vega Vinci (Armedia), Lina Rosales (Ramnis) with Raphael Duran, Anibal Vela, Nino, Renato Montalbano, Sergio Tefano, Nino Milano, Salvatore Furnari

The Roman tribune Marcus Numidius is sent to Armenia to subdue a revolt by rebel gladiators. Their leader, Asclepius, wins the tribune over to the rebel side and together they oppose the rule of the wicked Princess Amira. Marcus and Asclepius succeed in defeating Amira and her mercenaries but the brave gladiator is killed in the final battle. Above average peplum due to the ever reliable presences of leading players Georges Marchal, Ettore Manni and the ever-evil Gianna Maria Canale.

331 *The Warrior Empress*

(Saffo, Venere di Lesbo; Sappho, Venus of Lesbos)
Documento Films (1960) 87 min.
CinemaScope/Eastman Color
U.S.–Columbia

P–Gianni Hecht Lucari/D–Pietro Francisci/W–Ennio De Concini, Pietro Francisci, Luciano Martino/M–Angelo Francesco Lavagnino/C–Carlo Carlini/E–Nino Baragli/AD–Giulio Bongini/CD–Gaia Romanini

Cast–Kerwin Mathews (Phaon), Tina Louise (Sappho), Riccardo Garrone (Hyperbius), Antonio Battistella (Paeone), Enrico Maria Salerno (Melanchrus), Susy Golgi (Actis), Alberto Farnese (Laricus) Annie Gorassini (Dyla), Lilly Mantovani (Cleide) with Strelsa Brown, Aldo Fiorelli, Elda Tattoli, Isa Crescenzi, Audrey MacDonald, Jim Dolan

The original European title of *The Warrior Empress*, *Sappho Venus of Lesbos*, is far more appropriate as the story is about the poetess, with nary a warrior empress in sight. The plot is wholly fictitious and neglects the fact that Sappho is one of history's most famous lesbians. In this version, Sappho is a priestess of Aphrodite who helps the rebel leader Phaon. She is betrayed by Actis, another priestess who is jealous of Sappho's love for the young

Sappho (Tina Louise) prefers men and Kerwin Mathews in particular in *The Warrior Empress* (1960).

warrior. There is some implication that Actis is in love with Sappho, but this is never fully developed. After many hardships, the two lovers are reunited when Sappho renounces her vows as a priestess to marry Phaon. Kerwin Mathews and Tina Louise are extremely attractive performers and Mathews has the added bonus of being a very capable actor. Tina Louise possesses a spectacular face and figure that transcend acting ability. Most of her abbreviated costumes seem designed to provide the maximum amount of "jiggle" at all times. In addition to these sterling qualities, director Pietro Francisi has successfully incorporated many fantasy elements into the story, pushing it from history into the realm of mythology. This is a wise choice since most of the facts about Sappho are ignored anyway. *The Warrior Empress* also includes the requisite number of battle scenes and hungry lions, just in case you weary of the constant parade of pulchritude.

Modern Screen: Glorious seascapes, galloping horses, lavish sets ... the girls' generously revealed figures. At least, this is a decorative bit of foolishness, happily ignoring history.

332   Warrior Queen

Lightning Pictures-Vestron (1986) 79 min. Color
P–Harry Alan Towers/D–Chuck Vincent/W–Rick Mark, Peter Welbeck/M–Ian Shaw, Kai Joffee/C–Lorenzo Battaglia/E–Anthony Delcampo/PD/CD–Lucio Parise
Cast–Sybil Danning (Berenice), Donald Pleasence (Clodius), Richard Hill (Marcus), Josephine Jacqueline Jones (Chloe), Tally Chanel (Vespa), Suzanne Smith (Veneria), Stasia Micula (Philomena), David Haughton (Victo), Mario Cruciani (Roberto), Marco Tullio Cau (Goliath)

The absolute nadir of epic filmmaking. Harry Alan Towers, having previously produced inept remakes of such classic horror films as *Dracula* and *Dorian Gray*, turned his unwanted attentions to *The Last Days of Pompeii*. Produced during the mini-revival of peplum films in Italy during the eighties, *Warrior Queen* is little more than a soft-core porno film set in the city of Pompeii in August A.D. 79. This isn't too surprising as director Chuck Vincent had previously been responsible for such film fare as *Young Nurses in Love* and *Hol-*

lywood Hot Tubs. Cut to an R rating for the mercifully brief theatrical release, *Warrior Queen* was restored to its full length for the home video version. Approximately ten minutes had been cut, consisting of simulated sex scenes and excessive gore. The minimal story line concerns Berenice, a Roman dignitary visiting in the corrupt city of Pompeii. In her spare time she is also a vigilante who appears out of nowhere, swords flashing, whenever certain members of the cast are in danger. She is also the only female member of the cast who manages to keep all of her clothes on throughout. There is very little dialogue, which is a blessing considering the amateurish delivery. Once again Donald Pleasence proves he will do any part for money. Marco Tullio Cau is a Lou Ferrigno look-alike who plays the muscle-bound villain, Goliath. Steve Reeves should be given billing as he is visible in several scenes lifted from the 1960 version of *The Last Days of Pompeii*. They really don't get much worse than this.

333   The Warrior's Husband

A Jesse Lasky Production
Fox Films (1932)
P–Jesse Lasky/D/W–Walter Lang/Based on the play by Julian Thompson/C–Hal Mohr
Cast–Elissa Landi (Antiope), David Manners (Theseus), Marjorie Rambeau (Hippolyta), Stanley Sandford (Hercules), Ernest Truex (Sapiens) with Claudia Coleman, Maude Eburne, Helen Ware

In this whimsical version of mythology, the Greek army is threatening the Amazon capital and Queen Hippolyta is told by her advisors that the royal treasury is alarmingly short of money. In order to restore the gold necessary for a campaign against the Greeks, Hippolyta agrees to marry a man from a wealthy family. In the meantime, her sister Antiope has fallen in love with Theseus, a Greek soldier. When the mighty Hercules is taken prisoner by the Amazons, Hippolyta's new spouse emancipates the males by giving Hercules the Girdle of Diana. The loss of this sacred charm ensures the downfall of the Amazons. Despite the fact that Katharine Hepburn had originated the role of Antiope on Broadway with considerable success, when it came time for a film version of *The Warrior's Husband*, she was passed over in favor of Elissa Landi who was

David Manners and Elissa Landi in *The Warrior's Husband* (1932).

already an established film star while Hepburn was not. Had Hepburn made her screen debut in the role she had created, a place in film history would have been assured for *The Warrior's Husband*. As it turned out, the film is little remembered and seldom revived.

Time: The main trouble with *The Warrior's Husband* is that its theme lacks capacity for development. Once the original idea sinks in there is nothing very comical—unless you think a joke improves with repetition.

334 *When Dinosaurs Ruled the Earth*

A Hammer Film Production (1970) 100 min. Technicolor
U.S.–Warner Bros. (1971) 96 min.
P–Aida Young/D/W–Val Guest/M–Mario Nascimbene/C–Dick Bush/E–Peter Curran/AD–John Blezard/CD–Carl Toms/SVE–Jim Danforth
Cast–Victoria Vetri (Sanna), Robin Hawdon

(Tara), Patrick Allen (Kingsor), Drewe Henley (Khaku), Sean Caffrey (Kane), Magda Konopka (Ulido), Patrick Holt (Ammon), Imogen Hassal (Ayak), Carol-Anne Hawkins (Yani) with Jan Rossini, Connie Tilton, Maggie Lynton, Jimmy Lodge, Billy Cornelius, Ray Ford, Maria O'Brien

This is the second in Hammer's prehistoric trilogy; however, *When Dinosaurs Ruled the Earth* lacks the grittier aspects of the other two. Val Guest's approach is more light-hearted than Don Chaffey's, who directed both the other films in the series. The plot recounts the trials and tribulations of Sanna, a beautiful cavegirl whose blonde hair causes her no end of problems. She narrowly escapes being a human sacrifice, becomes the adopted offspring of a mother dinosaur, falls in love with a caveman named Tara, weathers a tidal wave on a raft and witnesses the birth of the Moon. Hammer executives had planned for Ray Harryhausen to do the special effects but

Prehistoric people never looked better: Victoria Vetri and Robin Hawdon in *When Dinosaurs Ruled the Earth* (1971).

he declined because of his involvement with another film about prehistoric monsters, *The Valley of Gwangi*. The stop-motion visual effects sequences in *When Dinosaurs Ruled the Earth* are the work of Jim Danforth, who supplies a fantastic array of creatures. Unfortunately, some of the proposed effects sequences had to be eliminated due to time and budget restrictions. Danforth was unable to work with Harryhausen's degree of economy and, to Hammer's dismay, it took him over 16 months to complete the effects work. Danforth was forced to eliminate a climactic battle between cavemen and giant ants and considerably more elaborate tidal wave effects. Victoria Vetri, of whom Hammer expected great things, is quite good but she inexplicably failed to make the impact that Raquel Welch had made in *One Million Years B.C.* A follow-up film titled *The Dinosaur Girl*, that was to star Vetri, was never made. Several nude scenes appeared in the European prints of *When Dinosaurs Ruled the Earth*, but these were cut for the American release. Considering the fairytale quality of much of the film they seem terribly out of place anyway.

AA Nomination: Best Special Effects

San Diego Union: When Dinosaurs Ruled the Earth is a mildly exciting prehistoric adventure movie. Special effects by Jim Danforth are first class.

New York Magazine: If you have a special taste for nonsense, there's a fine sort of idiocy about *When Dinosaurs Ruled the Earth*.

Films and Filming: This is life at the "dawn of history," comic-strip style. Its most engaging aspect is its special effects sequences.

335 *Wholly Moses!*

Columbia (1980) 109 min.
Panavision/Metrocolor

P–Freddie Fields/D–Gary Weis/W–Guy Thomas/M–Patrick Williams/C–Frank Stanley/E–Sidney Levin/PD–Dale Hennesy/CD–Guy Verhille

Cast–Dudley Moore (Harvey/Herschel), Laraine Newman (Zoey/Zeralda), James Coco (Hyssop), Paul Sand (Angel), Richard Pryor (Pharaoh), Jack Gilford (Tailor), Dom DeLuise (Shadrach), John Houseman (Archangel), Madeline Kahn (Witch), David L. Lander (Beggar), John Ritter (The Devil) with Richard B. Shull, Tanya Boyd, Ruth Manning, Andrea Martin, Stan Ross

Many of the top comedians of the time got together in this parody of biblical films in general and DeMille's 1956 version of *The Ten Commandments* in particular. The ironic thing about this comedy is that, despite all the talent involved, there is not a single laugh, chuckle or smile to be had during the entire running time. Dudley Moore once again portrays the beleaguered underdog role that he made a staple of his career. Harvey, a professor of languages, is on a bus tour of the Holy Land when he discovers an ancient scroll which tells the story of Herschel. Herschel was the son of the slave Hyssop. When the Pharaoh decrees that all the first born sons of the slaves be put to death, Hyssop places the infant Herschel in a reed boat and sets him on the Nile. Instead of being adopted by Pharaoh's daughter as Hyssop had hoped, Herschel is found by Senmut the Idol Maker. Through a series of mishaps, the adult Herschel incurs the anger of the Pharaoh and flees into the desert. He is taken into the household of Jethro, the sheik of Midian. Moses has already married one of Jethro's daughters and is now tending his father-in-

Dudley Moore and Richard Pryor in the unfunny *Wholly Moses!* (1980).

law's sheep. Herschel marries Zerelda, another of Jethro's daughters, and is given the task of rounding up the sheep which have strayed from Moses' flock. When Herschel overhears God speaking to Moses, he mistakenly believes that he has been chosen to lead the slaves out of Egyptian bondage. Herschel and his wife set out for Egypt but make a side trip to Sodom, where Zerelda is turned into a pillar of salt. Herschel arrives in Egypt too late and Moses has already led the slaves to freedom. As a consolation, God allows Herschel to carve the tablets of the Ten Commandments. Shockingly unfunny stuff.

Appendix 1:
Related Titles

336 Adam and Eve

Constelación-Film, Mexico (1956)
   76 min.
Widescreen/Eastman Color
U.S.–William M. Horne Films
P–Francisco Oliveros del Valle/D/W–Albert
   Gout/M–Gustavo Cesar Carrion/C–Alex
   Phillips/E–Jorge Bustor
Cast–Cristina Martel (Eve), Carlos Baena
   (Adam)

337 Caesar Against the Pirates

(Julio Cesare contro i Pirati)
C.A.P.R.I., Rome–Globus-Dubrava, Zagreb
   (1961) 90 min.
Eastman Color
P–Gastone Guglielmetti/D–Sergio Grieco/
   W–Gino Mangini, Fabio De Agostini,
   Sergio Grieco, Maria Grazia Borgiotti/
   M–Carlo Innocenzi/C–Vincenzo
   Seratrice/E–Enzo Alfonsi/AD–Alfredo
   Montori/CD–Giuliana Ghidini
Cast–Gustavo Rojo (Julius Caesar), Abbe
   Lane (Plauzia), Gordon Mitchell (Hamar),
   Piero Lulli (Edom), Franca Parisi (Cor-
   nelia), Susan Teri (Quintilla), Massimo
   Carocci (Publius), Ignazio Leone (Fron-
   tone) with Fedele Gentile, Erno Crisa,
   Rossana Fattori, Mario Petri, Pasquale
   Basile, Aldo Cecconi, Antonio Gradoli,
   Nando Angelini

338 Centurions of Rome

Uranus Films (1981) 84 min.
Color
D–John Christopher (Chris Corvino)/W–
Timothy Michaels/C–Larry Vincent
   Revene
Cast–George Payne (Demetrius), Eric Ryan
   (Commander), Scorpio (Octavius) with
   Myles Longue, David Morris, Michael
   Flent, Adam DeHaven, Ed Wiley,
   Guiseppe Welsh, John Kovacs, Roy Gar-
   rett, David Hadley, Ryder Jones

339 Challenge of the Gladiator

(Il Gladiatore che Sfido l'Impero/Hercules
   Against Spartacus)
Jonia Film S.R.L., Rome (1964) 90 min.
Totalscope/Technicolor
U.S.–American-International
P–Ferdinando Felicioni/D–Domenico
   Paolella/W–Domenico Paolella, Alessan-
   dro Fernau/M–Giuseppe Piccillo/C–
   Raffaele Masciocchi/E–Antonietta Zita
Cast–Rock Stevens (Spartacus), Piero Lulli
   (Metellus), Massimo Serato (Lucius Quin-
   tilius), Livio Lorenzon (Corbulius), Gloria
   Milland (Livia), Walter Barnes (Caius
   Terenzius)

**340 The Gospel According to
St. Matthew**

(Il Vangelo Secondo Matteo)
Continental Films (1964) 135 min.
P–Alfredo Bini/D/W–Piero Paolo Paso-
   lini/M-Luis Bacalov/C–Tonino Delli
   Colli/E–Nino Baragli/PD–Luigi Scac-
   cianoce/CD–Danilo Donati
Cast–Enrique Irazoqui (Jesus), Marcello
   Morante (Joseph), Margherita Caruso
   (Mary), Mario Socrate (John the Baptist),
   Alfonso Gatto (Andrew), with Susanna

Pasolini, Settimio Di Porto, Giacomo
Morante, Ferruccio Nuzzo

341   Nero and Poppaea

(Nerone e Poppea / Nero and the Whore of
   Rome)
Beatrice-Film Production (1981) 93 min.
CinemaScope / Color
D–Vincent Dawn (Bruno Mattei) W–Anto-
   nio Passalia / M–Giacomo Dell'Orso / C–
   Luigi Ciccarese / E–Bruno Mattei / AD–
   Amedeo Mellone
Cast–Rudy Adams (Nero), Patricia Derek
   (Poppaea) with Raul Cabrera, John
   Turner, Susan Forget, Anthony Freeman,
   Bruno Rosa, Guido Scalzone, Mario Nov-
   elli, Caterina Catambrone, Liliana Piras,
   Nicola Di Gioia

342   Nero and the Burning of Rome

(Nerone e Messalina; Nero and Messalina)
Spettacolo Film (1953) 97 min.
U.S.–Four Star
D–Primo Zeglio / W–Fulvio Palmierin, Ric-
   cardo Testa, Primo Zeglia / Based on the
   novel Nero and Messalina by David Bluh-
   men / M–Ennio Porrino
Cast–Gino Cervi (Nero), Paola Barbara
   (Agrippina), Milly Vitale (Acte), Carlo
   Tamberlani (Tigellinus), Steve Barclay
   (Aulus), Silvana Jachino (Eunice), Lud-
   milla Dudarova (Valeria Messalina),
   Jole Fierro (Poppaea) with Bella
   Starace Sainati, Lamberto Picasso,
   Loris Gizzi, Yvonne Sanson, Renzo
   Ricci

343   On My Way to the Crusades, I
Met a Girl Who...

(La Cintura di Castita; The Chastity Belt)
Warner Bros.–Seven Arts (1969) 93 min.
Technicolor
P–Francesco Mazzei / D–Pasquale Festa
   Campanile / W–Ugo Liberatore, Luigi
   Mangni, Larry Gelbart / M–Riz Ortolani /
   C–Carlo Di Palma / E–Gabrio Astori / AD–
   Piero Poletto / CD–Danilo Donati
Cast–Tony Curtis (Guerrando), Monica Vitti
   (Boccadora), Hugh Griffith (Ibn el Ras-
   cid), John Richardson (Dragone), Ivo Gar-
   rani (Pandolfo), Nino Castelnuovo (Mar-
   culfo) with Gabriella Giorgelli, Franco

Sportelli, Umberto Raho, Leopoldo Trieste, Francesco Mule

344   The Passover Plot

Atlas Films (1976) 108 min.
Color
P–Wolf Schmidt / D–Michael Campus / W–
   Millard Cohen, Patricia Knop / Based on
   the novel by Hugh Schonfield / M–Alex
   North / C–Adam Greenberg / E–Dov
   Hoenig / AD–Kuli Sander / CD–Mary Wills
Cast–Zalman King (Jesus), Scott Wilson
   (Judas), Harry Andrews (John the Bap-
   tist), Daniel Ades (Andrew), William
   Burns (Simon), Hugh Griffith (Caiaphas),
   Donald Pleasence (Pontius Pilate) with
   Michael Baseleon, Daniel Hedaya, Helena
   Kallianiotes, Kevin O'Connor, Robert
   Walker Jr.

345   The Return of the Strongest
Gladiator in the World

(Il Ritorno del Gladiatore Più Forte del
   Mondo)
Lea Film, Italy (1971) 93 min.
Eastman Colorscope
P–Emanuele Girogi / D / W–Al Albert (Bitto
   Albertini) / M–Sergio Pagoni / C–Alvaro
   Lanzoi / E–Lucia Luconi / AD–Fausto
   Ulisse / CD–Adriana Spadaro
Cast–Brad Harris (Marius), Massimo Serato
   (Quintillius), Michel Lemoine (Sevio),
   Maria Pia Conte (Licia), Paolo Rosani
   (Claudius) with Adler Grey, Alberto Far-
   nese, Margaret Rose Keil, Raffaele Baldas-
   sarre

346   Revak the Barbarian

(Revak, lo Schiavo di Cartageni; Revak, Slave
   of Carthage / The Barbarians)
A Galatea Production (1960) 84 min.
Technicolor
P / W–John Lee Mahin, Martin Rackin / D–
   Rudolph Mate / Based on the novel by F.
   Van Wyck Mason / M–Franco Ferrara / C–
   Carl Guthrie / E–Eugenio Ruggero / AD–
   Franco Lolli
Cast–Jack Palance (Revak), Milly Vitale
   (Creoa), Melody O'Brien (Tiratha), Aus-
   tin Willis (Varro), Guy Rolfe (Kainus),
   Richard Wyler (Lycursus) with John
   Alderson, Pietro Ceccarelli, Joseph Cuby,

George Ehling, Frederic Ross, Deidre Sullivan, Richard Watson

347   *Revenge of the Gladiators*
(La Vendetta dei Gladiatori)
Splendor Films, Italy (1964) 92 min.
Widescreen/Eastman Color
U.S.–American–International (1965)
D–Luigi Capuano/W–Luigi Capuano, Arpad De Riso, Roberto Gianviti/M–Giuseppe Piccillo/C–Raffaele Masciocchi
Cast–Mickey Hargitay, Jose Greci, Livio Lorenzon, Renato Baldini, Andrea Checchi, Roldano Lupi, Nerio Bernardi, Mirko Ellis, Aldo Canti

348   *Revolt of the Barbarians*
(La Rivolta dei Barbari/Los Barbaros Contra El Imperio Romano)
Protor Film, Italy (1964) 99 min.
CinemaScope/Eastman Color
U.S.–Trans America
P–Michaelangelo Ciafre/D/W–Guido Malatesta/M–Carlo Franci/C–Luciano Trasatti/E–Enzo Alfonsi/AD–Oscar D'Amico/CD–Vittorio Rossi
Cast–Roland Carey (Darius), Grazia Maria Spina (Lydia) with Susan Sullivan, Gabriele Antonini, Andrea Aureli, Erminia Pipnic, Mario Feliciani, Gaetano Scola, Franco Beltrame, Gilberto Galimberti

349   *Revolt of the Praetorians*
(La Rivolta dei Pretoriani)
F.I.A. Film, Italy (1964) 98 min.
Techniscope/Technisolor
U.S.–ABC Films
P–Carlo Vassalie/D–Alfonso Brescia/W–Gian Paolo Callegari/M–Carlo Franci/C–Pier Ludovico Pavoni/E–Nella Nannuzzi
Cast–Richard Harrison (Valerius), Moira Orfei (Artamis), Piero Lulli (Domitian), Giuliano Gemma (Fabius), Paolo Pitti (Lucilla), with Ivy Holzer, Fedele Gentile, Amedeo Trilli, Mirko Ellis, Aldo Cecconi, Salvatore Furnari

350   *Rome in Flames*
(L'Incendio di Roma/Fire Over Rome)
Cineproduzioni G.M.C. Italia (1963) 94 min.
Totalscope/Eastman Color
P–Giorgio Marzelli/D–Guido Malatesta/W–Giudo Malatesta, Giorgio Marzelli/

M–Gian Stellari, Guido Robuschi/C–Aldo Greci/E–Enzo Alfonsi
Cast–Lang Jeffries (Marcus Valerius), Miora Orfei (Poppaea), Cristina Gajoni (Julia), Mario Feliciani (Seneca) with Luciano Marin, Franco Fantasia, Massimo Carocci, Vladimir Medar, Vladimir Bacic, Evi Matagliati

351   *The Seven Revenges*
(Le Sette Sfide/Ivan the Conqueror)
Adelphia Compagnia Cinematografica (1961) 92 min.
Totalscope/Eastman Color
P–Emimmo Salvi/D–Primo Zeglio/W–Primo Zeglio, Emimmo Salvi, Sergio Leone, Roberto Natale/M–Carlo Innocenzi/C–Bitto Albertini/E–Franco Fraticelli
Cast–Ed Fury (Ivan), Roldano Lupi (Amok), Elaine Stewart (Tamara), Bella Cortez (Suani) with Furio Meniconi, Gabriele Antonini, Paola Barbara

352   *The Sword of El Cid*
(La Spada del Cid)
Alexandra Film, Rome–Cintora, Madrid (1963) 85 min.
Supercinescope/Eastman Color
U.S.–El Dorado Films Inc. (1964)
D–Miguel Iglesias/W–Ferdinando Baldi, Miguel Iglesias, Luis de Blain/M–Carlo Savina/C–Francisco Marin/E–Otello Colangeli/PD–Juan Alberto Soler
Cast–Chantal Denberg (Maria Sol), Roland Carey (Bernardo), Sandro Moretti (Ramon), Eliana Grimaldi (Bianca) with Andrea Fantasia, Daniela Bianchi, Andres Mejuto, Jose Luis Pellicena, Jeff Russel, Ray Myles, Nino Milano

353   *Sword of the Empire*
(Una Spada per l'Impero)
Assia Film, Italy (1965) 82 min.
Color
U.S.–American-International
P–Giorgio Marzelli/D–Sergio Grieco/W–Fulvio Tului/M–Guido Robuschi, Gian Stellari/C–Romolo Garroni
Cast–Lang Jeffries, Jose Greci, Enzo Tarascio, Renato Rossini, Mila Stanic, Nando Gazzolo, Elio Pandolfi, Angela Angelucci, Ignazio Leone

Lang Jeffries (left) portrays a Roman officer in *Rome in Flames*.

354   *The Tarter Invasion*

(Ursus e la Ragazza Tartara; Ursus and the
Tarter Princess)
Explorer Film '58, Rome–C.F.F.C. Film,
Paris (1961) 85 min.
Techniscope/Eastman Color
U.S.–Telewide (1963)
P–Nino Battiferri/D/W–Remigio Del
Grosso/M–Angelo Francesco Lavagnino/
C–Anchise Brizzi/E–Antonietta Zita/
AD–Antonio Visone
Cast–Joe Robinson (Ursus), Ettore Manni
(Steffan), Yoki Tani (Ela) with Akim
Tamiroff, Grazia Maria Spina, Roland
Lesaffre, Tom Fellegui, Andrea Aureli,
Ivano Staccioli, Jacopo Tecchio, Anita
Todesco

355   *Taur the Mighty*

(Taur, Il Re della Forza Bruta; Taur, King of
Brutal Force)
Italia Produczione Film–Cornet Produzioni
(1961) 89 min.
Totalscope/Eastman Color
U.S.–American-International (1963)
P–Livio Maffei/D–Antonio Leonviola/W–
Antonio Leonviola, Fabio Piccioni/M–
Roberto Nicolosi/C–Memmo Mancori/
E–Renato Cinquini/AD–Franco Ramacci,
Oscar D'Amico
Cast–Joe Robinson (Taur), Harry Baird
(Ubaratutu), Bella Cortez (Akiba), Thea
Flemming (Jia), Claudio Capone (Tuja),
Antonio Leonviola (El Kab) with Carla
Foscari, Alberto Cevenini, Isabella
Biancini, Erminio Spalla, Jose Torres

Appendix 2:
Epics That Never Were

While *I Claudius* and *Joseph and His Brethren* are the most famous unfilmed epics, there were many other projects announced that also never made it to the silver screen. Some of these were:

Alexander the Great (1954)
  20th Century–Fox
Produced by Frank Ross

Daniel and the Woman of Babylon
  (1953) Warner Bros.
Screenplay by John Twist

Empress of the Dusk (1953)
  Metro-Goldwyn-Mayer
CinemaScope and Color
Produced by Sam Zimbalist
Based on the novel by John W. Vandercook
Screenplay by Sonya Levien, William Ludwig
Starring Ava Gardner (as the Empress Theodora), Vittorio Gassman

The Galileans (1953)
  Universal-International
Technicolor
Produced by Aaron Rosenberg
Directed by Douglas Sirk
Based on the novel by Frank G. Slaughter
Starring Jeff Chandler

The Gladiators (1957) United Artists
Directed by Martin Ritt
Starring Yul Brynner (as Spartacus), Anthony Quinn

The Holy Grail (1953)
  Universal-International

Technicolor
Produced by Ted Richmond
Story by Jerome Wiedmann and Irving Wallace
Screenplay by Norman Corwin

The King Must Die (1972)
A Robert Fryer and Steve Fellouris Production
Directed by Jack Clayton
Based on the novel by Mary Renault
Starring Maggie Smith, Calvin Culver

King Solomon and His Thousand Wives (1954) United Artists
An Edward Small Production
Screenplay by Julius J. Epstein

King Solomon's Daughters (1953)
  Universal-International
Technicolor
Produced by Ted Richmond
Story by Joseph Gaer
Screenplay by John M. Lucas

The Last of the Pharaohs (1954)
  Columbia
Produced by Sam Katzman
Screenplay by Sam Roeca

The Legions of Hannibal (1954)
  Columbia

Produced by Sam Katzman
Screenplay by Jack Garis

Pilate's Wife (1954) R.K.O.
Produced and Directed by King Vidor
Original story by Clare Booth Luce

The Queen of Queens (1941–1942)
   Paramount
Produced and Directed by Cecil B. DeMille
Screenplay by Jeanie Macpherson, William
   Cowan

The Queen of Sheba (1954)
   20th Century–Fox
CinemaScope and Color
Produced by Samuel G. Engel
Screenplay by Czenzi Ormonde

Richard the Lion-Hearted (1954)
   Columbia
Produced By Fred Kohlmar
Screenplay by Aeneas MacKenzie

Salammbo (1960) 20th Century–Fox
Starring Harry Belafonte, Gina Lollobrigida

The Siren Jezebel (1954) Allied Artists

The Story of Jezebel (1954)
   20th Century–Fox

The Story of Mary Magdalene (1954)
   Columbia
Starring Rita Hayworth

The Wandering Jew (1954)
   20th Century–Fox
CinemaScope and Color
Produced and Written by Nunnally John-
   son
Original story by E. Temple Thurston

Young Moses (1954) United Artists
Produced by Leonard Goldstein
Written by Herb Meadow

Bibliography

Adkinson, Robert, and Allen Eyles. *The House of Horror: The Story of Hammer Films*. London: Lorrimer, 1973.

Archer, Eugene. "Hollywood and the Bible," *Show*. Dec. 1964, vol. 4, no. 11, pp. 30–36.

Belefonte, Dennis, and Alvin H. Marill. *The Films of Tyrone Power*. Secaucus, N.J.: Citadel, 1979.

Beuselink, James. "Mankiewicz's Cleopatra," *Films in Review*. Jan. 1988, vol. 39, no. 1, pp. 2–17.

Bodeen, DeWitt, and Gene Ringgold. *The Films of Cecil B. DeMille*. New York: Cadillac, 1969.

Brodsky, Jack, and Nathan Weiss. *The Cleopatra Papers*. New York: Simon and Schuster, 1963.

Butler, Ivan. *Religion in the Cinema*. New York: A.S. Barnes, 1969.

Capra, Frank. *The Name Above the Title*. New York: Macmillan, 1971.

Cary, John. *Spectacular!* London: Castle, 1974.

Connolly, William. "Tribute to a Big Man: The Films of Reg Park," *Spaghetti Cinema*. July 1991, vol. 8, no. 3, pp. 2–15.

Cook, Page. "Bernard Herrmann," *Films in Review*. August-September 1967, vol. 15, no. 7, pp. 398–412.

Costello, Donald P. *The Serpent's Eye: Shaw and the Cinema*. Notre Dame, Ind.: University of Notre Dame Press, 1965.

DeMille, Cecil B. *An Autobiography*. Englewood Cliffs, N.J.: Prentice-Hall, 1959.

Douglas, Kirk. *The Ragman's Son*. New York: Pocket Books, 1988.

Draper, Dave. *Brother Iron, Sister Steel*. Aptos, CA.: On Target, 2001.

Elley, Derek. *The Epic Film*. London: Routledge and Kegan Paul, 1984.

Eloy, Michael. "Images of Rome," *Peplum*. March 1981, no. 6, pp. 29–72.

Essoe, Gabe, and Raymond Lee. *DeMille: The Man and His Pictures*. Cranbury, N.J.: A.S. Barnes, 1970.

Fraser, George MacDonald. *The Hollywood History of the World*. New York: William Morrow, 1988.

Freedland, Nat. "Fellini Satyricon," *Entertainment World*. Jan. 23, 1970, vol. 2, no. 3, pp. 6–10.

Gabler, Neal. *An Empire of Their Own: How the Jews Invented Hollywood*. New York: Crown, 1988

Gillett, John, and Penelope Huston. "The Theory and Practice of Blockbusting," *Sight and Sound*. Spring 1963, vol. 32, no. 2, pp. 68–74.

Granger, Stewart. *Sparks Fly Upward*. New York: G.P. Putnam's Sons, 1981.

Griffith, Richard, and Arthur Mayer. *The Movies*. New York: Bonanza, 1957.

Hamilton, Edith. *Mythology*. New York: Mentor, 1963.

Harryhausen, Ray. *Fantasy Film Scrapbook*. New York: A.S. Barnes, 1981.

Hefner, Hugh M. "The New Italian Renaissance," *Show Business Illustrated*. Oct. 17, 1961, vol. 1, no. 4, pp. 30–35.

Heston, Charlton. *The Actor's Life*. New York: E.P. Dutton, 1978.

_____, and Jean-Pierre Isbouts. *Charlton Heston's Hollywood*. New York: GT Publishing, 1998.

Hickman, Gail Morgan. *The Films of George Pal*. Cranbury, N.J.; A. S. Barnes, 1977

Higman, Charles. *Cecil B. DeMille*. New York: Charles Scribner's Sons, 1973.

Hyams, Joe, and Walter Wanger. *My Life with Cleopatra*. New York: Bantam, 1963.

Jones, Lon. *Barabbas: The Story of a Motion Picture*. Bologna, Italy: Cappelli, 1962.

Koury, Phil. *Yes, Mr. DeMille*. New York: G.P. Putnam's Sons, 1959.

Kulik, Karol. *Alexander Korda*. New Rochelle, N.Y.: Arlington House, 1975.

Larkin, V.F., "The Cinema of Nicholas Ray," *Movie*. No. 9, pp. 5–24.

Lewis, Thomasine. *The Prince of Egypt: The Movie Scrapbook*. New York: Puffin, 1998.

Leyendeckner, Frank. "The Cycle of Biblical Films Continues," *Boxoffice*. July 10, 1961, vol. 79, no. 12, pp. 14–15.

Linet, Beverly. *Susan Hayward*. New York: Atheneum, 1980.

Lloyd, Ann, and David Robinson. *The Brave and the Bloodthirsty*. London: Orbis, 1984.

_____ and _____. *Movies of the Fifties*. London: Orbis, 1982.

McBride, Joseph. *Hawks on Hawks*. Berkeley: University of California Press, 1982.

McGee, Mark Thomas. *Roger Corman: The Best of the Cheap Acts*. Jefferson, N.C.: McFarland, 1988.

Madsen, Axel. *John Houston*. New York: Doubleday, 1978.

Moreno, Eduardo. *The Films of Susan Hayward*. Secausus, N.J.: Citadel, 1979.

Munn, Mike. *The Stories Behind the Scenes of the Great Epic Films*. London: Argus, 1982.

Naha, Ed. *The Films of Roger Corman*. New York: Arco, 1982.

Nash, Jay Robert, and Stanley Ralph Ross. *The Motion Picture Guide*. Chicago: Cinebooks, 1986.

Noerdlinger, Harry S. *Moses and Egypt*. Los Angeles: University of Southern California Press, 1956.

Robinson, Jay. *The Comeback*. Virginia: Chosen Books, 1979.

Rovin, Jeff. *From the Land Beyond Beyond*. New York: Berkley Winhover, 1977.

Rozsa, Miklos. *Double Life*. New York: Wynwood, 1989.

Sabatier, Jean-Marie. *Les Classiques du Cinéma Fantastique*. Paris: Ballard, 1973.

Shay, Don. "Willis O'Brien: Creator of the Impossible," *Cinefex*. Jan. 1982, no. 7, pp. 4–71.

Shipman, David. *The Great Movie Stars: The Golden Years*. New York: Crown, 1970.

Solomon, Jon. *The Ancient World of the Cinema*. Cranbury, N.J.: A.S. Barnes, 1978.

Valentino, Lou. *The Films of Lana Turner*. Secaucus, N.J.: Citadel, 1976.

Vermilye, Jerry, and Mark Ricci. *The Films of Elizabeth Taylor*. Secaucus, N.J.: Citadel, 1976.

Vidor, King. *On Film Making*. New York: David McKay, 1972.

Wanger, Walter. "The Trials and Tribulations of an Epic Film: Cleopatra," *Saturday Evening Post*. June 1, 1963, vol. 236, no. 21, pp. 28–52.

Weldon, Michael. *The Psychotronic Encyclopedia of Film*. New York: Ballantine, 1983.

Whitcomb, Jon. "Gina as Sheba," *Cosmopolitan*. August 1959, vol. 147, no. 2, pp. 12–15.

Williams, Lucy Chase. *The Complete Films of Vincent Price*. New York: Citadel, 1995.

Yordan, Philip. *King of Kings: A Novelization of the Screenplay*. New York: Permabooks, 1961.

Index

References are to entry numbers